A Ruined Fortress?

Governance in Europe
Series Editor: Gary Marks

A Ruined Fortress?

Neoliberal Hegemony and Transformation in Europe

Edited by
Alan W. Cafruny and Magnus Ryner

ROWMAN & LITTLEFIELD PUBLISHERS, INC.
Lanham • Boulder • New York • Toronto • Oxford

ROWMAN & LITTLEFIELD PUBLISHERS, INC.

Published in the United States of America
by Rowman & Littlefield Publishers, Inc.
A wholly owned subsidary of The Rowman & Littlefield Publishing Group, Inc.
4501 Forbes Boulevard, Suite 200, Lanham, Maryland 20706
www.rowmanlittlefield.com

P.O. Box 317, Oxford, OX2 9RU, UK

British Library Cataloguing in Publication Information Available

Library of Congress Cataloging-in-Publication Data

A ruined fortress? : neoliberal hegemony and transformation in Europe /
edited by Alan W. Cafruny and Magnus Ryner.
    p. cm. — (Governance in Europe)
Includes bibliographical references and index.
  ISBN 0-7425-1141-3 (cloth : alk. paper)—ISBN 0-7425-1142-1 (pbk. :
alk. paper)
  1. European Union. 2. Liberalism—Europe, Western. 3. Globalization.
4. Europe—Economic integration. 5. United States—Foreign
relations—Europe, Western. 6. Europe, Western—Foreign
relations—United States. I. Cafruny, Alan W. II. Ryner, Magnus, 1965–
III. Series.
  D1060 .R85 2003
  341.242'2—dc21
                                                                2003000520

Printed in the United States of America

♾ ™ The paper used in this publication meets the minimum requirements of
American National Standard for Information Sciences—Permanence of Paper
for Printed Library Materials, ANSI/NISO Z39.48-1992.

Contents

Preface

The title of this book, raising the question of whether European integration has generated a "fortress Europe" capable of challenging American supremacy in the world, appropriately reflects the general sentiment of the volume: If there ever were such ambitions in the re-launch of European integration in the 1980s, the project is now in ruin. Not seldom with regret, the contributors suggest that the EU, with all due recognition of the complexity of "multi-leveledness," is being subordinated into a much larger neoliberal, transnational, structural, and institutional ensemble under American leadership.

In line with the theoretical ambitions of this volume, the title also directs the reader to a deeper ontological and epistemological level. In particular, it is suggestive of a dialectical and critical-theoretical attempt to synthesize idealism and materialism. It was Denis de Rougemont who first invoked the phrase in contemporary discussions about European integration. He locates the term in the German idealist tradition and in the intellectual movement of Sturm und Drang arising out of the Revolutionary and Napoleonic Wars, which placed not only the "question of Germany" but also of Europe on the agenda. Goethe uses the term *verfallene Schloesser* to lament that the "weight of history" of national rivalries and protracted wars was preventing Europe from realizing the full potential of the Enlightenment that is its civilizational legacy. He thought that America "had it better" because it did not carry this weight. Hegel, however, put another slant on this sentiment. In a characteristically dialectical move, he asserted that the Revolutionary and Napoleonic Wars expressed the synthesis, and hence transcendence, of the "ruined fortress" and "Enlightenment." France's victory at the Battle of Valmy, and subsequently the conquests of Napoleon, would lead to European unification, the embodiment of the Idea of the Enlightenment, and "the end of history."[1] Of course, Hegel would be disappointed by the outcome of these wars, and his idealist-determinist interpretation of the dialectic is not used in this book.

Drawing not on Hegel, but rather on Gramsci, the authors in this volume suggest that the politics of Europe, which today has to assign central importance to the EU, is more open-ended and contingent on social struggle and compromises between social forces. It is developing in response to a complex interplay of material, ideational, and military factors (relations of force), of which the book offers an analysis. Although the question mark in the title is appropriate as a recognition of contingency (and as an implicit appeal for change in practices), the title suggests that the authors are more pessimistic than Hegel about the prospects of a European unification around a "civilizational ideal" and hence perhaps stick closer to Goethe's original sentiments. It is therefore apt that the picture on the cover is of one of the ruined fortresses of the Cathars in southern France, who were defeated around the twelfth century in the crusade against the Albigensian heresy. Although the Cathars were ardent believers in original sin, they also accepted the possibility of metamorphosis and salvation through a life of virtue. Gramsci invoked catharsis in his discussion of the political process of overcoming narrow self-interest in politics and attempting to forge an "ethico-political" conception—the defining feature of a hegemonic, or a counter-hegemonic, movement.[2] Since the EU's subordination to an American-centered neoliberal hegemony clearly does *not* represent such a catharsis, the ruined fortress of the Cathars serves as an appropriate symbol of our pessimism about the EU at the turn of the century.

The editors would like to thank Philip Cerny, Colin Hay, and Steven McGuire for serving as discussants on various conference panels in which contributors presented chapters of this book. Stephen Gill directed us to Denis de Rougemont and suggested the title. We thank Gary Marks (our series editor), Susan McEachern, Jehanne Schweitzer, and Matt Hammon at Rowman & Littlefield for their commitment to this project as well as their patience. Cheryl Adam and Dawn Woodward provided invaluable assistance on the manuscript.

NOTES

1. Denis de Rougemont, *Ouvres Completes de Denis de Rougemont III: Ecrits sur l'Europe*, vol. 1 (Paris: ELA/La Difference, 1994), inter alia 38–39, 598–645, esp. 634.

2. Antonio Gramsci, *Selections from the Prison Notebooks* (New York: International Publishers, 1971), 366–67.

Abbreviations and Acronyms

AMBO	Albanian-Macedonian-Bulgarian Oil Pipeline Corporation
BP	British Petroleum
CAP	Common Agricultural Policy
CBI	Confederation of British Industry
CDU	Christian Democratic Union
CEEP	European Center of Enterprises with Public Participation
CFSP	Common Foreign and Security Policy
CGIL	General Confederation of Labor
CGT	Confédération générale du travail
CSNEP	Common Strategy for National Employment Policies
CSU	Christian-Social Union
EADS	European Aeronautical Defense and Space Company
EBRD	European Bank for Reconstruction and Development
EC	European Commission
ECB	European Central Bank
ECJ	European Court of Justice
ECSC	European Coal and Steel Community
EEC	European Economic Community
EMF	European Metalworkers' Federation
EMS	European Monetary System
EMU	Economic and Monetary Union
ERM	Exchange Rate Mechanism
ERT	European Roundtable of Industrialists
ESCP	European Security and Defense Policy

ESDI	European Security and Defense Identity
ETUC	Congress of the European Trade Union Confederation
EU	European Union
EUREKA	European Research Coordination Agency
EWCs	European Works Councils
FDP	Free Democratic Party
FO	Force ouvrière
FSAP	Financial Services Action Plan
GDP	Gross Domestic Product
GDR	German Democratic Republic
GM	General Motors
IBM	International Business Machines
IFOR	Implementation Force
IGC	Intergovernmental Conference
IMF	International Monetary Fund
IO	International Organization
IPE	International Political Economy
IR	International Relations
JNA	Yugoslav National Army
KLA	Kosovo Liberation Army
MATIF	Marché à terme des instruments financiers
NAPs	National Action Plans
OECD	Organization for Economic Cooperation and Development
OSCE	Organization for Security and Cooperation in Europe
PDS	Party of Democratic Socialism
PHARE	Poland and Hungary Action for Economic Reconversion Programs
PS	Socialist Party of France
PSC	Political and Security Committee
SEA	Single European Act
SEM	Single European Market
SFOR	Peace Stabilization Forces
SIB	Securities Investment Board
SNCF	Société nationale des chemins de fer français
SPD	Social Democratic Party of Germany
SROs	self-regulation organizations
TEU	Treaty on European Union
TINA	"There is no alternative"
TNCs	Transnational Corporations
TUC	Congress of the British Trade Union Congress
UNDP	*Human Development Report*
UNICE	Union of Industrial and Employers'—Confederations of Europe
UNPROFOR	United Nations Protection Force
WEU	Western European Union
WTO	World Trade Organization

Introduction

⸙

The Study of European Integration in the Neoliberal Era

ALAN W. CAFRUNY AND MAGNUS RYNER

This book has been written from the premise that research on European integration has lagged behind theoretical developments in the fields of international relations, international political economy, and international organization that have been emerging since at least the mid-1980s. It seeks to remedy this shortcoming by presenting contributions to an analysis of European integration that draw on one of the strands of theoretical innovations of the last decade and a half: critical political economy, or transnational historical materialism.

"Eurosclerosis" is a term often used to describe the empirical state of European economics, politics, and society. We would suggest that it is more apt for describing the lack of adjustment of the conceptual frameworks of analysis of European integration. The state of theoretical sclerosis in the field of European integration studies can be illustrated by the fact that what it considers to be the theoretical state of the art—the neorealist/neoliberal debate—while still providing a useful set of perspectives, has not been the "state of the art" of IR, IPE, or IO since the mid-1980s. At that time, Friedrich Kratochwil and John Gerard Ruggie published an important review essay in *International Organization* that helped expand the ontological, epistemological, and methodological terms of debate in world politics but has not yet resulted in a corresponding widening in the subfield of European integration studies.[1]

In their review, Kratochwil and Ruggie took stock of the capacity of IR scholarship to make sense of important events in the international system such as the breakdown of the Bretton Woods system and oscillations in East–West conflict. These events, of course, would lead to even more profound changes that would

take the IR discipline completely by surprise. Kratochwil and Ruggie found the
state of the art wanting. What ought to have been fairly straightforward empirical questions, they wrote, had resulted in much puzzlement and debate: For example, did the Bretton Woods "regime" collapse in 1971–1973 or was the change
"norm governed"?[2] More recently, we can point to the inability to predict the
end of the Cold War and the erroneous and highly misleading thesis of America's hegemonic decline. Theoretically, Kratochwil and Ruggie pointed toward
the inadequacies of individualist and behaviorialist ontology and positivist epistemology to deal with the question. The analysis had led the discipline to a key
concept—regimes—which was inherently based on intersubjectivity ("we know
regimes by their principled and shared understandings of desirable and acceptable forms of social behavior"). Yet the discipline insisted on continuing—qua
positivism—to analytically separate the subject from the object and infer meaning from "objective" behavior.[3] This method of inquiry is useful when *ceteris
paribus* assumptions can plausibly be maintained, but when the broader social
context changes so profoundly that the interests and, indeed, very identities of
the principal actors of the system are in doubt, it becomes highly problematic.

To be sure, there has been some attention given to research in European integration from one of the perspectives that Kratochwil and Ruggie believed to be
among the most promising, that of liberal constructivism. However, little attention has been given to the other strand of thought on the nature of intersubjectivity that Kratochwil and Ruggie also considered to provide a way forward: that
is the unconventional historical materialism that in the 1980s had been articulated by Robert W. Cox, primarily through a retrieval of the thought of the Italian Marxist and theoretical founder of Euro-communism, Antonio Gramsci.[4]
The lack of attention is surprising in view of the growing literature on this perspective in the broader field of international political economy. It is the purpose
of this book to rectify this by providing a volume that analyzes developments in
European integration, and the foundation of the European Union, from such a
theoretical perspective.

An "unconventional historical materialist" perspective on the dynamics on
the European Union is worthy of consideration for a number of reasons. One has
to do with epistemology and methodology, which has been captured by Cox's oft-
quoted distinction between problem-solving theory and critical theory.[5] Positivist problem-solving theory, based on *ceteris paribus* assumptions, takes reality
as it finds it and concerns itself with problems of management of an established
system. For those purposes, this type of theory works well. However, when the
object of analysis is not the disequilibrium of an established system, but systemic
change, then critical theory, "which asks how orders have come about and how
they might change," is more appropriate. We take the view that the formation
and consolidation of the European Union takes place against the backdrop of a
set of secular shifts of world order, which includes the transition from Fordist production systems, the collapse of the Soviet Union, and the attendant end of the

Cold War. Hence, the epistemology and methodology of critical theory are apt for an analysis of the European Union.

A second reason for studying the European integration from the perspective of unconventional historical materialism has to do with ontology and what ought to be the fundamental object of political science: the study of the nature and dynamics of power. We know from the standpoint of common sense that European integration has in the 1980s and the 1990s been market-driven, that it is connected to a broader transnational phenomenon often referred to as "globalization," and that it has an attendant, essentially neoliberal raison d'être. This was not the least brought into focus by the Gothenburg Summit of 2001 and by the issues that were forced into the public arena by the so-called antiglobalization protests. Yet none of the aforementioned perspectives provide a satisfactory and comprehensive analysis of the nature of market power, which is constitutive of neoliberalism.

The inability of the theoretical mainstream adequately to address the question of legitimacy must be stressed. A growing number of scholars of European integration now assert that the European Union (EU) might be conceived of not as supranational organization, but rather as a polity in its own right. If these scholars are correct, there are nonetheless crucial differences between the EU and its constituent member states. Europe's nation-states experienced a significant degree of popular participation in the late nineteenth and twentieth centuries as universal suffrage and other democratic rights were achieved, working-class parties emerged, and welfare states were built and consolidated. The EU, by contrast, was built not by "the people," but rather by diplomats, bureaucrats, and multinational corporations. As the European Commission (EC) itself acknowledges in its use of the term "democratic deficit," the EU has experienced no comparable phase of democratization or socialization. During the first thirty years, working-class parties and trade unions either actively opposed the EU or were absent at its creation. If the EU is indeed a polity, it is, in Phillippe Schmitter's words, a "novel form of domination."[6]

The EU's elitist origins have greatly influenced mainstream scholarship. Despite their considerable differences, in many important respects the prevailing theoretical perspectives on European integration suffer from an excessive focus on institutions and ideas, while paying insufficient attention to the ways in which these institutions and ideas have during the last decade promoted a neoliberal agenda that has served to recast relations between capital and labor. In its most recent and significant phase of development, to be sure, governing social democrats have thoroughly embraced the EU. However, the emergent monetary union has resulted not in the democratization of the Union, but rather in a deepening crisis of legitimation as these parties have abandoned their distinctive commitments and traditional (albeit diminished) social bases.

The limitations of mainstream theory were perhaps less salient in the early years of the Union than at the present time. The focus on elite decision making, institutional spillover, and interstate bargaining made more sense when the European project itself had limited engagement with national societies and the content of comparatively modest European initiatives was consistent with the main political and economic contours of the postwar settlement. Rhetoric aside, prior to the completion of the single market and the Maastricht Treaty in the early 1990s the EU was not an important independent factor in European or world affairs. When European institutions did penetrate deeply into society, as with the Common Agricultural Policy, they did so not as externally constitutive policies but rather as internationally negotiated regimes designed to buttress existing corporatist settlements at the national level. More ambitious initiatives such as the Werner Plan for monetary union and the McDougall Report on the budget foundered on the rocks of national rivalry. Two decades ago it was plausibly argued that the corporatist networks established within the framework of European nation-states might prove resilient against the coming tidal wave of globalization. Yet, with the benefit of hindsight, it is clear that, notwithstanding given particularities of state–society relations, the European region as a whole is succumbing to this wave and has not, as yet, summoned either the will or the resources to develop an alternative strategy.

At the present time, however, the establishment of a monetary union, building on the unification of the market in goods and services, has brought about a novel and qualitative transformation in the nature of the Union. Such a transformation is important not primarily because it has triggered new forms of institutional deepening, as commonly understood. After all, from the point of view of traditional integration theory, the salience of these forms should not be exaggerated. Europe may now be understood as a complicated tangle of overlapping levels of governance, but national sovereignty has not died. As the Nice and Laeken Summits have clearly indicated, and as the convention presided over by Valery Giscard d'Estaing has confirmed, Europe seems bound to endure what amounts to a permanent constitutional crisis, one that is more likely to be exacerbated than transcended by further phases of enlargement. Although the contributors to this volume strongly assert the salience of trans-European business networks and the primacy of neoliberalism as a central organizing concept for the post-Maastricht European project, they do not claim that states have ceded their role as "masters of the treaties" or that state power is no longer relevant.

The significance of the current phase of the EU thus derives not only from the particular institutional and constitutional forms that are emerging, as much scholarship has assumed, but also from the socioeconomic content of current EU policies. The Maastricht Treaty and subsequent agreements designed to realize the monetary union have served to "constitutionalize" an emergent neoliberal European order. Yet this order is increasingly the subject of contestation and rebellion, as registered not only in the streets of Genoa and Gothenburg, but also in Irish and Danish referenda and in the recent reexaminations of key pillars of the Stability Pact. Although the problems that the national and supranational politics of neoliberalism raise are insufficiently addressed in the literature on European integration, they are central to the contemporary politics and future trajectory of the Union.

We would argue that the reluctance and incapacity to deal with these questions have to do with a priori assumptions. All versions of mainstream integration theory assume that market forces are expressions of an inner rationality of human nature, and that the market constitutes the "realm of freedom" standing in opposition to the state. Thus both intergovernmentalists of a realist persuasion and functionalists of a liberal internationalist bent assume that power and interest are strictly contained in the sphere of interstate affairs. The disagreement between these theoretical schools centers on the extent to which the "anarchy" of interstate relations limits the realization of a putative "inner rationality" inherent in market forces and free trade as the "motor force" of integration. The more recently developed theoretical perspectives of liberal constructivism and multilevel governance, despite other important contributions, do not overcome this blind spot with regard to power in neoliberalism.

PLAN OF THE BOOK

In chapter 1, Bastiaan van Apeldoorn, Henk Overbeek, and Magnus Ryner develop this argument in more detail in their critical review of integration theory, which concludes by setting out the basic theoretical foundations for a critical political economy approach to the analysis of European integration. Continuing to draw on Marx, but also on Polanyi, Braudel, and Gramsci, they conceive of market integration as a socially constructed process containing conflict and contradictions, power relations, and efforts to mediate and contain conflict in order to produce a social order—in the case of contemporary European integration, a transnational neoliberal socioeconomic order. The key concepts required for the difficult task of analyzing this process is hegemony, as understood in the Gramscian sense. The concept of hegemony draws attention to the continuities of economy, culture, state, and international order as well as the problems of maintaining coherence among these different "levels" of social order.

Whereas the first chapter situates critical political economy in relation to the limitations of other theoretical approaches and defines its basic ontological foundations, in chapter 2 Stephen Gill develops a more concrete set of concepts for the analysis of the historical situation. Drawing on Braudel's "dialectics of duration" and on Gramsci's "relations of force," Gill argues that the *Prison Notebooks* provide us with a set of flexible historicist concepts (such as "passive revolution," "historic bloc," "organic crisis," and indeed "hegemony") that can be elaborated so as to analyze different concrete socioeconomic and sociopolitical situations, whether they are national, international, or multileveled.

Gill then illustrates how one can make sense of European integration on the basis of this methodological injunction. He argues that European integration in the 1980s constitutes a moment in a broader transnational and trilateral neoliberal historic bloc that has been in formation since the 1980s, and that has been forged under the aegis of American state and civil societal leadership. Furthermore, this formation should be seen in the even broader historical time scale of the modern capitalist world system. In many respects, the present represents a return to the essential sociopolitical features established by the Glorious Revolution of 1688 in Britain: a subordination of politics to the power of property and capital and political oligarchy, expressed in a minimalist and constitutionalist state form. Hence, the welfare-nationalist and statist counter-tendencies associated with the "Fordist compromise" and "embedded liberalism," which in turn had resolved the organic crisis of capitalism in the 1930s, have been undermined.

Posing the transformation from the Luxembourg Compromise to the Maastricht accords in these terms, Gill argues that the present is characterized by "new constitutionalist" and "disciplinary neoliberal" forms of governance, which are embedding an increasingly inegalitarian and socially precarious shareholder capitalism, centered around the virtual accumulation of financial services. Juxtaposing this historic bloc with the organic crisis of liberal capitalism analyzed by Gramsci in the 1930s and the passive revolution underway in Central and Eastern Europe, Gill implicitly warns that the oligarchic nature of this bloc may not have a sufficiently strong social and ideological basis in Europe to acquire a "hegemonic aura." Indeed, it seems as if it depends on the welfarist arrangements it is itself eroding (e.g., unemployment insurance) to mediate its own social external effects. At the same time, history does not repeat itself but is always characterized by a dialectics between the old and the new. One decisive question of prospective stability of neoliberal Europe is the extent and salience of a new "rentier bloc." Apart from transnational capital, oriented around finance, this bloc includes privileged professional workers whose wealth is connected to global financial capital through, for example, private pension savings. They also share the *mentalities* of an emerging market civilization of commodified production and consumption. If this bloc is sufficiently extensive and if the material basis of its reproduction can be secured, then the supremacy of the neoliberal historic bloc, in which the EU of the Maastricht settlement is embedded, might be secured in Europe. This is, however, far from certain, and deficits of social representation generate vulnerabilities to challenges from the Left and perhaps even more from the Right.

In chapter 3, Otto Holman and Kees van der Pijl provide a more detailed and in-depth analysis of the nature of class leadership of the disciplinary neoliberal bloc in Europe. They contend that whereas in the 1970s and the 1980s one could discern tendencies toward a distinct European alternative to an Anglo-American, neoliberal economic strategy in continental Europe, the accumulation strategy of European capital is now firmly organized along neoliberal lines. On the other hand, although European capital no longer represents an alternative accumulation strategy (or, in their words, a "comprehensive concept of control"), one can discern the development of an integrated and coherent European capitalist class, organized on the macroregional European terrain. This is in contrast to the earlier state of affairs in which the power of European capital was constrained by the fact that it was organized on a national basis, and was integrated through a "hub and spoke" with American capital at its center. Hence, European capital does not represent an "ethico-political" challenge to the hegemonic order, but it does now constitute a strong competitor on the economic-corporate level to American capital. The one exception to this is British capital, which has not been integrated into European regional capital.

Within their chosen empirical domain, Holman and van der Pijl present a further refinement of the relations of force argument by Gill. Theirs is not an economic reductionist conception of class that can be inscribed in objective relations. Rather, it is formed through political struggles, often internal to capital itself between distinct fractions. Hence, there was nothing predetermined in the neoliberal nature of the comprehensive concept of control. Here they point to what they consider to be the strategic role of private planning bodies in European integration, such as the European Roundtable of Industrialists, which has served to strategically coordinate capitalist discipline in Europe through the Maastricht accords. This has primarily been realized through the European legal regime, centered around the Directorate-General of Competition and the European Court of Justice. It is important to note here that Holman and van der Pijl do not construct a simplistic or one-dimensional account of a "Europe of capital." They do indeed point to the continued importance of nation-states in social regulation and in the mediation of nationally specific compromises with subordinate classes and groups. Strategic coordination implies something more differentiated and multileveled, in which the legal regime ensures that nationally distinct modes of regulation are mediating nationally distinct class compromises with subordinate groups. However, the post-Maastricht legal regime ensures that the regulations of these nation-states are configured so as to internalize and extend capitalist discipline onto their social formations. Indeed, this noncorrespondence of the space of operation of capital, its strategic coordination, and national regulation with its attendant compromises can be seen as promoting the new constitutionalism and minimalism that Gill sees as constitutive of neoliberalism.

If transnational neoliberal hegemony is multileveled, this raises a key question: What is the configuration of levels? The question is further analyzed in chapter 4, where Alan Cafruny focuses on issues pertaining to the inner core of sovereign state power: military security issues. Cafruny concludes that contemporary transnational neoliberal hegemony is a "minimal hegemony," in which sovereign military power continues to be differentiated into individual state units. Focusing on the pivotal European security issue of the 1990s, the break-up of Yugoslavia, Cafruny argues that this is not least the case in Europe. As a result of narrow national concerns and interstate rivalry within Europe, the

Common Foreign and Security Policy (CFSP) failed to generate a morally credible and effective European response to the Yugoslav crisis, and the United States
instead took the lead. Paradoxically, this fragmentation consolidated neoliberal
hegemony. The Yugoslav crisis effectively ended any possibility that the EU
would develop a coherent policy through which a "European social model" might
have challenged U.S.-led neoliberalism via effective coherent political power
underpinning the launching of the euro. The implication of this is that there is
no correspondence between the incipient regional coherence of European corporate organization (see Holman and van der Pijl, chapter 3) and the organization of coercive state power.

The failure of a common European security policy was not simply a result of
American design. Rather, reflecting the reluctance of American society to risk
military casualties and the broader incapacities of the American political system
with respect to the establishment and maintenance of a global *imperium*, the
United States had hoped at the outset that the EU would have been able to cope
with the Yugoslav crisis. Hence, American policy to the crisis was reactive and
improvisational. Together with EU's lack of a common vision, the cost of the reactive nature of this policy was born by the victims of the conflict. Minimal
hegemony, then, is thin in terms of coherent ethico-political leadership. Sufficient consent is nevertheless ensured because of the absence of a credible socioeconomic alternative after the end of the Cold War, and the resilience of the
objective structures of the world market economy from which especially American political and civil society enjoys benefits. EU states and societies are relatively privileged but subordinate partners in this context.

The relationship between the transnational and the national is further explored by Leila Simona Talani in chapter 5. She approaches the topic from the
vantage point of what perhaps is the central organizational node of disciplinary
neoliberalism in Europe: the monetary regime that initially was organized
through EMS and that later became entrenched through the EMU. She does not
deny that neoliberalism is a common denominator in European monetary governance. However, variations in state policies toward the EMU need to be
explained, and the determinant for her remains relations of force and the modal-
ities of class alliance and class conflict within different nation-states. She sub-
stantiates her argument through an analysis of the different conclusions that
Italy and the United Kingdom drew from the financial crisis in 1993, which
forced the two states to withdraw from the Exchange Rate Mechanism. For the
UK, this led to a withdrawal from participation in the EMU project because of
the dominance and interests of financial capital centered in the City of London
and because monetarist discipline had already been established through the
Thatcherite revolution in the 1980s. Italy, however, had consistently depended
on an imported disciplinary neoliberalism through the EMS, and it required the
EMU to do the same to discipline organized labor and other social forces demanding social protection. Furthermore, in the absence of a global node of fi-

nancial capital comparable to the City of London, Italian productive capital constituted the dominant social interest.

Talani's most original contribution is, however, her refinement of the relations of force conception, which makes it amenable to short-term conjunctural analysis. Her dialectical distinction of a pure economic analysis (concerning short-term interests of different sectors and class fractions), pure political analysis (concerning the day-to-day considerations of the state), and political economy analysis (concerning the organic coherence of a historic bloc) allows her to explain the temporary convergence of British and Italian policy (the synchronization of entry and exit from the ERM). As pointed out, though, only in Italy was the conjunctural as well as structural (i.e., organic) configuration compatible with participation in the European monetary regime.

The question of rendering neoliberal hegemony organic in the EU is further explored in chapters 6, 7, and 8, which are concerned with the question of forging mass consent with neoliberalism and general social integration legitimacy— what Gramsci referred to as the "ethico-political moment." These chapters, in other words, begin to probe Gill's hypothesis that disciplinary neoliberalism may not be compatible with sufficiently broad-based social integration. They do so by analyzing what Gramsci called "political society": the actors and institutions charged with the task of integrating the administrative aspects of governance with civil society. This is primarily the terrain of mass parties and in some instances peak-level interest organizations, which continue to be organized primarily along national lines. Analysis in these chapters focuses on political society in the "big three" EU member states of Britain, France, and Germany.

As the site of a relatively undeveloped residual welfare state as well as the home of Thatcherism, Britain is the state–civil society complex associated with neoliberalism par excellence. Neoliberalism was organized domestically and organically by Thatcherism in the early 1980s. With a weak industrial structure, but a strong service economy centered around the City of London, its social formation provides a rather broad-based foundation for a *rentier* bloc and the ethos of shareholder democracy. This is the context in which the British Labour Party has been reformed to "New Labour" under Tony Blair. New Labour has not challenged neoliberal hegemony in Britain, but has rather consolidated it by forging an alliance between crucial elements of the Thatcherite bloc: white-collar professionals and working-class constituents.

In chapter 6, Colin Hay and Matthew Watson show how the social scientific discourse of globalization has been instrumental in the forging of the New Labour project. Hay and Watson's chapter contains a strong critique of the essentialist claims of globalization discourse in which globalization is depicted as an intransitive, technological, and socially neutral process. They demonstrate that because of the widespread acceptance of these claims, the power of the globalization thesis derives from its ideological and Sorelian mythological function of making social and political actors act *as if* globalization was an objective force.

In Britain, the contingent was rendered necessary when New Labour advanced a successful strategy around the slogan "There is no alternative" (TINA). Hay and Watson reject idealist accounts of this historical transformation. New Labour's discourse was forged against the backdrop of tremendous electoral payoffs as it allowed the Labour Party to occupy the center ground in a society with a strong rentier bloc. In this context, the logic of TINA allowed the New Labour leadership to resolve significant internal conflicts that had torn apart the Labour Party in the 1980s. The result was the construction of the broadly based social alliance that delivered the victory of 1997 and ensured that the British state remains the primary champion of U.S.–led transnational neoliberal hegemony in Europe.

Ben Clift's study of the economic policy of the French Socialists in chapter 7 points to a more complex and dialectical situation in a society with strong statist and "republican revolutionary" traditions, and where financial capital is not hegemonic. Quite clearly, since Mitterrand's U-turn in the early 1980s, French state strategy has been based on disciplinary neoliberalism as it has increasingly been configured along the lines of German monetarism and the norms of the EMS and EMU. Nevertheless, Clift shows that it is still important to make a distinction between active neoliberal policy and pronouncements by French Socialist ministers of finance and their strategy in what he calls "the long game." Although technocrats in the French treasury and the Bank of France, as well as some politicians of the right in the French Socialist Party, subscribe to new constitutionalism, others are biding their time as they wait for more opportune moments to restore *dirigisme* and the social market at the European level. Nevertheless, the long game demands that they pursue neoliberal policies in order to retain their credentials in the prevailing national and international order. Clift's account suggests that conformity to neoliberal governance may be less a matter of ideological conversion than of structural and institutional compulsion. It also highlights the serious legitimation problems for neoliberalism in continental Europe.

The question of the tension between the social market and disciplinary neoliberalism, as well as the question of whether monetary integration could serve as a Trojan horse against neoliberalism, is further addressed in Ryner's study of Germany in chapter 8. This study begins by identifying a German paradox. Germany has been the institutional guarantor of disciplinary neoliberalism (and hence blocked the long game of the French Socialists) through its leadership in the construction and the management of the EMS and the EMU. At the same time, Germany has one of the most entrenched sets of welfare-state traditions and institutions in Europe. Ryner argues that this combination of disciplinary neoliberalism and the social market has only been possible because of the exceptionally strong position of the German export sector. However, reunification, transnationalization of production, and post-Fordist restructuring are undermining this strong export position. As a result the neoliberal project is subject to increased contradictions in Germany that the mass parties and politicians find it increasingly difficult to mediate. Ryner shows that the defeat of Kohl represented the exhaustion of one strategy for resolving this tension while the Lafontainian challenge to disciplinary neoliberalism announced an alternative resolution. Had it proven successful, Lafontaine's project would have had wide-ranging ramifications for European and perhaps even transnational economic governance: It would have challenged the contemporary neoliberal configuration by providing the political basis for a revival of Keynesianism through the Franco-German axis. However, Lafontaine's removal, orchestrated indirectly within the SPD itself, is indicative of the ideological and political power of neoliberalism. Nevertheless, the contradictions remain. It is against this backdrop that one should read recurring signs by German politicians that they are tempted to loosen the strict criteria of the Stability Pact.

The book presents the European Union as a market-oriented, neoliberal hegemonic project. Chapters 9 and 10 address the question of whether initiatives on the EU level that are less obviously part of such "market making" contradict this approach. In chapter 9 Hans-Jürgen Bieling and Thorsten Schulten analyze the social dimension and European industrial relations, and they show that developments in these spheres are perfectly compatible with the EU's transition to neoliberalism. Indeed, notwithstanding the legitimation problems identified in chapters 7 and 8, one should not underestimate the capacity of neoliberal hegemonic strategies to draw on welfarist institutional forms in their efforts to sustain legitimacy.

Through an impressive summary of developments in the forging of European neoliberal hegemony, which in fact brings together the various facets that have been covered in this book, Bieling and Schulten argue that neoliberal hegemony should not be confused with the end of organized capitalism. First, their chapter invokes the dialectic of commodification and socialization already introduced in the chapter by Holman and van der Pijl. Trade unionism has become an institutional form that supports neoliberalism rather than challenges it. On the national level, trade unions have been forced to partake in a competitive corporatism that reproduces the logic of neoliberalism but also serves to socially integrate welfare-state constituencies into the emergent historic bloc. On the European level, Bieling and Schulten identify the European Social Dialogue as the center of a symbolic Euro-corporatism, which serves the same function. Despite the emptiness of real policy content of these measures, trade unions strengthen and legitimate European liberalization by participating in this forum. It is not that trade unionists are being ideologically converted per se. Rather, it is a combination of structural political weakness and the loyalty to a political institutional form that explains this acquiescence—or a lack of political alternative. It is possible that the pan-European cooperation between trade unions that this engenders will in the long run lead to a credible political challenge to neoliberalism. However, such a challenge is unlikely to emerge from the social dialogue and other measures sponsored by the Commission, but is more likely to emerge from autonomous coordinated action undertaken by the trade unions "spontaneously" in light of their common problems.

Beginning with chapter 5, the contributors have progressively expanded the analysis of the power bloc from its inner core of class and elite cohesion and strategy toward an analysis of mass politics and legitimacy. This culminates in chapter 10, in which Giles Scott-Smith broadens the discussion and explicitly addresses the question of legitimacy and citizenship with reference to culture. This, of course, is the terrain of the ethico-political moment par excellence. Scott-Smith also goes beyond the social realist analysis of the previous chapters of "what is" to address more normative questions head on. Again, drawing on van der Pijl's conception of socialization, Scott-Smith argues that the supranational forms of governance implied in the Maastricht agreements point to the fact that integration cannot be contained within the realm of the market. This, however, inherently leads to a problem of democratic legitimacy since supranational governance, in its technocratic corporatist manifestation removed from a mass base, is not grounded in such legitimacy. In his search for a potential resolution to this problem, he points to the progressive potential in the code of civic values found in the treaties, such as the Convention for the Protection of Human Rights and Fundamental Freedoms. These codes, when combined with a more developed form of European social citizenship, might provide the basis for a durable solution to the legitimation problem. The problem, though, is that such a development is hindered by the present-day neoliberal content of integration, and as a result EU culture policy aimed at forging a "European identity" has been, as Bieling and Schulten argued with respect to Euro-corporatism in chapter 9, a rather empty gesture.

Finally, in chapter 11 Alan Cafruny focuses on the core medium through which neoliberal governance is exercised, the EMU. Like its less ambitious predecessors, the EMU must operate within the context of transatlantic rivalry as well as unity. Although it is commonly assumed that the euro will ultimately place Europe on a more equal footing with the United States, the monetary union as presently constituted is subordinated to U.S. hegemony and contains the seeds of future conflict and instability. The lack of a common fiscal policy and adequate redistributive mechanisms, the absence of an authentic European public space, and the bitter fruits of monetarism—slow growth and uneven development—generate national rivalry and deepen the Union's crisis of legitimation. Neoliberalism does not provide an adequate economic or ethico-political basis for the further development of the monetary union or of a transnational European capitalist class.

NOTES

1. Friedrich Kratochwil and John Gerard Ruggie, "International Organization: The State of the Art of the Art of the State," *International Organization* 40, no. 4 (1986): 753–75.

2. Kratochwil and Ruggie, "International Organization," 764.

3. Kratochwil and Ruggie, 764.

4. Kratochwil and Ruggie, 763.

5. Robert W. Cox, *Production, Power, and World Order: Social Forces in the Making of History* (New York: Columbia University Press, 1987).

6. Philippe Schmitter, "The EC as an Emergent and Novel Form of Political Domination," *Estudio/Working paper* 1991/26, Center de Estudios Avanzados en Ciencias Sociales, Fundacion Juan March, Madrid, 1991.

I

⚜

THE EUROPEAN UNION AND NEOLIBERAL HEGEMONY

1

⁂

Theories of European Integration

A Critique

BASTIAAN VAN APELDOORN, HENK OVERBEEK,
AND MAGNUS RYNER

In this chapter we introduce the basic premises of the critical-theoretical frame-work that, with individual variations, underpins the contributions to this book. We show how our theoretical framework differs from mainstream theories of European integration and identify what we consider to be the essential weak-nesses of these theories. We then proceed to develop our critical theory, thereby setting the stage for the concrete empirical analyses contained in subsequent chapters.

Our basic argument is that mainstream theories, because of their basic con-ceptual design and assumptions, are unable to achieve what should be the fun-damental objectives of a political science of the European Union (EU): to understand the nature of power in the EU, including its organization and distri-bution, and to assess the implications of a given set of power relations for legiti-macy. In addition, if there is a contradiction between the actual practice of EU politics and the general principles of legitimacy in democratic society, then it is necessary to understand the conditions that might facilitate a resolution of this contradiction. We do not argue that mainstream frameworks are not interested in questions of power and legitimacy. We do claim, however, that by their very design they are unable to conceptualize adequately power relations that are constitutive of capitalist market structures. In other words, these mainstream theories fail to account for the *structural power* that determines the particular tra-jectory of European integration.[1]

Despite their important variations, all mainstream schools of thought—including neofunctionalism, realism, liberal intergovernmentalism, multilevel governance, and liberal constructivism—assume either explicitly or implicitly that market forces are expressions of an inner rationality of universal human nature that is held to be the essence of the realm of freedom in political affairs. This assumption makes these theoretical frameworks *inherently incapable of grasping fundamentally the structuration of power relations* on a social terrain, where market forces have come to constitute the dominant principle of social organization to which all other principles and media of social organization have become subordinated. There can be little doubt that this has become the case in the EU after the Single European Act (SEA), which affirmed and generalized the notion of mutual recognition in trade (enforced by the principles of direct effect, supremacy, and state liability in Community law), selectively reconfigured voting procedures for the passing of directives and regulations to facilitate the completion of the Single Market in 1992, and enshrined the four fundamental economic freedoms as the supreme rights to be protected above all else in a nascent economic constitutional framework. The essentially neoliberal content and social purpose of the "re-launch" of European integration was affirmed in the Treaty of Maastricht, which ensured that the Economic and Monetary Union would be organized to mobilize the disciplinary force of global financial markets and thereby to create an institutional framework of macroeconomic governance based on the ideas of sound money and finance.

Given the staggering amount of literature on European integration, it is impossible to provide an exhaustive review. As a result, we focus upon a few selected pieces, that are representative of the main theoretical tendencies. We begin our review by considering the oldest and most familiar debate in European integration studies: the debate between neofunctionalism and neorealist intergovernmentalism. Situating this debate in the more general context of the classical realist–liberal divide in international relations, we argue that, despite their important disagreements, the protagonists in this debate share certain problematic assumptions about a universal human nature. Both schools of thought employ utilitarian and individualist assumptions that have during the last two decades been subjected to criticism in the field of international relations for their failure to grasp the nature and central role of *social* power relations. Remarkably, these critiques have not been recognized and addressed in the subfield of European integration studies, and we suggest that it is high time that they were. From this vantage point, we proceed to criticize more recent theoretical approaches to the study of the EU, such as the multilevel governance approach and liberal constructivism. The former makes a singular contribution toward breaking down rigid distinctions among levels of analysis, and it generates considerable empirical insights concerning the internationalization of domestic politics. However, because it is fundamentally based on pluralist political and social science à la Parsons, Easton, Dahl, Lijphart, and others, this approach shares the limitations of the aforementioned liberal ontological assumptions of neofunctionalism and intergovernmentalism (with the partial and interesting exception of, as we shall see, Fritz Scharpf). Liberal constructivism, following the path of the likes of Ruggie, Kratochwil, Onuf, and Wendt in international relations theory, on the other hand, rightly engages the contingent, subjective, and social nature of identity formation. Therefore, it does represent a fundamental break with the transhistorical a priori utilitarian individualism of mainstream integration theory. However, the problem with this approach is that it (qua Parsons) implicitly maintains an untenable dualism between matter and ideas, which leads it astray from an analysis of the overdetermined social power relations that underpin identity and ideas.[2] Because this dualism has diverted the attention of liberal constructivism from the manner in which the economy is socially constructed, in practice liberal economics has remained uncritically accepted. Hence, its analysis of identity becomes little more than a "new idealism" that loses sight of the manner in which power and social interests are part and parcel of the hegemonic practices that constitute identity and ideas. Hegemonic practices are precisely the object of analysis of the critical political economy, the premises of which are outlined in the concluding section of the chapter.

THE "CLASSICAL" DEBATE OF EUROPEAN INTEGRATION: LIBERALISM VERSUS REALISM

Theoretical frameworks, through the logic of their internally consistent conceptual frameworks and their reflexivity with regards to assumptions, help us make sense of the nature and interconnections of reality. At the same time, insofar as hermeneutics (following a basic insight of Kant's) is correct to argue that observation cannot be separated from conception,[3] theoretical frameworks can also distort reality and prevent us from seeing things or even asking the important questions. If the fundamental problematic of a political science of European integration indeed is as we outlined in the introduction, then we would argue that the latter is to a large extent the case with the theoretical orthodoxy with which every student of EU politics is required to learn: the debate between neofunctionalism and neorealism.

These theories, steeped as they are in the scientistic and positivist tradition, are formulated in terms of general, universal, and objective propositions that are held to be affirmed or falsified as universal truths about "the order of things." However, the common *problématique* of these theories is in fact rather narrow, and it excludes adequate considerations of important sociopolitical questions about European politics. This common *problématique* emanates from a common premise, which is that market forces are expressions of an inner rationality of human nature and constitute the realm of freedom in political affairs. Power and special interests are strictly contained in the discrete realm of (inter)state affairs. The debate concerns the degree to which the "anarchy" of the international system manifests itself as an objective external reality that constrains the possibilities of realizing the alleged inner rationality inherent in market forces and free trade.[4]

Critical political economy rejects this axiomatic and transhistorical understanding of the interstate and market systems implied in this debate. Critical political economy, in contrast, recognizes the power relations, special interests, and arbitrariness contained in market forces and civil societal relations as well, and it seeks to relate these to state power.[5]

This allows critical political economy to move beyond a merely formal analysis of levels of governance, and in particular beyond the institutionalist focus on the *form* of the integration process of established integration theories, to identify the socioeconomic *content* of the integration process, or the social purpose underpinning political authority in the contemporary EU—a precondition for "understanding how the order came about and how it might be changed."[6] Understanding the social purpose underlying the emergent European order requires, we argue, an analysis of its social underpinnings, which remain hidden from established perspectives inasmuch as these narrowly define power in terms of political authority of either states or supranational/international public bodies. In order to overcome this narrow focus, we should add a concept of *social* power in both its material *and* ideological dimensions, deriving not from political authorities, nor from the state in a narrow sense, but rather from the social forces that underpin state power. It is thus that our *problématique* of the social purpose of European integration calls for an alternative approach to the study of European order.[7]

The neofunctionalist/intergovernmentalist debate, then, is strictly concerned with the form of governance, or even more to the point, with the level of authoritative decision making. One theory emphasizes its intergovernmental character and points at the limits to the process of supranational integration. The other theory takes the opposite view, stressing the supranational dynamics of European integration, seen by some in this tradition as leading eventually to a federal Europe.

The first tradition can be seen as being bound up with the (neo)realist paradigm and concentrates on interstate bargaining, the outcomes of which are determined by the distribution of relative power among the participating states. This leads to a focus on the most powerful member states, their national agendas, and their bargaining behavior. During the 1960s Stanley Hoffmann was one of the first IR scholars to write about European integration from this perspective,[8] but it was only in the early 1990s that intergovernmentalism came to dominate the debate.

The second tradition can be seen as partly related to the pluralist or liberal tradition in which the world is one of *complex interdependence* created by the beneficial effects (that is, "Pareto-optimalities" engendered by comparative advantage and other divisions of labor and scale economies) of the global market economy, creating the need for international institutions and regimes to manage this interdependence.[9] Whereas for realism the state is the primary if not the sole actor in international politics, the liberal tradition in principle allows for a conceptualization of a plurality of state and nonstate actors.[10] The liberal perspective tends to view economic integration as being driven by a logic of economic interdependence carried not only by states but also by nonstate actors such as economic interests groups.

Neofunctionalism may be regarded as one particular offshoot of the liberal tradition, but it has tended to develop, as Andrew Moravcsik has noted, into a "sui generis theory," explaining (often in a rather ad hoc way) the development of the EU in terms of its own unique, sui generis characteristics, rather than in terms of a general theory (of world politics).[11] At the core of neofunctionalist theory, as first of all developed by Ernst Haas, is the claim that integration is a self-sustaining process that propels itself forward to its assumed federal end goal.[12] Neofunctionalism was thus primarily concerned with institutional form rather than with socioeconomic content. To the extent that the emergence of some federal structure was thought to have a specific social purpose, neofunctionalists emphasized rational-bureaucratic technocracy as a benevolent social driving force. In fact, it was believed that the gradual evolution of a supranational political community would be in the interest of most societal and political actors and that they would thus come to support this process by "shift[ting] their loyalties, expectations and political activities toward a new center."[13]

Driving the alleged self-sustaining integration process was, according to the neofunctionalists, a mechanism called "spillover," referring first of all to a functionalist logic whereby the creation of a common policy in one sector generates the "need" to transfer policy making in related sectors to the supranational level as well. Apart from this functional spillover, there is also political spillover, whereby supranational institutions attain ever higher levels of policy-making autonomy, resulting in a situation in which the supranational executive sets the political agenda and independently carries the integration process forward, leading the individual member states rather than being led by them. Neofunctionalism also stressed the role of interests groups (especially organized business and trade unions) in this self-expansive integration process: "Any analysis of the political process must give a central place to phenomena of group conflict, to the beliefs, attitudes, and ideologies of groups participating in the process of policy formation."[14]

In the neofunctionalist perspective, the dynamics of interest group action are, however, very much bound up with the functionalist logic. European interest groups are seen as coming into existence as a functional response to the requirements of the benevolently unfolding supranational system. The new institutions generated by the integration process modify the interests, beliefs, and expectations of domestic socioeconomic actors in such a way that these actors will "tend to unite beyond their former national confines in an effort to make common policy" and in this way constitute an important force in support of further integration.[15] Once formed, European interest groups continue to be subject to the expansive logic of the integration process. Rather than playing an autonomous role, then, they are viewed as being instrumental to the self-expansive process of spillover, and hence to the achievement of what neofunctionalists have seen as the endpoint of European integration, a European supranational state. The fact that both societal actors and national governments often have conflicting interests and ideologies, potentially resulting in diverging strategies for European integration, was not deemed to be important with regard to the dynamics of the integration process. Nor did neofunctionalism pay much attention to the question of power within and between groups, of why some groups are more powerful than others and may thus be more successful in setting the agenda of European integration. As James Caporaso points out: "Neofunctionalism had no explanation for which groups should succeed, form coalitions, mobilize interests, have access to policymakers, and affect policy."[16]

Already in 1968, Haas himself acknowledged that his claim that the "inherent logic of the functional process" could push Europe in no other way than the gradual, and automatic expansion of supranationality was no longer tenable.[17] When in the 1970s—the era of "Europessimism"—the EC became bogged down in what seemed to be interstate politics, contradicting neofunctionalist predictions, Haas even declared that theorizing about regional integration was "no longer profitable as a distinct and self-conscious intellectual pursuit."[18] With supranationality apparently on the wane in EC politics, many scholars reaffirmed the primacy of the nation-state, and a realist critique stressing the intergovernmentalist dynamics of integration effectively buried neofunctionalism.[19] In the 1980s and 1990s, the (realist) intergovernmentalist perspective has in fact developed into the predominant approach to the study of European integration, although, as we shall see, a modified neofunctionalism has also reemerged in the more recent debate.

With the re-launching of the European integration process, the study of the EC also returned to the academic limelight, and the two theoretical traditions of realism/intergovernmentalism and neofunctionalism staged their comeback in the guise of what Andrew Moravcsik has denoted as an intergovernmental versus supranational institutionalist debate.[20] The former stresses the role played by interstate bargaining whereas the latter emphasizes the agency of supranational institutions (particularly the Commission) supported by various transnational actors.[21]

In the intergovernmentalist approach, the evolution of the EU is seen as having proceeded through a series of interstate bargains, which "reflect the relative power positions" and which tend "to converge toward the minimum common denominator of large state interests" as states eagerly protect their national sovereignty.[22] In the intergovernmentalist view, national sovereignty remains paramount even if strong supranational institutions (or regimes) are created. These are not seen as challenging the sovereignty of the member states but, on the contrary, as instrumental to "their control over domestic affairs, permitting them to attain goals otherwise unachievable."[23]

Defining the integration process in purely intergovernmental terms, this approach claims that Europe's re-launching was independent from any pressures of any of Europe's supranational institutions and their leaders, or from transnationally organized business groups.[24] Indeed, in the realist state-centric ontology of intergovernmentalism, social forces are excluded altogether from the analysis. The state is the central actor, and the state is seen as separate from society. The success of the SEA, for example, is explained as the result of an intergovernmental bargain between the three dominant EC states (i.e., Germany, Britain, and France). This bargain was made possible by a convergence of the national policy preferences of these three states.[25]

These national policy preferences are, however, not explained, but are taken as given. In line with the realist tradition, state interests are exogenous, determined by the balance of power of the anarchic state system. The state remains a black box. As such, this theory has no tools to conceptualize, let alone explain, any social purpose underlying European integration. At the most, interdependence is introduced as a condition with which these states had to contend. But this invocation is rather abstract. The meaning of interdependence is not discussed, nor is there an elaboration of what interdependence might mean for the assumption of anarchy that underpins this interstate perspective in the first place.

In contrast to intergovernmentalism, supranational and transnational actors are given central importance within the rival perspective of supranationalism. Thus, in the account of Sandholtz and Zysman, for example, the SEA is explained in terms of an "elite bargain" struck in response to structural changes in the world economy, the bargain being initiated by a transnational elite of European big business on the one hand, and the supranational Commission on the other.[26] Although Sandholtz and Zysman criticize neofunctionalism,[27] Moravcsik is right in arguing that their explanation of Europe's re-launch is in fact to a large extent compatible with neofunctionalist theory.[28] In line with the neofunctionalist theory of interest groups, the role of transnationally organized business is seen as a response not only to the international environment but also to institutional changes (i.e., the SEA) that were already taking place, leading to a new reality that was perceived as irreversible.[29] Although Sandholtz and Zysman tentatively suggest that big business might also have played a role in putting the internal market on the agenda, they interpret its role mainly in terms of supporting preexisting political initiatives taken primarily by the Commission, which sought to re-launch the European unification process.[30] In this way, the role of Europe's business elite is in fact reduced to that of a "political interest group [constituted] by community action,"[31] which is serving as a powerful constituency for the Commission. As Haas put it: "Group pressure will spill over into the federal sphere and thereby add to the integrative impulse."[32]

The crucial problem with supranationalism is that many important aspects of this approach remain rather undertheorized. For example, there is no explanation of where transnational interests come from and why they would be so powerful. Only the more recent volume edited by Sandholtz and Stone Sweet can be

said to seek to offer a *theory* on a par with intergovernmentalism, and in opposition to it.[33] Explicitly building on the legacies of Haas and Karl Deutsch (but
without their sociological attention to identity and culture), the core of this theory is the notion that integration, as an "inherently expansionary process," is
driven by the rise of cross-border transactions that will "increase the perceived
need for European-level rules, coordination, and regulation."[34] This approach
thus focuses on the quantitative phenomenon of cross-border movements and
their functionalist requirements, rather than on the formation of transnational
social forces as understood in the framework of this book. The supranationalist
theory of European integration remains one of liberal institutionalism in which
there are, on the one hand, economic agents conceived in rationalist and individualist terms, and, on the other hand, formal institutions (primarily supranational institutions) responding to the needs of those actors but also seen as
constituting "transnational society."[35] There is, moreover, hardly any attention
paid to the role played by global forces and processes in the constitution of this
thinly conceived transnational society. The EU thus remains a self-contained entity. In sum, although supranationalism does open the black box of the national
state (indeed, in this tradition the state never was a black box) by emphasizing
the role of transnational private actors, there is no conception of how social
forces may shape the socioeconomic content rather than only contribute to an
ever more supranational form of the integration process.

Seeking to go beyond both supranationalism and his own earlier formulation
of intergovernmentalism, Andrew Moravcsik's concept of "liberal intergovernmentalism" opens the black box of realism's unitary state with the explicit aim
of explaining "variation in substantive, as well as in institutional outcomes."[36]
Central to this approach is indeed the role of state–society relations in the formation of national preferences. Moravcsik conceptualizes the integration process
as proceeding in three stages. First, national preferences are formed at the domestic level by the aggregation of interests formulated by societal actors. In the
second stage, the member states of the EU bring their national preferences to
the European bargaining table. In a third stage, a certain choice is made for a particular institutional design: the delegation to or pooling of sovereignty in international institutions.[37] Although Moravcsik's explanations of the final two
stages are firmly grounded in neorealist state-centrism—with the critical (independent) variables being respectively "the relative power of nation-states" and
"efforts by governments to constrain and control one another," his focus on
state–society relations with regard to the first stage (or the "domestic sources" of
national preferences) constitutes an important step beyond neorealist orthodoxy.[38] Unlike neofunctionalism, it provides a theory of national preference formation and theorizes the possibility that given the divergence of interests
amongst societal actors involved in this preference-formation process, outcomes
of European integration can vary with regard to their socioeconomic content,
depending upon which domestic groups are more successful in setting the agenda

in the respective states. Moravcsik has thus sought to transcend the narrow *problématique* of conventional integration theory by bringing (domestic) society and the distributional conflicts of domestic politics back into the analysis.[39]

Underlying Moravcsik's theory, however, is a rather individualist conception of society and of state–society relations. Moravcsik employs a liberal-pluralist theory of state–society relations in which the units of society are "private individuals and voluntary associations with autonomous interests," the behavior of which is assumed to be determined by a rational choice logic of utility maximization.[40] Moreover, in his focus on interest groups, he does not go beyond an analysis of the relative strengths and weaknesses of what he calls "producer groups" that, he argues, the political system tends to favor over "consumers, taxpayers, third-country producers, and also potential future producers."[41] That producers' interests are also favored over those of workers is a point that Moravcsik does not seem particularly interested in; indeed, organized labor is mostly subsumed under the producer category. Moravcsik states that those groups who "stand to gain or lose a great deal *per capita* [from the integration process] tend to be the most influential."[42] That some groups (for instance, specific groups of workers) might lose a great deal but are nevertheless quite powerless when it comes to influencing national preference formation tends to be ignored here. There is no interest in the structural inequalities that are constitutive of the *balance* of social forces and how these forces change over time.

Liberal intergovernmentalism is hampered, then, by an unsatisfactory account of state–society relations. In the words of two sociologists who have criticized the current "theoretical retreat from society" found within the social sciences, society in such a conception tends to be reduced to a mere marketplace, in other words, toward the "instrumental, rational individual, whose choices in myriad exchanges are seen as the primary cause of societal arrangements."[43] There is no concept here of how historically constructed *social relations* (for example class relations) embed these actors and shape their identity and interests. Nor are intersubjective structures (e.g., ideas and ideologies) assumed to play a role in defining actors' interests and, therefore, in shaping their action. Society is thus emptied of most of its historically produced content. If we want to understand the social purpose underpinning European integration, such an atomistic conception of society, is, we would contend, not very helpful. Social purpose is more than an aggregation of individual preferences. It is located at the macrostructural level, as a structure that, although constituted through human agency, cannot be reduced to it and cannot be explained by adding up the actions of "private individuals and voluntary associations." Curiously, Moravcsik himself does not construct an empirically adequate account within a strictly utilitarian framework. For example, in his analysis of the Maastricht Treaty, he invokes "geopolitical ideology," which is, of course, ad hoc and inconsistent with his framework.[44]

Another problem with Moravcsik's domestic political approach is his assumption that social forces are contained within the boundaries of national states. Yet, given the centrality of transnational corporations in an era of glob-alization, what guarantees are there that social forces will be "contained" within the nation-state? Although Moravcsik acknowledges the transnational embeddedness of both governments and domestic groups, in practice all that is incorporated into the analysis is how international constraints created by economic interdependence affect the rational calculations of both societal and governmental actors.[45] The transnational society is no more satisfactory than that of national society. Moreover, transnational forces tend to be treated (if at all) as something external to national state–society complexes, whereas by definition they are also internal. Thus, in Moravcsik's theory, an understanding of domestic politics as determining national preferences is "a precondition to an analysis of the *strategic interaction among states*."[46] In this way, social forces are brought into the analysis but remain locked within na-tional state–civil society configurations. Liberal intergovernmentalism thus remains a very state-centric theory; indeed, for Moravcsik, "European inte-gration can be best explained as a series of rational choices made by national leaders."[47]

BEYOND THE CLASSICAL DEBATE: MULTILEVEL GOVERNANCE

In recent years, the terms of debate over European integration have expanded. An increasing number of authors have taken the position that the supranationalist-intergovernmentalist debate is restrictive and misleading.[48] The EU is becoming a new kind of polity. It transcends and thereby renders obsolete the simple inter-governmentalist model of the EU as an international regime (albeit a special kind of one) that in no way threatens the sovereignty of its member states. At the same time, the EU is different from a supranational (federal) state.

Marks, Hooghe, and Blank acknowledge that nation-states remain decisive ac-tors. At the same time, however, they assert that states neither possess the mo-nopoly of the EU's level of policy making nor of the aggregation of domestic interests anymore. The European Commission (as a delegated executive, with a distinct agenda-setting, administrative, and regulative role), the European Court (through direct effect), and even the European Parliament (through the codeci-sion procedure, in particular) have independent influence in policy making. Moreover, collective decision making now implies a significant loss of control of each *individual* state executive. The basic point made here is that the notion of discrete, or nested, political arenas, à la Singer's[49] discrete levels of analysis, no longer makes sense since policy initiation, decision making and implementation, and adjudication in the contemporary EU implies an *interconnection* of the sub-national, national, and supranational levels. In other words, the politics of the EU is not illuminated by identifying the level (e.g., supranational or intergov-ernmental) to be privileged, but by accounting for exactly how levels are connected in complex ways so as to constitute networks of governance. This is referred to as multilevel governance.[50]

Thus, the European integration process must not be regarded as being about the replacement of the national states by a federal superstate, but rather as entailing what Philippe Schmitter has called the emergence of "a novel form of political domination."[51] According to Schmitter, this novel polity is post-Hobbesian because military insecurity is no longer the "overriding motive/excuse for the exercise of political authority," which leads to "the changing relevance of territoriality to define its limits and capabilities."[52]

Thus, in the contemporary EU, political rule is no longer tied to fixed and mutually exclusive territories. Rather, it emerges both "above" (at the supranational level) and "below" (at the empowerment of local and regional government) the existing national systems, even if these systems do not dissolve into either of those two new levels of authority. Rather than witnessing the dissolution of the state in Europe, we are witnessing the transformation of the meaning of European statehood.

Multilevel governance is a rather new explanatory framework, and it is often confusing in its eclecticism. Hence, although it perhaps represents and describes the complex empirical reality that is the European Union, compared to the traditional theories it suffers from a lack of analytical clarity and parsimony, and as a result it is often unclear about what actually is *explained* through this approach. Recently, however, Simon Hix has made an admirable effort to move beyond this pretheoretical stage of the approach. Departing from the same premise as the one articulated by Schmitter, Hix suggests that once we accept the post-Hobbesian state of the Europolity (in which the locus of the exercise of political *authority* has been displaced from the [nation-state] site where the monopoly of legitimate *violence* is situated), we can treat the EU as a political system sui generis in which the traditional models of comparative politics are applicable. By this, he means the pluralist model of political science pioneered by Almond and Easton.[53] This is consistent with the aforementioned input–output model suggested by Marks, Blank, and Hooghe, if one adds the diffuse set of special interests and the electorate that in this model constitutes the site of input in the first instance and the site of feedback of the political system.

Hix demonstrates how this approach, combined with his impressive factual knowledge, can be used to shed fresh light on EU politics. In some respects, of course, Hix follows Robert Cox's pathbreaking analysis of the early 1980s, which also sought to break down distinctions between levels of analysis.[54] However, in a polity where the commodity economic logic of the market is so central, this approach can be subjected to exactly the same critique as that directed toward pluralist political science by neo-Marxists. Indeed, since the Euro-polity is much more purely neoliberal than the polities analyzed by the pluralists of the 1950s and the 1960s at the zenith of the Keynesian welfare state, this critique seems even more pertinent in the case of Hix's account of the EU (and, incidentally, to

Moravcsik's understanding of the domestic game that generates state preferences).

Following Ralph Miliband, we argue that pluralist theory is correct in arguing that liberal democratic states encourage a multitude of groups to organize themselves freely and to compete with each other so as to advance their own purposes. Pluralist theory is wrong, however, in implying that the competition of these interests takes place on equal terms on a politically neutral social terrain. Rather, the very structure of capitalism—which is unaccounted for in the actor-centered formal input–output model of Easton's "politics of allocation"—and the attendant economic dependence of the state on the tax revenue and future investment decisions of capitalist firms tend to make the political system treat the special interest of business as the "general interest."[55] Writing in the 1960s, Miliband recognized that the *structural power of capital* was greatly enhanced by the internationalization of capitalist economic relations, which gave capital the crucial exit option vis-à-vis the state. Therefore, it is incorrect to treat organized labor as a "veto-group" on par with business because the capitalist system does not provide labor, or any other social force, with the same kind of economic power that is inherent in the institution of private property and in the valorization process inherent in the market. This is not to suggest that there are no empirical insights to be gained from pluralist analysis concerning the relationship between the executive, legislative, and judiciary, or about different political cleavages and dimensions of conflict (that do not only pertain to class, but also to religion, region, gender, and race). The problem is that what Miliband and C. Wright Mills called the "abstract empiricism" of this theory distorts the socioeconomic context of this politics of allocation with its attendant social power relations as determined by the social relations of production.[56] We would argue that, despite their empirical merits, Hix's as well as Hooghe and Marks's analyses of the organization and allocation of formal political authority[57] can be criticized on similar grounds. Their analyses do not systematically incorporate an account of how the capitalist socioeconomic context systematically structures formal political authority. Hence, we maintain, the analysis remains in large measure epiphenomenal.

The point in question was in effect conceded in the latter work of Robert Dahl and Charles Lindblom, concerned as it was with economic democracy to rescue pluralism, but this concession has largely been lost in the way in which pluralism has been imported into EU studies.[58] In other words, in this respect, this theoretical framework of pluralist multilevel governance tends to reproduce the blind spots of liberal intergovernmentalism as well as supranationalism.

One interesting exception to this generalization is the "actor-centered institutionalist" work of Fritz Scharpf.[59] Actor-centered institutionalism focuses on the "output" or public policy side of the Eastonian model and asks whether there are limits to the extent to which the system can "steer" policy according to changes in politically articulated demands.[60] Scharpf has developed a rational choice model of post–SEA EU policy formation based on his previous work on German federalism, which pointed toward a "joint decision trap." According to Scharpf, this polity, through the principle of mutual recognition, has been designed to expedite negative integration, the removal of barriers against market forces. However, the decision-making structure is not set up to facilitate positive integration. Rather, the requirements for agreement lead to a joint decision trap and facilitate nondecisions in the area of positive integration—that is, it prevents positive agreement about authoritative statements and regulations that could regulate, constrain, and shape for social ends the forces unleashed on the economic space. According to Scharpf, this is an inherent feature of the economic constitution of Europe. We consider this to be a model, impressive in its clarity and parsimony, which describes essential features of the manner in which the structural power of capital operates. But reading Scharpf's account, however useful as the heuristic device it purports to be, is a bit like attending the screening of *Hamlet* without the ghost. The structural power is exogenous to the model and taken as given. The sociopolitical process that generated this economic constitution is never explained. Hence in this case Cox's aforementioned critique of problem-solving theory applies insofar as there is no probing of the social origins of the system nor of the conditions that may change the situation in question.[61]

BEYOND THE CLASSICAL DEBATES: LIBERAL CONSTRUCTIVISM

All the theoretical approaches considered thus far can be considered to be rationalist. Rationalism views politics as the outcome of the interactions between rational agents, calculating the most efficient means for achieving given ends. In such atomistic models of social action, there are only self-maximizing individuals, and any (social) outcome can be reduced to (the sum of) these individuals' rational actions. In this individualist conception, agency is ontologically prior, which means that agents and their identities and interests are taken as given (i.e., as constituted presocially). Constructivism seeks to propose a metatheoretical alternative to this rationalism underlying mainstream studies of international relations and the EU.

As individualism holds that all properties of social systems can be reduced to the attributes of individual agents, individualistic social theory has no concept of society or of "the social" as anything other than the aggregate of individual actions. It is thus denied that agents are embedded in social relations that actually shape their interests and identities. As Alexander Wendt puts it: "The consequence of making the individual ontologically primitive . . . is that the social relations in virtue of which that individual is a *particular kind of agent* with particular causal properties must remain forever opaque and untheorized."[62] In the constructivist view, in contrast, individuals must not be seen as presocial entities but as embedded within social relations, constituting individuals into a particular kind of agent.[63]

In a context of profound social change, it becomes increasingly problematic to assume a fixed identity to actors and to abstract their particular attributes from the social context. This is because social change alters the particularity of agents. The aforementioned insights on the relationship between structure and agency form the underpinnings of what has been termed the "constructivist turn" in IR theory.[64] Constructivism explicitly challenges the individualist and rationalistic understanding of social action underlying mainstream IR theory, while at the same time rejecting the structuralist alternative in which there is no room left for human agency. As constructivism tends to take agency seriously (in fact, more seriously than rationalist approaches do), it also draws our attention to the role of consciousness and ideas in social practice. In our view, the meta-theoretical assumptions underlying the critical political economy advanced here share these constructivist epistemological and ontological commitments. It is important, however, to differentiate from the outset our critical constructivism, which is grounded in historical materialism, with what we would call liberal constructivism.

The constructivist turn initially took off because of some rather embarrassing anomalies, paradoxes, and explanatory impasses that individualist-rationalist regime theory encountered in the mid-1980s, as pointed out with devastating effect by Kratochwil and Ruggie.[65] In this context, constructivists have drawn our attention to the *intersubjective* making of social reality, at which level we also find the role of ideas. Although ideas cannot be reduced to interests, they should also not (as in idealism) be reified as existing prior to practice. It is only in human activity that ideas are generated, and here the *structural conditions* in which this activity takes place must also enter into the analysis. Thus, a constructivist focus on the intersubjective making of social reality ought not to be taken to imply that there is no material dimension to social construction. As Robert Cox stresses, "Intersubjective making of reality is not a statement of philosophical idealism [because] these intersubjectively constituted entities have been created by collective human responses to the material conditions of human existence over long periods of time."[66] As Onuf points out, it is often difficult to draw a sharp distinction between material and social realities, but both are important: "The material and the social contaminate each other, but variably—and it [constructivism] does not grant sovereignty to either the material or the social by defining the other out of existence. . . . To say that people and societies construct each other is not to imply that this is done *wholly out of mind*."[67]

Unfortunately, this proposition, formulated at a high level of meta-theoretical abstraction, has not translated into the concrete research programs of what we call liberal constructivism, which in practice has tended toward idealism. A case in point is a recent special issue on constructivism of the *Journal of European Public Policy*.[68] Like the proponents of multilevel governance, the constructivists in this volume assume that the EU is already some kind of polity, the study of which thus requires tools beyond those of IR theory narrowly conceived. Their research agenda, however, is much more explicitly geared to understanding the nature of the broader European project, and in particular its transformative effects on identities and the behavior of collective social actors.[69] As Risse and Wiener point out, all of the contributors share a commitment to some kind of anti-individualist ontology.[70] In this respect, the constructivist approach favored by our critical political economy approach is in full agreement. Indeed, we would fully subscribe to the position of Risse and Wiener, who—basing themselves on an argument of Offe and Wiesenthal—in their defense of social constructivism state that

> the shared experience and social structure of a society contribute to whether, and if so how, actors *know* their interests. As Offe and Wiesenthal point out, the rationale of collective actors differs crucially. The difference is, however, not simply based on given interests. Instead, it changes according to experience, i.e. position in relation to other actors and in relation to larger structures.[71]

The question, however, remains, about which "larger structures" we speak—structures that influence the practices of actors, including discursive practices, and thus the construction of their interests—and about which social relations. Here, we would claim, a constructivism grounded in historical materialism provides us with an answer to these fundamental theoretical questions, and an answer that differs from the ones given for the liberal constructivism to which most self-proclaimed constructivists students of European governance appear to adhere.

The underlying idealism in the concrete research by liberal constructivists is also illustrated with reference to Thomas Risse et al.'s[72] study of the EMU. Risse et al. seek to explain "the variation of post-Maastricht elite attitudes towards the EMU in Western Europe" through a comparison of Britain, France, and Germany. They begin by separating material interests of the actors from visions about the European order, which give meaning to the EMU, which needs to be understood within the framework of identity politics. The latter can fruitfully be linked to "institutional accounts of path dependence" to provide a compelling explanation. The authors proceed by dismissing explanations based on material interests because "economic interests are indeterminate." They reach this conclusion by pointing to the fact that neoliberal economists disagree about the EMU and by engaging in a (rather stylized) cost–benefit analysis of the national economies of Britain, France, and Germany.

Risse et al. contend that at a critical juncture, a certain institutional trajectory is chosen "irrespective of its rationality," and it then tends to be followed over time irrespective of whether instrumental interests change. The commitment to EMU reached at the Treaty of Maastricht constituted such a choice. "Collective identities," by which they are clearly referring to national identities, are then invoked to explain the choices that have led to this path-dependent institutional development. In particular, they invoke social psychology "group identity." They emphasize the importance of historical, religious, and communal heritage (which includes liberal democracies and social markets). Based on this perspective, they seek to explain why Britain withdrew from the process in the wake of the EMS crisis of 1993, while Germany and France became even more determined to implement the EMU as laid out at Maastricht.

What we find particular striking and problematic about this analysis is its two initial conceptual moves: First, material interests and identity are treated as ontologically separate. Second, material interests are discussed (and dismissed) with reference to a priori fully constituted identities. Without any explanation, national economies are assumed to be these identities and to have indeterminate material interests. Why not, instead, choose classes, or even sectors, such as bankers versus industrialists? Contrary to what one would expect from a constructivist ontology, the analysis lacks a sociology of interest formation that is mediated by identity. As a result, it *leaves* the realm of matter and interest altogether and enters a discretely conceived realm of ideas and group psychology, sanitized of any interfering or awkward material interest and power relations. We do not dispute the importance of imagined communities, but they are hardly formed in Habermasian ideal speech communities. In our view, such an analysis is bound to reproduce the pitfalls of idealism and abstract from the overdetermined relations of material interest, power, and identity.

TOWARD A CRITICAL THEORY OF EUROPEAN INTEGRATION

Our emphasis on social critique, on the importance of the material context in social construction, and on the crucial role of the power of the market implies that we argue that a theory of European integration ought to take its point of departure from the Marxist tradition. However, it is equally important to acknowledge that this tradition has suffered from utilitarianism, economism, and reductionism that have only been redressed through a constructivist turn inspired by the reception of the work of Antonio Gramsci.[73] The contributions to this book are building blocks for such a more comprehensive, critical, transnational, historical, and materialist theory of European integration.[74]

We conclude this chapter by outlining the basic ontological and methodological premises of this approach, which with individual variations are fleshed out in the more concrete chapters of the book. These premises can be discussed under the headings of historical materialism, transnationalism, and neo-Gramscianism. The chapter concludes by deriving five central propositions on the nature of neoliberal hegemony, which the contributors to this volume believe characterizes the essence of the political economy of contemporary European integration. These propositions are intended to serve as hypotheses to be examined in further concrete research, some of which is presented in the remaining chapters of this book.

Historical Materialism

The historical materialist approach consists of:

- A materialist conception of history, which is to be found in classic texts by Marx and Engels such as *The German Ideology* and in the preface to *Contribution to the Critique of Political Economy*, which leads to the ontological primacy of the social relations of production.[75]
- A rejection of the separation between the subject and object, which is characterized by positivist social science, including all rationalist European integration theory and some constructivist theory. In contrast, historical materialism is based on a dialectic understanding of reality as a dynamic totality and as a unity of opposites: In the words of Lucien Seve, "When the attempt to grasp the essence of things leads us invariably to contradiction, it is because contradiction is in the essence of things."[76]
- The method of abstraction as outlined by Marx in the introduction to *Grundrisse*, but which also is implied in Fernand Braudel's conception of "social time" and the "dialectics of duration."[77] The adoption of a method of abstraction follows from the rejection of the subject–object distinction, which makes it impossible to assume that we can simulate laboratory conditions in social analysis. In other words, it is not possible to apply *ceteris paribus* assumptions and to isolate and treat all but selected dependent and independent variables as constant. Instead, a more holistic, multidimensional, and overdetermined conception of the constituent processes of social reality is accepted as inevitable. Abstraction in this context means "the activity of identifying particular constituents and their effects,"[78] and it implies a careful analytical reconstruction that, in thought, identifies particular determinants and their interrelations. This is an activity that is fraught with difficulty and that hardly can be truly objective. However, it is aided by the possibilities of observing recurrent regularities in history, which can be grasped as historic structures (see especially chapter 2).

Any analysis of the world we live in must, from the standpoint of historical materialism, be grounded in an understanding of the way in which human beings have organized the production and reproduction of their material lives. This applies to European integration and international relations as well, we would argue, and such analyses should depart from the premise that these processes are embedded in the dynamics of the *longue durée* of the capitalist mode of production.

From this vantage point, we can identify the fundamental epistemological and methodological distinction between critical transnational historical materialism and the mainstream theories. The latter, as argued earlier in this chapter, adopt the positivist method, intended as it is to reveal invariant causal relations, in order to support a certain transhistorical claim about human nature and its inner rationality. The former adopts a highly skeptical approach to the existence of an a priori human nature. Rather, it argues that humanity and its institutions are fundamentally determined by the historically contingent context of social relations they produce in their "making of history." These social relations, moreover, are riddled with contradictions. For example, evolving human aspirations for liberation and self-expression tend to stand in contradiction with instituted practices of material production and reproduction of class societies as well as political forms of domination. At the same time, the claim is that social-historical dynamics, which are the object of analysis of critical social science, are determined by the antagonisms that are generated by these contradictions. In this context, social scientific knowledge is not generated by the positivist identification of invariant laws, but rather through an intellectual conceptual "mapping" (or reconstruction) of contradictory social formations and their movement. This is the essence of the method of abstraction, which, however, is not to be understood merely as an abstract theoretical exercise, since it is liable to explain how reconstruction is based on identifiable historical events. Most fundamentally, however, drawing on the Frankfurt School and its adaptation of Hegel's master and slave metaphor, social critique implies identification of social power relations that are preventing humans from reaching their aspiration of self-expression and adequately achieving their needs.[79] For this reason, critical theory emerging in modern Europe has focused on the contradictions in modern western European society between its ideals of democracy, equality, and self expression and the at best only partial realization of these ideals, against the backdrop of alienating, often oppressive, and stratifying practices of the capitalist market and bureaucracies. In this context, the critical theoretical work to which we refer here is concerned with a more concrete analysis of the instituted social practices associated with European integration as a phenomenon that is a relatively autonomous regional expression of an emerging capitalist global political economy.

The most explicit attempts to construct a theory of the contemporary transnational political economy based on this departure point are to be found in the works of Cox, Mark Rupert, and Kees van der Pijl.[80] In his study of class formation on the Atlantic level in the years between 1945 and 1973, building on earlier work on European integration published in Dutch,[81] van der Pijl, for example, organizes the analysis around the "successive levels of decreasing abstraction,"[82] beginning with the production process, then turning to the circulation relations (i.e., how profit is validated in capitalism through commerce and finance) and the level of the profit distribution process at which concrete class fractions form (e.g., industrialists versus financiers). It is in the labor process where the real subordination of labor to capital, the precondition for extended capital accumulation based on profit, takes place. Van der Pijl assigns special importance to the shift from the production of absolute surplus value to the production of relative surplus value, that is, the introduction of new management techniques and production technology to improve the productivity of labor, which took place in the United States in the early decades of the twentieth century (e.g., Taylorism and Fordism). Fundamentally, he identifies the Marshall Plan and the European Coal and Steel Community as efforts to extend Fordism to Europe and as central to the forging of European "class compromises" based on the American New Deal model of a "politics of productivity," mass production, and mass consumption. These were based on a particular fusion of investment banking and industrialism, which combined liberalism in trade and nations' state-based economic regulation to sustain stable mass consumption (corporate liberalism).[83] Corporate liberalism experienced a crisis in the 1970s, and subsequent neoliberal developments represent a new constellation that assigns more importance to absolute surplus value (direct exploitation of workers through a reduction of wage rates relative to profit rates).

In van der Pijl's later work, the dynamics of contemporary social relations are traced to the contradictions engendered by two processes: commodification and socialization (or *Vergesellschaftung*). Commodification entails the incorporation of more and more dimensions of the lives of ever more people into "tendentially world-embracing market relations."[84] Socialization is the process (driven by the division of labor and the extension of commodification) in which individual integral labor is transformed into functionally differentiated specialized labor and in which individuals are drawn out of closed, self-sufficient, kin-ordered communities into wider circles of social interdependence and "imagined" communities. The process is contradictory, because commodification is based on individualism and the natural force of the market, which at times put the social interdependencies under threat. It is for that purpose that countervailing practices of social regulation have been developed to regulate market relations in modern capitalism, from the level of the corporation to the state and including international organizations, including European integration. The claim, then, is that at the most abstract level European integration can be understood with reference to this dialectic of commodification and socialization.

Transnationalism

Transnational historical materialism is characterized by the consistent treatment of social relations as being constituted transnationally, that is, in a spatial domain that is not defined in terms of national boundaries. This perspective is not universally shared among all the strands of historical materialism, but has nevertheless become widespread since the late 1970s.

The foundations for this transnational perspective are to be found in scattered fragments in the work of Marx on the world market. Capitalist expansion from Europe partly took place through the subordination of noncapitalist economies to the needs of capital accumulation in Europe. The understanding of capitalism as a global system, significantly weakened under the impact of Stalinism, was greatly enhanced by the world systems theory of Andre Gunder Frank and Immanuel Wallerstein.[85] The greatest promise of the world systems approach has been its recognition that capitalism and capitalist class relations were from their very inception located in a global context and not in the national economies. The dynamics of the global system are for Wallerstein to be located in the process of the international division of labor and the resulting patterns of trade and productive organization. However, political power is organized within national states, and since the rise of industrial capital in the nineteenth century especially, capitalists as self-conscious actors (classes *für sich*, as opposed to classes as structurally defined categories in the division of labor—*an sich*) are constituted on a national level.[86] Thus, the globalization of capital and the continued relevance of the state are one. In fact, the contradiction between the global and the national is the manifestation at the level of capitalism as a global system of the basic contradiction between socialization of productive forces and the private appropriation of surplus. By formulating our queries in this way, we make class our central analytic category. This enables us to transcend the distinction between the national and the international. The international division of labor then becomes the social network through which production relations spread and class formation is nationalized, in other words the process through which global class formation is articulated with the processes of nation building and state formation. Such a more dialectical view of the relation between the external and internal factors is essential for a better understanding of the nature of international relations and European integration.

The Essential Gramscian Dimension

The Marxist debate on the political articulation of class interests was long dominated by an instrumental understanding of the *Communist Manifesto* on the one hand and a structuralist view on the other.[87] Both of these views in their own way were rather deterministic, allowing little autonomy to the political and ideological spheres. The adoption of Gramsci's thought as developed especially in his *Prison Notebooks* was of crucial importance in overcoming this dichotomy.[88] Gramsci was concerned with rethinking political strategy in light of the very different experiences of the Russian and the West European revolutions of 1917–1919. It is really in the context of this project that all the concepts that have come to serve as keys to recognize neo-Gramscian work were developed (e.g., civil society, hegemony, historic bloc, organic intellectuals, passive revolution, *trasformismo*, war of movement, and war of position). Gramsci argued that in the West, the political power of the ruling class does not rest (exclusively or primarily) on the control of the coercive apparatus of the state, but is diffused and situated in the myriad of institutions and relationships in civil society. This form of class rule, hegemony, is based on consent and is backed up only in the last instance by the coercive apparatus of the state. Ideological and moral elements play a crucial role in cementing the historic bloc—that is, the synchronic and equilibrated configuration of economic structures as shaped by a paradigmatic set of productive forces and sociopolitical superstructures that draw on these productive forces to maintain social order and thereby also provide the necessary institutional framework for the economic structure (what regulation theory calls "the mode of regulation"). In Cox's words, the ideological and moral elements constitute a "configuration of social forces upon which state power rests"[89] and its hegemony in wider society.[90] Organic intellectuals of the dominant social groups formulate and disseminate these intellectual and moral ideas, transforming them into universal ones that bind subordinate groups into an existing social order.[91] More than anything else, the notion of organic intellectuals and their role in cementing and spreading the ideas of the historic bloc bring into view the importance of agency.

This essential Gramscian dimension allows us to further elaborate on the aforementioned dialectic of commodification and socialization. Socialization does not emerge as an automatic functional response to social disintegration engendered by commodification. Rather, these organizational superstructures are contingent outcomes that depend on concrete processes of struggle, contention, compromise, and osmosis of social forces. Fundamentally, in these processes the content of attendant knowledge—and ideological discourses—are formed and hence give direction, coherence, rationale, and legitimacy to the historic bloc or commodification-socialization configuration.

It is against this backdrop that the works of this book understand the re-launch of European integration in the 1980s and the 1990s with reference to a shift from an international configuration of historic blocs based on Fordism, Keynesianism, and "embedded" or "corporate" liberalism to a transnational neoliberalism. The so-called Amsterdam School[92] has focused on the process through which transnational class cohesion is generated, from diverging functional or fractional perspectives as well as national perspectives, around a common paradigm of economic organization, or comprehensive concept of control (see also Holman and van der Pijl, chapter 3). The formation of a neoliberal hegemonic bloc is more complex, however, since broader general consent in civil society requires a concept to transcend narrow class interests to form the general interest. In this context the state, and the diverging terms of legitimacy in diverging locales, has to enter the analysis, and this makes the anatomy of neoliberal hegemony more complex.

THE NATURE OF NEOLIBERAL HEGEMONY: FIVE PROPOSITIONS

On the basis of this presentation of basic ontological principles, we put forward the following propositions regarding neoliberal hegemony in Europe. These should be concretized, tested, and refined in empirical research.

1. The first point is to underline the complex and dialectical relationship between neoliberalism as process and neoliberalism as project. Crucial to a dialectic understanding of the relation between structure and agency is the notion that a hegemonic project is shaped, and continuously reshaped, in the process of struggle, compromise, and readjustment. In the words of Drainville: "Neoliberalism is both a broad strategy of restructuring and a succession of negotiated settlements of concessions to the rigidities and dynamics of structures as well as the political possibilities of the moment."[93] The contribution of the so-called Amsterdam school has been to concretely analyze how class formation develops in this context as a concrete accumulation strategy (or comprehensive concept of control) is forged. More explicit attention for the agency of subordinated groups and their ability to make an impact on the shaping of accumulation strategies and hegemonic projects is needed. We also need an analysis of the apparatuses of the state (and its extensions into civil society) as they seek to mediate these forces.

2. Following this, we must take into account the *phasing* of the process of global restructuring and the neoliberal ascendancy. Elsewhere, Overbeek has developed this point further.[94] It seems useful to distinguish three distinct moments in the trajectory of neoliberalism, namely:

   - Neoliberalism as a deconstructive project, in which neoliberalism emerges as the concept with the most convincing analytical and prescriptive framework of the crisis of Keynesianism and defeats corporate liberalism and social democracy in one country after another.

   - Neoliberalism as a constructive project, or the phase of the imposition of structural adjustment, liberalization, deregulation, and privatization; corporate liberalism is discredited, no new alternative can be articulated, and the tenets of neoliberalism are increasingly accepted as valid and legitimate.

   - Neoliberalism in its consolidation phase, in which, internationally as well as within the countries of the advanced capitalist world, any notion of an alternative to the global rule of capital has become utterly unrealistic and discredited, and neoliberal reforms are locked in or "normalized" in the Foucauldian sense.

3. The process of European integration must be situated in the context of transatlantic and transnational class formation, not as an autonomous process as is so often the case in mainstream theories of European integration. The foundation, development, and periodic expansion of European integration are fundamentally moments of the expansion of the transnational capitalist political economy, which has been in uneven formation since the Glorious Revolution, centered first around Great Britain and later around

the United States: a *Pax Anglo-Saxonica* of a "Lockeian heartland."[95] This process itself, although its rhythm is dictated up to a point by the dynamic of American capital, is contradictory. The transatlantic linkage fundamentally influences European integration, but European integration is not simply subject to or determined by American control. Prima facie plausibility for this proposition is, for example, given by the importance of the Marshall Plan for the Schuman Plan and the ECSC, which then established a relatively autonomous developmental trajectory for European integration.[96]

4. This brings us to the fourth point, namely to emphasize the need for a better understanding of what we mean by "transnational." Much space has been devoted in numerous writings to discuss the distinction between the international and the global, or between the international economy and the world economy, but one is hard pressed to find a good definition of *transnational*. Transnational, we would put forward, must not be juxtaposed to "national" (as if it is synonymous to international or supranational). Rather, we submit, the notion of simultaneity is crucial to an understanding of what is specifically transnational. Transnational processes are those that take place simultaneously in subnational, national, and international arenas. Their dynamic is not fundamentally defined by the existence of national boundaries (although these do exist and continue to be important; indeed, their particular configuration can play an important part in the transnational dynamic). Analogously, transnational *actors* are constituted and operative in a social space (Cox would say historical structure) that extends simultaneously beyond and within national boundaries, which still exist but have at best a second-order relevance when understanding their behavior.

5. Finally, the conceptualization of transnationality must also be brought into a fundamental rethinking of the concepts of sovereignty, governance, and statehood in the era of globalization. This is true for an understanding of what is called "global governance" but equally applies to our understanding of the exact nature of the emerging European polity. This is indeed a system of multilevel governance; but, as we argued above, theories of multilevel governance in Europe so far have been marred by a strong institutionalist bias, which ignores the embeddedness of the institutional architecture in the force field of social, economic, political, and ideological interests and conflicts as configured by the contemporary makeup of the capitalist mode of production. This is precisely where the challenge lies for a critical theory of European integration.

NOTES

1. Our conception of structural power is informed by Steven Lukes, whose ideas have been related to theories of international political economy by Stephen Gill and David

Law, *The Global Political Economy* (Baltimore, Md.: Johns Hopkins University Press, 1988), 71–82.

2. Following Louis Althusser, *For Marx* (London: Verso, 1990), we define overdetermination as a relation between A and B, in which the very being and identity of A depend on its relation to B (and, conversely, the being of B depends on its relation with A). This is very different from the positivist and atomist conception of determination, in which A and B, with discrete and independent existence, may impact on one another.

3. See Charles Taylor, "Interpretation and the Sciences of Man," *Philosophy and the Human Science: Philosophical Papers 2* (Cambridge: Cambridge University Press, 1985).

4. Magnus Ryner, Henk Overbeek, and Otto Holman, "Editors' Introduction," *Neoliberal Hegemony and the Political Economy of European Restructuring: International Journal of Political Economy* 21, nos. 1–2 (1998): 4. Also see Robert W. Cox, "On Thinking about Future World Order," *World Politics* 28, no. 2 (1976): 177–81.

5. Central here is the structural inequality involved in the capital–labor relation, questioning the extent to which the formal freedom of the capitalist wage labor involves any substantial freedom at all. Indeed, as is noted by Streeck, classical sociologists, including Max Weber for instance, have never been so unanimous as in their denunciation of the "free labor contract"; see Wolfgang Streeck, *Social Institutions and Economic Performance: Studies in Industrial Relations in Advanced Capitalist Economies* (London: Sage, 1992), 41. As Marx himself put it, "The worker whose sole source of livelihood is the sale of his labor power" is free to leave the individual capitalist, but he "cannot leave *the whole class of purchasers, that is, the capitalist class*, without renouncing his existence. He belongs not to this or that capitalist but to the *capitalist class*, and, moreover, it his business to dispose of himself, that is, to find a purchaser within the capitalist class"; see Karl Marx, *Wage Labour and Capital*, in Karl Marx and Friedrich Engels, *The Marx–Engels Reader*, 2nd ed., ed. R. C. Tucker (New York: W. W. Norton, 1978), 205.

6. Robert W. Cox, "Social Forces, States and World Order: Beyond International Relations Theory," in Robert O. Keohane, ed., *Neorealism and Its Critics* (New York: Columbia University Press, 1986), 208–9.

7. On this, see also Bastiaan van Apeldoorn, *Transnational Capitalism and the Struggle over European Order* (London: Routledge, 2002).

8. See Stanley Hoffmann, "Obstinate or Obsolete: The Fate of the Nation-state and the Case of Western Europe," *Daedalus* 95 (1966), 862–915.

9. Robert O. Keohane and Joseph S. Nye, *Power and Interdependence* (Boston: Little Brown, 1977).

10. Robert O. Keohane and Joseph S. Nye, eds., *Transnational Relations and World Politics* (Cambridge, Mass.: Harvard University Press, 1972).

11. Andrew Moravcsik, "Preferences and Power in the European Community: A Liberal Intergovernmentalist Approach," *Journal of Common Market Studies* 31, no. 4 (1993): 473–524.

12. Ernst B. Haas, *The Uniting of Europe: Political, Social and Economic Forces, 1950–1957* (Stanford, Calif.: Stanford University Press, 1968 [1958, with 1968 preface]).

13. Haas, *The Uniting of Europe*, 16.

14. Leon N. Lindberg, *The Political Dynamics of European Integration* (Stanford, Calif.: Stanford University Press/Oxford University Press, 1963), 9.

15. Haas, *The Uniting of Europe*, xxxiii.

16. James A. Caporaso, "Regional Integration Theory: Understanding Our Past and Anticipating Our Future," *Journal of European Public Policy* 5, no. 1 (1998): 1–16, esp. 9.

17. Haas, *The Uniting of Europe*, xxii.

18. Ernst B. Haas, *The Obsolescence of Regional Integration Theory* (Berkeley: Institute of International Studies, University of California, 1975), 1.

19. See S. Hoffmann, "Reflections on the Nation-State in Western Europe Today," *Journal of Common Market Studies* 21 (1982), 21–37; and Paul Taylor *The Limits of European Integration* (London: Croom Helm, 1983).

20. Andrew Moravcsik, "Negotiating the Single European Act," in Robert O. Keohane and Stanley Hoffmann, ed., *The New European Community, Decisionmaking and Institutional Change* (Boulder, Colo.: Westview Press, 1991), 41–84.

21. For the intergovernmentalist perspective see Moravcsik, "Negotiating the Single European Act"; and Geoffrey Garret, "International Cooperation and Institutional Choice: The European Community's Market," *International Organization* 46, no. 2 (1992), 533–60. Although Alan Milward writes as a historian rather than as a social scientist, claiming to formulate "laws" in a positivistic way, his work can also be argued to defend an intergovernmentalist interpretation of European integration; see Alan Milward, *The European Rescue of the Nation-State*, 2d ed. (London: Routledge, 2000). For the supranationalist perspective see Wayne Sandholtz and John Zysman, "1992: Recasting the European Bargain," *World Politics* 42 (1989): 5–128; Wayne Sandholtz, *High-Tech Europe: The Politics of International Integration* (Berkeley: University of California Press, 1992); and Wayne Sandholtz and Alec Stone Sweet, eds., *European Integration and Supranational Governance* (Oxford: Oxford University Press, 1998). See also J. Tranholm-Mikkelsen, "Neofunctionalism: Obstinate or Obsolete? A Reappraisal in the Light of the New Dynamism of the EC," *Millennium* 20, no. 1 (1991): 1–22.

22. Moravcsik, "Negotiating the Single European Act," 47.

23. Moravcsik, "Preferences and Power in the European Community," 507.

24. Moravcsik, "Negotiating the Single European Act," 64–65.

25. Moravcsik, "Negotiating the Single European Act," 48–53; and Garret, "International Cooperation and Institutional Choice," 540–48.

26. Sandholtz and Zysman, "1992," 116–17.

27. Sandholtz and Zysman, "1992," 98, 100.

28. Moravcsik, "Negotiating the Single European Act," 77.

29. Sandholtz and Zysman, "1992," 116.

30. Sandholtz and Zysman, "1992," 113–19.

31. Sandholtz and Zysman, "1992," 117.

32. Haas, *The Uniting of Europe*, xxxiii.

33. Alec Stone Sweet and Wayne Sandholtz, "Integration, Supranational Governance, and the Institutionalization of the European Polity," in Wayne Sandholtz and Alec Stone Sweet, eds., *European Integration and Supranational Governance* (Oxford: Oxford University Press, 1998), 1–26, esp. 3.

34. Sweet and Sandholtz, "Integration, Supranational Governance," 11, 25.

35. Sweet and Sandholtz, "Integration, Supranational Governance," 11.

36. Moravcsik, "Preferences and Power in the European Community," 479.

37. Andrew Moravcsik, *The Choice for Europe: Social Purpose and State Power from Messina to Maastricht* (Ithaca, N.Y.: Cornell University Press, 1998), 5–10, 23–76.

38. Moravcsik, *The Choice for Europe*, 7, 9.

39. Moravcsik, "Preferences and Power in the European Community," 479.

40. Moravcsik, "Preferences and Power in the European Community," 483.

41. Moravcsik, *The Choice for Europe*, 36.

42. Moravcsik, "Preferences and Power in the European Community," 483; see also 488.

43. R. Friedland and R. R. Alford, "Bringing Society Back In," in W. W. Powell and P. J. DiMaggio, eds., *The New Institutionalism in Organizational Analysis* (Chicago: Chicago University Press, 1991), 232–66, esp. 232.

44. Moravcsik, *The Choice for Europe*, 389–90.

45. Moravcsik, "Preferences and Power in the European Community," 483 and 485–86.

46. Moravcsik, "Preferences and Power in the European Community," 481, our emphasis.

47. Moravcsik, *The Choice for Europe*, 18.

48. Gary Marks, Liesbet Hooghe, and Kermit Blank, "European Integration from the 1980s: State-centric versus Multilevel Governance," *Journal of Common Market Studies* 34, no. 3 (1996): 341–78; Simon Hix, "The Study of the European Community: The Challenge to Comparative Politics," *West European Politics* 17, no. 1 (1994), 1–30; and Simon Hix, *The Political System of the European Union* (London: Macmillan, 1999).

49. David Singer, "The Level of Analysis Problem," *World Politics* 14, no. 1 (1961), 77–92.

50. Marks, Hooghe, and Blank, "European Integration from the 1980s."

51. Phillippe C. Schmitter, "The European Community As an Emergent and Novel Form of Political Domination," *Estudio/Working paper* 1991/26, Center de Estudios Avanzados en Ciencias Sociales, Fundacion Juan March, Madrid, 1991.

52. Schmitter, "The European Community," 12.

53. Hix, *The Political System of the European Union*, 2–5, 9–14. In Lisbet Hooghe and Gary Marks, *Multilevel Governance and European Integration* (Lanham, Md.: Rowman & Littlefield, 2001), the authors develop a similar and more explicit analytical framework.

54. Cox, "Social Forces, Forms of State and World Order."

55. Ralph Miliband, *The State in Capitalist Society* (New York: Basic Books, 1969).

56. Miliband, *The State in Capitalist Society*, 68–70, 131–39.

57. See Hooghe and Marks, *Multilevel Governance and European Integration*.

58. See, for example, Charles Lindblom, *Politics and Markets: The World's Political Economic Systems* (New York: Basic Books, 1977); and Robert Dahl and Charles Lindblom, *Politics, Economics, and Welfare* (New York: Transaction Books, 1992).

59. See Fritz Scharpf, "Negative and Positive Integration in the Political Economy of European Welfare States," in G. Marks, P. Schmitter, and W. Streeck, eds., *Governance in the European Union* (London: Sage, 1997).

60. See Renate Mayntz and Fritz Scharpf, eds., *Gesellschaftlige Selbstregelung und politische Steuerung* (Frankfurt: Campus, 1995).

61. The limitations of such an approach can be illustrated with reference to Robert Ladrech, *Social Democracy and the Challenge of European Union* (Boulder, Colo.: Lynne Rienner, 2000), 32. In discussing party-political convergence on macroeconomic policy in the 1990s, he is satisfied to point toward the "voluntary commitment to meet the convergence criteria set for monetary union." Apart from the empirical problems with this account (the "voluntary commitment" precedes the EMU; see chapters 7 and 8 in this

book), it begs the obvious question as to why social democrats would volunteer to these commitments. This, in our view, is part of what the Gramscian concept of hegemony sets forth to analyze.

62. Alexander Wendt, "The Agent-Structure Problem in International Relations," *International Organization* 41, no. 2 (1987): 335–70, esp. 343, our emphasis.

63. See on this, for instance, Roy Bhaskar, *The Possibility of Naturalism: A Philosophical Critique of the Contemporary Human Sciences* (Brighton: Harvester Press, 1979), 34–35; and Anthony Giddens, *The Constitution of Society* (Cambridge: Polity Press, 1985), 213–22. In this context, Roy Bhaskar remarks that "the real problem appears not so much that how one could give an individualistic explanation of social behavior, but that of how one could ever give a nonsocial (that is strictly individualistic) explanation of individual, at least characteristically human, behavior. For the predicates designating properties special to persons all presuppose a social context for their employment. A tribesman implies a tribe, the cashing of a check a banking system. Explanation . . . always involves irreducibly social predicates" (*The Possibility of Naturalism*, 35).

64. See Jeffrey T. Checkel, "The Constructivist Turn in International Relations Theory," *World Politics* 51, no. 1 (1998): 324–48; and Alexander Wendt, *Social Theory of International Politics* (Cambridge: Cambridge University Press, 1999).

65. Friedrich Kratochwil and John Gerard Ruggie, "International Organization: The State of the Art of the Art of the State," *International Organization* 40, no. 4 (1986), 753–75. To the explanatory impasses one can include the unresolved question as to whether the collapse of the Bretton Woods system represented regime change or "norm governed change." Another puzzle was the success of France in the wake of "1968" to acquire concessions from GATT simply on the basis of an appeal to "sympathy and solidarity," without any juridical basis or apparent interest by the other states.

66. Robert W. Cox, "Critical Political Economy," in Bjorn Hettne, ed., *International Political Economy: Understanding Global Disorder* (London: Zed Books, 1995), 31–45, 34.

67. Nicholas G. Onuf, *World of Our Making: Rules and Rule in Social Theory and International Relations* (Columbia: University of South Carolina Press, 1989), 40, our emphasis.

68. Thomas Christiansen, Christian Jørgensen, and Antje Wiener, eds., "The Social Construction of Europe," *Journal of European Public Policy* 6, no. 4 (Special Issue, 1999), 528–44.

69. Christiansen, Jørgensen, and Wiener, "The Social Construction of Europe," 528–44. With its emphasis on transformative effects, this approach relates to the so-called Europeanization literature; see Maria G. Cowles, James A. Caporaso, and Thomas Risse, eds., *Transforming Europe: Europeanization and Domestic Change* (Ithaca, N.Y.: Cornell University Press, 2001).

70. Cowles, Caporaso, and Risse, *Transforming Europe*, 776.

71. Cowles, Caporaso, and Risse, *Transforming Europe*, 780. For the argument of Offe and Wiesenthal, see Claus Offe and Helmut Wiesenthal, "Two Logics of Collective Action: Theoretical Notes on Social Class and Organizational Form," *Political Power and Social Theory* 1 (1979): 67–115.

72. Thomas Risse et al., "To Euro or not to Euro: The EMU and Identity Politics in the European Union," *ARENA Working Paper* 98/1.

73. Stephen Gill, ed., *Gramsci, Historical Materialism and International Relations* (Cambridge: Cambridge University Press, 1993); and Henk Overbeek and Magnus Ryner,

"Transnationaal historisch materialisme: De wederopstanding van marxisme en kritische theorie in de internationale politieke economie," *Vrede en veiligheid* 29, no. 2 (2000): 228–48. See also Henk Overbeek, "Transnational Historical Materialism: Theories of Transnational Class Formation and World Order," in R. P. Palan, ed., *Global Political Economy: Contemporary Theories* (London: Routledge, 2000), 168–83.

74. For some recent surveys of related approaches to the study of European integration, see A. Bieler and A. D. Morton, eds., *Social Forces in the Making of the New Europe: The Restructuring of European Social Relations in the Global Political Economy* (Houndmills: Palgrave, 2001); and also H-J. Bieling and J. Steinhilber, eds., *Die Konfiguration Europas: Dimensionen einer kritischen Integrationstheorie* (Münster: Westfälisches Dampfboot, 2000).

75. Karl Marx and Friedrich Engels, "The German Ideology," in *Marx–Engels Collected Works* (Moscow: Progress Publishers); and Karl Marx, *A Contribution to the Critique of Political Economy* (Moscow: Progress Publishers, 1971).

76. Lucien Seve, "De methode in de ekonomiese wetenschap," *Te Elfder Ure* 17 (1975): 676 (our translation).

77. Karl Marx, "Introduction," *Grundrisse* (Harmondsworth, UK: Penguin, 1973); and Fernand Braudel, "History and the Social Sciences: The 'Longue Durée,'" in Fernand Braudel, *On History*, trans. and ed. Sarah Matthews (Chicago: The University of Chicago Press, 1980). For an excellent exposition of the method of abstraction, see Andrew Sayer, *Methods in Social Science: A Realist Approach*, 2nd ed. (London: Routledge, 1992).

78. Sayer, *Method in Social Science*, 3.

79. Paul Connerton, "Introduction," *Critical Sociology* (Harmondsworth, UK: Penguin, 1976).

80. Robert W. Cox, *Production, Power and World Order* (New York: Columbia University Press, 1987); Mark Rupert, *Producing Hegemony* (Cambridge: Cambridge University Press, 1995); Kees van der Pijl, *The Making of an Atlantic Ruling Class* (London: Verso, 1984); and Kees van der Pijl, *Transnational Classes and International Relations* (London: Routledge, 1998).

81. Kees van der Pijl, *Een Amerikaans Plan voor Europa* (Amsterdam: SUA, 1978).

82. Van der Pijl, *The Making of an Atlantic Ruling Class*, 1.

83. This is what John Gerard Ruggie refers to as "embedded liberalism"; see "International Regimes Transaction and Change: Embedded Liberalism in the Postwar Economic Order," in Stephen Krasner, ed., *International Regimes* (Ithaca, N.Y.: Cornell University Press, 1983).

84. Van der Pijl, *Transnational Classes and International Relations*, 8.

85. See Andre Gunder Frank, *On Capitalist Underdevelopment* (Bombay: Oxford University Press, 1975); and Immanuel Wallerstein, *The Modern World System*, vol. 1 (New York: Academic Press, 1974).

86. Sam Pooley, "The State Rules, OK? The Continuing Political Economy of Nation-States," *Capital and Class*, no. 43 (Spring 1991): 65–82.

87. Remember the debate between Miliband, *The State in Capitalist Society*, and Nicos Poulantzas, *Les classes sociales dans le capitalisme aujourd'hui* (Paris: Le Seuil, 1974).

88. Antonio Gramsci, *Selections from the Prison Notebooks* (New York: International Publishers, 1971).

89. Cox, *Production, Power and World Order*, 105; see also 6 and 409 n. 10.

90. Gramsci, *Selections from the Prison Notebooks*, 161, 168.

91. Gramsci, *Selections from the Prison Notebooks*, 181–82.

92. See van der Pijl, *Een amerikaans plan*; van der Pijl, *The Making of an Atlantic Ruling Class*; Henk Overbeek, ed., *Restructuring Hegemony in the Global Political Economy: The Rise of Transnational Neo-Liberalism in the 1980s* (London: Routledge, 1993); Otto Holman, *Integrating Southern Europe: EC Expansion and the Transnationalization of Spain* (London: Routledge, 1996); and Bastiaan van Apeldoorn, *Transnational Capitalism and the Struggle over European Integration* (London: Routledge, 2002).

93. André Drainville, "International Political Economy in the Age of Open Marxism," *Review of International Political Economy* 1, no. 1 (Spring 1994): 116.

94. Henk Overbeek, "Globalisation and Britain's Decline," in R. English and M. Kenny, eds., *Rethinking British Decline* (Houndmills: Macmillan, 1999), 231–56.

95. The term was coined by van der Pijl. See, for instance, van der Pijl, *Transnational Classes and International Relations*.

96. This proposition is further elaborated in the chapters that follow, especially chapter 2 by Gill, chapter 3 by van der Pijl and Holman, and chapter 4 by Cafruny.

2

A Neo-Gramscian Approach to
European Integration

STEPHEN GILL

This chapter provides an outline for an analysis of European integration from a
transnational historical materialist perspective. It seeks to identify the particular conjunctures, moments, or turning points that may serve to redefine the
political—and thus the limits of the possible for collective action in the European
context today. The chapter should be read as a methodological outline for the kind
of critical-theoretical analysis that was schematically introduced in the previous
chapter. As such, it situates neoliberal hegemony and transnational/transatlantic
class formation in a broader conceptual and historical context.

After grounding the methodology in epistemology and ontology, we move to
the more concrete terrain of social and political analysis.[1] With the historical situation as our object of analysis, we will try to outline how political agency is constituted by what Gramsci called "the relations of force" and by what Braudel
called "the dialectic of duration."[2]

Our method may be applied to interpret rapid political transformations such as
the collapse of communist rule in the former East Bloc in 1989–1991. It can also
help explain crises (and their momentary conjunctures) that may last many decades.
Thus the method adopted here will seek to develop a perspective on the movement
of social and political forces in and across social and political space and time.

EPISTEMOLOGY, ONTOLOGY, AND HISTORICAL TIME

Similar to the critique of positivism outlined in chapter 1, my approach assumes
that "there is no symmetry between the social and natural sciences with regard to

47

concept formation and the logic of inquiry and explanation."[3] A key contrast between social and natural science is that the meaning of social relationships and social events are not principally functions of the scientist's theory, since social scientists confront what John Gunnell calls a second-order reality that has been predefined by human beings in social situations. Thus social science is concerned with a world that has been logically preordered by its participants, "in whose terms action is conducted and justified."[4] This implies that social scientific explanation entails limited generalizations and a conditional vocabulary. In order to avoid conceptual reification, this entails continual interaction between social scientific constructs and what can be termed "social reality." "Such a requirement," states Gunnell, "will be viewed as a limitation only if it is assumed that the science of physical mechanics must somehow serve as a standard for all explanation."[5] Underlying this contention is the argument that social science explanation cannot develop if it rests either upon a Cartesian dualism concerning subject and object or theorizes in terms of cause and effect.

Rather than following Descartes and a positivist search for invariant relationships that reveal a priori transhistorical human nature, I follow Giambattista Vico in assuming that knowledge about human affairs always is socially and historically contextual. As Vico observed, in the *New Science* of 1725, human beings make society and thus the social world is a human creation. Thus its explanation is to be "found within the modifications of the human mind" that configure action.[6] It was Vico, therefore, who first propounded the essential aspects of Marx's maxim that human beings make their own history but not necessarily under conditions of their own choosing. In this sense, we understand social structure as a conceptual abstraction that corresponds to how the collective agency of human beings produces regularities more or less institutionalized over time and space—as they struggle to objectify their social relations with each other and with nature.

In this vein, Braudel found a means to elaborate the idea of the "limits of the possible" or the conditions under which collective action was constituted.[7] His method encompassed all the ingredients of social reproduction: from the household to the patterns of global trade and investment. Braudel's work explored coordinates of space and time, production and power, and biological and ecological dimensions of social life. In doing so, he developed an elaborate, detailed, and differentiated social ontology, constructed for different regions of the world between the fifteenth and eighteenth centuries. Braudel used this apparatus to sketch a three-dimensional model of society, economy, and civilization.[8] Linked to this was a theory of time similar to that developed—albeit often more implicitly—by Gramsci in the *Prison Notebooks*.[9] In this theory, "events-time" (based on François Simiand's notion of *l'histoire événementielle*) is the easiest notion to grasp. It refers to the continual flow and succession of actions and events in the movement of history. By contrast, the *longue durée* involves sets of ideas, patterns of interaction, institutional forms, and a structure of experience that may persist "for an infinitude of generations." However, the latter may accelerate and broaden in its scope relative to the world's population over time as a result of time-space compression in modernity/postmodernity.

The historiography of conjuncture and the *longue durée* concerns derivation and abstraction of the principles that may account for the repetitions and cycles. Of course, events never return in the same guise, since the relationship between the three rhythms of social and political time is dialectical and transient. Also, in each conjuncture, elements of social structure that are specific need to be taken into account. For example, capitalism can be divided into different phases with different paradigmatic technologies, production, and consumption norms, associated with different forms of state and patterns of world order. On the other hand, at certain moments of fundamental crisis, events-time is connected to turning points or key moments in history—such as the French Revolution—when, in effect, key historical structures collapse and new structures are produced.

In some ways, therefore, the apparent continuities of history are associated with the *longue durée* and with the embedding of social structures. These structures appear to be of quasi-permanent character, even though, of course, they are governed by transience and mutability.

The *longue durée* involves the patterning of habits and expectations in everyday life involving repeated actions that form regularities. Braudel called these patterns *les gestes répétées de l'histoire*. Some sets of events and actions are characterized by certain regularities and express social practices that are institutionalized within identifiable epochs. It is, hence, these *gestes répetés* that form historical structures that constitute and constrain the limits of what is politically possible for different classes and social groups at a certain moment in time. Sets of historical structures, which are a form of power for some and sets of constraints for others, can be identified in the political economy and in broader patterns of civilization. Moreover, the *longue durée* also includes the persistence of philosophical and theological systems as well as conceptions of space and time.[10] Braudel points out that it is paradoxically more difficult to discern the *longue durée* in matters economic, since economic cycles, intercycles, and structural crises tend to mask the longer-term regularities.[11] Nevertheless, here we could cite the increasing monetization and commodification of socioeconomic relations as aspects of the economic *longue durée* of the political economy of modern capitalism. This is a process that began to accelerate in the nineteenth century with the consolidation of integral national states and the proliferation of international organization.[12]

Such distinctions of Gramsci and Braudel's provide us with meta-principles to explain and interpret the ontology of a given, historically specific configuration of world order. So what is ontology? Ontology involves shared understandings of the universe, the cosmic order, and its origins; thus of time and space, and the interaction of social forces and nature. That is to say, intersubjective frameworks

serve to constitute and reproduce patterns in social and political life, for example patterns of social reproduction, the political economy of production and destruction, and patterns of culture and civilization. Thus in this essay we seek to
identify what Braudel termed those "historical structures" that serve to constitute
the political economy, civilization, and forms of consciousness. One benefit of
this approach is that it may enable us to go beyond the conventional ways in
which social scientists define structure and agency—not as something separate
but as mutually constituted through collective action in sociohistorical time. So
what follows here is a brief summary of six elements, moments, or injunctions in
our method:

1. Social relations and social structures are the basic elements to be established, because they constitute the source of and limits to the possibility of
   social transformation in any given epoch.
2. Social structures and social relations are conditioned by the transience of
   social forms.
3. The historical situation, the interplay between different rhythms of social
   time and structural forces, constitutes the main object of analysis. It is
   within this situation—or configuration of world order—that the significance of events is to be interpreted and explained.
4. Historical events are produced by a range of social forces of varying intensity and duration, rather than of a single set of forces.
5. Social formations and world orders are formed by the dialectic between
   different sets of social forces and the dialectic of duration: between events-
   time and sociohistorical time (conjuncture and *longue durée*). This dialectic, involving agency and structure, may be located within a particular
   society or culture or across different civilizations.
6. Although society, economy, and the state, understood as distinct and separate entities, cannot exist unless they are reproduced through the actions
   and thoughts (intersubjectivities and particular ideologies) of individuals,
   the nature of these social institutions is such that they cannot be reduced
   to individual action. Gramsci called this the dialectic of the transformation
   of quantity into quality.[13]

THE OBJECT OF ANALYSIS OF POLITICAL SCIENCE: THE HISTORICAL SITUATION

In *The Modern Prince*, Gramsci sought to show that the theoretical and practical
object of political science is the historical situation. He compared the theoretical
and practical "object" of Machiavelli with that of Bodin (1530–1596), who was analyzing the *internal* class relations within a unified France. By contrast, Machiavelli
was dealing with a situation in which the political institutions of Italy between

1500 and 1700 were underdeveloped primarily because of the *primacy of international relations over internal relations*. In addition, I have elsewhere contrasted these two cases with the "century of revolution," 1603–1704, in Britain.[14] Whereas the Italian situation analyzed by Machiavelli is one of underdevelopment, that of France analyzed by Bodin is one of the consolidation of the absolutist state. The British situation concerns bourgeois state formation out of which emerged modern capitalist state forms and transnational capitalist relations. These were consolidated first through British, and later American, international hegemony. One interpretation of these hegemonies posits a discontinuous expansion of an *Anglo-Saxon heartland* of transnational capitalism—relative to rivalries with contender states—that has served to constitute processes of European integration.[15]

Gramsci points out that Machiavelli, as a "man of his times," sought to deduce the rules and principles for the foundation of a new form of state from the international context of his era—that is, in a Europe where absolutist and centralized state forms had been created in France and Spain but not in Italy. By contrast, Bodin was concerned not with the problem of founding a unified state but with "balancing the conflicting social forces within this strong and well-implanted state." His problematic was the construction of consent within France at the time of the civil wars, which required the formation of a new hegemony: a form of leadership that better incorporated subordinate classes. Thus Bodin laid the foundations of political science in France "on a terrain which is far more advanced and complex than that Italy offered Machiavelli." This also explains why Machiavelli's ideas were already at the "service of reaction" in France, which was dominated by the Third Estate operating through the rule of the absolute monarchy.[16]

Thus, at the very start of one of the key texts of Gramsci, we can see that what was really at issue for Gramsci was not the national or the international per se: It was the analysis of the effective reality of a concrete historical situation in order to clarify the political questions of today and tomorrow. In order to do this, Gramsci introduces his method of the relations of force.

RELATIONS OF FORCE AND THE PROBLEM OF HEGEMONY

In the *Prison Notebooks*, Gramsci asks whether fundamental historical events are caused by prosperity or economic malaise. His reply is that no general answer seems possible, and it is only part of "the equation of the relations of force." It is a question that cannot be reduced to the application of economistic forms of analysis of particular historical conjunctures: There is no necessary link between economic and political crisis.[17]

The relations of force operate at three interlinked levels:

1. **Structural**—These are social forces "closely linked to the structure," an objective relation that can be measured to estimate the formation of and

alignment of "groups in relation to production." This enables the examination of the question of whether "the necessary and sufficient conditions exist in a society for its transformation."[18] One way this could be understood is in terms of the much-debated conjunctural shift from what Gramsci called old-style Fordism to the new, and perhaps politically open-ended possibilities of post-Fordist forces of production and consumption in an interlinked set of network societies.

2. **Political**—This involves an assessment of the degree of homogeneity and political consciousness among different classes and political groupings, viz.:

   a. The primitive economic moment, reflected in awareness and solidarity couched in terms of what Gramsci referred to as corporate interests, for example between merchants or between manufacturers to advance their economic position. It is important to note that this is not the site of class formation for Gramsci (i.e., as a class *for itself*); rather, this happens as a result of mechanisms that promote solidarity, a solidarity that may have the potential to pose a real social and political alternative to the existing order.

   b. The attainment of solidarity; this poses the question of the state in terms of "rudimentary political equality," normally reflected in a politics of reform within an existing framework.

   c. The hegemonic moment, when there is a consciousness that corporate interests go beyond the specific confines of an economic group and can and must become the interests of the subordinate groups. This is the most purely political phase. It culminates in hegemony, which is posed on a universal plane insofar as a hegemonic order is one in which the subaltern classes accept their domination as legitimate. The characteristic ideas of the ruling class shape the life world of subaltern classes, such that their potential for political agency is constrained and channeled toward the reproduction of the existing order. Thus hegemony concerns the social structure of lived experience—or ontology—and it is simultaneously political, economic, and cultural. Also, while in a positive sense hegemony involves leadership, the active construction of consent, and the institutionalization of power (e.g., through the rule of law), in a more negative sense it involves when necessary the use of coercion (e.g., organized violence and incarceration by the state). It also is a process involving consistent attempts by ruling classes to both co-opt and marginalize different forms of opposition so that alternatives to the hegemonic social and political arrangements do not emerge. In sum, a hegemonic order is one in which consent, based upon the real inclusion of the interests of subordinates, characterizes the process of rule in ways that protect the basic mode of production and the hierarchy of social power.

3. **Strategic**—This primarily involves the relation of military forces, "which from time to time is immediately decisive." For example, the occupation of

one state's territory by another involves the former's subordination, as when an imperial state dominates a colony or when a conquering state occupies the defeated state,[19] as was in effect the case in Eastern Europe after the collapse of communist rule. Indeed, we might add that the strategic question is at the heart of any problematic for understanding and explaining European integration today.

It is worth noting that the structural and political changes in a given historical situation should be understood dialectically. For example, the advent of the network societies and the economies of post-Fordism under conditions of compression of time and space can allow, on the one hand, for extended apparatuses of intensified electronic surveillance of populations and transactions on the part of states and capital. On the other hand, such new structural capacities go with new political forms, including those that involve transnational linkages among subaltern groups in different settings. In this sense, the structural changes should always be linked to the possibility of new forms of political agency as well as the spread of new discursive forms and efforts to create an alternative social and political language that might help to constitute an alternative to the prevailing hegemony of liberal democratic capitalism in the OECD, and to passive revolution in much of the rest of the world.[20]

TWENTIETH-CENTURY CHANGE AND RELATIONS OF FORCE: A CONJUNCTURAL ANALYSIS

Taking a longer historical view enables us to bring into relief some of the important conjunctures in the twentieth century with respect to the relations of force, for example aspects of the *structure* as Gramsci defines it. Here it is worth noting that the nature of contemporary capitalism in Western Europe—in part because of the influence and power of the United States—is quite different from that in the 1930s. For example, despite the existence of mass unemployment in Europe today, the dislocations associated with contemporary capitalist development do not necessarily have the same material and political implications as in the 1930s. For example, at the time of the Wall Street Crash in 1929 the service sector in Western Europe and North America comprised approximately one-third of all workers, whereas at the beginning of the crash of 1987 two-thirds of all workers were in services, and half of those service workers were within the public sector. In 1929 transfer incomes in Western Europe amounted to less than 4 percent of GNP, whereas in 1987, because of unemployment benefits, pensions, and family and social security allowances, transfer payments amounted to 30 percent of GNP. Thus the scourge of mass unemployment today involves lower levels of social dislocation than in the 1930s, and despite the secular trend toward lower growth, few speak today of a crisis of capitalism.

With respect to the *political* level of analysis, or the second moment in the relations of force, if we contrast Europe's contemporary situation with that of the 1930s we see once again that the liberal democratic political form has been consolidated, and indeed has now become relatively universal in European politics (not only the EU, but also throughout most of eastern Europe), although this is not necessarily commensurate with the spread of substantive or direct democracy.

Indeed, in the West European context the main achievements of socialism and social democracy have been couched in terms of the corporate or reformist moments of consciousness, that is, with welfare nationalism understood primarily as a national project. The central goal of socialism and social democracy (and of some of the communist parties) seems to have been not the replacement of capitalism, but the civilizing of the capitalist mode of production, in effect conferring it with a *hegemonic* aura. Thus most of the institutional innovations associated with the postwar European welfare states, as well as the institutional order of the liberal international economic order that was restored after World War II, have been connected to the stabilization and legitimization of capitalism through the use of an expanding sphere of state regulation. That is, the hegemony of capital has been largely reinforced, although we have entered a period in which the nature of state forms is undergoing transformation.

If we survey the historical situation today, we might hypothesize that a central issue in the early twenty-first century concerns the nature and scope of a new phase of the bourgeois revolution, albeit on a more global scale than in the seventeenth century. The longer origins of this revolution lie in the early political forms of the Italian city states; the Dutch Republic; the French Revolution; and, especially, the American and the British Glorious Revolutions. In the context of the early twenty-first century, with the decline of the traditional organized Left (socialist and communist forces), we see an apparent consolidation of disciplinary neoliberalism. The latter can be understood as combining the old with the radically new, insofar as the new involves extended and accelerated commodification of social life and the biosphere, including processes of work, leisure, and political and cultural representation. Indeed, there has been an acceleration in the scope and intensity of change within given sociopolitical frameworks of modernity (e.g., the integral nation-state and interstate system, the spread and deepening of capital as a social relation, and processes of industrialization and rationalization) as well as a shift in forms of consciousness associated with this process.

This poses the question: Which other elements of the *longue durée* of capitalist political forms are significant for the analysis of the historical situation of European integration today? Here we might cite at least three: first, the effective restoration of the political power of the propertied; second, the increasing subordination of state forms to capital (following some socialization and nationalization of the means of production between 1917 and 1991); and last (but by no means least), the renewal of the process of primitive accumulation, with a lineage back to the seventeenth- and eighteenth-century enclosures and the fifteenth-century dispossession of the monasteries by Henry VIII of England (today's privatization). More generally, despite being accompanied today by a gradual extension of the franchise, liberal state forms are proliferating in the early twenty-first century. Today's social and political order, ultimately subordinated to the power of property (capital), has a long institutional and political lineage. Moreover, of course, communism in Europe, at least as a form of rule, has collapsed, and as such really existing alternatives to capitalism are notable by their absence. This is not to say that alternatives to the dominant political orthodoxy do not exist, especially on the Right.

With respect to the *strategic* or *military* level of force, perhaps the central feature of the last two decades is how the power and influence of the United States has increased. Here we understand the United States as a state–civil society complex, as a locus and model of accumulation and as a crystallization of military power and power projection capabilities. This is despite the efforts of other nations, for example China and Russia, to counterbalance some of this strategic power; and despite efforts to countervail American economic and monetary power through the process of European integration, for example by developing a single currency in EMU. One indicator of this relates to the redefinition and extension of NATO and its use in the Balkans, most recently in the former Yugoslavia and Kosovo. As Cafruny shows in chapter 4, most of this has occurred on American terms, showing once again the subordination of the European Union to American military supremacy.

The rest of the world is also subjected to the threats that emanate from American power projection and its capacity to sustain remote-controlled aerial warfare, irrespective of whether this power is sanctioned or legitimated by a UN mandate. Moreover, this has political implications for European integration. The penetration of European economic development by U.S. banks and corporations means that European integration is limited politically by America's relationship with each member state. This is despite the fact that the EU is creating autonomous institutional and political capacity in certain spheres of activity, such as the creation of a single currency and the day-to-day management of monetary policy by the ECB as well as effective European collective action in trade and investment negotiations.

PASSIVE REVOLUTION AND THE ABSENCE OF HEGEMONY: EVENTS-TIME AND THE RESTRUCTURING OF SOCIAL AND POLITICAL RELATIONS IN THE FORMER EASTERN BLOC

So far we have largely discussed the dialectic between capitalist hegemony and the subordination of socialism and social democracy to that hegemony. However, as was noted earlier, a key concept in Gramsci's lexicon relates to a situation associated with the creation of a new form of state characterized by the absence of the hegemony of a leading class. Gramsci called this a situation of passive revolution. For Gramsci, passive revolution generally refers to two sets of situations:

1. A revolution without mass participation that is often prompted by external forces. This type of revolution can often be rapid, involving what Gramsci called a "war of movement" that corresponds to the concept of events-time.
2. A capillary or molecular social transformation, which occurs more slowly and beneath the surface, particularly in situations when the most progressive class must advance its position surreptitiously. This may involve a different political strategy, or what Gramsci called a "war of position," which he often understood as something more long-term or conjunctural.[21]

The concept of passive revolution and the two strategic concepts (wars of movement and position) are derived from what Gramsci calls the "the two fundamental principles of political science":

1. No social formation disappears as long as the productive forces that have developed within it still find room for further forward movement.
2. A society does not set tasks for itself if the necessary conditions for their resolution have not already been incubated, etc.[22]

The notion of passive revolution is also crucial to Gramsci's analysis of transatlantic relations between complexes of civilizations, and it is used to characterize the dialectic between Americanism and Fordism, on the one hand, and the backward forms of political economy in Europe, notably in Italy, on the other. In the latter case, it involved efforts to introduce advanced methods of capitalist production in the absence of bourgeois hegemony, both before and immediately after World War II, the latter in the context of the American occupation and the Marshall Plan, when efforts were made to comprehensively introduce Fordist production under reformist conditions imposed from the outside in order both to preserve European capitalism and to subordinate it to American dominance. Indeed, the American forms of state, civil society, and mode of capital accumulation have become models for passive revolution elsewhere in the twentieth and twenty-first centuries. Moreover, since the 1940s, American military dominance in Europe, in part exercised through NATO, means that any discussion of European integration has to be placed in the context of what Gramsci called the relations of force. Thus economic, political, and military dimensions of European integration operate in and across different complexes of political and civil society and civilization.

As with the British colonies in the eighteenth and nineteenth centuries, the revolution of capital (albeit with its new conditions of extended liberal freedoms in the sphere of exchange and in electoral politics) is experienced in the periphery of Western Europe today as a "passive revolution." Passive revolution, according to Gramsci, occurs in a situation where (transnational) bourgeois class formations increase their social power in locations where no previous bourgeois hegemony has been consolidated. Thus in the former communist states after political domestication of the forces that propelled the revolutions that overthrew communist power in 1989 and 1990, we see a process allowing for the restoration of the power of capital. In the nineteenth century, British imperialism was the main vehicle for spreading the passive revolution of capital whereas, of course, in the twentieth century, the United States has been central and often decisive in this regard.

Thus it is noteworthy that the reform programs in the former East Bloc have been introduced very rapidly and have been imposed not only by domestic reformers but also by external forces drawn from Western Europe and from within the broader framework of the international institutional complexes of capitalism linked to the leadership of the United States in the G-7. What these processes have in common is that they exemplify the introduction and imposition of new constitutional and political forms from above. In this case, they serve the interest of advancing capitalism in the absence of a domestic capitalist class. Here the EU and its G-7 allies (what I call the "G-7 nexus") have acted to accelerate the transformation with the aim of restoring the rule of capital and providing it with legitimacy and protection through liberal constitutional state forms whose antecedents date back to the early Dutch and British forms of state.[23] Examples of such initiatives include the European Bank for Reconstruction and Development (EBRD), the Poland and Hungary Action for Economic Reconversion Programs (PHARE), the Accession Partnerships, and the Copenhagen Criteria of Accession. Although distinctly European, these programs and institutions are subordinate to American-style disciplinary neoliberalism.[24]

The new situation in the former East Bloc thus suggests the following interpretation. On the one hand, the desire for freedom and equality before the law meant that Western political models held out considerable long-term appeal to the populations of the East. The constitutions that marked the settlements following the revolution thus served to institutionalize a moment of consent that redefined the political limits of the possible. They also served to lock in the new property rights of capital. On the other hand, the conditionality that was imposed on the former East Bloc nations by the West left little choice. The consent of the populations was accompanied by coercive capacity since the former East Bloc either had to accept a Western liberal political and constitutional framework, with its absolute guarantees for private property rights, or Western aid would be denied and, indeed, those who refused might be severely punished as, for example, Serbia was. The tactics for this approach on the part of the West were established in restructuring programs for not only Poland but also, and perhaps more importantly, the restructuring of the former German Democratic Republic following its de facto annexation by West Germany.

Thus, the reforms were intended to domesticate radical democratic impulses and allow both the restoration of capitalism in the East (moment of revolution-restoration as an aspect of passive revolution) and the further weakening and incorporation of the enemy. The strategic aim was to extend the boundaries and political basis of the Western bloc and incorporate a newly created and empowered bourgeoisie in the East, as well as to subordinate or appropriate its military assets under NATO command. Indeed, the American interest was to prevent a purely European solution to the question of restructuring.

Today, a decade later, much of the evidence indicates that the restoration of capitalism has brought about a catastrophic decline in the standard of living and quality of life for the vast majority of the population in the former East Bloc, with women, children, and the elderly particularly hard hit. Not only has there been a decrease in life expectancy, especially in Russia, but also there has been a precipitate drop in the birth rate, as women, like men, experienced greater anxiety and insecurity about the post-communist future. Since 1989, there has been a steep increase in murder, suicides, crime rates, and domestic violence, and a rapid increase in income inequality.[25]

EUROPEAN INTEGRATION/DISINTEGRATION: BETWEEN HEGEMONY AND PASSIVE REVOLUTION?

When Gramsci sought to understand developments in Europe during the 1930s, the question posed was not of European integration but its opposite: the disintegration and destruction of European civilization. Gramsci argued that an organic or fundamental crisis was manifest. An organic crisis is a moment when a civilization and political form undergoes fundamental transformation, specifically involving the exhaustion of the old and its replacement by the new in a conjuncture that might last for decades. In a typically poetic way, Gramsci noted in the 1930s that the period following World War I was one of organic crisis: At that time, as he put it, the old was dying and the new was struggling to be born, and "in this interregnum" there arose many "morbid symptoms."[26] Of course, writing from prison, Gramsci could not be certain exactly how this transformation was occurring and precisely which new forces might be produced in the struggle—in this sense, the methodological distinctions between the different relations of force cannot be applied with any sense of historical determinacy because they involve situations in movement. Indeed, from the vantage point of the early twenty-first century, we might still pose the issue in the same terms: The dialectic between old and new continues with its particular morbid symptoms after the interregnum of state socialism and state capitalism posed temporary historical alternatives.

In the 1930s, no solution to the crisis was evident: The best that Gramsci could do from his prison cell was to invoke his favorite political slogan: to com-

bine "the pessimism of the intellect" with the "optimism of the will."[27] The crisis of the economic structure was a crisis of hegemony for capitalism as a system,
a general crisis of the state and of political authority. The "great masses" no
longer adhered to the orthodox political ideologies that legitimated the relationship between rulers and ruled.[28] Thus the coercive face of power came to the
fore and the ruling classes in many states were prepared to sacrifice constitutionalism and democracy at the altar of reaction and fascism.

Of course, it took the most destructive war in history for the organic crisis to
be (perhaps temporarily) resolved. The struggle did not produce an authentic
revolution against capital as such. In fact, in Western Europe, the defeat of fascism led to the restoration of capitalism and the rebirth of liberal democratic
constitutional forms supplanted or obliterated by authoritarianism and fascism
throughout much of the continent during the 1930s. The wartime alliance between Soviet Russia and the capitalist allies paradoxically allowed for the rele-
gitimating of capital in Western Europe under the aegis of the Marshall Plan.
The geopolitical context was the emergence of the Cold War following the de-
terioration of United States–Soviet relations after the use of atomic weapons by
the United States in Japan. Symptoms of morbidity between 1939 and 1945 involved the deaths of perhaps 50 million people.

Nevertheless, in his analysis of the condition of political life in the interwar
years, Gramsci posed the question of whether the advance of Americanism and
Fordism constituted the beginnings of a new historical epoch, or simply a combination of particular events that had no long-term significance. Indeed, he
posed the question relative to the forms of state and class structures of the old
and new worlds to ask whether the emergent historical bloc of American power
in the international relations of the interwar period was provoking a "transformation of the material bases of European civilization."[29] Even before his incarceration, Gramsci thought that the revolution in production in the new urban
centers of industrial capitalism clarified the class struggle and symbolized the fundamental political issue for the future of Europe.[30]

The dialectic between hegemony and passive revolution is a central theme of
Americanism and *Fordism*. For Gramsci, Fordism and Americanism represented
an acceleration of a new social form based upon a deep organic link
between form of state, civil society, and mode of production, and as such represented a new form of planned economy in which hegemony was based in the
forces of production and "was born in the factory." By contrast, the European
class structure involved many parasitic elements, which Gramsci indicated as he
unraveled the so-called Mystery of Naples.[31]

This situation was not unique to Italy since it was found throughout Old Europe and in an even more extreme form in India and China. As such, the bourgeoisie were not hegemonic in these societies. The transformations took the form
of passive revolution, and often dominance was manifested by a regressive Cae-
sarism in which order was imposed from above in a situation of deadlock between

contending old and new social and political forces, that is by dictatorship. Thus, in the situation of the 1930s in Italy, the productive apparatus of society was not shaped by the hegemony of capital in civil society but rather through control from above by the authoritarian state apparatus, mobilizing the petite bourgeoisie and repressing the working class as in fascism. As Gramsci put it:

> The ideological hypothesis could be presented in the following terms: that there is a passive revolution involved in the fact that—through the legislative intervention of the State, and by means of the corporative organization—relatively far-reaching modifications are being introduced into the country's economic structure in order to accentuate the "plan of production" element; in other words, that socialization and co-operation in the sphere of production are being increased, without however touching (or at least not going beyond the regulation and the control of) individual and group appropriation of profit.[32]

By contrast, Fordism had triumphed in the United States through a combination of *force* (destroying working-class unionism and solidarity) and *persuasion* (high wages, social benefits, and ideological and political propaganda) to create a new form of worker subjected to intense and puritanical moral and social regulation (requiring monogamy and freedom from alcoholism). However, Gramsci considered each of these weapons of exploitation as a double-edged sword: Workers resist the imposition of moral regimentation and identify the hypocrisy of the ruling classes with respect to sexual relations, and the workers gain "a state of complete [mental] freedom" after they have "overcome the crisis of adaptation" associated with repetitive mechanical work, so that they have "greater opportunities for thinking."[33]

Americanism and Fordism required a particular form of state and social structure, namely a liberal state based on free initiative and economic individualism and a corresponding form of civil society, but the very development of a planned economy and the need for social and moral regulation meant an increase in state intervention. Thus, the capitalist state can never be the same as before. The state increasingly intervenes in the process of production, even reorganizing productive processes according to plans and assuming the nationalization and socialization of risk. Thus the formal character of the liberal state is preserved within civil society at the level of freedom of initiative and enterprise but with its fundamental meaning reconfigured by statism, industrial concentration, and monopoly.

HISTORICAL BLOCS AND WORLD ORDERS

If Gramsci were alive today, it is likely that he would identify the central question of Europe by combining those posed earlier by Machiavelli and Bodin: how to create not a new form of state as such, but a new transnational political com-

munity in the European space; and how to construct radical democratic hegemony within that space, a problem involving past, present, and future, the old
and the new.

In this context, we now introduce what Gramsci called a historical bloc. The
concept helps to describe the basis of a form of state and its capacity for rule and
leadership.[34] A historical bloc may be formed "through a series of compromises
or force of arms." A historical bloc is, however, not simply the creation of leaders, since it also allows the collective will of groups to be realized as they seek to
forge their own personality; that is, it combines structure and superstructure, the
material and the ideological, in an organic way.[35] Indeed, as Gramsci shows,
the historical bloc is not something that depends upon a specific state for its existence as such. *The Modern Prince* principally explores the case of modern Italy,
which was a nation *before* it had a state, and, as such, the formation of a *blocco
storico* preceded the unification of Italy in the nineteenth century under
Garibaldi.

So here, in the spirit of Gramsci's conceptual elasticity, we use the idea of a
historical bloc to analyze forms of state or political association in a transnational
as well as national political framework, indeed, in and across what he called
"complexes of civilizations." We thus analyze historical blocs and their place in
the constitution of particular regional and world orders. World orders involve
potentials of power, production, and destruction, including the use of organized
violence, that configure the political and social relations between classes, states,
and societies in particular historical periods.

In this context, as we have seen, twentieth-century European development
and identity have been overdetermined by American globalism and Soviet
communism. The result for the EU is that its various national state–society
formations are penetrated by, or interpenetrated with, those of other nations
and international organizations. Of course, the United States is the imperial
sun in this respect, with its power radiating across the political universe of less
powerful states. Indeed, after World War II, in the context of the Marshall
Plan, NATO, and the emergence of the EEC, the *Pax Americana* involved an
international historical bloc built on Fordist foundations, and on the internationalization of aspects of the American New Deal state form, modified by
wartime mobilization and the subsequent establishment of the military-
industrial complex.[36] The new political settlements included moderate organized labor and big capital—as well as leaders from civil society in, for
example, the media, centrist political parties, and churches—in a series of European and transatlantic political settlements under American leadership. It
thus combined coercion and consent with Fordist accumulation and the legitimation of the material basis of the system through mass consumption. Its
ideological banners included the concepts of liberty, modernity, affluence,
welfare, and the "end of ideology," all fused into a concept of "the West" and
an anticommunist alliance. The transatlantic bloc balanced national

and transnational capital, organized labor, and the state. It was constructed during the late 1940s and 1950s, and it lasted until at least the late 1960s.[37]

Many of the events and phenomena associated with such developments are, of course, analyzed and debated by mainstream integration theory. Examples include the Schumann Plan and the formation of the European Coal and Steel Community (ECSC) at the Treaty of Paris, 1950–1951; The Treaty of Rome and the formation of the European Communities, 1957–1958; and the Empty Chair Crisis and the Luxembourg Compromise, 1965–1966. Each of these events, in the context of the postwar conjuncture of a reconstructed Cold War world order, constituted a distinct regional moment that served to define and to redefine this international historic bloc. The ECSC ensured European, especially French, consent to the American vision of the European order and the reconstruction and rearmament of West Germany. At the same time, on a sociopolitical level, the restructuring of the coal and steel industries by the High Authority ensured that especially the German industries, whose industrialists had had an authoritarian ethos, were subordinated to the Fordist mass consumption imperatives and the welfare liberal forms of state. With respect to this, intellectuals such as Jean Monnet, who because of their transatlantic activities and connections shared with the American leaders the norms of liberal internationalism, played a strategic leadership function and qualify for Gramsci's nomenclature as "organic intellectuals," in other words those close to the dominant elements in the bourgeois class formations.[38] The EC generalized and consolidated this formula. At the same time, the Luxembourg Compromise, which affirmed the principle of national veto and the intergovernmental procedure of passing EC legislation, underlined the importance of national state autonomy in the Fordist, Keynesian mode of regulation. John Ruggie has, with reference to the Bretton Woods system, described this balance of national autonomy and liberal internationalism in terms of the double screen of embedded liberalism.[39] The EC corresponded to this configuration in norms and functions.

Recently, political change and economic globalization have undermined this integral hegemony. For example, there has been an ideological shift toward neoconservatism in politics and neoliberalism in economics. Finance has taken the place of production as the main determinant of capitalist accumulation strategies. A political shift occurred that marginalized labor and social democratic parties from the inner circles of power (less so in some countries, such as Germany, than in others, e.g., the United States, UK, and Japan). What I call the "terrain of political contestability" has shifted to the right in the OECD countries since the early 1970s, and it has moved further in a neoliberal direction during the 1990s period of American triumphalism.[40]

Here the institutions and collective agency of large-scale capital have been important both within European political life and in transnational class formations, taking initiatives, forging compromises, and searching for a synthesis of positions in a long-term war of movement to restore the supremacy, if not the hegemony, of the power of capital, as I have elaborated at length elsewhere.[41] In time, therefore, with the emergence of a more integrated global political economy, the former postwar *international historic bloc* has today been transformed into an American-centric and American-led *transnational historic bloc,* by which organized labor has been virtually marginalized. In the vanguard of this bloc are elements in the leading states in the G-7 and capital linked to advanced sectors in international investment, production, and finance, and the accumulation patterns of virtual industries. Increasingly in the 1990s these have been American firms, partly reflected in the Wall Street boom.[42]

By contrast, one of the most salient features of the 1990s is an unprecedented increase in social inequality and an intensification of exploitation of both people and nature in an increasingly naked pursuit of profit, a development that is particularly noticeable in the United States.[43] At the same time, the neoliberal shift in government policies has tended to subject the majority of the population (most workers and small businesses) to the power of market forces while preserving social protection for the strong (e.g., highly skilled workers, oligopolistic corporate capital, and those with inherited wealth).

Again, the developments associated with the re-launch of European integration in the 1980s and the 1990s are the expression of a particular regional moment of this bloc. The re-launch started with the turnaround from "Eurosclerosis" to "Europhoria" at the 1984 Fontainebleu Summit. The principle of international market discipline associated with neoliberalism was then institutionalized when the SEA was ratified in 1987. The SEA entrenched the principle of mutual recognition in trade and capital mobility, and it instituted qualified majority voting *on issues pertaining to the realization of a single market by 1992.* These provisions have resulted in the concentration of vast regulatory powers to the technocrats of the Directorate-General of Competition of the Commission and to the European Court of Justice. The principle of disciplinary neoliberalism was then extended to the field of monetary policy by the Maastricht Treaty of 1992 and the Stability and Growth Pact, which instituted the EMU on the basis of the principles of the impeccably monetarist German *Bundesbank.* In this context, the nominal commitment to a social dimension and a federal Europe that might have balanced the primacy of the market was structurally hampered by both the problems associated with what has been called "negative integration" (the constraints of globalized markets, particular capital markets) as well as by lobbying and direct political intervention of the neoliberal forces that have gained increasing political primacy in the EU. The Delors Committee responsible for coming up with the blueprint for the EMU, for example, was dominated by the neoliberal "epistemic community" of central bankers who by then, through the Atlanticist fora associated with the BIS, the IMF, and the U.S. Treasury and Federal Reserve, had developed a market-monetarist, elite consensus.

At the same time, this European construct has failed to mobilize a mass, popular appeal, although it has some support from what might be called a *rentier* bloc of interests—including those of protected workers and professionals whose assets are tied up in mutual and pension funds, as well as in financial capital—that benefit most directly from the policies of low inflation and capital mobility associated with market monetarism. It is an open question as to whether this rentier bloc is a sufficient basis of social and political support for the Maastricht settlement. As I have noted elsewhere, there is a contradiction for citizens of countries where state assets are privatized (citizens are, in effect, buying assets that they own collectively). At the same time, however, privatization tends to promote a shift in *mentalités* as new shareholder interests are created (and as portions of state assets, including pension funds, are bought by institutional investors). These developments enhance the structural power of capital and shareholder forces in everyday life. Not surprisingly, interests and perspectives of many blue- and white-collar workers correspond to this *rentier* perspective. Such workers in the 1990s in Europe have been much less concerned with the unemployed than in maintaining their own living standards.[44] On the other hand, since the ratification process of the Treaty of Maastricht there is a widespread sense of alienation in the relationship between European elites and much of the populace. This was perhaps indicated by referenda in Denmark and France in the 1990s. In more recent times, the Irish referendum on the Treaty of Nice and the sentiments of the anticapitalist protesters at the 2001 Gothenburg Summit might be taken as continued expressions of a substantial legitimacy deficit.

In this context, we might say that the ideological hypothesis today is that neoliberal forms of accumulation are associated increasingly with a politics of supremacy, rather than hegemony. By a situation of supremacy, I mean rule by a nonhegemonic bloc of forces that exercise dominance for a period over apparently fragmented populations until a coherent form of opposition emerges, for example relative to the social disintegration in the former East Bloc and the divide between the employed and unemployed, and between "locals" and immigrants, in Western Europe. The supremacist bloc is based on giant oligopolistic firms that operate politically both outside and inside the state and form part of the local and global political structures. The central purpose of this bloc is the intensification of the discipline of capital within state and civil society in order to increase the rate of exploitation and long-term profit flows.

IMPLICATIONS FOR THEORIES OF EUROPEAN INTEGRATION

Any theory of European integration will only be fully complete if it is placed in the context of an analysis of the relations of force in the context of global, regional, national, and local politics in the past, present, and future, in other words the event, conjuncture, and *longue durée* that serve to constitute the political limits of the possible. Local changes interact with and overlay the specific national and international struggles to define the nature of the European integration project, as well as the constitutive frameworks of the globalization of capital and world order. In this sense, any theory of European integration is necessarily a theory of political and civil society as well as a theory of international relations and political economy and, indeed, of European civilization. Moreover, since the European question involves the future of European civilization, any theory that seeks to explain European integration must always be a theory in development—that is, one that is related to the concrete historical situation of Europe, a situation that is, by definition, in movement. What this actually means in practice depends on the different forms of state and capitalism in Western Europe and the balance or equilibrium of forces within and between them. Thus, the precise admixture associated with the neoliberal trend varies in different state–civil society complexes or in forms of what Gramsci called the "extended state." Gramsci's concept of the extended form of state (represented by the formula: state = political society + civil society) helps us to understand some aspects of this process. Political society includes the public sphere of government, administration, and law and order, as well as security. Civil society includes those elements normally considered private, such as free enterprise, political parties, churches, and trade unions.

So what is the contemporary and historical terrain upon which we might seek to build a theory of European integration? Put differently, what are the contemporary changes that are structural, or relatively permanent, and what changes are incipient as we enter the twenty-first century? Here I want to mention three sets of changes that combine coercion and consent that might be discussed, in addition to what has already been mentioned.

1. *The reconfiguration of patterns of accumulation and regulation* at the macroeconomic and microeconomic levels, associated with disciplinary neoliberalism. This involves the rivalries and collaborations between European and American capital in ways reminiscent of the earlier issues discussed relative to Americanism and Fordism. Part of what is at issue is a gradual, and still far from complete, redefinition of continental European corporate governance (with its involvement of stakeholders) in ways that prioritize shareholder value and the discipline of capital markets along Anglo-American lines. This trend allows for the power of capital (owners) to be exerted more effectively in the formation of macroeconomic policy (fiscal and monetary policy) as well as at the micro level of the firm or the individual. Indeed, I would argue that in the context of disciplinary neoliberalism a new form of society is being constructed in Europe, premised upon self-help and individualism, one in which market forces and processes of normalization discipline actors' outlook, expectations, and systems of incentives. In sum, what is at issue is a set of initiatives, which reformulate and redefine public policy and the rules for economic policy. Here it is important to stress that these initiatives and the policy discourses they entail involve

both macroeconomics (for example the main focus of EMU) as well microeconomics and structural policies (e.g., trade, labor market, and industrial policy).

2. *The reconfiguration of state forms* according to the principles and practices of new constitutionalism, thus indicating a gradual shift away from the social market as well as certain forms of planning, thus allowing for the consolidation or "locking in" of a more limited but still powerful neoliberal state form insulated from popular-democratic accountability. A central objective of new constitutionalism is to *prevent future governments* from undoing the commitment to a disciplinary neoliberal pattern of accumulation. In this way, the central purpose of new constitutionalism is to redefine and lock in the relationship between the political and the economic and, more specifically, to reconstruct the terms through which political action and regulation action are deemed possible in a capitalist society. Thus new constitutionalism is a more or less conscious effort to mobilize reforms that will define the limits of the possible for political agents both now and in the future. Indeed, the SEA and Maastricht are legal frameworks that seek to do just this. Institutional examples of the same trend include the independent European Central Bank, the trend toward greater centralization of power in the executive branches (e.g., the Economic Council of Ministers or Ecofin), and more generally in the largely unaccountable EU bureaucracy and in the Commission (e.g., the Directorate-General for Competition). The same would apply of course to more concentrated powers in largely unaccountable international organizations such as the World Trade Organization (WTO) that have some regulatory or legal jurisdiction over EU matters, as well as the many standards-setting bodies across a range of fields such as food safety, the environment, and securities regulation.

3. *The reconfiguration of civil society,* associated with the spread of possessive individualism, privatization, and the marketization of institutions in an emerging market civilization premised upon commodified desire as a means to generate consent. One indicator is the massive growth in private satellite TV and the proliferation of advertising and merchandising linked to not only soccer and other corporate products, but also to public institutions such as schools and universities.[45]

For example, the Maastricht Treaty expresses a characteristically European constitutional moment in the processes of global political restructuring and hierarchy. It reflects a synthesis between Western European and American interests in a pan-European historic bloc. Its constitutional project is primarily informed and led by *disciplinary neoliberal social forces.* As we have shown in an earlier work, EMU is commensurate with a neoliberal framework of governance: new constitutionalism, which restrains democracy, protects private property rights, and sets the governance frameworks that impose macroeconomic discipline under a regime of austerity.[46] Thus the dominant transnational historic bloc has a significant European basis.

Here our analysis dovetails with that of Magnus Ryner in chapter 8, which focuses on Germany. In sum, the characteristics of the pan-European transnational historic bloc include (a) a *relative* preponderance of export-oriented capital as well as a significant financial or *rentier* capital element and (b) the crucial importance of the social market to forge mass consent. Indeed, a stable compromise between market discipline, public goods provision, and welfare state entitlements seemed to have been reached by the late 1980s, combining social provisions and entitlements with market discipline: a combination that we call compensatory neoliberalism.

However, in some parts of the political spectrum this constellation is being called into question, partly because of continuing economic stagnation and partly because of mass unemployment. These questions frame the struggle, or, in Gramscian terms, a war of position between those forces advocating a purer and more disciplinary neoliberal reform (especially to impart flexibility or liberalization to the negotiated labor market) versus those that advocate a new Keynesian direction and thus emphasize the more compensatory aspect of neoliberalism. In this context, the German position in the EMU project becomes particularly interesting since social forces in Germany reflect both of these positions.

Thus the neoliberal trend varies in different state–civil society complexes or in forms of what Gramsci called the "extended state," and thus each requires careful empirical research, as do the forces—on the Right and on the Left—that oppose it. In the context of a hypothetical continuum, the UK gravitates most toward the more pure variant of disciplinary neoliberalism whereas the new German state with its strategy of progressive competitiveness seems caught between the Scylla of the social market and the Charybdis of neoliberal globalization.

NOTES

1. See the introductory chapters of Stephen Gill, ed., *Gramsci: Historical Materialism and International Relations* (Cambridge: Cambridge University Press, 1993).

2. Antonio Gramsci, *Selections from the Prison Notebooks of Antonio Gramsci,* trans. and ed. Q. Hoare and G. Nowell Smith (New York: International Publishers, 1971); and Fernand Braudel, *On History* (Chicago: University of Chicago Press, 1980).

3. J. G. Gunnell, "Social Science and Political Reality: The Problem of Explanation," *Social Research* 31, no. 1: 168.

4. Gunnell, "Social Science and Political Reality," 168.

5. Gunnell, "Social Science and Political Reality," 186.

6. Cited in Robert W. Cox, *Approaches to World Order* (Cambridge: Cambridge University Press, 1995).

7. Fernand Braudel, *The Structures of Everyday Life: The Limits of the Possible* (London: William Collins and Sons, 1981).

8. Fernand Braudel, *Civilization and Capitalism, 15th–18th Century* (New York: Harper & Row, 1982).

9. Gramsci, *Selections*.

10. Braudel points to the importance for modernity and capitalism of geometric pictorial space invented in the Renaissance. See Braudel, *On History*, 33.

11. Braudel, *On History*, 33.

12. Craig Murphy, *International Organization and Industrial Change: Global Governance since 1850* (Cambridge: Polity Press, 1994).

13. Stephen Gill, "Transformation and Innovation in the Study of World Order," in Stephen Gill and James Mittelman, ed., *Innovation and Transformation in International Studies* (Cambridge: Cambridge University Press, 1997), 17–18.

14. The English Revolution involved a radical restructuring of social and political relations and the emergence of a new social ontology and forms of consciousness. Also, the interplay between "domestic" and "international" aspects of British imperialism is crucial. See my *Power and Resistance in the New World Order* (Basingstoke: Palgrave Macmillan, 2003), 44–49. See also Christopher Hill, *The Century of Revolution—1603–1714* (London: W. W. Norton, 1980), 3–4; inter alia I. Deane Jones, *The English Revolution* (London: Heinemann, 1931), 55, 175, 182; Karl Polanyi, *The Great Transformation* (Boston: Beacon Press, 1957), 38; Eugen Rosenstock-Huessy, *Out of Revolution; Autobiography of Western Man* (Norwich, Vt.: Argo Books, 1969), 278, 280, 298; and E. P. Thompson, *The Making of the English Working Class* (Harmondsworth, U.K.: Penguin, 1980), 66.

15. Kees van der Pijl, *Transnational Classes and International Relations* (London: Routledge, 1998).

16. Gramsci, *Selections*, 142.

17. Gramsci, *Selections*, 181.

18. Gramsci, *Selections*, 179.

19. Gramsci, *Selections*, 181–82.

20. See Stephen Gill, "Toward a Post-modern Prince: The Battle in Seattle As a Moment in the New Politics of Globalisation," *Millennium* 29, no. 1 (2000): 131–41.

21. The main examples Gramsci gives are the bourgeoisie in Restoration France after 1815 and the emergence of Christianity within the Roman Empire. Gramsci also uses the concept relative to Italian fascism, which he interprets in a way similar to the role of Napoleon III in France. See Gramsci, *Selections*, 106–20.

22. Gramsci, *Selections*, 105.

23. By "nexus," I have in mind a grouping of social forces drawn principally from G-7 countries (Canada, France, Germany, Italy, Japan, the United Kingdom, and the United States, with the president of the European Union) but also from elites and ruling classes of many countries, as well as some representatives of organized labor. The basis of participation is primarily state power, private wealth, and certain forms of knowledge, and includes private councils such as the Trilateral Commission and World Economic Forum, as well as public multilateral institutions such as the World Bank, IMF, and WTO. The primary goals of the nexus include consolidation institutionalization of power of G-7 states and the establishment of a worldwide capitalist market economy to allow for deepening of the power of capital.

24. The material basis for the initiatives to extend and deepen economic globalization lies in the ownership, organizational control, and research and development functions of giant corporations mainly from North America, Western Europe, and Japan. These firms

investment and trade as well as the political networks of fractions of the ruling the triad and elsewhere.

UNICEF, *Women in Transition* (New York: United Nations, 1999).

"That aspect of the modern crisis which is bemoaned as a 'wave of materialism' is ed to what is called the 'crisis of authority.' If the ruling class has lost its consensus, is no longer 'leading' but only 'dominant,' exercising force alone, this means precisely at the great masses have become detached from their traditional ideologies, and no longer believe what they used to believe previously, etc. The crisis consists precisely in the fact that the old is dying and the new cannot be born; in this interregnum a great variety of morbid symptoms appear." Gramsci, *Selections*, 275–76.

27. This was the banner motto of the radical journal *L'Ordine Nuovo*, and Romain Rolland coined it.

28. Gramsci, *Selections*, 275.

29. Gramsci, *Selections*, 317.

30. For example, "Produzione e politica," *L'Ordine Nuovo*, 24–31 January 1920.

31. He noted that in contrast to America, where even millionaires worked until the day that they died, Naples represented the sad urban spectacle of a decaying and outmoded economic system presided over by *rentier* and unproductive classes. Southern landowners and the petite bourgeoisie exploited the producers, the peasantry, and went to Naples to spend the pensions and rents extracted from the peasants. Gramsci also noted how an enormous proportion of the Italian population, perhaps one-tenth of the total, lived off the state budget. By contrast, a modern industrial city like Turin was the locus where the struggle between capital and labor occurred—without the dead weight of the parasitic strata—and, as such, it indicated the social basis for the new society.

32. Gramsci, *Selections*, 119–20.

33. Gramsci, *Selections*, 310.

34. For a full elaboration of my conception of a historical bloc and its use in understanding international relations, see Stephen Gill, *American Hegemony and the Trilateral Commission* (Cambridge: Cambridge University Press, 1990).

35. Gramsci, *Selections*, 377 and 137ff.

36. Kees van der Pijl, *The Making of an Atlantic Ruling Class* (London: Verso, 1984).

37. Gill, *American Hegemony*, 49.

38. Van der Pijl, *The Making of an Atlantic Ruling Class*.

39. John G. Ruggie, "International Regimes, Transactions and Change: Embedded Liberalism in the Post-War Order," *International Organization* 36, no. 3 (1982): 379–415.

40. See Gill, *American Hegemony*. This work gives a sense of the history, structures, institutions, organizations, and actors that have "made" this history, such as the Trilateral Commission and other private bodies that serve to constitute what I called earlier the G-7 nexus. Indeed, the transatlantic historical bloc was unraveled in the 1960s and 1970s not by changes in the interstate distribution of power as such (remember that this was a period when American power was supposedly in relative decline), but by effects of the restructuring of capital both within and across states. This involved internationalization and gradual liberalization of production, capital and exchange markets, complex communications grids, rapid innovation, and diffusion of technology. Above all, change was accelerated by cumulative and accelerating growth in the globalization of finance with American capital at the vanguard, a process that was facilitated and promoted by both state power and resurgence in the power of capital.

41. Stephen Gill, "From Atlanticism to Trilateralism," in Steve Smith, ed., *I* *tional Relations: British and American Perspectives* (Oxford: Blackwell/British Internatio Studies Association, 1985), 185–212; Stephen Gill, "American Hegemony: Its Limits a. Prospects in the Reagan Era," *Millennium* 15, no. 3 (1986) 311–36; Stephen Gill, *American Hegemony*; and Stephen Gill, "Structural Change and Global Political Economy: Globalising Elites and the Emerging World Order," in Yoshikazu Sakamoto, ed., *Global Transformation* (Tokyo: United Nations University Press, 1994), 169–99.

42. In the 1999 *Financial Times Global 500 Survey*, the United States ranks highest with 244 American-owned and controlled firms (up from 222 in 1998) with a market capitalization of $7.3 trillion dollars, followed by the UK with fifty-three firms ($1.2 trillion), Japan with forty-six companies ($866 billion), Germany with twenty-three ($654 billion), and France with twenty-seven ($490 billion). Nine of the top ten corporations are American (Microsoft is number one), with banking, finance, insurance, business services, telecommunications, computer software, high technology, and pharmaceuticals the largest sectors.

43. UNDP, *Human Development Report* (1997); estimates from this report showed that the world's 225 billionaires had a combined wealth of over 1 trillion dollars, equal to the annual income of the poorest 47 percent of the world's people (2.5 billion). Indeed, the three richest people in the world had assets greater than the combined annual output of the forty-eight least-developed countries.

44. Backing for EMU was strongly linked to the interests of large financial houses and firms, government bureaucracies, and European Union organizations, with the governments of Germany and France pressing strongly for its realization. The wider transnational historic bloc associated with empowering corporate capital incorporates a wider range of interests and identities, including many privileged workers, members of the professions, and small business people (such as those who do subcontracting to large transnational corporations and those who run import-export businesses), as well as of course international and national firms in accountancy, law, consultancy, advertising, public relations, computing, stock brokering, and, increasingly, educational entrepreneurs, architects, urban planners and designers, and many of the top sports stars that serve to market corporate images and identities. The bloc comprises interests of both capital and labor and elements of the state apparatus, although the largest and most internationally mobile transnational firms dominate it.

45. For a fuller account, see Stephen Gill, "Globalisation, Market Civilisation and Disciplinary Neo-Liberalism," *Millennium* 23, no. 3 (1995): 399–423.

46. Stephen Gill, "European Governance and New Constitutionalism: EMU and Alternatives to Neo-Liberalism," *New Political Economy* 3, no. 1 (1998): 5–26.

3

᎒ᏰᏮ᎒

Structure and Process in Transnational European Business

OTTO HOLMAN AND KEES VAN DER PIJL

In this chapter, we analyze the transnationalization of European big business in terms of the evolution of an Atlantic class structure. As such, this chapter contributes to a substantiation of the propositions, developed in chapter 1, about transnational class formation and neoliberal hegemony as key determinants of European integration. Chapter 2 already contributed to such a task by providing a wide-ranging historical account of the *longue durée* of transnational class formation and by introducing the crucial Gramscian conception of "relations of force." We add depth to this analysis by focusing in more detail on the class basis, sources, and processes of the hegemonic leadership underpinning the "re-launch" of European integration since the mid-1980s. Hence, analytically we focus on the second level of Gramsci's relations of force (the formation of fundamental classes) as it has been generated through a dialectical interplay with objective structures (the first level) and the "ethico-political" (third) level.

Our argument is that European capital is showing an increasing regional cohesion within the wider world market structure of capital. This holds both for the structure of communication between companies (directly through corporate interlocks, and indirectly through transnational planning bodies), and for the relations to the political level. As rivalry with the United States increases, we suggest that European capital is not so much defending a different model of capitalism, but rather developing a transnational neoliberal strategy by marshalling its own regional cohesion. However, as we will show, British business is not part of this movement.

The chapter is composed of three sections. In the first section, we define our concept of class and class strategy. In the second section, we focus on the role of collective "organic intellectuals" in formulating transnational class strategy in Europe. In the third section, finally, we illustrate our argument of a growing regional cohesion of European capital by examining the structure of corporate interlocks for the year 2000 and the tensions that the growing cohesion of continental European capital produces in terms of Britain's European identity.

CAPITAL, CLASS, AND STRATEGY

Capital, in general, is a comprehensive social force that depends on the competitive exploitation of living labor power for profit. In this general sense, it is best understood as imposing a particular economic discipline on society. Particular capitals—the separate firms or otherwise single units of ownership that compete over the mass of profit generated by the exploitation of labor and nature—are the agents through which this discipline is enforced, although they, paradoxically, are equally subjected to it because if they stop competing, they cease to exist as capital. The state, in its capacity as trustee of the capitalist order as such, reinforces capitalist or market discipline with its own authority.

A class structure is the division of society into larger groupings, each of which occupies a different position in the productive relationship to nature. More specifically, a class society is shaped by (1) the ownership and control of property functioning as capital by a small minority in society and (2) the consequences of this unequal distribution of income-generating assets for the material well being of the majority of people.[1] In class society, the income-generating nature of capital assets is anchored in the labor process. That is, the level of income inequality (whether or not the result of direct ownership or control of capital assets) is correlated to the level of exploitation of labor power and the price it fetches in the market, like other commodities. This is no longer a matter of certain categories of people being exploited, as if they were a primary natural source, by others who are exempt from physical labor. But although the class structure of advanced capitalist societies is infinitely more complex, opaque, and fluid than that of early industrialization or of feudal society, this in itself does not invalidate the assumption that society derives its cohesion from its relationship to nature (that is, the degree to which it succeeds in developing, as productive forces for society, the inherent forces of nature including human nature), that this relationship is necessarily exploitative, and that all relations within society accordingly have an exploitative aspect that allows certain categories of people to live off the labor of others.

The capitalist class, then, is composed of those who, on account of their ownership and control of property functioning as capital, embody capital as a comprehensive social force. However, this is only the material foundation of their existence as a class, or what Gramsci calls "a relation of social forces which is closely linked to the structure, objective, independent of human will, and which can be measured with the systems of the exact or physical sciences."[2] "Structure" here refers to the quantitative distribution of assets (and their income-generating nature) in society that forms the basis on which exploitative relations take shape. By this measure, the capitalist class would include those who own and/or control substantial income-generating assets at the expense of others— through expropriation, unpaid (or surplus) labor, or unfair competition. Examples would include the historic founding dynasties of Europe's corporations who may or may not retain an active interest in these corporations (e.g., the Agnellis of Fiat, the Wallenbergs of Sweden, the Philipses, the Quandts of BMW, the Benettons, and so on); those who have inherited large fortunes from other activities and reinvested them at least partly in big blocks of corporate stock (such as big landowners and aristocrats, including the royal families of Europe); the lesser entrepreneurial and self-employed element, in other words, all those others owning (and managing) factories, banks, engineering or law firms, trading companies, and retail outlets, and the like. Finally, there is the remaining rentier element, that is, all those owning stock and bonds to an extent warranting their being identified as medium or small capitalists, in addition perhaps to being a public servant, a pensioner, or a manager.

Those functionaries of capital who control but do not necessarily own income-generating assets are capitalists only by delegation. They constitute a managerial cadre,[3] which is normally active in assisting the capitalist class proper in imposing the discipline of capital on the workers and on society at large. However, they perform this function not on account of property ownership but, rather, on account of their performing tasks of coordination and supervision within and between corporations, or their charge of upholding the normative and political-administrative structure of capitalist society. The cadre, too, are a varied lot. They range from top managers (e.g., a Percy Barnevik, who manages some of the interests of the Wallenberg family) who culturally and politically would seem identical to the capitalists proper and who, given current forms and standards of remuneration, will normally establish themselves and their descendants as hereditary members of the actual capitalist class; to national and local politicians and bureaucrats, middle managers, managing editors of print or audio-visual media, cadres of employers' organizations or trade unions, all categories of teachers, and a host of other functions, as long as there is a directive aspect to their activity.[4]

Let us now address the question of how the capitalist class actually constitutes itself as a conscious social force, which is unified in its attempt to present the existing distribution of income-generating assets as the general interest.

Class Formation and Strategy

Class rule is established in a process that goes beyond the structural properties of the distribution of assets. As Stephen Gill explained in the previous chapter, this process comes under the heading of relations of political forces, which Gramsci subdivides into three different moments of collective political consciousness. The most basic one of these is the economic-corporate level, by which he understands the mutual loyalties that unify, for example, shipowners, Wall Street bankers, and the like within a single interest group. These we call fractions, which are the building blocks of ruling class formation. The second moment is that in which consciousness of a common interest is no longer confined to a particular fraction, but extends to the class as a whole—albeit still of an economic nature. Only the third moment transcends the limits of one's own class in an economic sense and poses the problem of hegemony, which means the capacity to present one's particular interest as the general interest. As Gramsci puts it,

> This is the most purely political phase . . . bringing about not only a unison of economic and political aims, but also intellectual and moral unity, posing all the questions around which the struggle rages not on a corporate but on a "universal" plane, and thus creating the hegemony of a fundamental social group over a series of subordinate groups.[5]

Elsewhere we have termed the integral programs anchored in a particular class configuration, which play this role effectively, comprehensive concepts of control.[6]

Under capitalist conditions, ruling-class formation is a highly dynamic process that runs through and unifies these three moments. It involves the constant quest for solutions to challenges, be they in the form of actual resistance to capitalist discipline on the part of the exploited classes or societies, or in the form of objective contradictions potentially jeopardizing the rule of the upper stratum of the bourgeoisie such as inflation, war, or environmental and population crises of all kinds. The capitalist ruling class would already have been forgotten had its existence not been characterized, from its very rise to power in the nineteenth century, by the continuous quest to build coalitions with the lesser bourgeoisie; strike deals with the landowning classes, big and small; develop, especially in the twentieth century, the vast cadre of auxiliaries that it needs to deal with the expanding scale of its operations and the needs of coordination and supervision; and, occasionally, reach out even to segments of the working class. Building these class blocs, however, was never a matter of strategy in the sense of free choice. Rather, capitalist rule has to be investigative, exploratory, and responsive to real changes. "Strategy" is the capacity to guide the forces that the process of social change itself brings forth and lends strength, and to retain hegemony over the momentary array of classes by capturing its spirit.

The process of Western European integration has itself been a way of shifting the coordinates of class struggle. Europe was a key terrain of the struggles by which the capitalist class and its managerial cadre have sought to retain and enhance the hegemony of their social order. Indeed, from its inception, integration has been the project of the most enlightened and visionary elements within these classes (like, for instance, Jean Monnet at the creation of the European Coal and Steel Community), which alone were able to meet the challenges facing capitalist society by radically changing the terrain on which they were to be met: from the national state to the group of states sharing certain functions among themselves and submitting to a common discipline. Considered from the perspective of the longer time span outlined by Gill in the previous chapter, this was crucial in the consolidation of Fordism in Europe and in the overcoming of the organic crisis of the 1920s and the 1930s, as pointed out by Gramsci.

The shift to transnationality and integration was only obtained in constant struggles also within the capitalist class and the cadre. This brings us back to the internal constitution of these classes through the three moments of the relations of political forces and the way they achieve a measure of common purpose. As capitalist development passes through different phases of productive expansion by restructuring its production organization and technology, as well as the spatial coordinates of the accumulation process, capital as a collective social force is likewise engaged in a constant quest for deepening its discipline on society and nature. In the economic-corporate moment, the formation of fractions, it is not just the distribution of functional roles in the structure but also the particular role that one fraction plays in cementing the unity of the subsequent moments of class formation that may guide the entire configuration toward either intensive growth of capital (deepening the discipline on labor) or extensive growth (widening it by including new reservoirs of labor power). For instance, the postwar shift to mass production of consumer durables (Fordism) was critically influenced by the relevant industries (automobiles, electronics), whereas contemporary "globalization" is crucially driven by the financial fraction. But in the final moment, society as a whole has to be at least passively resigned to the particular course taken—if only because every four years, electoral confirmation has to be obtained one way or the other. But then, as Thomas Ferguson's investment theory of political parties maintains, there is little chance of radical alternatives to the hegemonic discourse to be taken serious by the electorate.[7]

The personalities who guide this process in the sense of formulating its momentary goals do so not as capitalists or managers embodying a particular particle of social capital, but rather in their roles as class strategists, as organic intellectuals in the sense Gramsci gives to this concept.[8] A crucial aspect of the role of the capitalist class in European integration has been that the organic intellectuals of the process have substituted, at critical junctures, a European for any national frame of reference. They (and here we should think of men such as Monnet, Robert Marjolin, Etienne Davignon, or Jacques Delors) projected class strategies beyond the confines of the existing states, as a *transnational* strategy, thus circumventing the national class configurations and any obstacles these might have put in the way of the project. Eventually, a real transnational fraction of the capitalist class, in other words those actively engaged in foreign direct investment or its financing, had to fill the social space projected by the architects of integration. Whether this new space was primarily Atlantic, drawing capital from Europe into a wider world market movement directly, or "European" in the sense of first gaining a certain cohesion at the Western European level, has varied in each phase.

However, any class strategy (of the ruling class or otherwise) can only be an inspired interpretation of the objective configuration of social forces, which in turn becomes a source of inspiration for others. Strategies that drift too far beyond the prevailing configuration lose their relevance for those whose interests are necessarily tied to the existing state of affairs—although, again, the transnationalization of a given configuration of forces is in itself a dramatic way of changing the frame of reference in which current assets and interests are evaluated.[9] In this chapter, we are especially concerned with the structure of the business network as one aspect of the configuration of forces determining class strategy, or as we term it, a comprehensive concept of control.

TRANSNATIONAL CLASS STRATEGY AND THE EUROPEAN CONSTRAINT

By European class formation and strategy we mean, concretely, the growth of social forces and the discovery of a route to maintaining and reinforcing the hegemony of the capitalist ruling class in postwar Europe that allows going beyond the reliance on the mobilization of national unity. International relations are not suspended by such a transnational strategy, as the architects of Western European integration were well aware. European capitalism after the war was still essentially national and state-contained (with the partial exception of Britain), and only elements of a transnational ruling class were in existence at the time. All along, therefore, integration developed also as a process of international relations, in which France could take the initiative as long as a divided Germany remained occupied by the victorious powers of World War II, who were themselves locked in a cold war between East and West. European integration in this perspective has developed under the dual auspices of the larger Western bloc organized by the United States, *and* as a French strategy to mobilize a bloc of states that resisted U.S. leadership of the capitalist alliance.[10]

Following the collapse of the Soviet bloc, a trend that had already been at work in the prior period, that is, the close integration between the United States and Britain, continued to develop. However, it remains to be seen whether the actual configuration of European capital, and British capital as part of it, will allow this development of a common Anglo-American global strategy to continue in this way. Or, alternatively, whether by the pull of its corporate embeddedness in a European structure, the British ruling class will eventually demand a shift away from too-intimate reliance on the United States. Let us first look at how and to what extent a European framework for ruling-class action is established at all.

Europe and the National States as Rival Frameworks

All action by classes draws in states, particular states, into rival strategies. Certainly, as the theory of state monopoly capitalism in the 1970s maintained, integration is a way of giving rivalry and redistribution a civilian form—it is no longer a matter of war being the final arbiter of imperialist rivalry, as Lenin maintained at the beginning of the twentieth century. Today, German capital can expand at the expense of French capital, Dutch relative to Italian, and the like, without the sort of friction that sparked off conflict in the imperialist age, because a substantial fraction of the bourgeoisie has itself become transnational because its assets are spread over several countries. The same holds for the cadre, a segment of which may work as easily for a French company as for a German company operating in France or elsewhere. But the complex of class compromises by which each national society is held together at any given point in time, and that upholds the legitimacy of the state and the hegemony of the ruling class, has a different history and remains different in key areas. Hence, in every country the free movement of capital and labor remains subject to all kinds of informal restrictions, and does not by itself suspend the differences. Therefore, European regulation tends to represent a kind of foreign influence in its own right, which may or may not for that reason be more acceptable than a real external force. As Cohen-Tanugi has argued, the prominent role of the European Court in the integration process has tended to foster a system of regulation that strongly resembles the U.S. federal system, undermining the strong state. Although some prerogatives of states have remained intact, the possibility of appealing to the European juridical authority has privileged a legal-administrative culture in which lawyers have become prominent as representatives of people's rights. This juridical Europe has been central in the consolidation in Europe of what Gill in the previous chapter defined as "new constitutionalism" and "disciplinary neoliberalism."

Juridical Europe has today become a reality much more important in daily life than political Europe, an evolution that is even more profound and irreversible because it establishes itself discretely. As in the history of American federalism, the recourse open to European litigation at the present stage permits establishing a direct relation between the nationals of a member state and the Community institutions, bypassing the state authorities. The result of this process has been, in the United States, the reinforcement of the federal government as a national government, albeit an incomplete one (because limited by the sovereignty of the states). A comparable trajectory in Europe would end in a Community government of which the modes of regulation will be mainly—and necessarily, as this is always the case when there is a plurality of powers to be regulated—juridical.[11]

The combination of a European legal space, with different national legacies that embody different national class compromises, has resulted in a patchwork of arrangements in which the idea of a closed block is receding. Already in the 1960s, the idea of a "Europe à la carte" was launched to open the possibility that member states might selectively participate in aspects of European integration rather than having to swallow the entire menu. This meanwhile has taken various forms, such as a Europe of two or more speeds, and in practice has been the pattern of progress anyway. The exceptional position of Britain on some issues, France on others, and, more recently, the Scandinavian member-states' exceptionalism have illustrated this trend. Indeed, many key developments of European integration such as early monetary integration (the EMS) or the control of illegal immigration and joint law enforcement (Schengen) have been organized by European countries outside the existing Brussels framework altogether. Once these key areas were incorporated into the European *acquis communautaire* (the official codex of integration achievements) in the Treaties of Maastricht (1991, signed 1992) and Amsterdam (1997), respectively, these exceptional positions were institutionalized through the so-called opt-out mechanism.

The basis for this patchwork in our view is that corporations and other investors make decisions to locate factories, invest money, and engage in joint production and related agreements by private profit and related class strategies. This produces complex webs of regulative structures in which the common European standard is compounded in every single national jurisdiction, because even the way a European regulation is applied locally, or enmeshed in other regulation, tends to be different in each of them. Integration then by necessity builds on different patterns of cooperation and coordination—say, in the armaments field (Germany and France, with the UK and Spain in junior roles) or in linking up capital markets (the attempted link between Frankfurt and London, *Euronext*).

Here we may see how the sovereignty of capital ultimately governs (informally) the institutional forms created to sustain its accumulation. As capital spreads over the globe, such patterns of regulation both coincide with political entities (national and supranational) and transcend them through direct world market competition.[12] European integration may be seen as a particularly dense network of flows of capital that at no point, however, is exclusively identical with the actual EU territory or jurisdiction.

If there is no identity between Europe and European capital, can we identify at all a single social force that is primarily European? It is our thesis that Europe, as any other context of international integration in principle, in this light constitutes the legal-institutional arena in which some form of coordination and regulation of the effects of private capital movements has to be created. This coordination in light of the density of capital flows in the region has become cumulative over time, and represents the substance of what we understand by European integration. There is no "Europe of capital" (at least, although there is a fraction of capital that in its scale of operation coincides with Europe, capital as such is transnationally integrated on a global scale), there is certainly no "Europe of the workers" (who have a more national or subnational identity) or of any other social force (e.g., farmers or intellectuals)—although there is perhaps a Europe of technocrats or cadres entrusted with managing the structures of regulation that have been created to serve transnational capital accumulation, and that require constant adjustment. European integration is very much the process by which European society has been transformed to allow the imposition of the discipline of capital on a scale beyond the national state. This task of guiding and institutionalizing coordination and regulation has typically been the task of a separate stratum of cadres, a European bureaucracy that is not confined to the actual Eurocrats. The decision-making processes, redistributive tasks, and support programs of the EU all reflect and reproduce this Euro-cadre class.[13]

European regulation, by cadres and by the rulings of the European Court, gradually have become a more important constitutive force of the political systems of the member-states and the EU as a whole than is often recognized, and a European common law, backed up by expert knowledge, has thus come into being that tends to put national legislation between brackets as soon a successful appeal to Europe has been made. This, then, is one aspect of new constitutionalism written by technocratic application of the discipline of capital. More recently, in the course of the 1990s, European integration has become the vehicle of neoliberal deregulation at the member-state level, particularly the deregulation of labor markets. That is, after and next to the (still ongoing) regulatory process of completing the Internal Market, a "new political wave in favor of deregulation" has come to the fore. As George Ross has argued,

> The social policy order of the day has shifted from constructing social regulatory policies at the European level, as attempted by Jacques Delors at the end of the 1980s and early 1990s, to reconfiguring labor market and other arrangements to allow the European economy to compete in the world market.[14]

It is around this comprehensive concept of competitiveness that a European quasi-state structure is being forged, characterized by a complex system of multilevel decision making in which national (and subnational) governments, bureaucracies, and business elites develop converging ideas and related interests in a widened neoliberal Europe. In this "emergent and novel form of political domination,"[15] the European Commission and the Euro-cadre play an essential role, both as the "guardians of the treaties" and in their policy-planning and agenda-setting capacities. The former role is basically about creating a system of credible commitments[16] in which the management of the structures of coordination and regulation can take place. The latter role is more proactive in the sense that new policies are initiated, notably in the field of labor market restructuring, with the explicit purpose of dismantling the so-called European social model along neoliberal lines. As indicated earlier, this more recent turn in European integration must be seen as a transnational class strategy, circumventing national class configurations, and supported (if not actively projected) by a real transnational fraction of the capitalist class. One of the most visible representations of this transnational class is the European Round Table of Industrialists. It is to this European planning forum that we turn now.

A EUROPEAN PLANNING FORUM
OF TRANSNATIONAL CAPITAL

The process of Atlantic and Western European integration, and today the projection of capitalist discipline to global proportions, is replete with consultative or planning bodies such as the International Chamber of Commerce, the European League for Economic Co-operation, the Bilderberg Conferences, the Trilateral Commission, and the World Economic Forum (to name only the most conspicuous ones), which function, as Stephen Gill has argued, as collective intellectuals preparing the consensus on which the momentary rule of the transnational capitalist class is predicated.[17] The actual *resumes* of those participating in this process of consensus formation are secondary, because they are represented here as class strategists or organic intellectuals. It is ultimately the process of real class struggle and fractional realignment that decides the epicenter of the next round of capital accumulation—socially, technically, and geographically.

In 1983, European capital, that is, industry from Western European countries including some not integrated into the then–EC, established a new transnational planning body to guide Western European policy in areas crucial to capital accumulation and ruling-class power, the European Roundtable of Industrialists (ERT). Originally composed of seventeen European captains of industry, the ERT in its first recommendation of 1984 advocated the construction of a continent-wide high-speed train network, and in 1985 it recommended a deepening of the intra-European division of labor; another report advised on how to tackle unemployment. Although some American companies such as Ford, GM, and IBM are major players in the European economy through their many subsidiaries, they were not members of the ERT. As the former secretary-general of the ERT recollects,

> From time to time the argument was heard that the head of a large U.S. multinational's European operations was running a business as big as many ERT members and making a major contribution to the European economy. Yet the answer always came that such a man . . . was only a divisional head, *not a bearer of global business responsibility.*[18]

In other words, the status enjoyed by ERT members did not just derive from the corporate statistics of one's managerial remit, but were of a class nature linked to the regional entity of the European Communities; only those business leaders who were also "citizens" of the emerging European political economy could legitimately aspire to act as the organizers of a consensus that then would find, in the European institutions, the channel through which it could be translated into policy. However, here precisely, the incomplete nature of the integration process and its meandering course between (predominantly) intergovernmental and supranational integration, between the corporate liberal strategy of class compromise (or, in Albert's nomenclature, "Rhineland" capitalism) and neoliberalism ("neo-American" capitalism), also undermined the European consensus.[19] Just as the integration process leaves the national states formally in place, members of the ERT could withdraw from it if the consensus moved too far away from the (national) vantage point from which they took part in the planning activities—and again turn to their own state to obtain the necessary cohesion and backing at the level of policy. This happened when the original ERT projects began to display a markedly protectionist aspect that resonated in the actual re-launch of the European integration process. Significantly, British and Anglo-Dutch corporations with a strong world market rather than a specifically European profile (e.g., Royal Dutch/Shell, ICI, and Unilever) left the ERT.[20]

An analysis of the supporters of the strategy for a restricted European market shows that they were concentrated in the European market industries (the so-called European Champions): strong, for example, in France, especially among industries that were vulnerable to extra–EC imports (including non-French companies such as Philips). As a result of fierce opposition to this corporate liberal, "Fortress Europe" strategy on the part of notably the British and West German governments, however, the ERT and the European Commission headed by Jacques Delors proved unable to influence the European Council to adopt its recommendations. Then the collapse of the Soviet bloc dramatically changed the terrain on which European integration was to proceed, and ERT strategy shifted to a more offensive, neoliberal strategy again—incidentally, with the defecting companies again on the membership list. In September 1991, a new ERT report, *Reshaping Europe*, recommended proceeding to monetary union and a common security and foreign policy, while leaving the institutional side of the actual Brussels apparatus for what it was. Matching the orientation of the incoming Clinton administration in the United States, the new ERT posture sought to balance the hypertrophy of financial flows through a more concerted industrial policy but one defined firmly within a free world market context, which among other things implied pressing for the flexibility of labor. The Maastricht Treaty broadly followed these recommendations, in effect terminating the Euro-Keynesian Fortress Europe experiment.[21]

Following on this major neoliberal breakthrough, the ERT proceeded to introduce concepts from neoliberal management consultancy such as benchmarking into the European policy vocabulary. The ERT report, *Benchmarking for Competitiveness*, of 1997 aimed at generalizing the idea of exposing all social and political activity to competitive pressures for which the norm was set by the market. To quote Richardson again, "Benchmarking passed into the main stream of EU thinking, and ERT pressure may have helped to ensure that the jobs summit of 1997 adopted a benchmarking approach, geared to such topics as entrepreneurship, skills and innovation, rather than a renewed round of social regulations as had at one stage seemed likely."[22] In fact, benchmarking (or "best practice") has become the leading principle of an emerging European employment policy, which aims to overhaul existing demand-side labor market practices by introducing European guidelines and recommendations—albeit nonbinding ones—distilled from best-practice comparisons.[23] Flexibility (or "adaptability," in the words of the Commission) takes a central position in these guidelines. Next to this, a change from passive to active labor market policies, through a reform of tax and benefit systems (making it more "attractive" for the unemployed to take up jobs) and an emphasis on lifelong learning (to improve "employability"), are other key elements of the European employment strategy. The twin goals of competitiveness and labor market flexibilization, so central to the ERT post-Maastricht discourse, have become the leading principles in a deregulatory social policy at the EU level.

In the 1990s, the ERT once again unambiguously stressed the need for deregulation and flexibility of labor markets. According to the ERT analysis, the causes of structural unemployment in Europe and the weak response of employment to economic growth were mainly due to institutional rigidities and high levels of social protection. This made it mandatory to deregulate labor markets and upgrade the supply of labor, to allow for more wage differentiation and more responsive, and, where necessary, to lower wages and nonwage costs. In the words of the ERT in its 1993 report, *European Labor Markets*: "Even painful measures should become socially acceptable, provided they contribute to a sustained improvement of the unemployment situation."[24]

A recovery of European industry's competitiveness, the same ERT report continues, can be realized only through adjustments in the supply side of the European economy, because "only a healthy, efficient and competitive private sector is able to provide sufficient jobs."[25] All decisions within the European Union have to be tested against this all-pervasive goal. In this context, in 1993 and 1994 the ERT proposed the establishment of a European Competitiveness Advisory Group, which would "act as a watchdog, by subjecting policy proposals and new regulations to the test of international competitiveness."[26] In 1995, this advisory group was established to keep competitiveness high on the EU policy agenda.

In June of that same year, the ERT published a working paper, *The 1996 Intergovernmental Conference and the Competitiveness of Europe*. In this document, five criteria were formulated on the basis of which policy proposals could be subjected to the test of international competitiveness. The IGC should result in policy recommendations:

- increasing the stability and reliability of structures (institutions and rules) relevant to business operations;
- contributing to an effective and durable currency system;
- extending the perspectives for Europe—especially through the rapid incorporation of the countries of Eastern Europe but not at the expense of an equally desirable opening up worldwide;
- improving the EU's ability to act; and
- leading overall to less and no more regulation.

In the meantime, several meetings were arranged with the chairman of the IGC, Carlos Westendorp; the president of the European Commission, Jacques Santer; and with a number of national politicians. The ERT delegation was headed by Helmut Maucher, CEO of Nestlé, president of the International Chamber of Commerce, and, since January 1996, chairman of the ERT. Its main objective was, again, to stress the overpowering importance of European industry's competitiveness.[27]

In this context, it is interesting to note that Maucher also served as the chairman of the ERT Working Group on Employment. In this capacity, he was responsible for its 1993 report on European labor markets. As indicated above, this report contained a set of quite explicit policy recommendations with respect to labor market flexibility and an improvement of the supply side of the European economies. Next to this, the report fulminated against the Social Charter—"with its inherent risk of uncontrolled momentum in EC social interventionism"—and against the proposal for a European Works Council.[28] Finally, the report expressed the ERT's fierce opposition to proposals directed at creating a European employment policy. "Experience shows that top-down bureaucracy in detailed matters and excessive central influence significantly slow any structural change. . . . There is little that can be done at the Community level to directly solve the unemployment problem."[29] The report therefore calls for strict "subsidiarity" in labor market policies; that is, wherever possible, leave the labor market to member-states.

More recently, the ERT, through its (former) Secretary-General Keith Richardson, again expressed its opposition to an active employment policy at the European level. In his view, European industry's competitiveness should be strengthened "by making it possible to build an integrated free market economic system, with a *maximum of flexibility and a minimum of regulation.*" And more explicitly: "Jobs cannot be created by laws or by writing some new clause or chapter into the Treaty. What is urgently needed is the deregulation of labor markets and better education and training. New jobs will then follow from economic growth and the creation of wealth by business."[30]

From the early 1990s onwards, the ERT acquired a strong neoliberal orientation, and few will dispute that this orientation reflects the universal preference of big capital in the current phase of globalization. However, the question of whether European capital can forfeit the specific cohesion and backing provided by the European states and Brussels, or if it wants to build on the regional constraint first before engaging in world market competition, has not likewise been settled. On this issue, shifts in the structure of European capital are particularly relevant. They seem to suggest, on the one hand, that European continental capital is marshalling its own regional cohesion. On the other hand, British capital, after having led the way into the neoliberal era as far as European business is concerned, has now become divided, with one segment drifting away from its previous anchoring in the American network of corporate interlocks. To this we turn in our next section.

RECENT SHIFTS IN THE STRUCTURE OF EUROPEAN CAPITAL

Both corporate liberalism and neoliberalism have spread within a geopolitics of capital in which the English-speaking world, with the United States at its center, continues to represent the most advanced stage of capitalist discipline over society. Hence in the 1980s, the United States once again acted as the spearhead of the newest capitalism (with Britain ideologically prominent, if materially confined, to the financial and militarist aspects of neoliberalism). Continental Europe on the other hand, like Japan and South Korea, remained entrenched in a corporate liberal configuration of forces, not least because of the continuing (defensive) strength of organized labor.

This applies in particular to Germany, the industrial core of the continent. Germany is still strong in the industries that belong to the corporate liberal set (automobile, engineering, and chemicals), while the United States has moved on to strength in industries of the future such as the information and biogenetics industries on which neoliberalism is grafted. Mid-1990s world trade shares in the former sector are 21 percent for Germany and 2 percent for the United States; whereas in the new industries, they are 14 percent for Germany and 28 percent for the United States.[31] Two-thirds of global profits made in the electronics and data processing industries between 1989 and 1994 went to American corporations.[32] This sectoral transition in the United States has been accompanied by a rising share of money capital in the profit distribution process to 58 percent of the total in 1990 (from 48 percent in 1975, and before declining again as neoliberal industrial capital came into its own in the 1990s); whereas in (West) Germany, the share of money capital was only 30.9 percent in 1975, 36 in 1990, and still increasing thereafter.[33]

Taking European capital as a whole, orientations vary around this German pattern. We may distinguish here between firms with a strong, mobile capital base relative to productive engagement, which can exploit labor and compete at the world market level directly, and hence are inclined to take their place in the configuration of forces expressed by the neoliberal concept of control; and firms relying more heavily on productive capital outlays, state support, regional cohesion, and other elements in the productive equations underpinning the corporate liberal concept. Thus if we look at the situation prevailing around 1990, the firms with the strongest mobile capital base were mainly British (with a few German firms), while the remainder of the biggest German firms were in the second division along with French and Italian companies.[34] This also would underpin the plausible assumption that within Europe, corporate liberalism retained its main stronghold in France, neoliberalism was strongest in Britain, and Germany was somewhere in between. Although this was brought out fairly clearly in each country's economic policy, there is of course also a geopolitical aspect that modulates economic interests and also influences perceptions of interests.

Networks of Interlocking Directorates

One channel through which company orientations become part of a wider class perspective is the international network of joint directorates. Such networks can be interpreted as structures of communication and strategy formulation, because the actual links are usually made not by managers but by so-called network specialists or "big linkers."[35] It is they who also often participate in informal planning councils such as the ERT, the Trilateral Commission, or the World Economic Forum. The more numerous the links of a particular corporation with others, the greater the extent to which the board meetings of that corporation already begin to approximate a planning body of sorts, no longer just an institution whose considerations are confined to the single firm. By this standard, the final quarter of the twentieth century displayed recurring shifts as to the relative centrality of American and European capital. As shown in table 3.1, the firms with the greatest centrality have moved between U.S. predominance and European ascendancy. To add information for the discussion that will follow, we distinguish between continental European and British firms.

Now with due caution given the differences in sample size and selection criteria for the first two, third, and fourth columns, we may note that in 1976 there was a marked increase in continental European firms relative to their U.S. counterparts: from two against four to four against four; in 1992, the tides seems to swing back to U.S. predominance; while for 2000, there is a resurgence of European capital again, from one against six to five against four. There is one British-Dutch or British firm in each list.

To draw conclusions, we should move beyond this very crude ranking and understand how corporations are actually linked. Here the British(-Dutch) firms, which we identified above as spearheading European capital toward matching the world market orientation of their U.S. counterparts, present a picture (if we confine ourselves to the 1992/2000 comparison) of first being interlocked with U.S. firms only, and then being divided into two categories: one interlocked with American capital, the other with the European core around Allianz.

Table 3.1. Most Centrally Located Firms in the International Network of Joint Directorates, 1970, 1976, 1992, and 2000

Rank	1970	1976	1992	2000
1.	J. P. Morgan (US)	Chase Manhattan (US)	Citigroup (US)	Citigroup (US)
2.	Chemical Bank (US)	Deutsche Bank (Eu)	General Motors (US)	Allianz (Eu)
3.	Chase Manhattan (US)	Canadian Imperial Bank (Can)	AT&T (US)	Chase Manhattan (US)
4.	Royal Dutch/Shell (Eu/GB)	Chemical Bank (US)	IBM (US)	Crédit Suisse (Eu)
5.	Deutsche Bank (Eu)	Dresdner Bank (Eu)	Crédit Suisse (Eu)	BP (GB)
6.	International Nickel (Can)	Ford (US)	3M (US)	Honeywell (US)
7.	AKZO (Eu)	J. P. Morgan (US)	Unilever (Eu/GB)	BNP Paribas (Eu)
8.	General Electric (US)	Swiss Bank Corp. (Eu)	Hewlett-Packard (US)	Nestlé (Eu)
9.		Volkswagen (Eu)		Siemens (Eu)
10.		Royal Dutch/Shell (Eu/GB)		Verizon (US)

Note: American (US), Canadian (Can), Continental European (Eu), and British (GB).
Sources: years 1970 + 1976: Meindert Fennema, *International Networks of Banks and Industry* (The Hague: Nijhoff, 1982), 117, 190 (based on 176 firms); 1992: Philip Mattera, *World Class Business: A Guide to the 100 Most Powerful Global Corporations* (New York: Henry Holt & Co, 1992) (100 firms); and 2000: *Financial Times,* "FT 500" (4 May 2000) (150 firms, data collected with the assistance of Stijn Verbeek). Lists are shorter if *ex aequo* ranked firms would exceed ten.

Let us work this out in some detail. We have taken the network of joint directorates of the one hundred most global corporations by the definition of Mattera[36] and looked at clusters of firms connected by two or more joint directors to raise the significance level of the link. This results in a series of clusters of mutually interlocked firms: for example, a cluster around Citigroup, one around GM, one around AT&T, and some lesser U.S. groups; as well as a number of European clusters to which we turn shortly.

Having obtained these clusters, we then have added those companies that have two or more links to the cluster (that is, to different firms within them; otherwise they would have been part of it themselves). In this way, one obtains a more detailed picture that yet retains a greater significance than drawing all the connecting lines between all corporations in the list. Thus AT&T, itself in one cluster, is also connected to two firms in the Citigroup cluster, and Exxon, which is not in a cluster of its own, is individually linked to two firms in the Citigroup cluster. So Exxon may be called a satellite of that cluster.

If we follow this method, we observe that the European companies in the 1992 sample are divided in three types: clusters linked to the United States, satellites linked to the United States, and clusters not linked to the United States (and with their own satellites). The result is given in table 3.2.

Thus British-Dutch firms Unilever and Royal Dutch/Shell, in addition to the cluster of Swiss firms around CS Holding, Nestlé, and Ciba-Geigy, are linked to, in this case, the central American core (configured around Citigroup). Other European firms listed by Mattera with two or more links (Deutsche Bank, Bayer, Daimler-Benz, Alcatel-Alstom, and Fiat) are not connected into the larger network at this (>1) level of multiplicity.

What has changed in the 2000 network, still in terms of clusters of firms linked by two or more directors and satellites linked by two or more to the clusters, is the much more prominent position of continental European capital in part because of the longer list. The Swiss cluster is still there, with L'Oréal of France part of it; the Deutsche Bank is now part of a cluster around Allianz, which contains the biggest German firms such as Siemens, Munich Re, and Deutsche Telekom. The French Alcatel cluster of 1992 in 2000 contains BNP Paribas, TotalFina, AXA, LVMH, and Aventis (the company formed by the merger of Rhône-Poulenc and Hoechst). Allianz has six links to the French cluster, though, but they are spread over different firms, so there is no Franco-German cluster, but a satellite connection. What has also been reproduced, in spite of the increased number of firms in the sample, is the isolation from the United States. Neither the French cluster nor the German one have a connection at the two or more level with a U.S. cluster (incidentally, the Swiss cluster is no longer connected to the United States at this level either). The German cluster has Daimler-Chrysler as a satellite, but this company, although containing a U.S. subsidiary, is not interlocked (at >1) with other American companies; it also contains Sprint, the U.S. telecom joint subsidiary with France Telecom

Table 3.2. Atlantic Differentiations in British and Continental European Capital, 1992

In U.S. Cluster	Satellite of U.S. Cluster	European Cluster Interlocked with U.S. Cluster	Satellite of European Cluster Interlocked with U.S. Cluster	Satellite of European Cluster Not Interlocked with U.S. Cluster	European Cluster Not Interlocked with U.S. Cluster
none	Unilever (Eu/GB)	Crédit Suisse (Eu) Nestlé (Eu) Ciba-Geigy (Eu)	Royal Dutch Shell (Eu/GB) Roche (Eu)	Deutsche Bank (Eu)	Bayer (Eu) Daimler-B (Eu) Alcatel (Eu) Fiat (Eu)

Note: Continental European (Eu) and British (GB).
Source: Philip Mattera, *World Class Business: A Guide to the 100 Most Powerful Global Corporations* (New York: Henry Holt & Co, 1992) (100 firms).

Table 3.3. Atlantic Differentiations in British and Anglo-Dutch Capital, 2000

In U.S. Cluster	Satellite of U.S. Cluster	European Cluster Interlocked with U.S. Cluster	Satellite of European Cluster Interlocked with U.S. Cluster	Satellite of European Cluster Not Interlocked with U.S. Cluster	European Cluster Not Interlocked with U.S. Cluster
BP	Glaxo	AstraZeneca LloydsTSB	none	Unilever British Telecom	Royal Dutch Shell (in cluster with ING) Vodafone (in cluster with Allianz a.o.)

Source: *Financial Times*, "FT 500" (4 May 2000) (150 firms, data collected with the assistance of Stijn Verbeek).

(itself a satellite of the Allianz cluster). Sprint is not connected with another American corporation either.

The overall picture is one of a European corporate "continent" pretty much isolated from the United States. However, British (including British-Dutch) corporations no longer provide the communication channel to the American network to the same degree they did in the smaller 1992 sample. Not constituting a single bloc comparable to the most densely connected German, French, and Swiss firms, British firms are instead spread across the Atlantic economy. Thus, BP is part of a U.S. cluster with SBC Communications and Morgan, Stanley, which has Bank of America, Dell Computer, and AOL–Time Warner (itself of the Citigroup cluster) as satellites. BP is linked as a satellite to a cluster that contains LloydsTSB, Ericsson, and AstraZeneca. Citigroup is also a satellite of this British-Scandinavian cluster. Glaxo, the pharmaceutical giant that has meanwhile merged with Smith-Kline Beecham from the United States, in the network still is a satellite of a small cluster of Canadian companies, Nortel and BCE. Royal Dutch/Shell is a separate small cluster with Dutch ING Bank. But Vodafone, the British mobile phone operator, is part of the Allianz network, after its takeover of Mannesmann, the steel tube maker turned phone company; while Unilever and British Telecom are both satellites of the Allianz cluster. So the British firms display a remarkable spread over all possible types of connection across the Atlantic, showing none of the cohesion of the other European companies. In table 3.3, this is summed up for the British companies.

European Integration as a Framework of Neoliberal Restructuring

A comparison of the 1992 and 2000 data presented above may be read as underpinning the plausible assumption that European capital is developing a transnational neoliberal strategy by marshalling its own regional cohesion in the deregulatory framework of an enlarging European Union. At the time of the collapse of state socialism in Eastern Europe and the post-Maastricht crisis, continental European capital was hardly European in any sense beyond plain geography. It is only in the course of the 1990s that continental European capital is rising to the occasion. The 2000 data show a strengthening of the three European clusters and, more importantly, a strong satellite connection between the German and French clusters. All three continental European clusters are isolated from the United States. This clustering of corporate Europe is very strongly related to the dramatic increase in (national and cross-border) mergers and takeovers throughout the 1990s. The concentration and centralization of European capital has been one of the side-effects of the extended re-launch of European integration: Both the completion of the Internal Market and the staged development toward monetary union—in short, the emergence of a European capital market—have clearly increased the transnational dynamics of European capital, frequent attempts of national governments to protect domestic industries from (hostile) foreign takeovers notwithstanding. British capital, on the other hand, seems to be more divided between an Atlantic and a European orientation. This British exceptionalism seems to reflect the ongoing debate in the British ruling class over its future commitment to the EMU.

At a more general level, the neoliberal turn in the process of European integration in the course of the 1990s seems to have enabled the West European ruling class to overcome the challenge of corporate liberalism, which a number of them, especially the German ruling class, would perhaps not have achieved if left on their own. Notably, the creeping dismantling of German Rhineland capitalism under the probusiness government of Gerhard Schröder would have been difficult without constant reference to the constraints imposed on Germany by its membership in the European Union. The convergence race in the context of EMU, the more recent Stability and Growth Pact, the deregulation of European capital markets, and the introduction of "best practice" in European labor market policies, are all cases in point. And even in France, the ruling class seems to accept the imperatives of neoliberal Europe. One of the representatives of the French establishment, Michel Albert, offers a striking example of this landslide change in class strategy. In his 1991 *Capitalism vs. Capitalism*, Albert was still arguing in defense of a European model of society, centered around Rhineland capitalism, and against the onslaught of neo-American shareholders' capitalism. More recently, he has become one of the members of the European Competitiveness Advisory Group, mentioned earlier in this chapter, and as such he fully underwrites the uncompromisingly neoliberal recommendations of that forum.

Finally, it is important to note that in the present phase of the European conjuncture European capital is expanding both intensively (deepening the discipline on labor) and extensively (widening it by including new reservoirs of labor power). Few would disagree that the current labor market flexibility program, which boils down to an aggressive recommodification of labor, is deepening the discipline imposed by capital. At the same time, the enlargement strategy of European capital is widening the structures of coordination and regulation—and the institutional framework underpinning them—toward Central and Eastern Europe. This is the true meaning of the widening/deepening debate within the European Union. Widening is part and parcel of a transnational strategy of continental European capital to increase its influence in the region at the expense of American capital. But widening also serves another purpose: Apart from including new reservoirs of labor power, it is conditioned upon dismantling the very few redistributive policies in place, notably the Common Agricultural Policy and structural funding. It is in this sense that European capital is marshalling its own regional cohesion while simultaneously deepening its inherently exploitative nature. "Widening versus social cohesion" is, then, the only debate that really makes sense.

NOTES

1. Erik Olin Wright, "The Continuing Relevance of Class Analysis—Comments," in *Theory and Society* 25 (1996): 693–716.

2. Antonio Gramsci, *Selections from the Prison Notebooks*, ed. and trans. Q. Hoare and G. Nowell-Smith (London: Lawrence & Wishart, 1971), 180.

3. Alain Bihr, *Entre bourgeoisie et proletariat: L'encadrement capitaliste* (Paris: L'Harmattan, 1992); and Gérard Duménil and Dominique Lévy, *Au-delà du capitalisme* (Paris: PUF, 1998).

4. However, as the examples of the trade union cadre and, less obviously perhaps, media managers illustrate, the direction provided by the cadre is not as straightforwardly incorporated within capitalist discipline generally as one would surmise when thinking of a corporate manager. Indeed, the role of the cadre as a functional "middle" class implies that it is, and because of its salaried status, *can* be potentially independent of the capitalist class of owners or at least can pursue interests other than those of capital. See Kees van der Pijl, *Transnational Classes and International Relations* (London: Routledge, 1998), chapter 5.

5. Gramsci, *Selections*, 181–82.

6. See van der Pijl, *The Making of an Atlantic Ruling Class* (London: Verso, 1984), chapter 1; Henk Overbeek, *Global Capitalism and National Decline* (London: Unwin Hyman, 1990), chapter 1; and Otto Holman, *Integrating Southern Europe: EU Expansion and the Transnationalisation of Spain* (London: Routledge, 1996), chapter 1.

7. Thomas Ferguson, *Golden Rule: The Investment Theory of Party Competition and the Logic of Money-Driven Political Systems* (Chicago: University of Chicago Press, 1995).

8. According to Gramsci, "Every social group, coming into existence on the original terrain of an essential function in the world of economic production, creates together with itself, organically, one or more strata of intellectuals which give it homogeneity and an awareness of its own function not only in the economic but also in the social and political fields." Gramsci, *Selections*, 5.

9. Tom Nairn, *The Left against Europe* (Harmondsworth, UK: Pelican, 1973).

10. De Gaulle's *Europe des Patries*, a "European Europe" keeping the United Kingdom out, is a clear case in point of the latter. See for instance Desmond Dinan, *Ever Closer Union: An Introduction to the European Community* (London: Macmillan, 1994), chapter 2.

11. Laurent Cohen-Tanugi, *Le Droit sans L'état: Sur la Démocratie en France et en Amérique* (Paris: PUF, 1987), 21–22. The European Court of Justice is first and foremost the European institution that guarantees the free movement of market forces in the Internal Market. It plays a central role in compelling compliance by member state governments with respect to the Union's *acquis communautaire* (which is mainly concerned with the completion of the Internal Market, and its institutional underpinnings).

12. Charles Bettelheim, "Theoretical Comments by Charles Bettelheim," in Arghiri Emmanuel, *Unequal Exchange: A Study of the Imperialism of Trade* (New York: Monthly Review Press, 1972), 295, appendix I.

13. See Justin Greenwood, "The Professions," in J. Greenwood and M. Aspinwall, eds., *Collective Action in the European Union: Interests and the New Politics of Associability* (London: Routledge, 1998).

14. George Ross, "Assessing the Delors Era and Social Policy," in Stephan Leibfried and Paul Pierson, eds., *European Social Policy: Between Fragmentation and Integration* (Washington, D.C.: The Brookings Institution, 1985), 388.

15. Philippe C. Schmitter, "The EC As an Emergent and Novel Form of Political Domination," *Estudio/Working paper* 1991/26, Center de Estudios Avanzados en Ciencias Sociales, Fundacion Juan March, Madrid, 1991.

16. Andrew Moravcsik, *The Choice for Europe: Social Purpose and State Power from Messina to Maastricht* (Ithaca, N.Y.: Cornell University Press, 1998).

17. Stephen Gill, *American Hegemony and the Trilateral Commission* (Cambridge: Cambridge University Press, 1990).

18. Keith Richardson, "Big Business and the European Agenda," in *Working Papers in Contemporary European Studies*, No. 35 (Sussex: Sussex European Institute, 2000), 6, emphasis added.

19. "Corporate liberalism" refers to the internationalized New Deal capitalism of the postwar period, based on the Fordist mode of production and class compromise within the framework of the Keynesian welfare state. See van der Pijl, *The Making of an Atlantic Ruling Class*. Albert's notion of Rhineland capitalism comes close to this definition inasmuch as it refers to the negotiated or consensual capitalisms in continental Europe, (West) Germany presenting the archetypal form of this "European welfare capitalism." Of crucial importance in this "stakeholders' capitalism" is the structural amalgamation between bank and industrial capital through long-term cross-shareholdings and interlocking directorates; see Michel Albert, *Capitalism vs. Capitalism* (New York: Four Walls Eight Windows, 1993).

20. Otto Holman, "Transnational Class Strategy and the New Europe," in *International Journal of Political Economy* 22, no. 1 (1992): 3–22. For a more detailed account, see Bastiaan van Apeldoorn, *Transnational Capitalism and the Struggle over European Integration* (London: Routledge, 2002).

21. For a comprehensive analysis of the importance of the ERT in the extended relaunch of European integration and its role in achieving the ideational and strategic unity of the emerging transnational capitalist class in Europe, see van Apeldoorn, *Transnational Capitalism*.

22. Richardson, *Big Business*, 4.

23. See also Bieling and Schulten in chapter 9 of this volume.

24. European Round Table of Industrialists, *European Labor Markets: An Update on Perspectives and Requirements for Job Generation in the Second Half of the 1990s* (Brussels: ERT, 1993), 2.

25. ERT, *European Labor Markets*, 9.

26. ERT, *European Competitiveness: The Way to Growth and Jobs* (Brussels, 1994), 3.

27. Interview conducted by one of the authors with Keith Richardson, secretary general of the ERT, and Assistant Secretary General Caroline Walcott, Brussels, February 2, 1996.

28. ERT, *European Labor Markets*, 12–13.

29. ERT, *European Labor Markets*, 9.

30. Keith Richardson, "Het Primaat van Concurrentievermogen: het Europese Bedrijfsleven en de Intergouvernementele Conferentie van 1996," in Otto Holman, ed., *Europese Dilemma's aan het Einde van de Twintigste Eeuw: Democratie, Werkgelegenheid, Veiligheid, Immigratie* (Amsterdam: Het Spinhuis, 1997), 64–65.

31. Ernst-Moritz Lipp, "Auf dem Weg zur transatlantischen Wirtschaftsgemeinschaft," in W. Weidenfeld, ed., *Partnershaft gestalten. Die Zukunftder transatlantischen Beziehungen* (Gütersloh: Bertelsmann Stiftung, 1997), 58.

32. Van der Pijl, *Transnational Classes*, 60, table 2.4.

33. Van der Pijl, *Transnational Classes*, 60, table 2.5.

34. Kees van der Pijl, "From Gorbachev to Kosovo: Atlantic Rivalries and the Reincorporation of Eastern Europe," *Review of International Political Economy* 8, no. 2 (Summer 2001): 282, table 1; cf. Otto Holman and Kees van der Pijl, "The Capitalist Class in the European Union," in G. A. Kourvetaris and A. Moschonas, eds., *The Impact of European Integration: Political, Sociological, and Economic Changes* (Westport, Conn.: Praeger, 1996), 68, table 3.4.

35. Meindert Fennema, *International Networks of Banks and Industry* (The Hague: Nijhoff, 1982), 208.

36. Philip Mattera, *World Class Business: A Guide to the 100 Most Powerful Global Corporations* (New York: Henry Holt & Co., 1992).

4

⚜

The Geopolitics of U.S. Hegemony in Europe

From the Breakup of Yugoslavia to the War in Iraq

ALAN W. CAFRUNY

As the previous chapters have intimated, but not fully explored, the contemporary transnational neoliberal hegemonic project entails a complex constellation of global unity and national specificity and fragmentation. Transnational agreements, and even a measure of class unity with regards to strategic coordination, go hand in hand with nationally and territorially specific formal and executive state power (see the previous chapter by Holman and van der Pijl). Indeed, this territorial noncorrespondence contributes to neoliberal hegemony because it ensures that state power is confined to the national level and thereby is functionally constrained to operate within the minimalist constitutionalist framework and to exert capitalist discipline. In addition, fragmentation under the unilateral military dominance of the state where the social base of neoliberalism is the strongest—the United States—ensures that coercive military action can be produced as required in the last instance to maintain neoliberal world order. This chapter contributes to our understanding of the nature of the consolidation and normalization of neoliberal hegemony in Europe by focusing on the geopolitical dimension that can generally be characterized by American supremacy, West European fragmentation and rivalry, and a "hub and spoke" integration with the dominant superpower.

American military supremacy implies that the exercise of the geopolitical dimension of hegemony expresses American national interests. This has not always been very palatable to the subordinate European allies. Immediately after the end of the Cold War, when a more independent model of post-Fordist development in the EU seemed feasible, the possibility of European military autonomy was resurrected out of the ashes of the European Defense Community. The Maastricht Treaty established the framework for a set of novel political and military institutions in a Common Foreign and Security Policy (CFSP). However, as Kees van der Pijl has shown, the consolidation of an enlarged Atlantic security zone under American tutelage reinforced the position of the neoliberal bloc in individual states and in the EU.[1]

The expansion of American power in Europe developed gradually after 1989 and was closely related to events in southeastern Europe. The improvisational and tentative nature of U.S. policy toward this region through the Dayton Agreement of November 1995, but still in evidence until the decision to deploy NATO forces against Serbia in the winter of 1998–1999, was a reflection of both conjunctural factors and more general considerations. Whereas the Bush administration was preoccupied with the break-up of the Soviet Union and with German reunification, the early Clinton administration emphasized economic aspects of neoliberal globalization and domestic fiscal retrenchment. More generally, U.S. foreign policy operated within a context of the post–Viet Nam fear of military engagement and casualties, a consideration whose significance was magnified by the relative unimportance of the western Balkans (as opposed to Kosovo and Albania) to either the European powers or the United States. In addition, the expansion of American power was a cause, but also in important respects an effect, of European weakness and fragmentation. As I show in the first part of this chapter, the United States encouraged the European powers, individually or collectively, to play the lead role when the Yugoslav Federation collapsed. The gradual projection of U.S. power in the Balkans developed primarily in reaction to a European security project that remained stillborn as a result of persistent national rivalries. In the second part of this chapter, I analyze the development of instability in Kosovo and the complex chain of events leading up to the seventy-eight-day American-led bombing of Serbia that served further to consolidate American power with respect not only to Europe but also to Russia. The third part addresses recent trends in the establishment of a European Security and Defense Policy (ESDP), including attempts to foster trans-European military-industrial cooperation. Despite its rhetorical appeal, ESDP is fatally weakened by insufficient levels of defense spending and the limited integration of European defense industries.

The implication of my analysis is that EU states lack the commitment required to fulfill their nominal ambitions, even in the European space itself, to a security order underpinned by cosmopolitan human rights norms and international law. Rather, they accept by default American supremacy and protection, with all that that implies for the organization of the global and European political economy and subservience to the United States' conception of its own national interest. The failure of the EU to develop a morally credible and effective security response to the Balkan crisis and the improvisational nature in which the United States entered to fill the vacuum reflect the minimalist nature of U.S.–led neoliberal hegemony. "Minimal hegemony" implies a reduced need to secure international political coherence and consent in the absence of any serious ideological challenge to a market-based order in which the United States enjoys formidable structural power.[2]

THE UNITED STATES, EUROPE, AND
THE BREAKUP OF YUGOSLAVIA

Since the end of World War II, political-military rivalry among Western Europe's leading powers has undermined efforts to achieve regional autonomy. The failure of the European Defense Community in 1954 made it clear that Western European security policies would be developed within a national framework and organized by NATO, while integration would proceed primarily by means of economic cooperation. With the exception of Britain, Western European states limited their defense spending in exchange for U.S. occupation of the western half of a militarized continent. Geopolitical weakness diminished the ability of Western European states individually or collectively to challenge core U.S. interests or, with the exception of sub-Saharan Africa, to retain primacy in former colonies. America's threat to withdraw troops from Europe helped to enforce European adherence to the dollar–gold standard during the 1960s, and defeated French attempts to break the Anglo-American control of international oil markets during the 1970s.

The contrast between the EU's strong bargaining position in international trade and relative geopolitical weakness has given rise to the concept of civilian power. Yet, the concept is ultimately misleading because it makes an artificial distinction between economic and political power. The Bretton Woods system was both economic imperium and an expression of America's political-military supremacy. The privileged position of the dollar made it possible to finance the construction of a military colossus while defense expenditure and research and development generated massive economic benefits and served as a powerful Keynesian stimulant. By contrast, the EU has been unable to develop mutually reinforcing structures of economic and political power. The fiscal and monetary constraints of the Economic and Monetary Union (EMU) have greatly impeded the development of a common foreign and security policy. If the euro were to challenge the primacy of the dollar, Europe would need to build a polity that is both economically and politically independent of the United States.

When the European continent became indivisible as a result of the collapse of the Soviet Union, it appeared that the basic contours of such a polity were forming. The Maastricht Treaty codified ambitious plans for a Common Foreign and Security Policy (CFSP). As a European constitutional process began to unfold, many observers discerned the outlines of an emergent system of multilevel governance, the formation of an embryonic European transnational class, and even the "birth of a polity."[3] A unified Europe was assumed to be a necessary (but not sufficient) condition for the defense of a distinctive European social market against neoliberalism[4] and a more humanitarian foreign policy based on principles of international law.[5] Throughout the decade of the 1990s, moreover, the institutions of a CFSP gradually emerged, including the appointment of a high representative for the CFSP, the expansion of the Western European Union (WEU), and a rapid reaction force. These developments, in turn, were accompanied by a degree of transnational consolidation of European defense industries, including large collaborative projects such as the Eurofighter and the Airbus A400 military transport aircraft.

The crisis of Yugoslavia developed concurrently with the Maastricht Treaty negotiation. The global recession of the 1980s had served to intensify the political and economic contradictions of Yugoslav market socialism. Confronted with pressures for structural adjustment arising from an international debt exceeding $22 billion, a contraction of export markets in Western Europe, and the return of "guest workers," the individual republics of the Yugoslav Federation began to pursue their own methods of dealing with the resulting economic shocks and political unrest. As relations among the republics deteriorated in the first half of 1991, both the EU and the United States proclaimed their support for federal Yugoslavia. Preoccupied with the breakup of the USSR, they believed that encouraging secessionist tendencies in Yugoslavia would spill over there and in Europe and would impede structural adjustment and debt repayment. Consequently, neither the EU nor the United States took preventive measures or seriously considered Slovenian and Croatian proposals for transforming what was essentially a one-party state into a democratic confederation. The EC offered Yugoslavia an association agreement and $4 billion in aid for the preservation of the federation. U.S. Secretary of State James Baker's meeting with Slobodan Milosevic in Belgrade in June left Serbian generals with the impression that "the US had no intention of stopping them by force" if they took military action against secessionist republics.[6] When Serbian units of the former JNA attacked the provisional Slovenian militia, Jacques Poos, president of the Council of the European Union, asserted, "This is the hour of Europe. It is not the hour of the Americans." The collapse of Yugoslavia was widely viewed as an opportunity for the assertion of European power and independence.

The EC's mediation ended the fighting between the JNA and the Slovenian militia, effectively severing Slovenia from the rest of Yugoslavia. But the cease-fire freed JNA troops for an attack in August on Croatia , where Milosevic had already been fomenting rebellion among local Serbs and where local militias supported by Belgrade had proclaimed a "Republic of Serbian Krajina." In response, the EC asserted a principle of the inviolability of internal borders, stating a determination "never to recognize changes of frontiers that have not been brought about by peaceful means."[7] On September 1 the negotiation of a cease-fire agreement allowed EC monitors—five of whom would subsequently be shot down by Serb forces—to be sent into Croatia, but the cease-fire did not hold. At this point France, Yugoslavia, and other countries requested the involvement of the UN Security Council.

In September 1991 the EC convened a peace conference on Yugoslavia's future and established an Arbitration Commission to make recommendations on the recognition of sovereignty in the various republics. The EC's envoy to the peace conference, Lord Carrington, sought to secure agreement on a loose confederation of all the republics along with the protection of minorities and the principle of the inviolability of borders. Before it could render an opinion, Germany declared its intention on the eve of the Maastricht conference unilaterally to recognize Slovenia and Croatia.

The Crisis of German Recognition and Intra-European Rivalry

Although Germany initially followed the U.S. and EC consensus on the inviolability of the Federation, as the war progressed in Croatia there was a great deal of support in Germany for recognition. The support derived from several domestic sources, including the presence of large numbers of Croatian émigrés, the recent experience of reunification, strong support from Bavarian Catholics, and Foreign Minister Genscher and Chancellor Kohl's desire to raise Germany's diplomatic profile.[8] British and French interests were formulated within a framework that included a strong fear of Germany in the immediate aftermath of reunification, anti-Islamic sentiment, and the desire to maintain ties with Serbia.

Attacks on German policy revealed less about the realities of an imploding Yugoslavia than it did about fears of German revanchism in the immediate aftermath of the fall of the Berlin Wall. The harshest criticisms emanated from London, Paris, and of course Belgrade. French Foreign Minister Roland Dumas claimed that Germany "bore a crushing responsibility in the speeding up of the crisis."[9] Critics argued that recognition was premature for two reasons: First, it ignored the reservations issued by the Arbitration Commission concerning Croatia's human rights record with respect to the Serbian minority in the Krajina; second, it served to provoke both Bosnian Serbs and the JNA, thereby making war in Bosnia inevitable. Serbian propaganda echoed this general line, citing German support for the *ustashe* during World War II and claiming that Germany sought to establish a sphere of influence in the Balkans. Fearing the rise of German power, French and British leaders condemned Germany even as they acquiesced in recognition. The German insistence on recognition came to be seen as a cause of the Serbo-Croatian war and the subsequent war in Bosnia, providing alarming evidence of an aggressive post-unification foreign policy.[10] Hence, the conflict over recognition led to intensified rivalry among the European powers and effectively put an end to the project of a common foreign policy. A subsequent myth of German responsibility also helped to provide a rationale for the de facto pro-Serbian policies of France and Britain during the 1992–1994 period.[11]

Germany's decision to recognize Croatia was motivated not by the desire to establish a Balkan sphere of influence but rather by domestic public opinion and strong currents of euphoria in post-reunification Germany that were reflected in Genscher's policies. Germany had concluded that Yugoslavia had collapsed not as a result of secessionist movements but rather as a result of the Serbian massive offensive against Croatia that predated German and EU recognition by three months. As the German Foreign Ministry noted, "The JNA was not only unable to prevent interethnic conflict but as a part of the Serbian war of conquest and expulsion, it even abetted these clashes initially, then intervened, and finally took the lead in them." Nonrecognition, moreover, "had an increasingly adverse effect on the efforts to bring about peace; it only reinforced the Serbian leadership's expectation that the international community would accept a Greater Serbian policy of force under a Yugoslav guise."[12] Recognition, on the other hand, allowed the conflict to become internationalized, thereby making possible the entry of UN peacekeepers and EC cease-fire monitors. Although the EC did, as a result of recognition, finally elicit guarantees from Croatian President Franzo Tudjman concerning the treatment of ethnic Serbs, this fell short of the guarantees asked for by the Arbitration Commission, as Croatia's subsequent conquest of the Krajina and expulsion of Serbs showed. Yet prolonging the recognition process was a delaying action that would only have guaranteed further Serbian aggression. In any case, the ethnic Serbs of the Krajina and Eastern Slavonia, highly mobilized and already implicated in widespread paramilitary activities and crimes, were unlikely to settle for anything short of *anschluss* with Serbia.

Early recognition did encourage a cease-fire in Croatia that was enforced by 10,000 peacekeeping troops, as arranged by UN Special Envoy Cyrus Vance in January 1992, but it came too late to allow for international action to deter Serb attacks on Croatia. The cease-fire was not permanent because it did not resolve the question of Serb minorities in Croatia; Serb militias were not disarmed, and the minority rights of Serbs were not guaranteed. Germany's subsequent policy in former Yugoslavia does not, however, support the contention of German revanchism or a U.S.–German division of southeastern Europe. After the recognition of Croatia in December 1991, Germany did not undertake new diplomatic initiatives in the former Yugoslavia. It has failed to support Croatian membership in the EU, and its foreign direct investment in Croatia has been negligible.[13] The crisis over recognition indicated that Franco-German cooperation over monetary union could not be extended to a more comprehensive vision of a united Europe, even at a time when American policy toward Europe lacked coherence.

Following recognition, all European countries sought to avoid military engagement even as they requested UN involvement and supported an arms embargo designed ostensibly to keep the conflict localized. The problem with German policy was not the recognition of Croatia because Serbia's attack occurred at a time when Germany still supported the Federation. Because Germany applied the principle of nonaggression selectively; if the threat of recognition itself was not sufficient to deter Serbian attacks against Croatia, it was demonstrably insufficient to deter them against Bosnia. Once Germany joined the Franco-British consensus on neutrality and nonintervention, it was no longer possible to protect Bosnia from Croatia and Serbia; Germany would subsequently half-heartedly endorse U.S. calls to lift the arms embargo on Bosnia. But the strategy of ethnic partition that all European powers (with the partial exception of Germany) endorsed either explicitly or implicitly would be pursued with devastating results. A "common foreign and security policy" was achieved by acquiescing to the dismemberment of Bosnia.

U.S. Intervention

Croatian independence placed Bosnia in an untenable position. By the spring of 1992, the JNA had withdrawn its heavy weapons to Serbia, and Bosnian Serb paramilitary forces were mobilizing in conjunction with the JNA. At the same time, Croatian forces were also planning a program of expansion and ethnic cleansing in Herzegovina. Croatian President Tudjman met with Serbian President Milosevic in September 1991 in what was widely considered to be a plan to divide Bosnia-Herzegovina between Croatia and Serbia.[14] Bosnian President Izetbegovic had publicly warned that, in the absence of international security guarantees, Croatian independence posed a grave danger to Bosnia. In February 1992, Carrington requested that the Portuguese presidency convene a conference on Bosnia's future, the outcome of which was a proposal for a system of ethnic cantons that was both highly unrealistic and ultimately unacceptable to Izetbegovic. Following a referendum, Bosnia declared its own independence and received EC recognition. Bosnian Serb units attacked government forces throughout Bosnia. By the summer of 1992, these units, closely supervised and supported by Belgrade, had overrun 60 percent of Bosnian territory, laid siege to most major cities including Sarajevo, and carried out a campaign of ethnic cleansing and extermination. In the autumn of 1992, Bosnian Croats embarked on their own project of ethnic cleansing and territorial conquest, leaving the Bosnian government in control of less than 20 percent of its own territory.

In August 1992 a special conference was convened in London, and a negotiating team chaired first by Carrington and later Lord David Owen (representing the EU) and Vance (representing the UN) was established in Geneva. In October, 8,000 UN troops were sent to Bosnia in order to facilitate food shipments to major cities including Sarajevo. Britain and France provided large contingents to UNPROFOR, which eventually expanded to 22,000 troops, strictly limited to humanitarian aid whose underlying rationale was partly public relations and partly designed to prevent large-scale migration of refugees to Western Europe. The unwillingness of EU and UN negotiators to identify the Serbs as aggressors led them to adopt a position of neutrality with respect to all parties, and to advance successive plans for ethnically based provinces. Ethnic cleansing was encouraged by the willingness to redraw maps to take account of territorial conquests.[15] In January 1993 Vance and Owen put forward a plan for de facto ethnic partition that not only rewarded (and therefore provoked further) ethnic cleansing but also encouraged Croatia to enter the war against Bosnia.[16] Bosnian President Izetbegovic reluctantly accepted the plan, but the Bosnian Serbs refused to follow suit. Croatia and Serbia formed a united front in June 1993 that included military cooperation, a meeting between Tudjman and Milosevic, and a Serb-Croat plan for partition that became the basis of the Owen-Stoltenberg plan.[17]

The increasing involvement of the UN was necessitated by the renationalization of EU policy and the refusal of Britain or France to undertake military intervention.[18] The United States continued to limit its own involvement, with two notable and revealing exceptions: First, at the end of 1992, Bush delivered a strong warning to Milosevic that further moves in Kosovo would lead to U.S. military intervention, a warning that was repeated by Clinton in 1993.[19] Second, in July 1993, Clinton sent 500 troops to Macedonia to serve as a "trip-wire" to guarantee against Serb intervention. These warnings and policies, which were especially clear and unambiguous given the usual torrents of empty rhetoric, sharply defined the U.S.'s essential interest in establishing a bridgehead in the Albanian diaspora and preventing the spillover of conflict to Turkey, Greece, Albania, Macedonia, Bulgaria, or Hungary.

As the war continued and the scope of atrocities and ethnic cleansing became widely publicized American and European views began to diverge, but the differences were more rhetorical than real. During the 1992 presidential campaign Clinton called for lifting the arms embargo on Bosnia and for more robust action against Serbia including air support. The EU, now reflecting the views of Britain and France, rejected the use of force unless the United States was willing to provide its own troops. In fact, the rhetoric obscured a carefully choreographed transatlantic performance, even if the lines were at times delivered spontaneously. The Europeans were fully aware that Clinton would not commit troops; for his part, Clinton recognized the impossibility of intervention given strong opposition from all military branches, and indeed his administration veered between a rhetorical policy in favor of Bosnia, especially when atrocities were widely publicized, and claims that the war was grounded in "ancient hatreds," which served to dampen enthusiasm for military intervention.[20] In June 1993, the United States introduced a resolution to the UN Security Council to end the arms embargo on Bosnia. Germany supported it, but Britain and France (along with Russia) abstained and the resolution did not pass; further initiatives were stifled by the threat of French or British vetoes. At this point, the United States declared that it had no vital interest in the war in Bosnia.[21] But the arms embargo impeded the ability of the Bosnian government to defend itself,[22] and the humanitarian effort had become a means of "managing" the war and resisting public demands for intervention. The UN took on an expanded humanitarian role and implemented a disastrous policy of establishing safe havens. When the Serbs carried out their "final solution" at one such "safe haven," Srebrenica, in July 1995, expelling 23,000 Bosnian Muslim women and children and killing 7,000 men, Dutch forces immediately capitulated and the French commander refused to allow air strikes.[23]

The conjunction of several factors in early 1994 marked a new phase in the war, characterized by the entry of the United States and the formation of a "Contact Group" (Germany, Britain, France, Russia, and the United States), in which European actions would be dependent on American military power. Continuing atrocities, including the Serbian bombing of the marketplace in Sarajevo in February 1994, vividly illustrated the bankruptcy of the safe haven strategy and generated increased international public pressure for the use of force against the Serbs, especially in the United States. At the same time, it became clear that the assumption of an eventual Serbo-Croatian partition had been rendered moot by the tenacity of the Bosnian forces, whose growing strength threatened to provoke direct military involvement by Belgrade, thereby risking an expansion of the war beyond the borders of the former Yugoslavia. The threat of wider instability led to U.S. diplomatic and military intervention within the framework of NATO and coincided with a developing consensus within the Clinton administration that NATO should be expanded into Central and Eastern Europe. The centerpiece of U.S. diplomacy was the establishment of a federation between Croatia and Bosnia. The federation permitted more heavy weapons to flow to the Bosnian military forces, thus helping to change the balance of power on the ground, but it also allowed for greater U.S. influence over the Bosnian government. The Bosnian Serb rejection of effective partition, coupled with continuing attacks on safe areas, led to the incremental use of air power by NATO's southern command against Bosnian Serb targets.

U.S. efforts to forge a Muslim-Croat alliance gradually produced a new military situation; by the summer of 1995, the situation on the ground was transformed. With the fall of Srebrenica, Zepa, and Gorazde, the Serbs had realized long-standing war aims. The U.S.–sponsored Croatian offensive in the Krajina, which led to the expulsion of 200,000 ethnic Serbs from their homes, represented the denouement of the Serbo-Croat War of 1991. At the same time, the Bosnian Army showed that even without heavy weapons it was capable of defending existing government-held territory and, with help from Croatia and limited U.S. air power, recovering territory in northwest Bosnia. The resurgence of the Bosnian Army, coupled with the NATO action "Deliberate Force" of July 1995, gravely damaged the Bosnian Serb military infrastructure and convinced Belgrade that a settlement was preferable to continued bombing. On the one hand, the Bosnian Serb army had by the fall of 1995 failed to conquer Sarajevo. At the same time, the Serb conquests of Srebrenica, Zepa, and Gorazde eliminated these areas as negotiating issues. A joint Croat-Bosnian offensive (Operation Storm) in northwestern Bosnia threatened to liberate the whole region, including Banja Luka, from Serb control while Croat forces overran the Krajina and captured Western Slavonia (Operation Flash), thereby resolving on the ground most of the important remaining disputes between Croatia and Serbia.

The Dayton Agreement of November 1995 essentially ratified the existing balance of forces. It called for the positioning of 50,000 troops under NATO command (IFOR and later SFOR) and guaranteed by 10,000 U.S. soldiers. Although the accord provided for the existence of a nominal Bosnia-Herzegovina, the underlying reality has been one of ethnic partition and the consolidation of ethnic power in both cantons. Although NATO forces have largely kept the peace, they have not guaranteed wholesale repatriation of refugees nor have they promoted multiethnic democracy.[24] As an exercise in de facto partition, the Dayton agreements sought to preserve the battlefield status quo and indeed may have prevented the Bosnian Army from exploiting its successes on the battlefield and recovering more territory.

FROM DAYTON TO RAMBOUILLET: THE POLITICAL ECONOMY OF NATO'S WAR AGAINST SERBIA

Kosovo itself occupied an idiosyncratic position within the Yugoslav Federation. During the 1970s, demands for greater Albanian autonomy were repressed by Tito, although the province was granted limited autonomy. In 1989, even this limited autonomy was revoked as the province was reincorporated within Serbia and treated as a de facto colony. As the rest of Yugoslavia disintegrated, the repression of ethnic Albanians, who constituted 90 percent of the population, threatened to inflame the entire Albanian diaspora. With support from Italy and, after 1993, the United States, the Berisha government in Albania had been able to seal off its borders with Kosovo and Macedonia. The overthrow of Berisha in 1997 opened up the borders to population flows as well as 750,000 Kalashnikov rifles.

The United States recognized that it had crucial economic and political interests in Kosovo. As David Gompert, special assistant for national security affairs to Bush, wrote:

> The chief American strategic concern during the Bush administration and later under Clinton was to keep the Yugoslav conflict from spreading southward, where its flames could leap into the Atlantic alliance. Therefore, while the Bush administration was not convinced of the need to intervene in Bosnia, it took a markedly different attitude toward Kosovo. Washington feared that a Serbian assault against the Albanian Kosovars would consume the entire southern Balkan region in a conflagration that would pit one NATO ally against another. Hostilities in Kosovo would probably spill into Albania proper. This in turn could incite the large Albanian minority in Macedonia and lead to a Serbian or Greek intervention there.

Bulgaria and Turkey would then feel pressure to act in order to prevent Greek control of Macedonia. Whereas the Bosnian war could be contained, conflict in Kosovo could not.[25]

As noted above, despite strong public resistance to the deployment of ground troops, in July 1993 the United States did send 500 troops to Macedonia under UN auspices to act as a "trip wire" in case of Serbian invasion. In October 1993 the United States established military ties with Albania. Bush's "Christmas Warning" of 1992 that Serbian aggression in Kosovo would provoke U.S. military force—a warning reaffirmed by the Clinton administration—was intended to let Milosevic know that whereas the United States had exercised restraint in Bosnia, it would not do so in Kosovo. Within Kosovo, a pacifist opposition under the leadership of Ibrahim Rugova organized shadow institutions designed to accommodate Albanian participation in public life without provoking Serbia into open conflict. The United States sought to obtain concessions from Serbia while warning Rugova that independence was not an option. In this context, the decision at Dayton to ignore Kosovo was a reflection of the reluctance of either the United States or the European powers to undertake military intervention in the face of what would almost certainly have been Serbian resistance. At Dayton, the United States urged Milosevic to use restraint in Kosovo, hoping that the province would remain quiet. Yet, within weeks after the Dayton Accord, the Kosovar Albanians began to mobilize behind the KLA and Rugova's strategy of nonviolence gradually lost credibility.

From early 1996 until the conference at Rambouillet in January 1999, the policy of the United States and the key European powers toward Kosovo was essentially reactive, based on the premise that military intervention would be costly and dangerous to the fragile peace in Bosnia, and that the best hope lay in restraining Milosevic while also seeking to limit the activities of the KLA. Short of military intervention, the only real means of influence was an outer wall of sanctions provided for in the Dayton Accord.[26] Although the agreement contemplated the possibility of lifting UN sanctions on the Federal Republic without regard to the situation in Kosovo, the outer wall would maintain a degree of leverage until Serbia addressed concerns in Kosovo as well as with the War Crimes Tribunal. But the sanctions had little effect on Serbia, and the cycle of KLA-led guerilla attacks and Serb retaliation intensified. Although both the United States and the Europeans hoped that the stalemate between the KLA and Milosevic would continue indefinitely, France, Italy, and Germany tended to favor greater passivity, while beginning in 1998 the U.S. Secretary of State Madeleine Albright escalated the rhetoric of threat.

Despite Albright's bluster, however, at times the United States also encouraged Serbian attacks on the KLA, provided these did not destabilize the political situation or provoke world public opinion. On February 23, 1998, for example, Gelbard lavished praise on Milosevic for his cooperation with the

Dayton Accord, declaring that the "KLA is without any questions a terrorist group" and that the U.S. "condemns very strongly terrorist activities in Kosovo."[27] These statements gave Milosevic a pretext for launching subsequent massive attacks on KLA positions.

Racak and the Drive to War

The U.S. policy of diplomatic neutrality regarding Kosovo was necessitated by the unwillingness of either the United States or the European powers prior to the latter part of 1998 to extend the existing NATO operation beyond Bosnia or commit ground forces to Kosovo or Serbia. As late as September 1998, for example, Albright assured the U.S. Congress that the Clinton administration had no plans to send ground troops to Kosovo, even as peacekeepers. But this type of engagement required the maintenance of a delicate compromise between Serbia and an enlarged and increasingly well-armed KLA. The United States would continue to uphold Serbian sovereignty provided the Serbs showed restraint, but the strategy also required restraint on the part of the KLA. As noted above, at times it required the United States to encourage limited Serbian attacks on the KLA. However, as the situation on the ground became more problematic and Rugova's pacifist policy appeared increasingly unrealistic to Kosovar Albanians, the United States began to escalate the rhetorical campaign against Serbia and to tilt to the KLA. Thus when Serb forces carried out large-scale attacks on the KLA in October 1998, Albright declared that "the United States and its allies are moving NATO activities from the planning stage to readiness to act" and "the activation order is on the table."[28] Holbrooke eventually secured an "October Agreement," which called for a cease-fire, troop withdrawals, elections, limited autonomy for Kosovo, and 2000 unarmed OSCE cease-fire monitors under U.S. leadership. NATO extended the bombing deadline two weeks, and after Serbia began withdrawing thousands of security forces from the province Albright stated that Milosevic's compliance with UN Security Council Resolution 1199 was "sufficient to justify not launching air strikes."[29]

The killing of forty-five Albanians in the village of Racak by Serb paramilitary forces in January 1999, as documented by the OSCE Verification Mission, set in motion a chain of diplomatic and military moves culminating in the abortive negotiations at Rambouillet and, from March to June 1999, the subsequent civil war between the KLA–led Kosovar Albanians and JNA forces, which broke out in the wake of NATO bombings. Whereas by following Holbrooke's last-minute intervention in October 1998 the Serbs had been able to avoid bombing, the United States now began to carry out a strategy whose logic would lead inexorably to war. Although there are many questions about what happened in Racak, it is clear that the OSCE Verification Mission was becoming an instrument of U.S. support for the KLA, as evidenced by growing conflicts between the United States and Europe over the OSCE's activities and statements.[30] As a result of the Racak killings the Contact Group, at U.S. initiative, summoned Serbia and the KLA to talks at Rambouillet to a conference cochaired by French Foreign Minister Hubert Vedrine and British Foreign Minister Robin Cook. Albright warned that further conflict would be likely to spread beyond the borders of Yugoslavia; that Greece and Turkey would be drawn in; and that Serbian failures to comply with UN Security Council Resolutions undermined NATO's credibility.[31] Thus the conference at Rambouillet was presented to Belgrade as a final opportunity to avoid war.

The interim agreement that the United States presented to the Serbs and the KLA at Rambouillet expressed a clear shift in U.S. strategy. Consistent with existing U.S. policy, it refused to accept the demands of the KLA for self-determination. Serbia was, however, to permit a far-reaching autonomy for the Kosovar Albanians, including self-governing democratic institutions, a withdrawal of most security forces, and the acceptance of a peace implementation force under NATO command that would enjoy freedom of maneuver throughout the Federal Republic, including Serbia. The KLA was asked to accept continuing status as a Serb province, and to cease all military activities against the Serb forces.

The argument that Rambouillet was designed to establish a pretext for war by giving the Serbs an ultimatum they could not accept is consistent with the overall trend of U.S. diplomacy in the region, which appears by late 1998 to have become predicated on the necessity of at least some level of military involvement subsequent to the abandonment of neutrality in favor of the KLA. Although the interim agreement contained provisions that were clearly unacceptable to the Serbs,[32] Milosevic did not attempt to negotiate changes in the text while continuing to mass troops in Kosovo and escalate attacks on KLA guerillas as well as civilians.[33] Both Milosevic and the United States made significant miscalculations: Based on past experience, Milosevic probably believed that the bombing would be light and of short duration and hoped for Russian support; the United States clearly also anticipated that a short campaign would compel capitulation or compromise.[34] Once the war had begun, however, the United States recognized that the failure to defeat Serbia would endanger "NATO credibility," which was by now indistinguishable from America's broader geopolitical objectives in Europe and Eurasia.

War and American Power in the Balkans

As the first wave of U.S. warplanes attacked Serbia, Clinton reiterated his long-standing pledge not to place ground troops in Europe: "I do not intend to put our troops in Kosovo to fight a war."[35] Clinton's statement—which clearly damaged the war effort by encouraging the Serbs—reflected the profound unpopularity of intervention within the United States as well as the estimate that Milosevic would capitulate after a few days of limited bombing. In fact, the Serbs did not capitulate, but rather, as had been predicted, implemented a massive campaign of expulsion of 850,000 Kosovar Albanians to Macedonia and Albania.

The war itself indicated the novel transatlantic division of labor. U.S. military power was clearly in the forefront, and the imbalance between Europe and the United States was striking: U.S. forces flew 80 percent of air combat missions and supplied 85 percent of munitions. The United States deployed 150 tankers while France and Britain deployed twelve each.[36] Whereas at the outset Britain and France had sought to exclude Germany from the Rambouillet negotiations, as the bombing campaign intensified Germany emerged as a central factor in the war effort.[37] While Britain's Prime Minister Tony Blair served as the principal NATO cheerleader, in fact Bonn served as the "nerve center" of diplomacy, a role that had been unacceptable to Britain and France at the beginning of the decade. Thus the Blair–Schroeder "third way" economic initiatives, announced in the immediate aftermath of the war, had their counterpart in the ascendance of the Atlanticist vision of foreign policy that emerged in the mid-1990s in the context of debates over the enlargement of NATO, and were now consolidated through the maintenance of NATO's "credibility." Atlanticism was confirmed by the ouster of Oskar Lafontaine, who strongly opposed the war and favored an independent European military force.[38] Foreign Minister Joschka Fischer's strong support for bombing, similarly, exposed deep divisions in the Green Party, and the party leadership eventually abandoned its pacifist stance as opponents of Atlanticism were marginalized.

The refugee crisis, the failure of planning, and the unwillingness of the United States to deploy ground troops exposed the hypocrisy of the humanitarian rationale. With respect to the case for external military intervention, moreover, there were morally and politically relevant differences in the nature and level of violence in Kosovo and Bosnia. In Bosnia, a society that had achieved a high level of assimilation, the project of Serbianization necessitated ethno-religious fascism and genocide. In Kosovo, by contrast, ethnic Albanians and Serbs were already living separately in an essentially colonial situation.[39] The campaign of repression against ethnic Albanians, while at times undeniably massive and violent, was not strictly speaking genocidal and was often—especially after 1997—provoked or instigated by the KLA. In any case, to the extent that U.S. (or European) policymakers believed their own human rights rhetoric, their adherence was highly selective: The war was clearly to be fought with the absence of American casualties, regardless of the consequences either for refugees or for civilian victims of bombing raids flown from 15,000 feet beyond the range of anti-aircraft guns. The progress of the war, moreover, provoked Russian and Chinese intransigence. By May, it became clear that a strategy of limited air power alone could not compel the Serbs to withdraw from Kosovo in time to repatriate refugees before winter. NATO softened its diplomatic stance by accepting a fig leaf UN administration for postwar Kosovo but also greatly expanded the scope of bombing raids to include civilian targets including roads, bridges, power sources, and factories. Following Blair's statement that ground forces should be deployed, on May 18 Clinton declared that "all options are on the table" and approved plans for positioning 45,000 NATO troops, including 7,500 Americans, in Macedonia either as an occupation force if Milosevic capitulated or as an invasion force if he did not.[40] The escalation of bombing, the threat of ground troops, and the realization that Russia would not support him convinced Milosevic on June 3 that the time was right for a settlement, which resulted in the Military Technical Agreement between NATO and the Federal Republic of Yugoslavia.

The recognition of military weakness and dependence on the United States generated support for a "European Security and Defense Identity" (ESDI) and a substantial reconstructive effort. Although technically under the authority of the UN Mission in Kosovo (UNMIK), Kosovo, like Bosnia, would effectively be governed as a NATO protectorate, although some Russian and other non-NATO forces would be present. The EU announced a Stability Pact for South-Eastern Europe, which promised high levels of assistance to the whole region. Sanctions were not lifted and funds for Serbia were not released until Milosevic was removed from office in the 2000 elections and sent to the Hague.

Whereas the war was fought largely with American forces, the United States clearly envisaged a postwar transatlantic division of labor in which peacekeeping was to be a European problem. U.S. Deputy Secretary of State Strobe Talbott declared that the "ultimate status of Kosovo" was "a question for the future," but that it was "first and foremost a challenge for the Europeans in general and the EU in particular."[41] The EU and United States pledged through the European Agency for Reconstruction to provide an initial sum of $1 billion in humanitarian and reconstruction aid, followed by an additional $12 billion over the next six years as reconstruction aid while through the Stability Pact for the Balkans to establish a political administration.[42] By mid-2002, however, it had become apparent that there were limits to the resources Europe (or the United States) was willing to devote to the Balkans.[43] The U.S.–brokered Ohrid Agreement has not eliminated ethnic tensions in Macedonia, and the United States has only a symbolic presence among the 5,000 troops of Operation Essential Harvest, NATO's response to the outbreak of civil war in Macedonia, which is under German command and is scheduled to be taken over by the EU. During his presidential campaign, George W. Bush pledged to withdraw troops from the former Yugoslavia, and after September 11 the United States proposed significant cutbacks.[44] By November 2002 the U.S. troop presence in Bosnia had declined to 1,800, but exceeded 5,000 in Kosovo.

Kosovo and Macedonia have implications for the international political economy that are notably lacking in Bosnia. A comprehensive explanation for U.S. power projection in the region must include the geopolitical imperatives of the struggle for control over oil and gas reserves and transit routes. The defeat of Serbia and the pacification of Kosovo not only served to restore the credibility of NATO and stabilize its eastern Mediterranean flank, but they also advanced the interests of the Anglo-American multinational oil companies. By the mid-1990s, it had become clear that both the United States and Western Europe were becoming increasingly dependent on the Middle East, and that diversification of supply was necessary to ensure continued U.S. dominance of international oil.[45] The vast undeveloped energy reserves of the Caspian Sea basin have generated fierce international competition, and the United States has sought to destroy the Russian monopoly over both production and transportation of Caspian oil and gas. Western companies have invested $18 billion in Azerbaijan and Kazakhstan since the mid-1990s, and strong efforts have been made to detach these key former Soviet republics from Russia.[46] U.S. multinationals have been discouraged from building pipelines through Iran, despite their commercial viability, and alternative routes, some of which are commercially unprofitable and opposed by the oil companies, have been supported. At various times the United States government has both promoted and discouraged plans to build pipelines to the heavily trafficked Bosporus.[47] Although geographically distant from Central Asia, Kosovo and Macedonia straddle or lie adjacent to an alternative transit route from the Caspian Sea to Western Europe, Corridor VIII, which has been designated by the EU as a strategic transportation route.

In September 2000, the Albanian-Macedonian-Bulgarian Oil Pipeline Corporation (AMBO), an Anglo-American firm based in New York, signed memoranda of understanding with the three countries for exclusive rights to a project for a 900-kilometer pipeline from Burgas, Macedonia, to Vlore, Albania, which runs adjacent to the Presevo Valley and Camp Bondsteel, built by Halliburton in 1999 as part of a $330 million contract and now the largest U.S. military base in southeastern Europe with permanent housing for 7,000 troops. The project, which originated in 1996 but faces numerous difficulties owing to the difficult terrain, has been supported by the U.S. government as a means of circumventing an alternative Burgas–Alexandroupolis route financed by Greek and Russian interests.[48]

THE LIMITS OF EUROPEAN MILITARY INTEGRATION

As war progressively enveloped all of the republics of the former Yugoslavia, NATO, and not the EU or individual European powers, has become the key unit of political-military stabilization. NATO has now conducted extensive air, land, and sea campaigns and has established a substantial military presence in Bosnia, Serbia (Kosovo), Albania, and Macedonia. Summing up the experience of the past decade, two distinctive trends can be identified: first, the fragmentation of the EU at the political level and the further consolidation of a hub and spoke system connecting European powers to the United States; and second, the development of an embryonic ESDP. However, ESDP is evolving under the umbrella of the United States and serves to institutionalize Europe's subordinate position in the transatlantic relationship.

U.S. Power versus the European Security and Defense Policy

The institutional framework of ESDP formed in the late 1980s as a result of a Franco-German project that recognized the integral relationship between monetary and political union. Even at the outset, however, the debate over institutions reflected the sharp conflicts of interest among European countries. In contrast to France, which has traditionally favored independence, Britain and Germany required any such defense identity to be within the NATO framework. In response to the Reagan–Gorbachev summit in Reykjavik in 1987, a WEU Summit declared, "We are convinced that the construction of an integrated Europe will remain incomplete as long as it does not include security and defense," and called for a "more cohesive European defense identity." But the declaration did not specify the precise nature of the relationship between the WEU and NATO. In 1992 the Eurocorps was launched as part of a Franco-German initiative, later including Belgium, Spain, and Luxembourg. However, the Eurocorps has essentially been a paper organization comprising units assigned to it from national forces, and it does not have credibility outside of NATO. In December 1998, Blair and Chirac agreed at the St. Malo Summit that the EU should have the capacity for autonomous action. Notably, however, Britain's willingness to participate in an EU security structure was predicated on the claim that it was spearheading a more effective European wing of NATO, and was cooperating more closely with Germany.

Following the war, the Cologne European Council Summit in June 1999 produced a commitment to "a capacity for autonomous military action backed by credible military forces." European leaders including the UK agreed that the Western European Union would be collapsed into the EU. The former secretary-general of NATO, Javier Solana, was appointed EU high representative for the CFSP, and was answerable to the Council of Ministers and also the WEU. In December 1999, a joint Anglo-French declaration supplementing the St. Malo proposals stated that the EU would develop an autonomous capacity to take decisions and that where NATO was not engaged, the EU could launch military operations on its own. There were also bilateral meetings between France and Germany, resulting in a joint declaration that the two countries would seek to build an air transport command. Finally, at the Helsinki EU Summit of December 1999, European leaders established a further set of European institutions, including a permanent structure, the Political and Security Committee (PSC) modeled on NATO with a military committee and military staff. At the same time, a rapid reaction force of 60,000 troops and 500 aircraft will be established by 2003. Nevertheless, all of these agreements assume that the EU will uphold all NATO obligations. The Prague NATO summit of November 2002, moreover, authorized the establishment of a 20,000-troop "rapid reaction" force under NATO command.

It has been argued that these institutional and bilateral developments promise a dramatic breakthrough in European unity. Solana himself has stated his intention to transform the EU into "a more active and influential global power."[49] Yet, such a development is in fact more consistent with the desire of the United States to limit the costs of geopolitical dominance while ensuring that the European "pillar" is planted within the framework of Atlanticism. Three factors point in this direction: first, the continuation of intra-European rivalry and conflicts of interest; second, the technological and economic realities of military procurement; and third, the success of the United States in extending NATO deep into Central and Eastern Europe.

Although St. Malo did indicate Britain's willingness to join defense structures independently of NATO, it did not authorize the EU to act outside of the framework of NATO or U.S. policy, or for tasks other than those defined as humanitarian. All of the ESDP structures report to the Council of Ministers, and not to the Commission. NATO consent would need to be secured for any use of NATO assets. At the same time, there is no evidence that the huge gap in military technology between Europe and the United States—highlighted by the war against Serbia—will be closed as a result of autonomous European efforts. European defense budgets declined by 22 percent between 1992 and 1999. Defense spending of NATO's European members is less than one-half of that of the United States, but spending on R & D and weapons procurement is less than one-quarter of U.S. levels. German military spending has declined to 1.5 percent of GDP.[50] Increases in defense spending are ruled out by the generalized fiscal constraints and slow growth resulting from the Growth and Stability Pact.[51]

There is, furthermore, little evidence that the gap in technology can be closed as a result of European regional initiatives. The process of cross-border mergers and acquisition in the European defense industry not only continues within the context of national rivalries but also contains a strong transatlantic dimension, which appears to be necessary for research and development as well as to achieve economies of scale. The Eurofighter remains perhaps the key example of European defense collaboration, but even the success of this emblematic project was called into question as a result of the battle over whether to arm it with European or U.S. missiles.[52] The establishment of the European Aeronautic Defense and Space Company (EADS) in 2000 indicates the emergence of an embryonic European defense industry. However, BAE's limited involvement and relatively low levels of European defense spending will greatly constrain the development of EADS's military sector.[53] The planned European-wide Battlefield Taxi program has been scaled down dramatically.[54] The Horizon Frigate program under which the UK, France, and Italy were to build missile-carrying ships has collapsed.[55] In 1999 Britain withdrew from a joint military satellite program.[56] Although regional defense cooperation has slowed, the United States has sought to promote greater transatlantic technology sharing and mergers. EADS is becoming increasingly dependent on the U.S. market, including ballistic missile defense. BAE sells more to the Pentagon than to the British Ministry of Defense.[57] The numerous statements of support for European defense initiatives from within the U.S. defense and foreign policy establishment make sense only when viewed in this context.[58] The process of cross-border mergers and acquisitions has not resulted in the cutting of the transatlantic umbilical cord. As Christophe Cornu writes, "American industrial strategy in recent years has essentially been to increase the number of agreements so that American interests become a part of the fabric of European industry, and thus retain access to European markets in all sectors."[59]

U.S. hegemony is reinforced, finally, by the eastward movement of NATO, which remains one step ahead of the EU's own enlargement. NATO's expansion into Central Europe and the subsequent enlargement into Eastern Europe and the Baltic states ratified by the Prague Summit of November 2002 entrench American economic and military power on the EU's eastern flank. Lockheed Martin's $3.5 billion contract with Poland for the F-16 fighter cemented close U.S.–Polish relations and serves as a template for further U.S. defense industry involvement throughout Central and Eastern Europe.[60] The potential for Franco-German collaboration within an alliance whose newest members are politically and economically dependent on the United States is also correspondingly weakened.

The U.S. Offensive after September 11: From Belgrade to Baghdad

Washington's campaign against the Taliban and the subsequent planning for a Middle Eastern offensive during 2002 and early 2003 served to define more sharply the specific parameters of American hegemony with respect to Europe. Although NATO responded to the war in Afghanistan by invoking Article 5 (mutual defense) for the first time in its history, the United States typically preferred to fight an air war largely on its own while using local proxies in order to avoid casualties and maintain its freedom of action. Despite Schröder's opposition to war with Iraq, Germany sent 1,200 peacekeeping troops to Afghanistan immediately after the general election of September 2002. Blair's attempt after September 11 to convene an exclusive inner council of EU great powers at Downing Street antagonized many of the smaller member states. Russia abandoned long-standing commitments to Serbia while during the course of 2002 it made overtures to U.S. multinationals to develop Caspian as well as Siberian oil and gas. The United States began negotiations for a string of new military bases in the former Soviet republics of Central Asia, including Uzbekistan, Kyrgyzstan, Tajikistan, Kazakhstan, Armenia, and Azerbaijan. By detaching NATO from its regional context and giving it a global mission, the United States sought to incorporate Europe more fully into an America-led international division of labor.

Prior to September 11, 2001, George W. Bush maintained a delicate balance between the Republican realism that informed his father's cautious policies of containment and multilateralism and the messianic unilateralism favored by neoconservatives who sought to mobilize America's unprecedented economic and military superiority behind a "war on terror" and a forward strategy in the

Middle East. The gradual emergence of a consensus on Iraq within the administration appeared to confirm the ascendancy of the neoconservatives. Bipartisan support for "regime change" in Iraq suggested, moreover, that there were few remaining practical differences between the emergent Republican synthesis and the "neoliberal cosmopolitanism"[61] that had developed among Democratic party leaders during the Clinton years.

The Anglo-American invasion of Iraq deepened transatlantic tensions even as it opened up new economic and political fault lines within Europe. By announcing a novel doctrine of "preemption" and unilateral action the United States served notice that it would not make significant concessions to gain UN Security Council or NATO approval for future military interventions. As with the war against Serbia, the rapid conquest of Iraq demonstrated America's unprecedented global military supremacy. Nevertheless, as neo-conservatives in the Bush administration turned their attention to Tehran and Damascus, the postwar occupation promised to be difficult.

Although commercial interests undoubtedly played a role in the French and German (and Russian) opposition to a political-military offensive designed to eliminate all challenges to American primacy in the Persian Gulf, the decision to withhold UN and NATO endorsement also expressed widespread resistance to the American imperium. Yet, the improvised Franco-German initiative did not constitute a pan-European ethico-political alternative to U.S.-led Atlanticism. The ability of the United States to obtain consent for the war from many EU and NATO states in Eastern and Southern Europe, despite overwhelming popular opposition, indicated the depth of Europe's crisis of political representation.

NOTES

1. Kees van der Pijl, "From Gorbachev to Kosovo: Atlantic Rivalries and the Reincorporation of Eastern Europe," *Review of International Political Economy* 8, no. 2 (Summer 2001). See also Peter Gowan, *The Global Gamble: Washington's Faustian Bid for Global Dominance* (London: Verso, 1999), especially chapter 12; and Peter Gowan, "The Euro-Atlantic Origins of NATO's Attack on Yugoslavia," in Tariq Ali, ed., *Masters of the Universe: NATO's Balkan Crusade* (London: Verso, 2000).

2. Alan Cafruny, "A Gramscian Concept of Declining Hegemony: Stages of U.S. Power and the Evolution of International Economic Relations" in David P. Rapkin, ed., *World Leadership and Hegemony* (Boulder, Colo.: Lynne Rienner, 1990).

3. See, for example, Liesbet Hooghe and Gary Marks, "Contending Models of Governance in the European Union" in Alan Cafruny and Carl Lankowski, eds., *Europe's Ambiguous Unity: Conflict and Consensus in the Post-Maastricht Era* (Boulder, Colo.: Lynne Rienner, 1997); Liesbet Hooghe and Gary Marks, "Birth of a Polity: The Struggle over European Integration" in Herbert Kitshelt, Peter Lange, Gary Marks, and John Stephens, eds., *Continuity and Change in Contemporary Capitalism* (Cambridge: Cambridge University Press, 1999); and

Baastian van Apeldoorn, *Transnational Capitalism and the Struggle over European Integration* (London: Routledge, 2002). See also Holman and van der Pijl in chapter 3 of this volume.

4. Alan Cafruny, "Social Democracy in One Continent?" in Alan Cafruny and Carl Lankowski, eds., *Europe's Ambiguous Unity* (Boulder, Colo.: Lynne Rienner, 1997).

5. See for example Oskar Lafontaine, "May Day Speech at Saarbrucken," in Tariq Ali, ed., *Masters of the Universe*; and Hubert Vedrine, *France in an Age of Globalization* (Washington, D.C.: Brookings Institution Press, 2001).

6. Warren Zimmerman, *Origins of a Catastrophe: Yugoslavia and its Destroyers—America's Last Ambassador Tells What Happened and Why* (New York: Basic Books, 1996), 137.

7. Mark Weller, "The International Response to the Dissolution of the Socialist Federal Republic of Yugoslavia," *The American Journal of International Law* 86 (1992): 553.

8. Beverly Crawford, "German Foreign Policy after the Cold War: The Decision to Recognize Croatia," Center for German and European Studies, *Working Paper* No. 2.21 (Berkeley: University of California, 1993).

9. O. Lepick, "French Perspectives," in A. Danchev and T. Halverson, eds., *National Perspectives on the Yugoslav Conflict* (New York: St. Martin's, 1996).

10. Beverly Crawford, "Explaining Defection from International Cooperation," *World Politics* 48, no. 4 (July 1996), 482, 490–92. Other critics of German policy included Misha Glenny, *The Fall of Yugoslavia: The Third Balkan War* (London: Penguin, 1993); and Susan Woodward, *Balkan Tragedy: Chaos and Dissolution after the Cold War* (Washington, D.C.: The Brookings Institution, 1995). For a characteristic misreading of German policy, see W. Grieger, "Towards a Gaullist Germany? Some Lessons from the Yugoslav Crisis," *World Policy Journal* 11 (Spring 1994). On French policy, see O. Lepick, "French Perspectives"; and on British policy, see J. Gow, "British Perspectives," in Danchev and Halverson, *National Perspectives*.

11. On the pro-Serbian sentiments in the British Foreign Office, see, for example, Daniele Coversi, "Moral Relativism and Equidistance in British Attitudes to the War in Former Yugoslavia," in Tom Cushman and Stipe Mestrovic, eds., *This Time We Knew: Western Responses to the War in Bosnia* (New York: New York University Press, 1996).

12. German Foreign Ministry, "Recognition of the Yugoslav Successor States: Position Paper of the German Foreign Ministry," 10 March 1993, 2, 3. See also Michael Libal, *Limits of Persuasion: Germany and the Yugoslav Crisis, 1991–2* (Westport, Conn.: Praeger, 1997).

13. Slovenian membership in NATO was championed by France and opposed by Germany. Between 1993 and 1998, total foreign investment in Croatia was less than $1.8 billion. See Christopher Civic, *The Background to the Investment Climate in Slovenia, Croatia, and the FRY* (Rome: Istituto Affari Internazionali, 1998).

14. Susan Woodward, *Balkan Tragedy: Chaos and Dissolution after the Cold War* (Washington, D.C.: The Brookings Institution, 1995), 172; and Sabrina Ramet, *Balkan Babel: The Disintegration of Yugoslavia from the Death of Tito to Ethnic War* (Boulder, Colo.: Westview, 1996), 50.

15. The European Parliament condemned the Vance–Owen Mediation, noting that the strategy of ethnic partition "constitutes an extremely dangerous precedent" that condones "the destruction of a multiethnic society in Bosnia-Herzegovina and legitimizes the violent aggression that has taken place there." See "Resolution on the Situation in Bosnia-Herzegovina," *Official Journal of the European Communities* C 268/160 (April 10, 1993).

16. Radha Kumar, *Divide and Fall? Bosnia in the Annals of Partition* (London: Verso, 1997), 59–62.

17. Ramet, *Balkan Babel*, 251.

18. James Gow, *Triumph of the Lack of Will: International Diplomacy and the Yugoslav War* (New York: Columbia University Press, 1997), 174–83.

19. Richard Caplan, "International Diplomacy and the Crisis in Kosovo," *International Affairs* 74, no. 4 (1998): 753.

20. On May 19, 1993, for example, Secretary of State Warren Christopher declared, "This is at heart a European problem" and that Bosnia had become "a morass of ancient hatreds, a war between all, against all, with all parties guilty of atrocities." *The Times of London*, May 20, 1993, 3. During the 1999 bombing campaign against Serbia, President Clinton apologized for having adopted this view: "There are those who say [ethnic conflicts] are the inevitable results . . . of centuries-old animosities. . . . I myself have been guilty of saying that, and now I regret it." *New York Times*, May 14, 1999, 7.

21. Sabrina Petra Ramet, *Balkan Babel: The Disintegration of Yugoslavia from the Death of Tito to Ethnic War*, 2nd ed. (Boulder, Colo.: Westview, 1996), 251.

22. At the outset of war, Bosnian military forces had two tanks; Bosnian Serbs had 300 and maintained close logistical ties to the JNA. Alan Cafruny, "The European Union and the War in Former Yugoslavia," in Alan Cafruny and Patrick Peters, eds., *The Union and the World: The Political Economy of a Common European Foreign Policy* (The Hague: Kluwer Law, 1998), 139.

23. David Rohde, *Endgame: The Betrayal and Fall of Srebrenica—Europe's Worst Massacre since World War II* (New York: Farrar, Straus & Giroux, 1997); J. W. Honig and N. Both, *Srebrenica: Record of a Warcrime* (London: Penguin, 1996); and Report of the Secretary-General Pursuant to the General Assembly Resolution 53/35 (1998), *Srebrenica Report* (New York: United Nations, 1998).

24. See especially David Chandler, *Bosnia: Faking Democracy after Dayton* (London: Pluto Press, 1999). A recent report of the International Crisis Group states, "Today Bosnia and Herzegovina has three *de facto* mono-ethnic entities; three separate armies, three separate police forces, and a national government that exists mostly on paper and operates at the mercy of the entities. Indicted war criminals remain at large and political power is concentrated largely in the hands of hardline nationalists. The effect has been to cement wartime ethnic cleansing and maintain ethnic cleansers in power within mono-ethnic political frameworks. . . . A thorough examination of the Dayton Peace Accord annex by annex indicates that the ethnic cleansers are winning the battle to shape postwar Bosnia." See "Is Dayton Falling Apart: Bosnia Four Years After the Peace Agreement," www.crisisweb.org/projects/bosnia/reports (February 2000).

25. David Gompert, "The United States and Yugoslavia's Wars," in Richard Ullman, *The World and Yugoslavia's Wars* (New York: Council on Foreign Relations Press, 1996), 136–37.

26. E. Hasani, "The Outer Wall of Sanctions and the Kosovo Issue," *Perceptions* 3, no. 3 (September-November 1998).

27. Richard Caplan, "International Diplomacy and the Crisis in Kosovo," 753.

28. "Observer Mission Documents Mass Killings of Civilians; NATO Challenges Milosevic by Approving Air Strikes; Belgrade Averts Strikes by Removing 4,000 Serbian Police," *Foreign Policy Bulletin* 9, no. 6 (1998): 32.

29. Remarks by Secretary of State Madeleine Albright, October 27, 1998.

30. The Verification Mission was led by William Walker, a veteran U.S. diplomat who had been ambassador to El Salvador during the extreme phase of U.S.–supported terror in

that country during the late 1980s. According to America's Watch, Walker attempted to cover up the murders of six Jesuit intellectuals in 1989. See Jeffrey Smith, "This Time, Walker Wasn't Speechless; Memory of El Salvador Spurred Criticism of Serbs," *Washington Post*, January 23, 1999, 7.

31. Madeleine Albright, "The Importance of Kosovo," *U.S. Department of State Dispatch* 10, no. 1 (January 1999).

32. Appendix B of the "Implementation" chapter of the Rambouillet Accord states that "NATO personnel shall enjoy, together with their vehicles, vessels, aircraft, and equipment, free and unrestricted passage and unimpeded access throughout the FRY, including associated airspace and territorial waters." This argument is advanced by, among others, Noam Chomsky, "The Kosovo Peace Accord," in Ali, *Masters of the Universe*; and Chomsky, *A New Generation Draws the Line: Kosovo, East Timor, and the Standards of the West* (New York: Verso, 2001). Henry Kissinger wrote in *Newsweek* (May 31, 1999), "Rambouillet was not a negotiation—as is often claimed—but an ultimatum. This marked an astounding departure for an administration that had entered office proclaiming its devotion to the U.N. Charter and multilateral procedures. Quoted in Gilbert Achcar, "Rasputin Plays at Chess: How the West Blundered into a New Cold War" in Tariq Ali, ed., *Masters of the Universe*, 82.

33. Tim Judah, *Kosovo: War and Revenge* (New Haven, Conn.: Yale University Press, 2000), 219; and H. Daalder and Michael E. O'Hanlon, *Winning Ugly: NATO's War to Save Kosovo* (Washington, D.C.: The Brookings Institution, 2000), 14, 15. James Rubin, a key U.S. negotiator at Rambouillet, insisted that the United States was prepared to be flexible, including with respect to the military annex. James Rubin, "A Very Personal War, Part II," *Financial Times*, October 6, 2000, sec. B1. However, arguments concerning the specific intentions and "premeditations" of U.S. diplomats at Rambouillet must be placed in the broader context of the decision to remove Serbian forces from Kosovo that was reached in the fall and winter of 1998. Because this decision could never have been acceptable to Belgrade, military action was sooner or later inevitable, although its precise form was of course unpredictable.

34. The CIA is said to have concluded that "Milosevic doesn't want a war he can't win. After enough of a defense to sustain his honor and assuage his backers he will quickly sue for peace." Cited in Elaine Sciolino and Ethan Bronner, "How a President, Distracted by Scandal, Entered Balkan War," *New York Times*, April 18, 1999, 5. See also Steven Erlanger, "NATO Was Closer to Ground War in Kosovo Than Is Widely Realized," *New York Times*, November 7, 1999, 4.

35. Erlanger, "NATO Was Closer to Ground War," 4.

36. In seventy-eight days of air strikes, NATO forces flew 32,000 sorties and dropped 21,000 tons of bombs on Serbia, Montenegro, and Kosovo. Various estimates of civilian casualties run from 1,000 to 2,000 killed and 3,000–6,000 injured. The war left 1 million homeless and produced widespread environmental damage. The systematic bombing of bridges across the Danube crippled the Serbian economy. The United States did not have a single casualty.

37. *The Economist*, "Germany Comes Out of Its Post-War Shell," July 10, 1999, 43.

38. Anne-Marie Le Gloannec, "Germany and Europe's Foreign and Security Policy: Embracing the British Vision," in Carl Lankowski, ed., *Break Out, Break Down, or Break In? Germany and the European Union after Amsterdam* (Washington, D.C.: American Institute for Contemporary German Studies, 1998). On the ouster of Lafontaine, see also Kees van der Pijl, "From Gorbachev to Kosovo," and chapter 8 of this volume.

118 *Alan W. Cafruny*

39. In Bosnia more than 145,000 people, the great majority of them Muslim or Bosniak civilians, died between 1991 and 1995. Two and a half million were driven from their homes as a result of "ethnic cleansing." Data on casualties are from the Carnegie Endowment for International Peace, *Unfinished Peace: Report of the International Carnegie Commission on the Balkans* (Washington, D.C.: Author, 1996). The Bosnian government provides an estimate of 300,000 killed.

40. Erlanger, "NATO Was Closer to Ground War," 4.

41. Deputy Secretary of State Strobe Talbott speech, August 24, 1999, Official U.S. Policy Materials on Kosovo, igeuweb@exchange.usia.gov.

42. European Union in the United States fact sheet, "European Union's Contribution to the Balkans," August 12, 1999, www.eurunion.org.

43. Stephen Fidler, "Albright Irked by Kosovo Funds Delay," *Financial Times*, January 28, 2000, 5.

44. Alexander Nicoll, "U.S. Moots NATO Exit from Bosnia," *Financial Times*, December 21, 2001, 5.

45. Gawdat Bahgat, "Pipeline Diplomacy: The Geopolitics of the Caspian Sea Region," *International Studies Perspectives* 3, no. 3 (August 2002).

46. Neela Banerjee, "U.S. Remains Dependent on Oil from Mideast but Is Diversifying," *New York Times*, October 22, 2002, sec. B1.

47. Marika S. Karayianni, "Caspian Oil Seeks Safe Transit Route," *Alexander's Oil and Gas Connections* 6, no. 20 (October, 24, 2001). In conjunction with the Export-Import Bank and the Overseas Private Investment Corporation, the U.S. Trade and Development Agency sponsored numerous feasibility studies for pipelines from the Black Sea to Western Europe, including the AMBO pipeline.

48. "ExxonMobil and Chevron Consider Trans-Balkan Pipelines," *Alexander's Gas and Oil Connections* 7, no. 5 (March 6, 2002).

49. Remarks to the press by Javier Solana, secretary-general of the Council and high representative of the EU for the Council of the European Union (CFSP), October 18, 1999, www.eu.int/pesc.

50. American Institute for Contemporary German Studies, "Germany and Macedonia: The Struggle over Strategy" (Washington, D.C.: Author, 2001). The report cites the conclusion of the inspector-general of the Bundeswehr that the German army "has financially been cut to the bone" and "does not have the staying power for another Kosovo-type operation" (2).

51. International Institute for Strategic Studies, *The Military Balance 1999/2000* (Oxford: Oxford University Press, 1999).

52. Each aircraft uses Litton avionics worth $1 million and supplied either directly from the United States or from Litton's European subsidiarity. See Gordon Adams, Christophe Cornu, and Andrew James, *Between Cooperation and Competition: The Transatlantic Defense Market, Chaillot Paper* 44 (Paris: International Institute for Strategic Studies, Western European Union, 2001). The U.S. defense manufacturer Raytheon lost out in a direct competition with the Anglo-French joint venture Matra BAE Dynamics over the provision of missiles for Britain's Eurofighter in a bidding process that was viewed as a test of Europe's capacity to develop an integrated military-industrial complex. Manfred Bischoff, chief executive of DaimlerChrysler Aerospace, part of the consortium led by Matra BAE, called the decision "a litmus test of how far the British government is serious about its intention to strengthen the European defence industry and exports." Alexander Nicoll,

"Pressure Grows over Missiles for Eurofighter," *Financial Times*, January 3, 2000, 3. Although the deal may have represented a tactical victory for European defense autonomy (and New Labour's European strategy), it is unlikely to interrupt the long-run tendency toward transatlantic mergers. See, for example, David Gow, "Politics Proves the Most Powerful Weapon," *Guardian City Pages*, May 17, 2000, 17.

53. Roxana Tiron, "European Firms Energizing U.S. Defense Market," National Defense Magazine, Dec., 2002, www.nationaldefensemagazine.org.

54. Alexander Nicoll, "France Backs Out of Battlefield Taxi Project," *Financial Times*, September 24, 1999, 3.

55. Alexander Nicoll, "Collaboration Is Stumbling," *Financial Times*, June 14, 1999, 11.

56. Nicoll, "Collaboration Is Stumbling," 11. One important example of European cooperation is of course the Airbus A440 M military transport aircraft, a $16 billion production contract involving eight governments.

57. *The Economist*, "The Defense Industry's New Look," October 6, 2001, 57; Tiron, "European Firms Energizing U.S. Defense Market," 3.

58. See, for example, John Deutch, Arnold Kanter, and Brent Scowcroft, "Saving NATO's Foundation," *Foreign Affairs* 78, no. 6 (November-December 1999); and also Elizabeth Becker, "Defense Department Urges Industry to Cooperate With Europe," *New York Times*, July 7, 1999, 5. As Burkard Schmidt noted, "Whether it is a question of military equipment planning, harmonization of regulation, research and development cooperation, or regulatory issues, the absence of a common position weakens the European position *and* makes Euro-American cooperation difficult." See Burkard Schmidt, "Conclusion" in Adams, Cornu, and James, *Between Cooperation and Competition*, 134.

59. Christophe Cornu, "Fortress Europe: Real or Virtual?" in Adams, Cornu, and James, *Between Cooperation and Competition*, 65.

60. *The Guardian* (London), December 27, 2002. The U.S. Committee on NATO was founded in 1994 by Lockheed Martin Vice President Bruce Jackson.

61. Peter Gowan, "Neoliberal Cosmopolitanism" *New Left Review* 11 (September-October, 2001).

II

NEOLIBERAL HEGEMONY
AND THE STATE

5

⁂

The Political Economy of Exchange Rate Commitments

Italy, the United Kingdom, and the Process of European Monetary Integration

Leila Simona Talani

Transnational neoliberal hegemony entails a complex amalgam of interrelated global, macroregional, and national practices. Chapter 2 by Gill and chapter 3 by Holman and van der Pijl focused on the global and macroregional dimensions of the forging of a neoliberal intersubjective framework, which in turn reflected dominant class interests associated with an emerging finance-led "virtual accumulation regime." However, they also recognize that the "transnational historic bloc" also has nationally segmented dimensions and that capitalist regulation depends on relatively autonomous state practices that continue to mediate nationally specific class compromises and conceptions of the general will.

As with the previous chapter by Cafruny, this chapter contributes to an understanding of the continuing relevance of the "national dimension" in the consolidation and normalization of transnational neoliberal hegemony in Europe, even for the practices at the very core of this project—financial, monetary, and exchange rate policy. Thereby, I seek to advance a conceptual refinement of the Gramscian "relations of force" framework outlined by Gill, Holman, and van der Pijl. "Neoliberalism" is, after all, a general articulating principle, which is commensurate with a wide range of concrete policy positions. This is not the least exemplified in the contrasting cases of Italian and British state strategies toward the ERM and the EMU, which are the objects of analysis of this chapter. Hence, a more refined and conjunctural analysis needs to be advanced if we are to be able to make sense of why different neoliberal strategies lead to different policy outcomes. This is not the least important in the EU, where questions about the nature and viability of the EMU are central to the process of neoliberal consolidation and normalization.

This chapter, then, seeks to elucidate the reasons why governments decide to commit themselves to a system of fixed or quasi-fixed exchange rates and the underlying socioeconomic conditions grounding the credibility of similar commitments, as well as the conditions under which markets decide to bet on the lack of such credibility.[1] There are few political science contributions to these issues, since the subject has traditionally been considered much more suitable for a purely neoclassical economic approach. Economists have sought to understand the rationale for the formation of market expectations on exchange rate credibility, and their debates have concerned the question of the rationality or irrationality of markets' behavior. Political scientists, on the other hand, have emphasized the interpretation of exchange rate commitments as international economic commitments and have applied the theoretical tools offered by the discipline of international political economy to explain governments' decision to adhere or not adhere to an exchange rate regime. This contribution will approach the issue of British and Italian governments' position toward the process of European monetary integration from this latter point of view.

The first part of this chapter considers the various explanations that the mainstream IPE approaches have provided for the process of European monetary integration but concludes that each of these explanations has serious limitations. The second part identifies a critical political economic approach to the study of exchange rate policy making that integrates the notion of socioeconomic interests and historically defined power relations between socioeconomic actors into the analysis that accords with the theoretical concerns of this book. In the final part, I show that the critical political economic approach provides a more satisfactory and comprehensive explanation for Italian and British policies toward the European monetary integration.

MAINSTREAM APPROACHES TO EUROPEAN MONETARY INTEGRATION

Neofunctionalism

The theoretical debate over the issue of the European monetary integration is traditionally characterized by the dichotomy between neofunctionalism and intergovernmentalism.[2] As noted in chapter 1, Ernst Haas and other neofunctionalists sought to explain integration through the concept of "spillover." Integration in one issue area will generate functional linkages to other issue areas; as a result, the desire to obtain the full benefits of integration in the first area will produce pressures for integration in a second linked area. Neofunctionalists identify two types of spillover, each of which deepens and widens integration by working through interest group pressure, public opinion, elite socialization, or other domestic actors and processes. The first, functional spillover, is economic and occurs when incomplete integration undermines the ability to achieve all the benefits of the existing policies both in the areas that are already integrated and in related sectors of economy, thus automatically creating the need for further cooperation among the EC countries. The second, political spillover, is linked to the fundamental role of existing EC institutions in giving impetus to a self-reinforcing process of institution building.

When applied to EMU the concept of spillover, in its milder, political form, implies that the 1992 single-market process increased the level of support among the public opinion and the EC governments for all those EC initiatives that could enhance the gains coming from the single-market program. In terms of economic spillover, the Treaty on European Union (TEU) was portrayed by the EC Commission, and by Jacques Delors in particular,[3] as functionally linked to the internal market process and necessary for its success. The Commission's case rests on the argument that the completion of capital liberalization in July 1990 coupled with exchange rate stability, as provided for by the EMS, is incompatible with autonomous national monetary policies.[4] In fact, in an environment of capital liberalization, there is a sort of a trade-off between stable exchange rates and independent national monetary policies. As Tomasso Padoa-Schioppa argues,[5] since the first brings about gains in efficiency and transaction costs savings, considered particularly important for a single market to work properly, the only viable solution is the pooling of national monetary policies in a monetary union.

However, the determinist economic argument for the functional linkage between the internal market and the process of monetary union is not convincing, as demonstrated by the alternative proposals to EMU in the context of the internal market based on the notion of currency competition. Similar proposals were officially presented by the British government on the summer of 1990[6] and later on developed into the Treasury's proposal of a thirteenth competitive European currency, the hard ECU, issued and managed by a special central bank.[7] Moreover, the UK successfully remained in the single market after the establishment of the European Monetary Union, thus preferring monetary independence to the transaction gains provided by the adoption of a single currency.[8] Finally, the spillover argument implies a learning period: Once an integrative step has been taken, the actors discover that they must integrate further in order to fully gather its benefits. In the case of the EMU, however, this learning period did not elapse since the internal market became fully operative only on December 31, 1992, when the TEU had already been approved. In other words, the relationship between the single market and monetary union is more contingent than the concept of neofunctionalism might suggest.

Intergovernmentalism

Intergovernmentalist integration theory postulates that nation-states dominate EC politics and that outcomes directly reflect the interests and relative power of the member states. Thus intergovernmentalists explain the development of supranational institutions in terms of strategies pursued by rational governments acting on the basis of their preferences and power. Andrew Moravcsik, for example, has sought to demonstrate empirically that the primary source of integration lies in the interests of the states themselves and in the relative power each brings to Brussels, although he also recognizes the important role played by supranational institutions in cementing existing interstate bargaining as the foundation for renewed integration.

Intergovernmental institutionalism is based on three principles: intergovernmentalism, lowest common denominator bargaining, and strict limits on future transfer of sovereignty. As Moravscik himself notes,[9] intergovernmental institutionalism is based on neorealist assumptions: States are the principal actors of the international system, interstate bargains reflect national interests and relative power, and international regimes shape interstate politics by providing a common framework that reduces the uncertainty and transaction costs of interstate interactions.

David Andrews has applied an intergovernmentalist approach to the origins and development of EMU.[10] He argues that the Maastricht Treaty resulted from a confluence of interests between the French and the German governments. Changes in the international system, including the collapse of the Soviet Union and the consequent reunification of Germany, opened a window of opportunity for France and Germany to come to an agreement on the substance of the EMU. However, since the window of opportunity created by the diplomatic imperative for France of binding Germany to the community following German unification closed after 1992, the implementation of the EMU project faced increasing difficulties in its ratification phase, hence the ERM crisis of 1992–1993.

Although Franco-German relations clearly played an important role in the development of EMU, they do not in themselves explain the origins of the EMU movement, especially the interest shown by Belgium, Italy, and other countries in 1988 and in early 1989. Moreover, the intergovernmental explanation does not account for the central role played by some domestic[11] and transnational socioeconomic actors[12] in promoting the goal of the Economic and Monetary Union. Nor is it clear how the fear of German unification, in the absence of other motives, could compel the other EC states to overcome the difficulties involved in designing supranational institutions and transferring monetary sovereignty to them. A more comprehensive and complete explanation requires an analysis of domestic interests.

The need for such an analysis was indeed noted by Moravcsik himself. Building on his earlier intergovernmentalism, he proposed a novel "liberal intergovernmentalism,"[13] which refines the theory of interstate bargaining and institutional compliance and adds an explicit theory of national preference formation grounded in liberal theories of international interdependence.[14] Liberal intergovernmental-ism contains three essential elements: the assumption of rational state behavior, a liberal theory of national preference formation, and an intergovernmentalist analy-sis of interstate negotiation. The model of rational state behavior on the basis of domestically constrained preferences implies that international conflict and coop-eration can be modelled as a process that takes place in two successive stages: First, governments define a set of interests, and then they bargain among themselves in order to realize those interests. Thus as Moravcsik acknowledges, the question fac-ing international relations theorists is no longer whether to combine domestic and international explanations, but how best to do it.

One solution to the problem is Robert Putnam's two-level games theory.[15] Putnam first defines the conceptual framework applicable to all kinds of issues including foreign economic policy ones. Then, he seeks to show how and when domestic politics and international relations become entangled. Putnam's ap-proach rests on the metaphor of the two-level game for domestic-international relations: At a national level, domestic groups pursue their interests by pressur-ing the governments to adopt favorable policies, and politicians seek power by constructing coalitions among these groups; at the international level, national governments seek to maximize their own ability to satisfy domestic pressures while minimizing the adverse consequences of foreign developments. Since each national political leader appears at both game boards, international relation scholars can ignore neither of the two games.

With reference to European monetary integration, different scholars have fo-cused their attention on different aspects of the integrated international-domestic politics approach, often reproducing the institutionalist/intergovernmentalist di-chotomy at one or both levels of analysis. Some applications of the two-level game approach focus on the institutional implications of bargaining links, arguing that is important to view the debate over EMU as embedded in an institutional pattern of interstate cooperation on many dimensions.[16] Others adopt an institutionalist approach at the national level and an intergovernmentalist one at the interna-tional level.[17] Finally, some scholars use an intergovernmentalist application of the integrated international-domestic politics approach to the process of European monetary integration.[18]

Wayne Sandholtz has provided a synthetic account of the process of European integration by simply juxtaposing the three main theoretical approaches to the process of European monetary integration—namely the intergovernmental ap-proach, the institutional approach, and the domestic politics one—and claiming that each of them explains a different aspect of the overall phenomenon. Sand-holtz also grounds the discussion of the Maastricht Treaty in the conversion to neoliberal monetary discipline in several European countries during the 1980s. The convergence to low inflation rates that occurred in the EMS during this pe-riod, in fact, was not due to any EMS change that rendered it more effective.

Rather, the success of the EMS derived from the new inclination of a number of EC countries, particularly the weakest ones, to commit to low inflation policies. This line of thought is also the basis of neoconstructivist or liberal constructivist reconstructions of monetary integration,[19] whose discussion has already been dealt with in chapter 1.

However, the one author who has contributed substantially to the development of political scientists' approach to exchange rate credibility from within a two-level game theoretical framework is Jeffrey Frieden.[20] Indeed, Frieden has proposed a "two-step" model of national economic policy making based on domestic sectoral interests. According to Frieden, two interrelated dimensions of policy choice are especially important in an environment of increasing capital mobility:[21] the degree of exchange rate flexibility and the level of the exchange rate itself. With regard to the first dimension, in a Mundell–Fleming world[22] with full capital mobility, a country faces a trade-off between exchange rate stability and monetary policy autonomy:[23] The more the country's exchange rate is held constant, the less its monetary policy can deviate from that of the rest of the world.[24] Thus, while some actors will favor a low degree of exchange rate flexibility, such as a system of pegged but adjustable exchange rates as the EMS or fixed-rate regime as the EMU despite the loss of monetary policy autonomy, others will be willing to accept a higher degree of exchange rate flexibility, ranging from a freely floating rate solution to a two-tier EMU, in exchange for policy-making autonomy.

Fixing the rate in a world of mobile capital implies foregoing national monetary policy autonomy in favor of greater certainty about the value of the currency. In other words, it gives priority to a stable exchange rate over the ability of national policy to affect domestic macroeconomic conditions. This is especially attractive to two groups of actors whose economic activities directly involve international trade and payments and who, therefore, are highly sensitive to currency fluctuations: international traders and investors and the producers of export-oriented tradable goods. Both of these groups tend to suffer from exchange market volatility, since it makes their business riskier.[25] In turn, these actors are relatively unconcerned about domestic macroeconomics conditions, since they can respond to depressed local demand by shifting their business to other countries. Conversely, two other groups of actors tend to be concerned about domestic macroeconomics conditions and thus favor the national monetary policy autonomy made possible by a flexible exchange rate. The first of these groups comprises producers of nontradable goods and services. Since their business does not involve the use of foreign exchange and since currency volatility has at best only indirect effects on them, they tend to have no clear preferences for stable exchange rates. The second group consists of producers of import-competing tradable goods for the domestic market. This group tends to be relatively indifferent about exchange rate volatility because it may even reduce import pressure inasmuch as it makes importing riskier, but is primarily concerned about policy-making autonomy.

However, during the implementing phase of monetary arrangements, in which the actors are much more concerned about the level of exchange rates, the political cleavages are likely to change since the interests of the various economic sectors will be affected by relative price changes involved in depreciation or appreciation of the currency. From a differential distributional point of view, the lower or more depreciated the exchange rate, the higher is the price of tradable goods relative to nontradable ones.[26] This, in turn, tends to favor the producers of tradable goods, whose output prices rise more than the prices of the nontradable inputs they use, and to hurt producers of nontradable goods. Producers in the tradable sector, therefore, gain from depreciation while producers in the nontradable sector generally benefit from currency appreciation. Moreover, international traders and investors, who are interested in purchasing assets abroad, favor a strong currency. These varying exchange rates level preferences, in turn, affect preferences about different macroeconomic policies: The actors who gain from a strong currency will prefer macroeconomic policies consistent with the commitment to the ERM that caused, from its outset, an overvaluation of the weakest currencies,[27] while producers of tradable goods will prefer a depreciation of the currency.

From an operational point of view, it is possible to identify the import-competing producers of tradable goods for domestic market as the producers of standardized manufactures, that is, with the manufacturing sector. The export-oriented producers of tradable goods can be operationalized as the big, international companies; producers of nontradable goods and services with the public sector; and, finally, the investors with the financial and banking systems.[28]

Yet, the cases of Italy and Britain show[29] that Frieden's model is not exhaustive regarding the complex political issues arising at the domestic level from the international economic phenomena, nor does it succeed in predicting the actual positions adopted by the domestic economic interest groups. To be sure, Frieden proposes economically plausible hypotheses concerning the exchange rate preferences of various economic sectors. In the absence of power struggle among different social and economic actors in the political arena, these hypotheses might prove effective in explaining and even predicting interest groups' positions toward the issue of exchange rate level and regime. However, because Frieden's model does not take account of these historical struggles, it offers little explanatory or predictive value. Indeed, the model is essentially static: It does not contemplate the possibility of a change in the actors' attitudes and is, consequently, unable to explain why change actually occurs.

A CRITICAL POLITICAL ECONOMIC APPROACH TO EUROPEAN MONETARY INTEGRATION

The critical political economy approach to the credibility of exchange rate proposed in this chapter challenges the mainstream assumption that markets in general and financial markets in particular stand aside of history and society and behave independently from social and political considerations. The approach proposed here grounds financial markets' behavior in the underlying political economy structure of capitalist economies subordinating their expectations to the interests of the hegemonic (in the Gramscian sense) socioeconomic groups.[30] It challenges the assumption of the infallibility of the markets and of their independent "inner rationality," and it proposes an alternative political economy rationality, which embeds markets' expectations into a given socio-economic structure.

This political economy approach to the credibility of exchange rate commit-ments and of the rationality of financial market behavior transcends the ahistor-ical and abstract explanations provided by mainstream accounts without falling into the trap of historical or cultural relativism. It also provides the theoretical underpinnings for a rigorous analytical framework consisting of different levels of explanations structured in a clear-cut hierarchy. By introducing the crucial as-sumption that power relations are, eventually, the main heuristic tools in any at-tempts to explain socioeconomic events, it inserts the notions of power and power struggles into the analysis. These power struggles are not, however, as-sumed to be confined to the state, but rather extend to the socioeconomic groups that define the particular capitalist structure of a given nation-state. Purely eco-nomic explanations or purely political ones are not, of course, discarded, but are integrated within the analysis of the underlying political economy structure.

The political economy approach adopted in this chapter is based on three dif-ferent levels of analysis, which correspond to three different levels of explana-tion. The first level of analysis, which might be called the "political economy analysis," corresponds to a synthetic conception of Gramsci's relations of force as presented in chapter 2 by Gill. It is represented by an organic analysis of the domestic structure of capital and of power relations between the various socio-economic actors as historically developed. It represents the limits within which further developments must necessarily take place. This first level of analysis, then, allows for the identification of what Gramsci called the "historic bloc," the power relations among the social forces under consideration within a given mode of production and historical conjuncture. It also provides a basis for com-parison with different sets of power relations in different countries. However, these kinds of structural considerations cannot account for the entire history of Italian and British stances in the process of European monetary integration. Nor can they provide the basis for reliable predictions of future behavior. Therefore, it is necessary to connect this first level of analysis with the more conjunctural analysis of the second and the third levels, in order to obtain a dynamic picture of the phenomenon under consideration. The second level, that of "purely eco-nomic analysis," separates out the first level of Gramsci's relations of force and focuses on the identification of the concrete interest groups' preferences within a restricted time period. It focuses on the concrete struggle for economic power, and particularly on the competition among interest groups to obtain favorable economic policies. It is at this level that classifications of socioeconomic preferences toward exchange rate levels and regimes can be tested empirically.[31] Finally, the third level, that of "purely political analysis," focuses on the day-to-day political struggles or the specific means by which economic interests become policies after having been processed through the political and institutional system. It is here that the political bargaining process, the role of political parties and leaders, and the incentive–disincentive mechanism are taken into consideration. This conjunctural analysis, then, follows conceptually the formal separation between the economy and the state in capitalism. Ultimately, however, it has to be connected to the integral and organic political economy analysis, where the mediation of fundamental class conflict and hegemony is considered.

A comprehensive explanatory model requires a synthesis of each of these levels in order to provide the most reliable possible picture of the phenomenon under analysis. This reflects the fact that in the real world there are overlapping relationships of mutual reciprocity between the economic structure, the economic interests promoted by socioeconomic groups, and the political and institutional life. Thus, for example, the Italian decision to enter the ERM can be analyzed as a political decision in the framework of the day-to-day political life. However, it has also much deeper roots in the underlying struggle for power among the different Italian economic interest groups, mainly trade unions and the employers' organizations. On the other hand, the British decision to enter the ERM was primarily a function of day-to-day political life and the need to gain political consensus on the eve of a general election.

THE POLITICAL ECONOMY OF EXCHANGE RATE CREDIBILITY: EXPECTATIONS AND INTERESTS

This analytical framework makes it possible to derive a "phenomenology of credibility" of the international economic commitments and in particular of exchange rate commitments. Credibility is not based on pure economic expectations, but rather on a much more complex set of political economy considerations. In particular, it is possible to hypothesize that the more foreign economic commitments in general, and exchange rate policies in particular, are rooted in the interests of a given hegemonic bloc, the more these commitments are credible. That is, in the case of fixed exchange rates or target zone commitments, the more they can count in the consensus of the most powerful sections of society, the less likely they are to be challenged by the markets. Indeed, there is a dialectic relation between interests and expectations; expectations of the markets are deeply influenced by the interests and preferences of the leading socioeconomic sectors of the country under consideration. Market expectations, and thus also market behavior, are crucially affected by considerations about something "more fundamental than the fundamentals": the economic structure and the way in which it is reflected in economic and political life. This definition is perfectly consistent with the political scientists' view that exchange rate commitments are international agreements and therefore need to be based on the existence of a domestic consensus rooted in the interests of domestic actors.

From the economists' standpoint, this approach to the credibility of exchange rate pegs could help in reconciling the two opposing theories on speculative attacks. The contemporary debate in exchange rate economics is in fact characterized by the opposition between "fundamentalists," in other words supporters of the thesis that real exchange rate fluctuations largely reflect changes in macroeconomic fundamentals,[32] and those who believe that "foreign exchange markets behave more like the unstable and irrational asset markets described by Keynes than the efficient markets described by modern finance theory."[33]

The latter approach assumes that speculative attacks are self-fulfilling, or that in a multiple equilibria environment, the markets produce their own exchange rate expectations without any intelligible connection with fundamentals.[34] In turn, these expectations produce speculative attacks, which ultimately compel governments to abandon the exchange rate peg and to adopt ex-post softer monetary stances. A compromise approach has been proposed that allows for multiple equilibria only within a certain range of fundamentals' performance.[35] Alternatively, economists tend to overcome the problem by lifting the assumption of market participants' complete information on the performance of economic fundamentals.[36]

This chapter argues, however, that the failure of the fundamentals to explain speculative attacks does not necessarily imply that exchange rate markets act "irrationally" or "inefficiently" or that they are constrained by the lack of information. It can also mean that the markets, in deciding which of the multiple equilibria is more likely to be adopted by the government after a speculative attack, evaluate a wide range of events, including sociopolitical and structural ones. Thus the credibility of an exchange rate commitment crucially depends on the behavior and interests of socioeconomic actors in a particular historical moment.

Adopting a similar political economy definition of credibility, Italian commitment to the ERM may be considered very credible. Indeed, it was rooted not only in the pure economic interests of the hegemonic bloc but also in their desire to shift the balance of power from the national to the European level in order to maintain their leading position. When the consensus faded, the only obvious conclusion that the markets could draw was to attack the lira in the ERM. However, that the consensus had faded only at the second level of analysis, that is, at the level of pure economic considerations and not of structural ones, is demonstrated by the fact that Italian commitment to the realization of EMU did not disappear despite the ERM crisis. On the other hand, the British decision to enter the ERM was far less credible because it conflicted with the more structural interests of its leading fraction, which were then reaffirmed in the British government's opposition to EMU.

Of course, this model is not static and changes may occur at each level of analysis. At the first level of analysis, changes are certainly long-term ones and are represented by substantial transformation of the underlying structure of power. Italy, for example, experienced a decline of the power of trade unions and strengthening in the power of the industrial and banking organizations from the second half of the 1980s onwards. In Britain, a change in power relationship among economic interest groups occurred after 1931 when the City surrendered its power to the industrial sector and did not fully recover until the 1960s.[37]

At the second level of analysis, the preferences of the socioeconomic groups considered may vary from time to time and from country to country. Indeed, in 1979 neither of the British economic sectors showed an overwhelming enthusiasm for the making of the European Monetary System (EMS). However, by 1985 the British industrial sector, as represented by the Confederation of British Industry (CBI), started to push for British entry in the ERM, while from the late 1980s the British Trade Unions have (with some exceptions) supported entry into the monetary union. Similarly, the Italian CGIL, once one of the most convinced opponent of the European monetary integration process, eventually endorsed the EMU as envisioned at Maastricht.

Finally, at the third level, changes are linked to the decline of the leadership of given political parties or leaders. The end of the Thatcher era and the *tangentopoli* revolution in Italy are clear examples of changes at the third level of analysis. Their importance, however, must not be overestimated since, in the lack of more structural changes, their consequences appear rather superficial.

ITALY, BRITAIN, AND THE PROCESS OF EUROPEAN MONETARY INTEGRATION

The foregoing argument suggests that the credibility of a government's exchange rate commitments derives neither from market fundamentals nor from the putative interests of specific sectoral groups. Rather, such credibility is linked to the existence of consensus within the socioeconomic hegemonic bloc. Italian and British policies toward the ERM and EMU have reflected the particular interests of this hegemonic bloc in three crucial historical occasions: entry into the ERM (or "the birth of consensus"), abandonment of the EMS (or "the death of consensus"), and the making of the Maastricht Treaty and EMU (or "the new consensus").

Birth of Consensus in Italy and the UK

The three main actors in the Italian decision to join the ERM were the state, the trade unions, and private capital, particularly big industry.[38] These actors were crucial not only in the debate over the issue of joining the ERM but also more generally in the struggle for power beginning in the late 1970s to the present time, or what Peter Lange has called "the end of the Unions' era."[39] In this context, the shift of the power struggle from the domestic to the European level was the only way for the Italian banking and industrial sectors to obtain the implementation of macroeconomic policies designed to reduce public sector spending and discipline the trade unions at a time when they still had significant bargaining power. More generally, where the militancy of the labor movement has been the strongest, as in Italy and France (see Clift, chapter 7), the imperatives of the EU have been used to counterbalance that militancy.

Indeed, had the Italian industrial and banking sectors sought a direct confrontation with the trade unions and their political counterparts, the most likely result would have been what they were determined to avoid: a strengthening of working-class militancy. Therefore, the issue of the ERM was the battlefield where the struggle for power was conducted among domestic actors in a context in which political power was still fully exercised at the domestic level. The nature of the agreement on exchange rate constraints, given the kind of macroeconomic policies it implied and its inherent reduction of state autonomy in the monetary policy decision making, had straightforward consequences for the other two actors of the Italian scene. Indeed, it dealt a decisive blow both to the possibilities of state intervention in the economy and to the bargaining power of the trade unions. Thus, in the course of the 1980s the interests of the various economic, social, and political groups, which represented the bases of the Italian consensus to the ERM, were revealed with great clarity. Participation in the ERM reflected the domestic balance of forces and thereby constituted the political guarantee that the commitment to the ERM was credible.

The case of the United Kingdom reveals a very different political economic context. For Britain, monetary policy needs to be understood within the context of the long-standing historical division between the City and the industry and the hegemony, of financial capital over the productive capital, with all that it implied in terms of commitment to the pursue of laissez-faire and strict monetary policies.[40] At the same time, the strength of the labour movement in Britain had been reduced by the mid-1970s, to a much greater degree than in Italy.

Since the leading sectors in the UK did not need to shift the power struggle to the European level to pursue those macroeconomic policies necessary to maintain their economic and political power, entry in the ERM was not a significant issue in British politics during the late 1970s. This was clearly demonstrated by the lack of interest in the issue of the ERM shown by almost all sectors of British economy and British political system during the negotiations leading to the establishment of the new European monetary arrangements.[41]

Similarly, the British government's decision to enter the ERM in 1990 resulted from the evolution of the relations between the two components of capital: the productive and the financial one. The trade unions were excluded from the decision-making process because their political power had been greatly diminished during the course of the 1980s. Indeed, the government's decision to enter the ERM did not reflect any shift of power from the leading socioeconomic group to a coalition of the two sides of the productive sector. Neither did it imply the strengthening of industrial capital over finance capital. The latter had even undergone in the course of the second half of the 1980s a major structural change, the so-called City revolution that, far from decreasing, substantially increased its preeminence in the British economic and political context. Thus, the interests underlying the decision to join the ERM reflected a change of macroeconomic policy preferences of the dominant socioeconomic groups, namely the financial community and the City of London, which sought to continue pursuing anti-inflationary policies in the face of clear signs of overheating of the economy and to influence the negotiations over EMU.

Regarding the first dimension, the decision to join the ERM did not require abandoning monetarist practices and aims. It merely represented a final stage in the move from domestic monetarism, a policy that had by the late 1980s fewer adherents, to the international version of that doctrine, the pragmatic monetarism of the Bundesbank. Despite the fact that this policy was still extremely controversial, both within the City and within the Conservative party, its implementation was triggered by the exceptional commitment of the other European countries to monetary union. Yet, the balance in favor of the external version of monetarism through the commitment to the ERM was very unstable. It was doomed to be overthrown soon after the failure of the British government to secure the interests of the dominant socioeconomic group in the negotiations at Maastricht in 1991. The death of consensus led to the loss of credibility of both British and Italian governments' commitments to the ERM. This triggered the logical reaction of the markets and ensuing crises of the lira and sterling, ultimately leading to their withdrawal from the system.

The Death of Consensus

The analysis of Italian entry in the ERM has led to the conclusion that a major role was played by Italian industrial sector interests, particularly "big industry," which is intimately connected to the interests of the banking sector.[42] In particular, the attitude of big Italian enterprise toward the whole process of European integration, and, to a greater extent, toward the process of European monetary integration in the last twenty years may be summarized in the claim: "Let's bring all problems to Brussels since it will be much easier to solve them there than in Rome."[43] For Italian big industry, Brussels provided the opportunity to exert the most effective pressure for the acceptance and implementation of those national economic policies most opposed by the Italian trade unions. This had been the case with the Italian entry in the ERM, and this continued to be the case throughout the 1980s. However, the issue of exchange rates has always been a very delicate one for the Italian industrial sector because of the close linkage between the level of exchange rate and the performance of the exports. Although the linkage could be ignored or set aside in periods of sustained internal demand, it caused many problems in periods of recession. To the extent that exports represented a substantial part of the industrial sector's activity, whenever the commitment to fixed or quasi-fixed exchange rates collided with the need to improve economic performance, Italian industry traditionally insisted on the need to devalue.

As a result, the attitude of Italian industry toward the process of European monetary integration has always been geared to the attempt to balance two inconsistent strategies. On the one hand there was the "political economy" strategy to shift the power struggle from the national to the supranational level with the aim of overcoming internal opposition to the implementation of fiscal and monetary orthodoxy. On the other hand, there was the "purely economic" strategy to keep exchange rates in line with the desired performance of the exports. During periods of acute industrial militancy or when the business cycle allowed industry to sustain the commitment to quasi-fixed exchange rates, as the second half of the 1980s, the first consideration prevailed over the second. In periods of recession, however, the contradiction was bound to explode, and it did explode at the beginning of the 1990s, triggering the withdrawal of industrial support for the European monetary arrangements and the monetary crisis. However, the fact that the consensus faded only at the second level of analysis, that is, at the level of purely economic considerations and not of structural ones, is demonstrated by the fact that Italian commitment to the realization of EMU did not disappear despite the ERM crisis.

In contrast to the situation in Italy, in the British case the consensus on the ERM was not based on an overarching stable compromise among the leading actors. Rather, it reflected exclusively (and short-term) political and pure economic considerations and contrasted with the more structural interests of its leading faction, which were then reaffirmed in the British government's opposition to EMU. Underlying all this, there was the City's fear of losing its economic power, that is, its dominance of the European financial markets and its competitiveness in the international financial markets in favor of a German-dominated ECB based in Frankfurt. The City also feared that joining EMU would reduce its domestic political power, especially its ability to influence monetary and exchange rate policies.

The dilemma for both the City of London and the British Government, which led to the insistence on an opt-out clause at Maastricht, was that the UK could not remain outside the process. Some of the consequences of EMU, including the loss of domestic macroeconomic policy power, could be avoided by remaining outside. Others, however, including de facto German political dominance, the loss of the City's European financial primacy, or the loss of international competitiveness, were linked to the process itself, and could be avoided only by stopping it. The solution to the dilemma was to destroy or at least to delay the process leading to EMU by attacking the credibility of the whole EMU project.

Because the route to monetary union hinged on the survival of the ERM, one of the ways to achieve this objective was to undermine the credibility of the British commitment to the ERM. This could be done through voicing the British financial community's discontent with the working of the European monetary arrangements. Entry into the ERM in October 1990 had in fact signalled both the City's wish to be at the center of Europe and to secure low and stable inflation after the errors and the convulsions of the 1980s. Whereas by the signing of the Maastricht Treaty the second objective could be considered successfully achieved, in the first area the British government had not been able to influence effectively the future of European monetary integration. Ultimately, it had relegated itself to a rear-guard, though important, battle over an opt-out from EMU, an option which, incidentally, was welcomed by the British financial sector but opposed by both sides of the industrial sector. Indeed, it is clear from the whole analysis of sterling's experience in the ERM that the British government did not take into consideration the needs of British industry. The whole ERM episode had, in fact, been characterized by the preponderance of financial sector preferences over any other consideration. British entry into the ERM had been called for by the employers' major organization since 1985. However, the British government had endorsed it only when the failure of the monetarist practices of the 1980s had created a vacuum in the British government's anti-inflationary stance that the British financial community could hardly conceive.

Yet, the acceleration of the process of European monetary integration with the publication of the Delors report on EMU had disclosed to the City of London the dismaying likelihood of losing its dominance of European financial markets, as well as its international competitiveness. The report thus also hastened the need for the City of London to influence or somehow to delay a process that clearly clashed with British financial interests.[44] However, given the power and interest of continental industrialists, particularly the Germans and the French, the British government had limited ability to shape events, and the Maastricht negotiations did not constitute a major success from the British point of view. The disillusionment with its outcome within the City, as well as the repeated attacks on the existing European monetary arrangements, revealed to the international financial markets the weakness of British commitment to the ERM. This led to an epilogue of Sterling's experience in the ERM that was far from being unwelcome.

New Consensus

As the last section shows, the analysis of the Maastricht Treaty in both Italy and the United Kingdom cannot be disentangled from the broader issues arising from the establishment in Europe of a common currency area. In the case of Italy, the government's decision to endorse and actively pursue the policies implied in the Maastricht agreement on EMU was based on an extremely broad socioeconomic consensus. Indeed, it is worth asking why Italian industry was so willing to surrender its autonomy in determining monetary policy and, to a very large extent, fiscal policy by shifting it to the European level. From the point of view of Confindustria, the maintenance of independent monetary and fiscal policies was seen more as a problem than as an advantage because it allowed for the persistence of significant interest rate differentials with the other European countries, thus undermining Italian industry's competitive position in Europe.

At the outset, adherence to the ERM in a situation of acute social and political conflict had facilitated the adoption of macroeconomic policies in line with Italian industry's primary aim to boost its competitive position. However, in the course of the 1980s adherence began to contradict such an aim. Indeed, the excess of credibility that the participation to the European monetary arrangements granted to Italian national monetary and budgetary policies led to an overvaluation of the exchange rate that, as was already seen, proved unsustainable for the Italian industrial sector that, consequently, withdrew its support for the ERM.

However, it had become increasingly clear that, in the longer term, the solution to Italian competitiveness could not be found in a system of floating exchange rates since this produced chronic domestic struggles between capital and labor over the implementation of strict monetary and budgetary policies aimed at the achievement of low inflation and interest rates. Moreover, it left unsolved the problems of intra-European and extra-European competitiveness, which were becoming increasingly important in the context of regionalization and intensified global economic competition. As a result, neither a system of freely floating exchange rates nor one of quasi-fixed exchange rates could solve Italian industry competitive problems. Even a system of nonadjustable fixed exchange rate would not be enough, since it would always leave some scope to the implementation of divergent monetary and budgetary policies that would necessarily spill over to interest rates, creating differentials and, ultimately, exchange rate instability.

The interests of Italian industry within a specific sociopolitical context thus clearly indicate that there was in fact no contradiction between its withdrawal of support to the ERM and its promotion of EMU. Italian capital continued to seek to shift policies from the national to the European level. When the ERM had proved insufficient, support was shifted to the far more satisfactory solution of EMU. Unlike the ERM, the EMU framework allowed for a more stable pursuit of orthodox fiscal and monetary policies because it institutionalized them at the European level and insulated them from the instabilities and uncertainties of day-to-day national political life. Indeed, it is possible to claim that the ERM and the EMU embodied two different ontological plans. This clearly explains why it was perfectly logical for Italian industry to gather the fruits of the collapse of the ERM and, at the same time, call for the establishment of EMU.

The Italian case reveals a strong coincidence of interest among the Italian and banking sector concerning EMU. In contrast to banking sector profits in Britain, those in Italy are structurally dependent on industrial performance.[45] Therefore, it is possible to hypothesize the existence of a strong consensus on the part of Italian industrial and financial capital in favor of the establishment of a single currency area in Europe, based on strict monetary and fiscal policies. This consensus in itself could be enough to understand the Italian government's unconditional decision to enter EMU from the outset. However, to have a more complete answer to the question of why Italy was so eager to enter EMU immediately, it is also necessary to consider the position of the trade unions.

As noted above, the decision of Italian industrial capital to shift to the European level the decision on a set of politically sensitive orthodox macroeconomic policies was by no means abandoned as a result of the failure of the ERM. On the contrary, it has been institutionalized throughout the adoption of the Maastricht criteria as well as the approval of the Stability and Growth Pact,[46] with evident consequences for the trade unions. Indeed, the path to EMU, as defined by the Maastricht Treaty and by the subsequent Stability Pact, affects directly and substantially the powers and prerogatives of trade unions.[47] In particular, the statutory ECB goal of a low and stable inflation rate has undeniable consequences on the limits within which trade unions are able to conduct wage policies. Moreover, the implementation of monetary policy by the ECB, through the decisions over the level of European interest rates, undoubtedly affects investment decisions and, consequently, the level of unemployment. Finally, the rigid limitations on the conduct of national fiscal policy, imposed by the Maastricht Treaty for the transition to EMU and by the Stability Pact for its aftermath, profoundly influenced the terms of the debate over the survival of the welfare state in all its components. Given their limited power, the trade unions confined themselves to a rear-guard struggle over the social dimension of EMU, whose achievement implied a general acceptance of the Maastricht clauses on the single currency. Therefore, the trade unions' support for EMU must be understood in terms of exchange between a more "monetarist" Europe and a more "social" Europe. Here the trade unions sought in what Bieling and Schulten (see chapter 9) show was a compensatory but largely symbolic attempt to reproduce the corporatist structure of the domestic governance system and thus regain some the terrain lost since the beginning of the process of monetary integration.[48]

With the analysis of the trade unions, the picture of the Italian socioeconomic sectors' stance toward the Maastricht Treaty and EMU is complete and shows a widespread socioeconomic consensus on the goal of EMU. Indeed, it has been on the basis of this consensus that the Italian government's commitment to the Maastricht criteria has become credible and that Italy has been able to reach its goal of a deficit-to-GDP ratio of 3 percent.

The British case offers an interesting and instructive contrast with that of Italy. The deep fissures in British society—including among various fractions of capital—persist and continue to structure the debate over entry into the EMU. As this analysis has made clear, the British financial community in general and the City of London in particular emerge as the main domestic counterparts of the government with respect to foreign economic policies. From these premises it is possible to infer that also the British government's position toward the making of EMU is likely to have been deeply affected by the City's preferences and interests. Indeed, the establishment of a single currency area in Europe poses direct competitive threats to the City of London by itself, irrespective of British participation. Within euroland, the elimination of barriers to trade in many relevant City markets, as well as the development of new financial instruments denominated in the common currency, increase the ability of other European financial centers to grasp new market opportunities. This could undermine the City of London's until now undisputed financial leadership in Europe.[49] Although British participation would at least eliminate the possibility for the EMU countries to adopt protectionist measures, entry into the EMU poses a substantial threat to the position of London as a leading international financial center.

Because of London's unique international orientation, entry would entail significant restrictions on the working of its markets and institutions. A more general threat is the submission of the City of London to exogenous controls, which would circumscribe the City's unparalleled freedom of action. Indeed, in the British regulatory environment, controls for the wholesale money markets are only represented by a discretionary supervisory role of the Bank of England. On the other hand, capital markets after the Big Bang are self-regulated through the endogenous organizations of the Securities Investment Board (SIB) and of SROs. Moreover, EMU will affect the City's international primacy by eliminating the possibility for London to develop as the main offshore market in euro or in euro-denominated assets, an activity that, were the UK inside EMU, would certainly be developed by one of its major world competitors. The domestic economic consequences of joining a monetary union are generally assessed within the all-embracing expression of "loss of sovereignty." In the case of the City of London, they have the clear-cut meaning of the loss of the ability to influence domestic monetary and exchange rate policies, with all that it implies in terms of loss of domestic political power.

Just as the Thatcher government's "wait and see" attitude toward the ERM perfectly matched the British financial sector's preferences for a set of monetarist practices inconsistent with the pegging of the exchange rates,[50] the lack of commitment of the Blair administration to EMU conceals the substantial opposition to entry within the City of London. It is not by chance, indeed, that prominent among the five economic tests put forward in 1997 by Chancellor of the Exchequer Gordon Brown is the impact of EMU on the British financial sector. That the City's preferences might change in the future is, of course, a possibility implicit in the approach adopted in this chapter. However, from the evidence it is possible to infer that the City of London would prefer the British government to avoid committing the UK to EMU. Since the success of the City of London has always been linked to its ability to adapt to the changing environment, its markets and institutions will certainly be able to grasp the business opportunities coming from the establishment of a single currency area even while remaining outside it. Moreover, they will certainly be able to take advantage of the problems that even a successful union will have to tackle.

THE POLITICAL ECONOMY OF MONETARY POLICY

The critical political economy approach to the credibility of exchange rate proposed in this chapter challenges the mainstream theory belief that markets in general and financial markets in particular stand aside of history and society and behave independently from social or political considerations. On the contrary, the approach proposed here explains the behavior of financial markets in terms of the underlying political-economic structure of capitalist economies. The assumption of the infallibility of the markets and of their independent "inner rationality" is rejected in favor of a political economic rationality, which embeds markets' expectations into a given socioeconomic structure within a given historical conjuncture.

A political economic approach to the credibility of exchange rate commitments and of the rationality of financial market behavior helps to transcend the limitations inherent in the debate between neorealist and institutionalist accounts of European monetary integration without falling in the trap of historical or cultural relativism. It provides a systematic and rigorous analytical framework consisting of different levels of explanations structured in a clear-cut hierarchy. It also introduces the crucial assumption that power relations constitute the main heuristic tools in any attempts to explain socioeconomic events. It thus inserts the notion of power and, in particular, of power struggles into the analysis without confining them to the state, but rather by extending them to the socioeconomic groups defining the capitalist structure of a given nation-state. Purely economic explanations or purely political ones are not, of course, discarded, but they are inserted into the structured analytical framework.

Given the nature of the questions posed in this chapter, this analysis has limited itself to the power struggles within the borders of the nation-state and between domestic socioeconomic groups. However, in principle it is possible to apply the theoretical framework to the power struggles between transnational socioeconomic groups to the extent that the decision-making level shifts from the national to the regional or to the international level. This is indeed the most likely scenario if the process of EMU results in greater political integration at the European level.

The political economic approach to monetary policy adopted in this chapter makes it possible to account for phenomena that would, otherwise, appear rather obscure. In particular, it is possible to explain why, even if usual economic measures of credibility did not show evident signs of any financial markets' loss of faith in the British commitment to the ERM, the pound sterling was driven out of the ERM by speculators. Indeed, the credibility of the sterling exchange rate peg was undermined by the lack of a structural consensus about its permanence in the ERM, a lack of consensus that was easily detected by the financial markets. On the basis of similar considerations, this approach helps to explain why two different countries, with two completely different positions within the ERM, were compelled to take the same decision at the same moment. In fact, both countries experienced the same loss of socioeconomic consensus to pegged exchange rates at the same time, though this loss was of a more structural nature in the case of the UK. Finally, this approach allows the analysis to be extended to the making of the EMU, and to the position adopted by the two countries toward the establishment of the European single currency area. In the UK, the loss of consensus was structural and was rooted in the consideration that further steps in the process of European monetary integration substantially endangered the interests of the British dominant socioeconomic groups, helping to explain the subsequent deep hostility of the UK toward EMU. By contrast, in Italy the loss of consensus was of a more contingent nature and did not generate substantial opposition to the establishment of the single currency alongside the lines decided upon at Maastricht.

NOTES

1. The chapter summarizes the argument of a research project outlined at greater length elsewhere. For the complete analysis see my *Betting for and against EMU* (London: Ashgate, 2000).

2. See W. Sandholtz, "Choosing Union: Monetary Politics and Maastricht," *International Organization* 47 (1993): 1–39.

3. See European Communities Council, *Report to the Council and the Commission on the Realisation by Stages of Economic and Monetary Union in the Community* (Werner Report, definitive text) (Luxembourg: European Communities Council, 1970), in which the case is put for the need of a parallel approach to the process of economic and monetary integration; see also CEC (Brussels: Commission of European Communities, 1990), 17: "The economic advantages of the Single Market are certainly not fully achievable without a single currency."

4. See CEC, 17: "If the move to EMU were not to take place, given 1992, it is quite likely that either the EMS would become a less stable arrangement or capital market liberalization would not be fully achieved or maintained."

For further analysis of the economic mechanism, see T. Padoa-Schioppa, "The European Monetary System: A Long Term View," in F. Giavazzi, S. Micossi, and M. Miller, *The European Monetary System* (Cambridge: Cambridge University Press, 1988), 373–76.

5. See T. Padoa-Schioppa, "The European Monetary System."

6. See HM Treasury, "Economic and Monetary Union," *Treasury Bulletin* (Summer 1990).

7. See HM Treasury, "The UK Proposal for a EMF and a Hard ECU," *Treasury Bulletin* (Autumn 1990). The economic argument in favor of a greater currency competition is based on the early works by F. A. Hayek: F. A. Hayek, "Toward a Free Market Monetary System," *Journal of Libertarian Studies* 3, no. 1; F. A. Hayek, "Denationalization of Money," *Hobart Paper Special*, no. 70 (October 1970); and F. A. Hayek, "Choice in Currency: A Way to Stop Inflation," *IEA Occasional Papers*, no. 48 (1976). For further reading on the subject, see M. De Cecco, *Monete in concorrenza* (Bologna: Il Mulino, 1992); and D. Currie, "European Monetary Union or Competing Currencies: Which Way for Monetary Integration in Europe?" *Economic Viewpoint* (September 1989).

8. This is mainly due to the fact that a reduction of transaction costs and the elimination of hedging expenses are particularly appealing to the industrial sector and, mainly, to those manufacturing companies particularly involved in intra-European trade. On the other hand, the financial sector, which, incidentally, has much to earn from the instability of exchange rates, is much more interested in keeping an independent monetary policy in an environment of loose regulatory constraints. Given the relevance of the financial sector for the British economy, and the declining importance of the manufacturing sector, it appears less puzzling why the UK could profit from the single market without being compelled to join EMU. For more detail on the subject see Talani, *Betting for and against EMU*.

9. Andrew Moravcsik, "Negotiating the Single European Act: National Interests and Conventional Statecraft in the European Community," *International Organization* 45, no. 1 (Winter 1991): 27.

10. See D. M. Andrews, "The Global Origins of the Maastricht Treaty on EMU: Closing the Window of Opportunity," in A. Cafruny and G. G. Rosenthal, eds., *The State of the European Community: The Maastricht Debate and Beyond* (Boulder, Colo.: Lynne Rienner, 1993). See also D. M. Andrews, "Capital Mobility and State Autonomy: Toward a Structural Theory of International Monetary Relations," *International Studies Quarterly*, no. 38 (1994): 193–218.

11. See this chapter below and Talani, *Betting for and against EMU*, for more details.

12. For example, the role played by the Association for Monetary Union, set up in 1987 and including the main representatives of the European Multinationals. See Talani, *Betting for and against EMU*. Similar considerations can be made about the role of the European Round Table.

13. See van Apeldoorn, Overbeek, and Ryner, in chapter 1 of this volume.

14. See A. Moravcsik, "Preferences and Power in the EC: A Liberal Intergovernmentalist Approach," *Journal of Common Market Studies* 31, no. 4 (December 1993): 474.

15. See Moravcsik, "Preferences and Power," 9.

16. See L. Martin, "International and Domestic Institutions in the EMU Process," *Economics and Politics* 5, no. 2 (1993).

17. See G. Garret, "The Politics of the Maastricht Treaty," *Economics and Politics* 5, no. 2 (1993); T. Wooley, "Linking Political and Monetary Union: The Maastricht Agenda and German Domestic Politics," *Economics and Politics* 5, no. 2 (1993); Sandholtz, "Choosing Union"; and D. M. Andrews, "The Global Origins of the Maastricht Treaty."

18. See Wooley, "Linking Political and Monetary Union."

19. See K. McNamara, *The Currency of Ideas: Monetary Politics in the European Union* (Ithaca, N.Y.: Cornell University Press, 1998). See also T. Risse et al., "To Euro or Not to Euro: The EMU and Identity Politics in the European Union," *ARENA Working Paper* 98/1 (1998).

20. See J. Frieden, "Invested Interests: The Politics of National Economic Policies in a World of Global Finance," in *International Organization*, no. 45 (Autumn 1991). See also J. Frieden, *The Impact of Goods and Capital Market Integration on European Monetary Politics*, unpublished manuscript (August 1994).

21. Incidentally, the issue of European monetary union has been addressed for the first time in the context of the European community exactly at the beginning of the 1970s with the Werner Plan, since the Treaty of Rome, in its original version, did not contain any reference to the goal of monetary union. Although many authors, like T. Padoa-Schioppa (see Padoa-Schioppa, "The European Monetary System"), claim that this was due to the collapse of the Bretton Woods system, some evidence may be found that this debate over monetary arrangements was urged by the growing impact of greater capital mobility. See, for references on this subject, Bank for International Settlement (BIS), *Sixtieth Annual Report* (Basle: BIS, 1990).

22. The Mundell–Fleming model is a macroeconomic model that links together the monetarist economic equilibrium, that is, the equilibrium of monetarist variables, given by the equilibrium between the money supply and demand, summarized in the so-called L/M curve, and the real variables equilibrium, the equilibrium between investments and savings, summarized by the so-called I/S curve. The model does include also the equilibrium of the external economic relationships in the form of the balance of payments equilibrium, summarized in the so-called B/P curve.

23. See also Padoa-Schioppa, "The European Monetary System."

24. In fact, in the Mundell–Fleming model, if the exchange rates are held constant, any monetary expansion causes the interest rates to decrease and the capital, given the assumption of its freedom of movement, to outflow until the interest rates reach their original level without any rise in the domestic demand. Thus, if the exchange rates are fixed, any expansionary monetary policy is ineffectual in stimulating national economy, while monetary policy can be effective if the value of the currency is allowed to vary.

The reverse is true for fiscal policies, since, given capital mobility, in a fixed exchange rates regime, bonds floated to finance increased government spending are bought by international investors and there is no effect on interest rates that are set globally. If exchange rates vary, as foreigners buy more government bonds the resultant capital inflow causes a currency appreciation that tends to reduce domestic demand for domestically produced goods and thus to dampen the fiscal expansion. Therefore, in conclusion, any autonomous national macroeconomic policy in a world of capital mobility does not affect interest rates, in other words, does not produce any effective change in domestic economy, while it can result in changes of the exchange rates.

25. It is true that it is possible to cover exchange rates risks by recurring to the forward exchange rate market, but this is neither costless nor available for all currencies.

26. In fact, the real exchange rate can be expressed as the relationship between the price of nontradable goods and that of tradable ones: P\P*xe. By assumption, the price of tradables, P*, is set on world markets and cannot be changed, in foreign currency terms, by national policy. Depreciation makes tradables relatively more expensive in domestic currency terms, while nontradables become relatively cheaper; appreciation has the opposite effect.

27. See A. Walters, *The Sterling in Danger* (London: Collins, 1990), chap. 5.

28. See J. A. Frieden, "Invested Interests: The Politics of National Economic Policies in a World of Global Finance," *International Organization*, no. 45 (Autumn 1991).

29. See Talani, *Betting for and against EMU*, also as reported further on in this chapter.

30. See S. Gill, "Historical Materialism, Gramsci and International Political Economy," in C. N. Murphy and R. Tooze, eds., *The New International Political Economy* (Boulder, Colo.: Lynne Rienner, 1991).

31. See, for example, Frieden, "Invested Interests"; Frieden, *The Impact of Goods and Capital Market Integration*; and J. Frieden, *The New Political Economy of EMU* (Oxford: Rowman & Littlefield, 1998).

32. For more details see P. De Grauwe, *International Money* (Oxford: Oxford University Press, 1996), 71.

33. See P. Krugman, "The Case for Stabilising Exchange Rates," *Oxford Review of Economic Policy* 5 (1989): 61–72.

34. For a detailed account of the approach see De Grauwe, *International Money*, 75.

35. See R. P. Flood and N. P. Marion, "Speculative Attacks: Fundamentals and Self-fulfilling Prophecies," in *National Bureau of Economic Research*, Working Paper 5789 (Cambridge, Mass.: NEBR, 1996).

36. For an application of this approach to the 1987 crash see D. Romer, "Rational Asset-Price Movements without News," *The American Economic Review* 83, no. 5 (1993): 1120–30.

37. See G. Ingham, *Capitalism Divided? The City and Industry in British Social Development* (London: Macmillan Education LTD, 1984).

38. See for example A. Martinelli and M. Chiesi, "Italy," in T. Bottomore and J. Brym, eds., *The Capitalist Class: An International Study* (London: Harvester Wheatsheaf, 1989); and A. Martinelli, "Organised Business and Italian Politics," in P. Lange and S. Tarrow, eds., *Italy in Transition* (London: Frank Cass, 1980).

39. See P. Lange, G. Ross, and M. Vannicelli, *Unions, Change and Crisis: French and Italian Union Strategy and the Political Economy* (London: Allen and Unwin, 1982).

40. J. Coakley and L. Harris, *The City of Capital* (Oxford: Basil Blackwell, 1983); and G. Ingham, *Capitalism Divided? The City and Industry in British Social Development* (London: Macmillan, 1984).

41. See Talani, *Betting for and against EMU*.

42. See C. Crouch and W. Streeck, *Le capitalismes en Europe* (Paris: La Decouverte, 1996).

43. See Talani, *Betting for and against EMU*.

44. The British "Hard Ecu" alternative to EMU, proposed by the City of London and immediately endorsed by the new Major government, clearly represented an attempt to stop, or at least delay, the process of European monetary integration. See HM Treasury, "Economic and Monetary Union," *Treasury Bulletin* (Summer 1990).

45. See Crouch and Streeck, *Le capitalismes en Europe*.

46. The Stability Pact confirms the objective of a deficit-to-GDP ratio not exceeding 3 percent and commits EMU member states to a medium-term budgetary stance close to balance or in surplus. It also defines the terms and sanctions of the excessive deficit procedure. Exemption from respecting this fiscal criterion within EMU is allowed only in case of a decline in GDP of 2 percent or more and of a temporary and small excess deficit. With a GDP declining by between 0.75 and 2 percent, the decision on exemption from

sanctions is left to the Council of Ministers. With lower decreases in GDP, the excessive deficit procedure will be implemented in any case, and countries are obliged to keep up to 0.5 percent of their GDP in non-interest-bearing mandatory deposits with the ECB until excess deficit is reabsorbed. If this does not happen within two years, deposits are transformed into outright transfers.

47. For more information see L. S. Talani, "Mediterranean Labour and the Impact of EMU: Mass Unemployment As the Price for the Euro" in H. Overbeek, ed., *The Political Economy of European Unemployment: European Integration and the Transnationalisation of the Employment Question* (London: Routledge, 2003).

48. Indeed, the Social Charter, whose proposal was the result of the bargaining process going on between the two major European social partners (UNICE and the ETUC) in parallel with the IGC on EMU, contains the embryo of a European corporatist system, which, however, has not developed further thereafter. See Bieling and Schulten's argument in chapter 9.

49. A meaningful example of the loss of London primacy in favor of its continental competitors is represented by the derivatives exchanges. Eurex, a screen-based derivatives exchange born on the joint initiative of the French, the Germans, and the Swiss, demolished the European leadership of the London's floor-based Liffe, which lost its near-monopoly in the German Bund futures contract in a matter of months. See *The Economist*, "A Survey of Global Equity Markets," May 5–11, 2001.

50. Reference is made here to the adoption by the Thatcher government of monetary aggregates and interest rate targets, which in a world of capital mobility is inconsistent with the pegging of the exchange rates.

6

⁓ ⧉ ⧉⁓

Diminishing Expectations

The Strategic Discourse of Globalization
in the Political Economy of New Labour

COLIN HAY AND MATTHEW WATSON

Globalization is increasingly seen to circumscribe the parameters of the politically and economically possible. Heightened capital mobility, labor market deregulation, and financial liberalization, it is argued, conspire to announce not only the end of the "embedded liberalism" that came to characterize the postwar years, but also a positive agenda for welfare reform, an active and interventionist role for the state, and, indeed, social democracy itself. In the face of this mounting list of casualties, there is nothing that can be done save lament the inevitable. Or so we are told. The political practices and ideologies that served to sustain welfare capitalism are typically believed to have been cast on the pyre of Keynesian social democracy, an inferno fanned by global economics.

In this chapter, we break from this conventional wisdom to suggest that the impact of globalization may be more rhetorical than substantive. It is the political discourse of globalization rather than globalization per se, we argue, that summons the inexorable "logic of no alternative" (of welfare retrenchment, labor market deregulation, and fiscal conservatism writ large). We illustrate this argument with respect to the British case, and demonstrate how this logic has come to define hegemonic common sense. In other words, we demonstrate the discursive mechanisms through which what Gill in chapter 2 called "disciplinary neoliberalism" and "new constitutionalism" has permeated, from the narrow confines of a class-based "accumulation strategy" and policy, into mass politics in broader civil society. (This is what Gramsci called the "ethico-political moment.") Nationally based mass parties remain crucial in this context. Research on Thatcherism has illustrated this with regard to the formative phase of neoliberalism. However, neoliberal hegemony has been consolidated and normalized in Britain through the transformation of "New Labour."

It should be noted that it is *not* our claim that the impact of globalization is any less real for its rhetorical origins. The political deployment of the discourse of globalization is real in itself, and rather than the transformation of the international economy that such a discourse purports to represent, it itself is the most significant factor in restricting the parameters of that considered politically and economically possible. In this way, the highly contingent, though now ascendant, politics of neoliberalism is rendered necessary by the discourse of globalization. We illustrate this argument with reference both to the downsizing of New Labour's aspirations in the two years prior to the 1997 general election and to its subsequent conduct in office, revealing and scrutinizing the narrative of globalization upon which this has been publicly predicated.

We locate the British variant of neoliberalism at its consolidation phase (on the phases of neoliberalism, see chapter 1 of this volume), and we suggest that New Labour's globalization discourse has been crucial to the momentum of that recent consolidation. Labour used its globalization discourse to enforce the impression of its own potential governing "competence," in circumstances in which it understood competence solely in terms of the efficiency with which it could manage the prevailing socioeconomic settlement in Britain. There were clear electoral payoffs. The deconstructive phase of neoliberalism had long since been established and had been guided by the decisive political interventions of the preceding Conservative administrations. Labour's appeal to the structural realities of globalization served to highlight the futility of assuming that political and social time could simply be reversed in order to undo the deconstructive phase of neoliberalism in Britain. Hence, neoliberalism was validated and normalized in British society.

We conclude that Labour internalized the nonnegotiable economic imperatives that are so frequently associated with globalization, *specifically* in order to make its revised economic priorities palatable to the widest range of potential voters. Firstly, it made the party's revisionism easier to sell to its core constituencies of traditional "Old" Labour supporters. New Labour could not be held responsible for its failure to introduce a more progressive alternative—or so it claimed—in circumstances in which there were, in any case, no viable progressive alternatives available. Secondly, it allowed the party to broaden the social basis of its support amongst those constituencies who had found their interests to be furthered during the preconsolidation phase of the neoliberal project. New Labour deployed its globalization discourse to liberate itself from popular expectations that the party could, and indeed would, lead a successful counter-mobilization against neoliberalism. In the process, it picked up large numbers of new voters not predisposed to support a counter-hegemonic project.

THE POLITICAL LOGIC OF GLOBALIZATION

> The explanation itself has become a political force helping to create the institutional realities it purportedly merely describes.
>
> —Frances Fox Piven[1]

The political logic of neoliberal convergence announced by the "business globalization" literature is now so familiar and so widely discredited in the secondary literature that it may seem peculiarly perverse to begin an analysis of globalizing tendencies by once again revisiting such arguments. In theoretical and, perhaps more importantly, empirical terms, the crude globalization thesis of Kenichi Ohmae and other "globalization gurus" may well be as dead as Francis Fukuyama's sense of history. Yet rumors of its declining political salience are, as yet, greatly exaggerated. Globalization is one of the myths by which we live. It is this that makes the political logic of globalization so familiar. As Linda Weiss notes,

> Political leaders . . . have themselves played a large part in contributing to [the] view of government helplessness in the face of global trends. In canvassing support for policies lacking popular appeal, many OECD governments have sought to "sell" their policies of retrenchment to the electorate as being somehow "forced" on them by "global economic trends" over which they have no control.[2]

Such an expedient logic is undoubtedly widely utilized. In the qualitatively new environment summoned by globalization, nation-states have no choice but to seek to position themselves as competitive economic spaces by virtue of the enticements of macroeconomic stability they might offer potential investors. The heightened mobility of capital has radically curtailed the parameters of political choice. If national, regional, and local economies are to prove competitive in the market for inward investment, they must effectively guarantee a context in which consistently high returns can be anticipated. In this way, governments have been locked in to a game of competitive arbitrage—the winners being those deemed most likely to provide the biggest subsidies, the lowest taxes, and the most flexible and cheap supply of docile labor. Fiscal austerity, welfare retrenchment, and the removal of "supply-side rigidities" (such as trade union rights) thus delimit the full extent of legitimate state intervention. The welfare state, social democracy, and full employment are revealed as indulgent luxuries of a bygone era, which must now be downsized in accordance with the overriding imperative of economic competitiveness. Globalization, thus understood, announces the global diffusion of neoliberalism; there is simply no alternative.

This is perhaps the public face of the globalization thesis, reflected in the editorial columns and in the financial and business pages of the tabloid and broadsheet media alike. Yet, it is by no means the only path to the conclusion that financial liberalization, heightened capital mobility, and a more integrated and competitive global economic environment serve to summon a logic of "neoliberal necessity" on whose altar the social munificence of a welfare society must be sacrificed. We now move from analytical assumptions that originate in the business studies literature to those whose roots lie in academic political economy. No less significant, indeed perhaps rather closer to New Labour's understanding of globalization, is the "modified structural dependence thesis" advanced by Adam Przeworski and Michael Wallerstein.[3]

The thesis is a simple one: It concerns the state's supposed structural dependence upon capital and, in particular, the consequences of heightened capital mobility for this relationship. As Przeworski and Wallerstein themselves note, "Politicians seeking reelection must anticipate the impact of their policies on the decisions of firms because these decisions affect employment, inflation, and the personal income of voters: vote-seeking politicians are dependent on owners of capital because voters are."[4] The state is thus dependent upon capital in the sense that the revenue basis on which its very function is predicated is reliant upon its ability to secure conditions conducive to investment and capital accumulation. In an era of enhanced exit options, capital mobility, and potential flight, this places considerable constraints on the political latitude of parties vying for state power. If we can assume that capital is likely to associate the election of a social democratic administration with higher levels of domestic taxation and, in an integrated global economy, enjoys near perfect mobility, then the merest hint of the election of a social democratic government is likely to be accompanied by a rapid and destabilizing exodus of capital. Social democrats must accommodate themselves to the perceived interests of capital. If they fail to accept "commonsense" demands for low taxation, labor market deregulation, welfare retrenchment, and fiscal austerity, the very suggestion of their election is likely to precipitate disinvestment, currency speculation, and subsequent economic crisis. Once again, within the parameters of such a thesis, there is simply no alternative to neoliberalism within contemporary capitalism.

What is so remarkable about such a thesis is the extent to which it seems to capture New Labour's strategic assessment of the context in which it found itself in 1995–1996—an assessment it has come to share with an array of sister parties around the western world. New Labour has behaved in a manner entirely consistent with how a utility-maximizing social democratic party *would* act *were* the structural dependence thesis valid. This, as Wickham-Jones's careful and important analysis makes clear,[5] can be seen in its studious courting, since 1992, first of domestic industry, then the City, and, eventually, international investors from Wall Street to Singapore. Of course, the fact that Labour acts as if the "modified structural dependence thesis" were true is not in any sense confirmation of such a thesis. What it does suggest, however, is that Labour accepts and embraces the economic logic of structural dependence, and is content to be seen accepting the political logic of no alternative that the assumption of structural dependence conjures.

Central to such a conception of political-economic constraint is the concept of capital flight. The suppositions on which the idea of exit is grounded are rendered most explicit in the rational expectations theory of macroeconomic policy making. This is a theory with a somewhat checkered history. Academically de rigueur in the early 1980s, it sanctioned strict monetary targets in macroeconomic policy. At the same time, the fact that governments acted as if the rational expectations hypothesis were true provided additional impetus for its embedding as the dominant perspective on policy-making theory. All this was to change, however, with the conspicuous failure of attempts to target essentially arbitrary monetary indicators. However, despite its waning popularity as a theoretical model, the assumptions on which the rational expectations hypothesis is based have been "smuggled" back into the policy-making arena in the guise of the conventional wisdom on globalization.

Here, then, we turn from an analysis of globalization's perceived logic of neoliberal necessity rooted in academic political economy to one rooted in economic theory. It is, however, in the assumptions shared by all of the perspectives reviewed that globalization's logic of no alternative is conjured. These assumptions are perhaps most clearly stated in the rational expectations hypothesis. They are, essentially, six-fold: (a) that capital will invest where it receives the greatest return on its investment; (b) that capital is blessed with perfect information of the conditions likely to prove most conducive in maximizing returns on that investment; (c) that capital has a singular and homogeneous interest that only it can best perceive; (d) that this interest is undifferentiated with respect to sector (there being no distinction drawn between financial and industrial capital, for instance) and over time (there being no conflict envisioned between the short-term interest of individual capitals and the long-term collective interest of capital per se); (e) that capital mobility is perfect, instantaneous, and without cost; and (f) that capital has unhindered access to information about future government policy and is able to translate this into rational expectations about the costs and benefits of exit.[6]

At best these assumptions are crude and simplistic. At worst they are demonstrably false, as we go on to suggest in later sections of this chapter. For the time being, it is merely important to reiterate that it is in such premises, particularly in the assumption that disinvestment and exit are without cost to both financial and industrial capital, that globalization's logic of inevitability resides. Soften and render more complex the assumptions and the predictive power of the model may have gone, but so too is the political fatalism that such a model engenders. The significance of this point can scarcely be overstated.

Much of the political fatalism that attends Labour's understanding of globalization derives from the association it draws from such assumptions between competitiveness in an era of heightened capital mobility and labor market flexibility. Moreover, such flexibility is here invariably held synonymous with the suppression of labor costs. The rational expectations hypothesis reappears in such reasoning, suggesting that financial liberalization has served to create a global capital market capable of "policing" social relations in line with labor market flexibility. The truly global circuit of capital, which rational expectations theory merely assumes and globalization is believed to provide, essentially imposes strict macroeconomic orthodoxy.

As we later argue, this assumption cannot be corroborated empirically—even in a context in which concerted political interventions facilitate financial globalization.[7] Nonetheless, to concentrate solely on empirical denials of the rational expectations hypothesis may be to miss the point. This is because the assumption of perfect capital mobility remains integral to political projects that, like New Labour's, seek to place "the market" at the heart of economic policy. Indeed, they underpin the very notion of a self-adjusting market equilibrium. Within this pervasive paradigm, temporary disturbances within the economic environment have no long-term effects on equilibrium levels of output and employment in the absence of market distortions that subvert automatic adjustment mechanisms. Consequently, Blair's frequently reiterated commitment that the new Labour government will aim to "work with the grain of global change" initiated by the market suggests a commitment to supply-side reforms focused on removing market rigidities. In arguing that his administration will "accept, and indeed embrace, the global market," he consistently stressed that New Labour does not view the processes of globalization as imposing long-term disequilibrating effects on the British economy.[8] In fact, New Labour claims to harness the globalization process to facilitate smoother adjustments between short-term market equilibria.[9]

It is important at this point to emphasize the distinctiveness of the rational expectations hypothesis. Even in neoclassical theory, macroeconomic analysis tends to assume wage–price *stickiness*; it is only once neoclassical assumptions are traded for those of rational expectations that the notion of wage–price *flexibility* is introduced.[10] Viewed in this way, legitimate economic governance is only conscionable to the extent that it is required to enforce flexibility norms. Furthermore, given the current financial context, it is thought that governments have no choice but to allow flexibilization to impact in a systematically asymmetric manner to the detriment of labor. As such, in its emphasis on flexibility, the Labour Party has internalized not only a dominant economic orthodoxy but also one with unevenly distributed social and political consequences. The financial system has become increasingly inelastic in response to demand shocks; vast sums of capital are now prepared for the sole purpose of defending real monetary values. With monetary prices being policed by short-term flows in this way, they have become progressively more *in*flexible. As a result, the burden of flexibility has increasingly fallen on labor. The market economics that the Blair government has implemented in response to globalizing tendencies thus necessitates an ever more coercive regulation of wage relations.

The justification for such a stance is that, in an era of global financial relations, the state's structural dependence on capital is most acute in financial sectors. This assumption lies at the heart of the government's decision, taken within a week of its election victory, to depoliticize monetary policy relations by ceding operational responsibility for interest rates to the Bank of England.[11] As Labour's leaders thought could be seen quite clearly by the observed pattern of currency speculation, foreign exchange traders appear consistently to indicate a preference for currencies backed by anti-inflationary policies. Liquidity crises in domestic banking sectors are consequently triggered by speculators moving out of domestic currencies en masse on the expectation of imminent inflationary tendencies. Accordingly, the search for counter-inflationary credibility has become a cornerstone of New Labour's economic management. Its "tough on inflation, tough on the causes of inflation" stance was the key consideration behind the decision to absolve the government of all further responsibility for the "technicalities" of interest rate settings.

This brings us to the crux of the matter. Whilst the Labour government has *acted* tough, its anti-inflationary credibility has been built primarily by *talking* tough, that is, by sending the correct signals to those in the international financial markets who effectively serve as the guardians of national liquidity. Speculative flows of short-term financial assets are now triggered increasingly by *expectations* of likely future government policy (whether formed rationally or otherwise). To a significant extent, then, the "demands" of a global era have been understood so as to suggest that the execution of a "successful" macroeconomic policy relies upon the execution of a "successful" *discursive* strategy. In this way, macroeconomic policy enters the realm of symbolic politics.

In this final articulation of a logic of no alternative, the "inevitability" of welfare retrenchment is conjured rather differently than it is in the literatures reviewed previously. Here it owes its "necessity" to the need to satisfy the anti-inflationary preferences of the global foreign exchange markets. Yet, though the path is different, the destination is the same. It would indeed seem as though all intellectual routes converge on a similar diagnosis—New Labour exists in a hostile and unfriendly environment defined, as it is circumscribed, by a set of "harsh economic realities." In such a context, governments simply have no choice but to announce the end of punitive tax regimes on business, to promote aggressively inward investment (whatever the costs in terms of subsidies and labor market deregulation), and to render the welfare state both residual and increasingly functional in terms of national competitiveness.

NEW LABOUR'S "NEW TIMES"

> The economy is becoming ever more global. Trade is growing at twice the speed of production. British Airways does its backroom work in Bombay, while a baker in South Yorkshire is taking on fifty new staff because his baguettes are selling so well in France. Yesterday's solutions will not work for tomorrow.
>
> —Robin Cook[12]

An image of inexorable economic forces is often summoned in order to explain the emergence of globalization's logic of inevitability. Once a more dialectical understanding of the relationship between the material and the ideational is emphasized, however, a rather different picture emerges.[13] Political outcomes are not structurally determined by a globalization process for which there is, in any case, only superficial evidence. The political is far more than merely residual to a determining economic essence. Indeed, in the absence of decisive, facilitating political interventions, the material processes of globalization would in all likelihood be unsustainable.[14] Consequently, just as crucial as the empirical indices of globalization are conceptions of such a process. For, ideas are far more than mere post hoc rationalizations of preexisting structural logics. An understanding of the government's discursive construction of globalization is a necessary, though clearly insufficient, condition of an adequate understanding of the processes of change visible in contemporary Britain.

That New Labour chooses to deploy the rhetoric of globalization is undeniable. It is crucial, then, that we establish *on what terms* it chooses to do so. The dominant suggestion, rhetorically, is one of a qualitative break with the past. The economic logic of the latest phase of capitalist development is assumed by the Labour Party to mark a clear transition with the postwar years. Moreover, as this logic has diffused and penetrated political structures, it is further assumed to have swept away the sedimented institutions and dominant conventions of a now bygone era. Even the now familiar addition of the prefix "new" to the party's name— emphasized most deliberately in the prime minister's post-election invocation: "We have been elected as New Labour; and we will govern as New Labour"[15]—is testament to such an assumption. The implicit suggestion is that we have witnessed a paradigm shift in the organization of economic relations, requiring a similarly dramatic shift in the politics of economic regulation. "In a global economy," Tony Blair argued in a speech to the Singapore Business Community, "the old ways won't do. . . . In reality, in a modern economy, we [do not] need old style dirigisme."[16] In a similar vein, Gordon Brown argued at the final CBI Annual Conference before the 1997 general election, "We understand that in a global market place, traditional national economic policies—corporatism from the old left—no longer have any relevance."[17] As such,

> The key to new Labour economics is the recognition that Britain . . . [has] to compete in an increasingly international market place. . . . Today's Labour Party, new Labour, is the political embodiment of the changed world—the new challenges, the new policies and the new politics.[18]

However else New Labour subsequently markets itself, the first image that it wishes to convey is that it is qualitatively distinct from its former self.[19] The "newness" of New Labour is juxtaposed to Old Labour, just as the supposedly unique attributes of globalization are emphasized in order to differentiate the logic of the current phase of capitalist development from the logic of capitalism per se. Within such a characterization, the predominant line of causation runs unequivocally from the economic to the political. It is political actors that have had to "respond" to the "challenges" posed by the "new realities" of changed economic circumstance. In this respect, Blair's warning to party supporters with reservations about the pace of New Labour's political transformation "to stop living in the past and move with the times" is typical.[20] So, too, is his similarly phrased assessment of Lionel Jospin's hopes, expressed at the Congress of Socialist Parties in Malmo in June 1997, that a more aggressive and interventionist European stance on unemployment would be tolerated by Europe's new and nominally social democratic governments.[21] The "new times" of which Blair speaks are primarily new economic times; as such, a residual economic determinism characterizes New Labour's own accounts of its "modernization."

According to Blair, "there are three obvious changes in the post-war world" that are demanding new political norms, the first and most important of which is that "the economy is global."[22] The new structure of the international economy is seen to constrain, in particular, those parties most traditionally associated with the ethos of active government (however misplaced that association is). While, in the academic literature, this tends to be stated bluntly as the assumption that globalization sounds the death knell for social democracy, New Labour's articulation of such an assumption is expressed in rather more moderate language. "In the complex and increasingly integrated world economy," Gordon Brown told the party's influential Finance and Industry Group while still in opposition, "we need a clear appreciation of the role—*and the limits*—of government."[23] Interestingly, this conception of the essential fallibility of government was introduced as an immediate precursor to the section of the speech headed, "No return to past failures." In contrast to the "failed" world of Old Labour, the "future" world of New Labour was to be one in which there is no place for an overactive government. "Good government" of the economy is "minimal government" of the economy, a conception clearly highly compatible with the spirit of both the rational expectations hypothesis and the structural dependence thesis. The space for alternatives, in such a schema, no longer exists as globalization has ensured that "choices are constrained" in line with a best-practice neoliberalism. Above all else, globalization ensures that "there are no panaceas." Consequently, expect that "the solutions adopted by left and right may often overlap."[24] In this way the rhetoric of Anthony Giddens's "future of radical politics"—a politics beyond the old binary oppositions of left and right—is summoned by New Labour.[25] Moreover, this is a rhetoric that is deployed across the whole of the ideological spectrum of New Labour, from Robin Cook— "Because the world is changing fast [and] the economy is becoming ever more global . . . yesterday's solutions will not work for tomorrow"[26]—to Peter Mandelson—"New Labour does not accept the classic view of the left-right divide in which both sides are locked in permanent conflict."[27] This latter assumption is captured even more vividly in the prime minister's insistence that "[New Labour] means a politics no longer scarred by the irrelevant ideological battles of much of the 20th century [because] most of the old left/right tags today are nothing but obstacles to good thinking."[28]

What is clear, however, is that the context within which "overlapping solutions" are to be found lies on a terrain that was until recently exclusively dominated by the class strategies of the right. In an analysis that represents little more than a subtle reinflection of the arguments of Kenichi Ohmae and Francis Fukuyama, the economic rhetoric of New Labour conflates the "era of globalization" and, if not quite the "end of history" per se, then certainly the end of the history of social democratic economic policy making in Britain. In all three accounts, the traditional tensions between the state and the market as the most efficient means of organizing economic activity have been resolved irrevocably in favor of the latter. As a result, the Labour party's discursive positioning in relation to the market has shifted from outright hostility to general skepticism, and from there to grudging acceptance and finally open embrace. "Modern government has a strategic role," the Labour Party declared in its 1992 election manifesto, "not to replace the market but to ensure the market works properly."[29] This is a theme that Tony Blair in particular has since picked up on with some vigor. "The modern function of government," he has argued, "is not to second-guess the market."[30] In this respect, New Labour's understanding of the imperatives of economic governance endorses the move away from discretionary policy making, a move made explicit in economic theory grounded in the rational expectations hypothesis. Instead of adopting a discretionary policy that seeks actively to shape market outcomes, the limit of acceptable government intervention in macroeconomic relations is now assumed to be set by the implementation of a rules-based policy. Here, the government feeds the market with information about its intentions by publicizing a series of medium-term targets for the economy. In its desire to foster market expectations that it has created, in Gordon Brown's words, "a credible framework for monetary discipline,"[31] the "first goal of policy" has become the perceived need to "set an explicit target for low inflation."[32] In turn, the suppression of inflationary tendencies is assumed to entail a commitment to "lay down rules" for being "fierce in controlling public spending."[33] To this end, the chancellor "has published explicit spending targets, in order that "nobody should doubt [his] iron resolve for stability and fiscal prudence."[34]

Once again, the rhetoric of globalization is deployed by New Labour in order to explain the shift in macroeconomic focus from employment to inflation imperatives. Thus, as Blair himself has suggested, in the new economic environment, "low inflation is not simply a goal in itself, it is the essential prerequisite both of ensuring that business can invest and that supply-side measures can work to raise the capacity of the economy to grow."[35] Those operating within global foreign exchange markets are now assumed to be able to exercise considerable restraint over the policy autonomy of individual national governments that do not appear to be as inflation-sensitive as they are. As the chancellor has argued, financial capitalists now have

> more choice and freedom than ever before, and day to day flows of capital are greater and faster than ever before. . . . Today, the judgement of the markets—whether to punish or to reward government policies—is as swift as it is powerful.[36]

To a large extent, therefore, the Labour party's rapprochement with the market is a reaction to assumptions about *global* market relations. Viewed through this perspective, any outward display of diffidence toward the market—or, more accurately, toward the concerns for price stability of those operating within the currency markets—is thought, quite simply, to force financial activity offshore. For investment to be retained onshore, governments "must convince the markets" of their reputation for being tough on inflation.[37] As such, it is assumed that:

> Credibility has become the keystone of policy-making in the nineties. A credible government is a government that pursues a policy that is "market friendly"; that is, a policy that is in accordance with what the markets believe to be sound.[38]

By delegating operational control of interest rate policy to the Bank of England, the Blair government has effectively externalized the responsibility for anti-inflationary credibility. This deliberate attempt to depoliticize domestic monetary policy relations can only have been guided by the assumption that "the City . . . believes that the Bank will be a lot less tolerant about inflation than any government could be."[39] Indeed, on the day that the reforms were announced, John Sheppard, then chief economist at the ill-fated Japanese securities house, Yamaichi International, commented that "the government's credibility has been vastly improved by this bold step." Similarly, Andrew Roberts, bond analyst at the Swiss Bank, UBS, remarked, "It is unbelievable to gain so much financial market credibility with such a simple move."[40]

The government explained the new institutional arrangements for the conduct of monetary policy as a necessary condition for remaining competitive within the global economy.[41] National competitiveness has increasingly become a central preoccupation of governance strategies, to the point at which it has ceased to be a means to a wider economic, far less social, end. It has become a political end in itself. As Riccardo Petrella observes, "Competition has acquired the status of a universal credo, an ideology."[42] In Tony Blair's terms, "Economically, the challenge [of globalization] can be summed up in a single word: competitiveness"[43]; and, in Bob Jessop's terms, competitiveness has now been constituted as *the* national economic interest.[44] As such, Labour's economic policy proposals are now almost exclusively "aimed at increasing the competitiveness of British companies in increasingly competitive markets."[45] In this respect, there is little difference between the government's aims and its predecessor's attempts to generate "the right climate . . . to help business to help itself."[46] The basis of successive governments' competitiveness strategies has been to foster an economic climate that is looked upon favorably by the managers of both national and multinational capital. No clearer indication could be given that the government believes that rationally acting financial investors are now able at will to confirm the state's structural dependence on capital through threats of disinvestment. At the macroeconomic level, New Labour routinely argues that its competitiveness strategies are facilitated by its "determination to create a modern monetary framework that [can] command confidence and credibility"[47]; a "stable low inflation environment" is assumed to act as the "platform . . . from which we can build our industrial strength."[48]

The stated goal of the Labour government is to construct that new "industrial strength" via strategic microeconomic interventions. Thus, its loud proclamations of the limits of government are translated rather unevenly into practice. Although New Labour respects such a restricted view of the legitimate role of government in the sphere of macroeconomic policy, this is in marked contrast to its attempts forcibly to impose itself on the microeconomics of the labor market. This graphically reveals perhaps the most common misunderstanding of the whole globalization debate: Namely, the popular mythology that globalization (or at least, the context in which globalizing imperatives are freely invoked) spells the demise of the political efficacy of national governments. In practice, what we are seeing is not the withering of the state so much as the wholesale redefinition of its form and function.[49] From a previously active state at the macroeconomic level, we now see the emergence of states whose competencies have been rearticulated in order to be able to intervene in line with perceived microeconomic imperatives. New Labour's interpretation of the new economic functions of the state is articulated most frequently in the presumed need to enhance economic competitiveness; its principal response to turn its attention to supplyside constraints operating in the labor market.

In this respect, British workers have increasingly been subjected to statesponsored forced flexibilization. The aim of the government's policy has been to integrate an increasing proportion of the workforce into the low-skill, low-wage sectors that, in terms of job creation at least, are currently the most dynamic in the "global" economy. This new politics of flexibilization is a direct reaction to the view that, under conditions of globalization, British workers in relatively unskilled sectors now face direct wage competition from workers whose rates of pay are substantially lower than their own. In the words of the "Road to the Manifesto" documents, under a New Labour government,

> What there will be is a new deal for people at work. . . . [The] world is changing. . . . Companies need both the capability and the flexibility to succeed in this new world. . . . We must avoid rigidity in labor market regulation and promote the flexibility we require.[50]

Similarly, when he has entered the debate on global economics from his position at the Foreign and Commonwealth Office, Robin Cook has done so on almost identical terms:

> Britain is a global player. . . . Companies must be able to adapt to a fast-changing market. Otherwise, they stop being competitive and cannot create jobs. . . . We must guarantee [that government legislation does not] over-burden business and destroy jobs.[51]

The rhetoric of globalization is here deployed to justify a shifting of the burden of market forces from productive capital to labor in the name of national competitiveness.[52] Moreover, this is a strategy that New Labour has felt sufficiently confident to attempt to export it to its European partners:

> We have shown that alongside low inflation and sound public finances, Europe needs a new approach to employment and growth, based on British ideas for competitiveness, including more flexible labor markets and employability.[53]

Once again, the overall message is a simple one. Globalization, financial liberalization, the imperatives of competitiveness in a more open international market place, and the exhaustion of the "golden age" of Keynesian welfare states and Fordist capitalism leave no room for the distinctly "old" politics of social provision, the correction of market failures, and a positive agenda for welfare reform. If we accept that the parameters of the possible have been circumscribed in this way, we can once again interpret New Labour as exhibiting radicalism—albeit a radicalism carefully fashioned for "new times." However, there may well be good reasons of an empirical nature for dismissing precisely such a depiction. It is to this line of argument that we turn in the following section.

THE MYTHOLOGY OF GLOBALIZATION

> The truth effects of discourses of economic globalization are somewhat independent of the veracity of the analysis.
>
> —Nikolas Rose[54]

New Labour systematically recast its social and economic priorities in the face of "imperatives" that appear to have little basis in fact. When attempts are made to translate the globalization thesis into a series of empirical statements, it becomes immediately apparent that the rhetoric of globalization is only tangentially related to the realities of the contemporary international economy. Reaching a similar conclusion, Will Hutton advises us that every time we hear talk of such "imperatives," we should "blow a big raspberry."[55] Cathartic perhaps, yet hardly sufficient for globalization continues to dominate political rhetoric relating to current economic circumstances. Moreover, until now, where this rhetoric has led, the politics of neoliberalism have seemingly followed. It is time to move beyond mere raspberry blowing and to start telling some altogether different stories about the pattern and trajectory of supposedly global economic integration.

Crucially, such stories must start to bear a rather closer relation to empirical realities. The most common assumption of the more extreme variants of the globalization thesis is that "capital" now enjoys unlimited exit options, roaming freely around the globe in diligent pursuit of labor market flexibility, investment incentives, and low rates of corporate taxation. It is capital's new "hypermobility" that effectively disempowers those clinging to a nostalgic, if touching, desire to impart social democratic dynamics onto the structures of a capitalist economy.

A number of points can here usefully be made. First, we should be wary of the analytical virtues of arguments that talk of capital in the singular. Capital is not a homogeneous entity that might display a static and undifferentiated interest. Indeed, the concerted liberalization of the financial markets has produced a situation in which different capitals now operate more independently of one another than perhaps ever before.[56] The deregulation of the international financial services sector has, for instance, served to exacerbate the effects of the divergence in the interests of financial and productive capital. The liquidity ratios associated with capital investments in productive capacity are, consequently, now very different to those associated with capital investments in financial assets. Consequently, the rationality exhibited by financial managers is at best wholly independent of—and, in many cases, directly contrary to—the interests of productive managers. This difference is reflected in the contrasting time horizons over which returns accrue to financial and productive investments. The short-term nature of financial investments allows capital to be retained in the money markets in essentially fluid form. The speed with which financial assets can consequently be traded serves to sustain the depiction of capital as hypermobile.

The same cannot be said, however, of capital invested in new productive capacity. The longer-term nature of industrial investments requires dedicated rather than fluid capital. As such, productive capital is locked into distinct social and economic loci. Indeed, it is a condition for the success of such investments that firms seek to build a stock of good will with the local community that acts as their host economy.[57] This they tend to do by sealing off many of their own future exit options; the sunk costs incurred by the initial investment make it significantly less rational for industrial capital to play the mobility card as distinct, say, from *threatening* to play the mobility card—at any time thereafter.[58] In seeming confirmation of this, there is precious little evidence of productive capital utilizing its much-vaunted mobility. In no sense, then, should we understand productive capital as essentially rootless, forever on the move in search of lower unit costs, and leaving an ever-widening track of devastation and unemployment in its wake. Business managers may well have a clear strategic stake in talking up their exit options in the hope of brokering a more favorable deal, especially in the run-up to an election in which a genuine social democratic alternative is perceived to exist. Yet, this hardly guarantees concerted disinvestment in the postelection period. As far as we are aware, no case of such coordinated exit exists.

It is, then, imperative to distinguish clearly between financial and productive capital. Financial transactions are both geographically and functionally mobile.[59] Such flexibility and mutability has resulted in a substantial erosion in transactions costs. This has triggered a massive increase in the volume of assets changing hands on any given market on any given day. Moreover, over two-thirds of all flows of financial funds are now considered to be flows of effectively "stateless money."[60] Financial capital thus appears to operate within a spatial context from which the concept of territory has been largely abstracted.[61] Purely national regulatory measures are therefore likely to prove ineffective.[62] In the absence of coordinated and multilateral moves toward currency controls, New Labour may be well advised to continue to construe the "statelessness" of financial capital as a structural constraint on its monetary policy. Altogether more problematic, however, is its assumption, made most explicit in Kenichi Ohmae's "borderless world" thesis, that production relations are now *also* played out on a "supraterritorial plane."[63]

Production relations continue to be territorially specific. Indeed, even the globalization orthodoxy hints at this: The very notion of globalizing tendencies summons the image of flows, be they of capital, people, information, or ideas. And flows imply direction; direction in turn implies geography. At least in terms of production, then, it would seem premature to write off the relevance of national economic spaces amidst misplaced talk of the "end of geography."

Moreover, notions of a postgeographic world summoned by globalization are hardly commensurate with the claims invariably made as to the strategic significance of foreign direct investment (FDI)—often held as the clearest indication of genuine economic globalization and attendant global economic convergence. A note of cautious realism is quickly sounded when it is recalled that domestic consumption demands continue overwhelmingly to be satisfied via the domestic circuit of capital.[64] Furthermore, these domestic producers remain predominantly domestically owned. Thus, despite efforts to render domestic stock markets more penetrable to interdependent trading, the typical exchange on such markets continues to be that of a domestic investor selling stock in a domestic company to another domestic investor. The presence of foreign investors within domestic markets may well make for headline news—as it did, for instance, when foreign investors found themselves overexposed in certain markets when the Asian financial crisis first struck—yet it is hardly representative of the modus operandi of such markets. As Frances Fox Piven notes, for any given year of the 1990s, the trend pattern of trading on Wall Street—assumed to be the most "open" stock exchange in the world—shows that at least nine out of every ten investments by American citizens were in stocks or bonds of U.S. firms.[65] Far from inhabiting a "borderless" world defined purely by global economic relations, then, invested capitals continue to circulate primarily within the more familiar confines of national economic spaces. As Linda Weiss argues, the postwar trend toward greater trade integration has slowed significantly throughout the 1980s and 1990s, a period that is commonly assumed to be the "take-off" stage to globalization. World trade growth remains stronger than world output growth, yet such a ratio has declined by around 20 percent as the embedded liberalism of postwar reconstruction gradually has been dismantled in favor of a neoliberal accumulation regime.[66]

More significantly still, confirmation of an increase in traded volumes is not unambiguous evidence that there is now a truly global circuit of trade. Insofar as such increases have impacted only minimally on the spatial distribution of trade flows, that impact has not been to *widen* the dispersion of trade. Recent patterns of trade point to a *reconcentration* of capital within the Triad, with non-Triad shares of world trade having diminished markedly since the 1960s.[67] Interregional trade has also failed to develop in a manner consistent with the globalization hypothesis. Indeed, exports from each unit of the Triad—North America, Western Europe, and East Asia—have now stabilized at around 10 percent of GDP.[68] Viewed historically, there is nothing remarkable about such a figure. It has been exceeded at the national level in more years of the twentieth century than it has not.[69]

What is perhaps remarkable here, then, is not the extent of globalization, but the extent to which the Blair government has been successful in making the conventional wisdom of globalization resonate in public policy-making discourse in the face of such contrary evidence. New Labour's focus on the systemic "imperative" of increasing labor market flexibility is based almost entirely upon the assumption that British workers are now locked into direct competition with workers from newly industrializing economies. For such an assumption to hold requires trade patterns so interdependent that labor market asymmetries would become an active element of trade competition. Yet there is no evidence of this. Trade interdependencies simply do not conform to assertions of globalization. Neither, for that matter, do investment interdependencies.

Recent increases in inward investment penetration have taken place within distinct spatial limits. Again, southern regions of the globe seem to have been conspicuously bypassed by "globalizing" trends. The south's share of the world FDI stock fell by a third in the twenty years to 1990—the period most frequently associated in the conventional wisdom with the onset of globalization.[70] The sudden surge in FDI in the 1980s led to the further concentration of investment within the Triad. Around 85 percent of all inward investment flows during globalization's "take-off" stage were both sourced and received by advanced industrialized economies.[71] There is, then, a well-defined, consistent, and well-documented sense of directionality in aggregate patterns of FDI flows; it does little to sustain appeals either to globalization's logic of no alternative or, indeed, to globalization itself.[72]

Irrespective of the claims embodied in the globalization hypothesis, therefore, geography is still intrinsically important to the location of productive investment.[73] It is the specificities of the social contexts in which the development of individual production technologies is set that ensure that capital assets that are invested in fixed form production outlets tend to remain where they are. Despite the importance that the Blair government has attached to the attraction of supposedly "stateless" flows of inward investment, the concept of a national economic space remains relevant. Moreover, though difficult to reconcile with the economic rhetoric, it is supported by much of the available empirical evidence. When expressed as a proportion of GDP, for example, today's flows of FDI are merely comparable with those of 1913.[74]

Admittedly, such a statistic, in itself, tells us next to nothing about the character of foreign direct investment or, then, of the domestic political constraints it implies. Yet it does problematize claims of qualitative novelty that provide much of the rhetorical force of the conventional wisdom. There exists a clear gap between the discourse and the reality of globalization. In the absence of such a gap, we should expect a steady increase in the significance of FDI on a global scale. Yet, that is not what we see. In fact, the growth of FDI flows in the pre-globalization era (1967–1980) was higher than that for the following ten years—a decade most commonly caricatured as that in which globalizing tendencies were increasingly institutionalized. Given these figures, it should come as no great surprise that inward investment remains of only marginal importance in relation to the overall functioning of the British economy.

It is also apparent that FDI flows reveal a highly distinctive geographical distribution *within* Britain. Contrary to assumptions about the increasing irrelevance of geography, inward investment into Britain tends to flow down spatial gradients to those areas in which deindustrialization has brought both unemployment and lower union densities. A disproportionate number of high-profile inward investors coming to Britain in recent years have chosen to locate in South Wales for precisely such reasons. That said, the manufacturing employment generated by this transfusion of FDI has accounted for only around 1 percent of the Welsh workforce, even in those years in which the imminent completion of the European Single Market sparked a one-off acceleration in inward investment activity. Significantly, such transplant manufacturing sectors have consistently paid below average Welsh wage rates. Accordingly, the 1 percent of the Welsh workforce that has been employed by such companies has earned a mere 0.7 percent of Welsh consumption potential.[75]

Such statistics hardly point to productive capitals taking advantage of unlimited exit options to locate wherever perceived competitive advantage draws them. What is clear is that multinationals have a vested interest in playing up their footloose image in order to win concessions (direct and indirect subsidies) from government. Yet the threat of exit should not be confused for the capacity to exit. What is certainly true is that the assumption that productive capital now seeks out the lowest unit labor costs anywhere in the world is flatly contradicted by the evidence that suggests that inward investors rarely look beyond the Triad for their adopted homes. Almost 90 percent of FDI flows since 1981 have been conducted within and between the relatively high-wage, high-cost regions of North America, Western Europe, and Southeast Asia.[76] FDI flows may well be spatially concentrated in the lowest cost local labor markets within Britain, but there is a big difference between this spatial patterning within a distinct national capitalism and the assumption of a complete global diffusion of production structures. The mobility of productive capital is routinely overemphasized in popular debates on globalization. Consequently, so too is the extent to which mobility disciplines government activity.

At this point it is important to emphasize that although the Blair government perceives increasingly fluid production relations to be a constraint on its policy autonomy, it appears to be more fearful still of prompting mass capital flight within the financial markets. Again, however, the empirical evidence suggests that financial capital's hypermobility is somewhat exaggerated. So, while Labour may well be wise to be sensitive to the constraints on its policy-making autonomy arising from financial liberalization, it would be equally wise not to overstate the nature of such constraints. In the conventional wisdom, financial assets are moved instantaneously around the world as a series of electronic impulses, driving a convergence in financial commodity prices. This view is grounded in the assumption of such perfectly integrated capital markets that demand and supply reflects a single equilibrium price. Yet this should lead us to expect a rapid international convergence of interest rates—something flatly contradicted by the empirical evidence. The correlation between short-term interest rates in the world's major financial centers is no greater in our "virtual" age than it was in the Victorian age.[77] That is, international investors have tended to limit their exposure to international markets, preferring instead to concentrate their activities within domestic markets. Some recent studies even suggest that the concentration of activities within domestic markets has added a new element of *divergence* to short-term interest rates.[78] As Tamim Bayoumi concludes, amongst those who have used macroeconomic tests to investigate capital mobility, assumptions of continuing differentials have now become "a 'stylized fact' about the international economy."[79]

Conventional assumptions of financial globalization notwithstanding, then, it is not surprising that a statistically significant correlation remains between the rate of domestic investment and the rate of domestic saving.[80] It is simply wrong to assume that supposedly "global" investments are sourced from a "global" pool of savings.

All the evidence thus suggests that, far from long-term financial assets moving freely across borders on a supraterritorial plane throughout all markets, globalizing tendencies are only evident in the short-term speculative flows that typify the currency markets. Unless reserved solely to describe behavior on the foreign exchanges, then, globalization is a singularly inappropriate term to describe the mobility of financial assets. In the words of The Economist, "despite all the hyperbole, a global capital market does not yet exist. . . . [C]apital markets do not fully transcend national boundaries."[81] Indeed, had such a market existed there would, presumably, have been no need for the government to grant operational independence to the Bank of England.

As the above paragraphs suggest, governments are not the unwitting victims of the exogenous economic processes that they so often make themselves out to be. Here New Labour's stance with respect to calls for the reregulation of financial markets is surely telling: It has consistently sided with those for whom any new financial architecture should be grounded in more rather than less liberalization. In the debates on reregulation that have followed the Asian financial crisis, for instance, the Blair government was conspicuous for its enthusiastic endorsement of the Washington Consensus. The U.S. administration was the only other western government to have given such unreserved support for increased capital market "transparency" to make the wheels of international finance run more smoothly.

Such actions are not, we suggest, indicative of a government unaware of the political implications of its interventions. New Labour has acted in the explicit knowledge that its adopted stance makes possible the continued use of the international financial markets as an automatic pilot for the reproduction of the policy preferences of its new target constituencies.

RENDERING THE NECESSARY CONTINGENT

When even The Economist is prepared to concede that capital markets do not yet fully transcend national boundaries, the space for political and economic alternatives may be somewhat greater than is often assumed. If we follow John Allen and Grahame Thompson in suggesting that "the stress placed upon the erosion of national regulatory barriers and the free movement of economic activities across national boundaries is what distinguishes a global from an international economy,"[82] then New Labour inhabits an environment whose parameters are circumscribed by an international, but not as yet, a global economy. Accordingly, the fatalistic, profoundly pessimistic, and essentially antipolitical conclusions of those anxious to capitulate to rampant and inexorable globalizing tendencies are in need of revision.

The discourse of globalization by which New Labour policed, disciplined, and ultimately downsized its expectations for government is based upon a series of profound misconceptions of the international economy. Once one attempts to reconcile the claims made by Labour about globalization with the empirical evidence, the disparity is starkly exposed. The constraints imposed by financial liberalization, international economic integration, and heightened capital mobility, however considerable, are far less restrictive than Labour consistently implies.

If there is to be a future for social democracy in Britain, as indeed in Western Europe, North America, and the Antipodes, then this is just as well. For, within the conceptual universe that New Labour inhabits, there is simply no alternative to neoliberalism within the contours of contemporary capitalism. It is only if Labour can break the spell of the discourse of globalization, and hence the largely self-imposed shackles of neoliberal economics, that a stable and long-term growth trajectory can be restored to British capitalism.

Yet, after over a term of Labour government, is not everything rosy in New Labour's economic garden? Here our judgment may sound harsh. Such success stories as there are have been largely superficial. They are attributable, for the most part, to the relatively benign international context in relation to short-term inflationary expectations that Labour has enjoyed to date, rather than anything more proactive that the government has done to "turn the economy around." The structural weaknesses of the British economy remain much as they were at the time of New Labour's first election victory in May 1997. The evidence to back such a claim can be found in no less reliable a source than the chancellor's budgets. In each of his first three budgets, Gordon Brown made reference to the fact that the British economy is being run over and above the maximum capacity that the economy can sustain beyond the short term. Moreover, the underlying capacity constraints were reported as more pronounced at each successive budget.[83]

The analytical case for alternatives to New Labour's neoliberalism is, we argue, largely unanswerable.[84] Indeed, to suggest that the international political economy can sustain only one governance strategy—that of "neoliberal necessity"—is merely to reveal, we think, a startling lack of political and economic imagination. Nonetheless, it is not an *analytical* case for an alternative that New Labour requires if it is to rediscover its former social democratic sensitivities or to remain true to its rhetoric of "national renewal"; what it requires is a *substantive* alternative.

It is not the purpose of this chapter to present such a vision. Yet, it is perhaps important that we conclude by pointing to what we regard as various fruitful lines of further enquiry.

In recent years, and particularly in response to a growing frustration with the crude logic of globalization often conjured to absolve the state of economic responsibility and political culpability, a range of alternatives have begun to emerge. Two complementary strands can, in particular, be identified: the former concerned principally with domestic measures to restore an indigenous investment ethic to British capitalism, the latter with multilateral strategies to reregulate the global financial markets through the imposition of capital controls.

The first literature is diverse, ranging widely from Will Hutton and the New Cambridge economists, via institutionalist variants of comparative political economy to Marxist-inspired accounts of British "exceptionalism." Its authors nonetheless converge on very similar conclusions. Refusing to accept a necessary trade-off between unemployment and inflation, they argue that in a more inter-dependent international economic environment, any persistent failure by the state to intervene in a concerted fashion is likely to be penalized very severely. Three generic forms of intervention in particular are emphasized: The first stresses the need to alleviate market failures, the second to rectify long-term structural weaknesses on both the demand- and supply-side of the economy, and the third to secure the conditions conducive to sustaining high levels of productive investment. Pointing to the specificities of the British economy, they identify persistently low levels of dedicated productive investment and a sadly depleted capital stock. Accordingly, they prioritize the creation of additional industrial capacity and the expansion of the capital stock, measures that they perhaps rather optimistically argue might restore a high-wage, high-skill yet full employment growth dynamic to the British economy. Specific proposals concentrate on reform of the traditional, and now profoundly pathological, relationship between the City of London, the Bank of England, and the Treasury; a relationship that has seen economic policy consistently favoring financial over industrial interests. In particular, its advocates favor systematic reform of the law governing institutional investors (such as pension funds) to secure a dedicated supply of long-term productive indigenous investment, as well as a complex repertoire of national and regional investment banks and development agencies.[85]

The second strand of literature is rather different in its emphasis, concentrating on multilateral strategies to reregulate the financial markets through the imposition of capital controls. Advocates of such a response to a *politically* engendered financial liberalization draw upon and develop proposals for a Tobin-style tax designed to throw "sand in the wheels of international finance."[86] Amongst those who regard such a transfer tax as desirable, there is considerable controversy about the feasibility and practicality of such a measure. In particular, skeptics argue that the effectiveness of a regime of extensive cooperative controls (even if the political will for such controls could be established) is, in a context of very rapid financial innovation, at best likely to be partial and temporary.[87] Nonetheless, as Eric Helleiner notes,

> The objective is not to stop every international financial transfer but rather to limit the bulk of them. . . . [T]he globalization trend would certainly not be nearly as extensive nor would it have proceeded so rapidly if a regime of either cooperative controls . . . or tight unilateral exchange controls had been in place during the previous three decades.[88]

Our own view is that, so long as they are not revered as the ultimate panacea to all economic ills, such measures are indeed feasible. Moreover, it is also likely that there could be an increasing amount of political will to *make* them still more feasible as ever-intensifying speculation threatens yet further currencies and exposes as vulnerable continued U.S. growth, which is grounded in ever expanding asset prices on Wall Street. In addition, such measures are necessary if the deflationary pressures of the 1980s and early 1990s are to be reversed; certainly given the recent emergence of external conditions that have seen systemic demand under pressure in markets throughout East Asia as well as in various "emerging" markets in South America and Eastern Europe.

Ultimately, then, these are political rather than technical issues. We are confronted, then, with a clear *political* choice; there is no logic of economic necessity here.

A continued and unquestioned belief in globalization's logic of no alternative can only threaten to make what is now contingent a future necessity. As Peter Evans notes, "The danger is not that states will end up as marginal institutions but that meaner, more repressive ways of organizing the state's role will be accepted as the only way of avoiding the collapse of public institutions."[89] The stakes of the globalization debate could scarcely be higher.

NOTES

1. Frances F. Piven, "Is It Global Economics or Neo-Laissez Faire?" *New Left Review* 213 (1995): 108.

2. Linda Weiss, "Globalisation and the Myth of a Powerless State," *New Left Review* 225 (1997): 126.

3. Adam Przeworski and Michael Wallerstein, "Structural Dependence of the State on Capital," *American Political Science Review* 82 (1988): 11–29.

4. Przeworski and Wallerstein, "Structural Dependence," 12.

5. Mark Wickham-Jones, "Anticipating Social Democracy, Preempting Anticipations: Economic Policy-Making in the British Labour Party, 1987–1992," *Politics and Society* 23 (1995): 465–94; and Mark Wickham-Jones, "The Ties That Bind: Blair's Search for Business Credibility," unpublished manuscript (Bristol, UK: University of Bristol, Department of Politics, 1996).

6. See, for instance, Przeworski and Wallerstein, "Structural Dependence," 14–15, 20–21.

7. Eric Helleiner, "Explaining the Globalization of Financial Markets: Bringing States Back In," *Review of International Political Economy* 2 (1995): 315–41.

8. Tony Blair, Speech to Singapore Business Community, January 8, 1996.

9. Matthew Watson, "Globalisation and the Development of the British Political Economy," in D. Marsh et al., eds., *Postwar British Politics in Perspective* (Cambridge: Polity, 1999).

10. D. Laidler, "Wage and Price Stickiness: Historical Perspective," in F. Capie and G. Wood, eds., *Monetary Economics in the 1990s* (London: Macmillan, 1996).

11. Colin Hay, "Negotiating International Constraints: The Antinomies of Credibility and Competitiveness in the Political Economy of New Labour," *Competition and Change* (2001).

12. Robin Cook, speech to the Institute of European Affairs, Dublin, November 3, 1997.

13. For an elaboration of such an ontological position see Colin Hay, "Continuity and Discontinuity in British Political Development," in D. Marsh et al., eds., *Postwar British Politics in Perspective* (Cambridge: Polity, 1999); and Colin Hay and Daniel Wincott, "Structure, Agency and Historical Institutionalism," *Political Studies* 46 (1998): 951–57.

14. Piven, "Is It Global Economics or *Laissez Faire?*"; Helleiner, "Explaining the Globalization of Financial Markets"; Weiss, "Globalization and the Myth," esp. 20, 23; and Peter Evans, "The Eclipse of the State? Reflections on Stateness in an Era of Globalization," *World Politics* 50 (1997): 62–87.

15. Tony Blair, speech to party workers, Royal Festival Hall, London, May 2, 1997.

16. Tony Blair, speech to Singapore Business Community, January 8, 1997.

17. Gordon Brown, speech to CBI Annual Conference, Harrogate, November 11, 1996.

18. Tony Blair, speech to the BDI Annual Conference, Bonn, June 18, 1996.

19. Colin Hay, *The Political Economy of New Labour: Labouring under False Pretences?* (Manchester: Manchester University Press, 1999), chap. 1.

20. *Sunday Times*, interview with Tony Blair, September 1, 1996.

21. Lionel Jospin, speech to the Congress of Socialist Parties, Malmo, June 6, 1997.

22. Tony Blair, *Socialism* (London: Fabian Society, 1994).

23. Gordon Brown, speech to the Labour Party Finance and Industry Group, May 17, 1995; emphasis added.

24. Tony Blair, speech to the BDI, Bonn, June 18, 1996.

25. Anthony Giddens, *The Third Way: The Renewal of Social Democracy* (Cambridge: Polity, 1998).

26. Robin Cook, speech to the Institute of European Affairs, November 3, 1997.

27. Peter Mandelson and Richard Liddle, *The Blair Revolution: Can New Labour Deliver?* (London: Faber, 1996), 17.

28. Tony Blair, speech to the Lord Mayor's Banquet, Guildhall, November 10, 1997.

29. Labour Party, *It's Time to Get Britain Working Again: Election Manifesto* (London: Labour Party, 1992), 11.

30. Tony Blair, speech to the BDI, June 18, 1996.

31. Gordon Brown, speech to the Labour Party Finance and Industry Group, May 17, 1995.

32. Tony Blair, speech to the BDI, June 18, 1996.

33. Gordon Brown, speech to the CBI Annual Conference, November 11, 1996.

34. Gordon Brown, press conference, reported on BBC TV, April 28, 1997.

35. Tony Blair, Mais Lecture, May 22, 1995.

36. Gordon Brown, cited in Eric Shaw, "The Trajectory of New Labour: Some Preliminary Thoughts," paper presented at the American Political Science Association annual conference, Washington, D.C., 1997.

37. Tony Blair, speech to the Singapore Business Community, January 8, 1996.

38. John Eatwell, cited in Wickham-Jones, "The Ties That Bind."

39. *Daily Telegraph*, May 7, 1997.

40. Both cited in *Financial Times*, May 7, 1995.

41. See Gordon Brown's letter to the Governor of the Bank of England, Eddie George, explaining the decision to depoliticize interest rate policy, transcribed in full, in *Financial Times*, May 7, 1997.

42. Riccardo Petrella, "Globalization and Internationalization: The Dynamics of the Emerging World Order," in R. Boyer and D. Drache, eds., *States against Markets: The Limits of Globalisation* (London: Routledge, 1996), 62.

43. Tony Blair, speech to the BDI, June 18, 1996.

44. Bob Jessop, "Towards a Schumpeterian Workfare State? Preliminary Remarks on Post-Fordist Political Economy Studies," *Lancaster Papers in Political Economy* 40 (1993): 5.

45. Labour Industry Forum, *Winning for Britain* (London: Labour Party, 1996), 2.

46. White Paper, *Competitiveness: Forging Ahead, Cm 2867* (London: HMSO, 1996).

47. Gordon Brown, interview with the *Financial Times*, May 7, 1997.

48. Gordon Brown, speech to Labour Finance and Industry Group, May 17, 1995.

49. Matthew Watson, "Globalisation and the Development"; and Bob Jessop, "Changing Forms and Functions of the State in an Era of Globalisation and Regionalisation," in R. Delorme and F. Dopfer, eds., *The Political Economy of Diversity: Evolutionary Perspectives on Economic Order and Disorder* (London: Edward Elgar, 1994).

50. Labour Party, *Building Prosperity: Flexibility, Efficiency and Fairness at Work, Road to the Manifesto Document* (London: Labour Party, 1996), 1.

51. Robin Cook, speech to the Institute of European Affairs, November 3, 1997.

52. Matthew Watson, "International Capital Mobility in an Era of Globalisation: Adding a Political Dimension to the 'Feldstein-Horioka Puzzle,'" *Politics* 21 (2001): 82–93.

53. Tony Blair, statement to the House of Commons on the European Council meeting, Amsterdam, June 18, 1997.

54. Nikolas Rose, "The Death of the Social? Re-Figuring the Territory of Government," *Economy and Society* 25 (1996): 354.

55. *The Observer*, November 17, 1996.

56. L. Budd, "Globalization and the Crisis of the Territorial Embeddedness of International Financial Markets," in R. Martin, ed., *Money and the Space Economy* (Chichester, UK: John Wiley, 1999).

57. Daniel Drache, "From Keynes to K-Mart: Competitiveness in a Corporate Age," in R. Boyer and D. Drache, eds., *States against Markets: The Limits of Globalisation* (London: Routledge, 1996); and K. Cox, "Globalization and the Politics of Distribution: A Critical Assessment," and M. Meric Gertler, "Between the Global and the Local: The Spatial Limits to Productive Capital," both in K. Cox, ed., *Spaces of Globalisation* (New York: Guilford Press, 1997).

58. Colin Hay, "Anticipating Accommodations, Accommodating Anticipations: The Appeasement of Capital in the Modernisation of the British Labour Party, 1987–1992," *Politics and Society* 25 (1997): 243; and R. Wade, "Globalisation and Its Limits: Reports of the Death of the National Economy Are Greatly Exaggerated," in R. Boyer and D. Drache, eds., *States against Markets*.

59. R. Harrington, "Financial Innovation and International Banking," in H. Cavanna, ed., *Financial Innovation* (London: Routledge, 1992); and S. Bonetti and D. Cobham, "Financial Markets and the City of London," in D. Cobham, ed., *Markets and Dealers: The Economics of the London Financial Markets* (Harlow, UK: Longman, 1992).

60. Gugelielmo Cardechi, "Financial Crisis, Recessions and Value Theory," *Review of International Political Economy* 3 (1996): 529.

61. Matthew Watson, "Re-thinking Capital Mobility, Reregulating Financial Markets," *New Political Economy* 4 (1999): 55–75.

62. Robert O'Brien, *Global Financial Integration: The End of Geography* (London: Pinter, 1992), 1; and G. Epstein, "International Capital Mobility and the Scope for National Economic Management," in R. Boyer and D. Drache, eds., *States against Markets*; and Geoffrey Garrett, "Capital Mobility, Trade and the Domestic Politics of Economic Policy," *International Organisation* 49 (1995): 657–87.

63. Jan Aart Scholte, "Beyond the Buzzword: Towards a Critical Theory of Globalisation," in E. Kofman and G. Youngs, eds., *Globalization: Theory and Practice* (London: Pinter, 1996).

64. A. Busch, "Unpacking the Globalization Debate: Approaches, Data and Evidence," in C. Hay and D. Marsh, eds., *Demystifying Globalisation* (Basingstoke, UK: Palgrave, 2000); and B. Steil, "Effective Public Policy in a World of Footloose Finance," in *International Financial Market Regulation* (London: John Wiley, 1994).

65. Piven, "Is It Global Economics or Neo-Laissez Faire?" 111.

66. Weiss, "Globalisation and the Myth," 7.

67. R. Wade, "Globalisation and Its Limits," in R. Boyer and D. Drache, eds., *States against Markets*; and J. A. Frankel, *Regional Trading Blocs in the World Economic System* (Washington, D.C.: Institute for International Economics, 1997).

68. P. Hirst, "The Global Market and the Possibilities of Governance," paper presented to the conference on *Globalisation: Critical Perspectives*, University of Birmingham, March 14–16, 1997, 8.

69. Calculated from Michael Chisholm, *Britain on the Edge of Europe* (London: Routledge, 1995), 15.

70. K. Griffin and A. R. Khan, "Globalisation and the Developing World: An Essay on the International Dimension of Developments in the Post–Cold War Era," *Human Development Report Occasional Papers*, New York: United Nations Development Programme/ Human Development Report Office, 1992.

71. P. Bairoch, "Globalisation Myths and Realities: One Century of External Trade and Foreign Investment," in R. Boyer and D. Drache, eds., *States against Markets*, 183.

72. P. Krugman, "History and Industry Location: The Case of the Manufacturing Belt," *American Economic Review* 81 (1991): 80–83.

73. See, in particular, P. Hirst and G. Thompson, *Globalisation in Question*, 2nd ed. (Cambridge: Polity, 1999).

74. Bairoch, "Globalisation Myths and Realities," 188.

75. Matthew Watson, "The Changing Face of Macroeconomic Stabilisation: From Growth through Indigenous Investment to Growth through Inward Investment?" in J. Stanyer and G. Stoker, eds., *Contemporary Political Studies 1997* (Oxford: Blackwell/ PSA, 1997).

76. Hirst, "The Global Market," 8.

77. R. Zevin, "Are Financial Markets More Open? If So, Why and with What Effects?" in T. Banuri and J. Schor, eds., *Financial Openness and National Autonomy* (Oxford: Oxford University Press, 1992).

78. Wade, "Globalisation and Its Limits."

79. T. Bayoumi, *Financial Integration and Real Activity* (Manchester, UK: Manchester University Press, 1997).

80. M. Feldstein and C. Horioka, "Domestic Saving and International Capital Flows," *The Economic Journal* 90 (1980): 14–29; G. Garrett, "Capital Mobility, Trade and the Domestic Politics of Economic Policy," *International Organisation* 49 (1995), 657–87; and

J. A. Frankel, "Quantifying International Capital Mobility in the 1980s," in *On Exchange Rates* (Cambridge, Mass.: MIT Press, 1993).

81. "Capital Goes Global," *The Economist,* October 25, 1997.

82. John Allen and Grahame Thompson, "Think Globally, Then Think Again— Economic Globalization in Context," *Area* 29 (1997): 213–27, esp. 214.

83. Matthew Watson, "Adopting and Appropriating Conservative Common-Sense," unpublished paper, University of Birmingham, 1999.

84. Colin Hay, "Anticipating Accommodations, Accommodating Anticipations: The Appeasement of Capital in the Modernisation of the British Labour Party, 1987–1992," *Politics and Society* 25 (1997): 234–56; and L. Panitch and C. Leys, *The End of Parliamentary Socialism* (London: Verso, 1997), esp. 262–71.

85. Colin Hay, *The Political Economy of New Labour: Labouring under False Pretences?* (Manchester, UK: Manchester University Press, 1999), chap. 6.

86. B. Eichengreen, J. Tobin, and C. Wyplosz, "Two Cases for Sand in the Wheels of International Finance," *The Economic Journal* 105 (1995): 162–72; J. Tobin, "A Proposal for International Monetary Reform," *The Eastern Economic Journal* 4 (1978): 153–59; Y. Akyüz and C. Cornford, "International Capital Movements: Some Proposals for Reform," in J. Michie and J. G. Smith, eds., *Managing the Global Economy* (Oxford: Oxford University Press, 1995).

87. P. Garber and M. P. Taylor, "Sand in the Wheels of Foreign Exchange Markets: A Skeptical Note," *The Economic Journal* 105 (1995): 173–80; G. Albo, "A World Market of Opportunities? Capitalist Obstacles and Left Economic Policy," in L. Panitch, ed., *The Socialist Register 1997* (London: Merlin, 1997); J. Goodman and P. Pauly, "The Obsolescence of Capital Controls? Economic Management in an Age of Global Markets," *World Politics* 46 (1993): 50–82; and S. Strange, *Casino Capitalism,* 2nd ed. (Manchester, UK: Manchester University Press, 1997).

88. E. Helleiner, "Explaining the Globalization of Financial Markets," 338.

89. P. Evans, "The Eclipse of the State? Reflections on Stateness in an Era of Globalisation," *World Politics* 50 (1997): 64.

7

⁂

The Changing Political Economy of France

Dirigisme *under Duress*

BEN CLIFT

Contemporary developments at the national, and indeed European, level can only be understood in the context of an ascendant transnational neoliberalism. Structural developments have reinforced shifts at the ideological level, shifting incentives structures in a manner consistent with the priorities of neoliberalism as a "constructive project" (see chapter 1). The previous chapter began to explore in more detail how these shifting structures play themselves out in mass politics with reference to British New Labour. This chapter continues to explore this dynamic with reference to the French case, where, due to a more statist and Republican tradition, neoliberalism encounters more resistance.

The pressures in question have fundamentally altered key aspects of the French model, and significantly hemmed in the French state's *volontariste* potentialities. Neoliberalism as a project interacted with the French state apparatus, characterized by a *dirigiste* model that suffered from partial internal dysfunctionalities in the 1970s, rooted in the misallocation of funds that owed more to political expediency than economic strategy. These problems were exacerbated by the emergence of a neoliberal "deconstructive project" that sought to explain problems facing the French model in terms of a neoliberal analytical and prescriptive framework (see chapter 1) whose a priori superiority was asserted over both Keynesian and *dirigiste* paradigms.

It is not inconceivable that restructuring could have occurred, over time, *within* the extant French model. Indeed, the Mauroy government after 1981 was initially strongly committed to *dirigisme*. However, neoliberalism as a "deconstructive project" powerfully influenced how the difficulties faced by the French model in an adverse international economic climate were interpreted. Affirming the thesis as formulated in previous chapters, with reference to the French state apparatus, the neoliberal ideological agenda dovetailed with domestic impetus for change among key "conservative liberal" administrative elites within the (increasingly empowered) Tresor and Banque de France.

The dynamics of French neoliberal restructuring were conditioned by the results of the partial dysfunctionality of the model, notably the cavernous trade gap and the serious balance of payments problems. This created powerful external pressures, and underlined the mismatch with a changing international economic context that undermined the French model, contributing as it did to a fiscal crisis of the French state. This was exacerbated by funds being diverted to defending the franc against repeated speculation. Deregulated financial markets did not deem the *dirigiste* policies of the Mitterrand experiment sustainable or credible, and their structural and disciplinary power as discussed in previous chapters constrained the French Socialist government. The only way of regaining a degree of economic policy autonomy, it was felt, was by securing financial credibility—the linchpin of French monetary policy regime after the 1983 decision. This was achieved through an emulation of German monetary arrangements, which concretized the shift from neoliberalism as a constructive project to its consolidation phase. After 1983, the French Socialist governments' desire to facilitate European construction and shift the macroeconomic framework consistent with European priorities was reinforced by the structural constraints of the international political economic context, and by budgetary constraints.

Thus focusing only at national and EU levels cannot provide an adequate explanation of France's evolution and the nature of its advocacy of the EU project. This change in conditions coincided with changing priorities of a policy elite. European construction presented an opportunity for evolution, but the collective action conditions under which this could proceed were predicated upon German Ordo-liberalism. The coincidence with the domestic priorities of conservative liberals engendered a particular reading of the implications of changed conditions in the international political economy. This locked in the neoliberal path of development, "normalizing" it in the Foucauldian sense.

European integration, however, remained a contested process. Resistance to the neoliberalism was graphically demonstrated in the public sector strikes of 1995. Given the new constraints imposed by changed international economic context, French Socialists attempted to build on this resistance, conceiving European economic integration and EMU as a long-run game. Accommodation of the German model was sought, on the understanding that increased influence once European integration advanced would offer more scope for moving the goalposts in the direction of growth, employment, and a more creative role for fiscal policy. Bérégovoy, like other French Socialists, saw Ordo-liberalism as a necessary means to achieve European integration, and thence, eventually, to recover Keynesian economic sovereignty.

There was also an element of ideological conversion to the constructive project of neoliberalism on the part of Socialist elites in the vigor with which they "tied themselves to the mast" of competitive disinflation, involving austerity, a strong currency, and balanced budgets in the context of high and rising structural unemployment. The restructuring of the French financial system, furthermore, was seen by key actors such as Delors as a means of relieving the burden of industrial financing from an overburdened state. The attendant loss of strategic influence was deemed a price worth paying.

This highlights the interaction of international external constraints with a shift in the domestic microeconomic policy agenda. This aspect of the French model displays a much more direct European-level influence on developments. The U.S.–influenced antitrust, anti-*dirigiste* bias of the neoliberal Single European Act (SEA) and its competition regulation, policed by the Commission, have blunted some of the French model's traditional policy instruments. Illustrating the interaction of domestic European and transnational factors still further, the liberalization of France's financial markets, and the resultant inflow and outflow of foreign direct investment, further undermined *dirigiste* policy mechanisms, and increased the influence of Anglo-Saxon norms on French corporate governance.

The first section sets out the core features of the French model. This is followed by a section exploring the macroeconomic policy dimensions of the French model's accommodation to neoliberalism. Domestic political support for the project amongst key policy elites for post-1983 "competitive disinflation," Ordo-liberalism, and EMU is placed in the context of a changing international political economy. The mounting opposition to the neoliberal, monetarist foundations of EMU in the mid-1990s then provide the context for analysis of attempts by the Jospin government to reconcile this neoliberal bias to the French social model and social democratic aspirations for the euro area. Thus, in macroeconomic terms, while elements of the French model endure, notably aspirations for the political direction of macro policy toward the goals of jobs and growth, the model faces tighter constraints than previously. The anti-inflationary sound money and balanced budget model set in marble at Maastricht bars Keynesian counter-cyclical policy.

The chapter then explores the microeconomic dimensions of the French model's evolution. Here the SEA and financial deregulation hinder traditional French mechanisms of state influence over industry. However, while state allocated credit has largely disappeared from the *dirigiste* arsenal, public procurement and protection of key sectors (such as energy) have proved more resilient. Quiescence to neoliberalism was challenged with increasing vigor in the Jospin era, particularly in the field of the *services publiques*. Some limited *dirigiste* "policy space" still exists, but new techniques must be developed to pursue quasi-*dirigiste* strategies.

THE FRENCH MODEL AND ITS CRISIS

The *dirigiste* French model, underpinned by the Republican state tradition, was predicated upon a set of coordinating and steering mechanisms in the postwar era. The policy mechanisms included, firstly, price, credit, and exchange controls; and *tutelle* (or hands-on supervision) over key (public and private) industries, involving

> an intricate network of commitments on the part of private firms. . . all in return for favours from the state . . . [and] the habit of the exercise of power by public officials over the private sector of the economy.[1]

The final element was state orchestration of industrial finance through *le commissariat du Plan*. In addition to the "economy of administered finance," a further characteristic of this French model was that the state had difficulty controlling the growth of credit, and thus of inflation. This inflationary pressure was compounded by "the consensual refusal of the state, the trade unions, and the employers to control nominal changes in incomes and prices."[2]

Central to France's *dirigiste* interventionism was the state's role in providing funds for industrial investment.[3] The state's centrality to the system of "institutionally allocated credit" from private and public banks gave the French state extraordinary leverage, acting as gatekeeper to strategic, cheap capital. State loans tended to be conditional upon meeting specific restructuring targets, incorporating subsidiaries into parent companies, or merging with other big firms. After 1971, the French government's complex credit rationing scheme (*encadrement du crédit*) controlled the direction of financial flows, but left many areas of the French economy undercapitalized and hindered the development of capital markets.

It was not that administered credit system *could* not work, but that capital allocation in France in the 1970s did not always display the logic and virtues highlighted by Zysman.[4] Often state funds did not feed a dynamic industrial core, but delayed layoffs and restructuring in industries whose collapse was deemed too politically costly in the short term. The problem became acute in the wake of the 1974 industrial crisis; the chronic lack of investment in many areas led the French economy to be caricatured as "capitalism without capital."[5] As we shall see later, these problems were compounded by a growing fiscal crisis of the French state, leading many to question whether the French state could afford to play its traditional role, *even if* it could be done effectively.

France's *dirigiste* model of economic policy making in the postwar era was predicated upon "embedded liberalism" as discussed by Gill in chapter 2. This context, and the "competitive devaluations" and levels of state spending and state debt it permitted, were a necessary condition of the success of France's "inflationist social compromise."[6] As that system unraveled amidst the Nixon shock, oil crises, and advancing liberalization and deregulation in the 1970s, it necessitated a realignment of France's engagement with the international economic order. This realignment underwent fairly radical shifts in direction between 1976 and 1983, but after the latter date the essential contours were set and have become the de facto parameters of all subsequent governments.

After Bretton Woods collapsed and deregulation gained momentum, governments have found themselves constrained to pursue tight monetary policies in order to avoid incurring a "risk premium" imposed on borrowing by investors suspicious of potentially inflationary macroeconomic stances. Increased capital mobility has structurally empowered investors vis-à-vis governments because, under deregulated conditions, holders of currency and securities denominated in domestic currency (government bonds, bank deposits, or corporate stocks) have many more exit options and lower exit costs than before. Thus, on a global level, the changing international political economy of the 1970s and 1980s presaged a shift away from the French model of the 1950s and 1960s. Furthermore, international financial liberalization rendered the *dirigiste* approach (*encadrement du crédit*) increasingly unworkable.[7] This culminated in the monetary policy-making system being overhauled, phasing out of the *encadrement du crédit* in favor of open market operations, and Banque de France manipulation of interest rates as a means of controlling the money supply.

Focusing only at national and EU levels cannot provide an adequate explanation of France's evolution and the nature of its advocacy of the EU project, since that ignores a transnational neoliberal orthodoxy that shaped both European and French developments. As Lordon notes of the 1983 U-turn,

> This major shift, in fact, corresponds to the acknowledgement by the Socialists of the new rules of opened and internationalized economies. . . . The 1983 decision was grounded on a strong—even if somewhat fuzzy—European commitment, based on an acceptance of the evolution of the world economy.[8]

As the Parti Socialiste's *Projet socialiste* put it, "Socialism . . . is developing at the heart of a globalized capitalism which today restricts our vision, but not our will to act."[9] Ever since the U-turn of 1983, the "external constraints" of international economic context have become commonplace in French policy discourse. However, there has been evolution in how those external constraints are constructed, or conceived, and in the policy implications that flow from them. As we shall see, competitive disinflation and EMU were two versions of a similar construction—known as *la pensée unique*—but there were other voices.

PENSÉE UNIQUE AND VOLONTARISME: DISCOURSES
AND PRACTICE OF "NECESSARY" ADJUSTMENT

The impact of the new international political economy on the French model can only be discerned by appreciating how these structural mechanisms interacted with ideological developments. Some have sought to present the changes heralded by French economic integration within the EU as "internalizing" the external economic "imperatives" of globalization. From a critical political economy perspective, this requires qualification. What was at hand was the internalizing of *one interpretation* of such imperatives. In the French case, this vision was most explicitly distilled by Alain Minc—France's most famous neoliberal hyperglobal thinker, propagating neoliberalism as a constructive project. Howarth notes how "the EMU project has been an explicitly manipulated driving force behind financial market liberalization, budgetary, fiscal and welfare state, administrative and labour market reforms—most prominently in the 1994 Minc report."[10]

Minc epitomizes *la pensée unique*, the French translation of a hyperglobal[11] neoliberal model, which claims that "there is nothing to be done" but accept the free play of global economic forces. According to critics, the process of European construction in the Single European Act and preparation of Maastricht phases was used as a means of framing *that* vision of globalization. Furthermore, this vision was presented as a neutral mechanism, involving a purely technical debate, largely abstracted from the ideological position that underpinned it. In the 1990s, debate within the Socialist party—and beyond—explicitly rejected *this* "technical" view of economic policy making and European integration built on monetarist assumptions about the role of government, the primacy of sound money and finances and free markets, and the overriding importance of tackling inflation above all other economic ills.

In 1993, the Socialist Party Conference final text observed of the 1983 U-turn that

> this choice did not instigate an authentic economic policy debate concerning the use of the available room to manoeuvre. . . . As a result, we were too ready to believe that the economy was not a matter of politics but rather of technical management.[12]

The party's 1997 election manifesto reprised these themes. The Parti Socialiste, or PS, under Jospin became increasingly critical of the neoliberal agenda, seeking a more preponderant role for the state, in particular in generating employment security and protecting cherished public services and welfare provision. In macroeconomic policy, "monetarist" myopic concentration on inflation rates has been sidelined, but there was no return to calls for state-led reflation, and the PS remain committed to deficit reduction, sound public finances, and price stability, all needed to secure financial credibility. These commitments reflect both changed economic realities in the global economy (see later in this chapter), but they are also justified in terms of the "long game" that French Socialists are playing in seeking to create a Euro-Keynesian economic space as a context for national policy activism.

This more critical engagement with the notion of the economic imperatives of globalization was foregrounded by Prime Minister Jospin's own evaluation[13] and the distinctively French take on the economic realities of a globalizing world characterized by a dominant neoliberal economic paradigm. Jospin couched this skepticism about liberal orthodoxy in "realist" terms. His "conceiving of the real" sought to discern the extent to which realism is distorted by neoliberal economic thought; thus concepts such as "economic realism" cannot be taken at face value, but must be interrogated.[14] This was reiterated when Jospin asserted, "If . . . the Third Way involves finding a middle way between social democracy and neoliberalism, then this approach is not mine."[15] This problematic was at the heart of the critiques of economic policies in the later Bérégovoy era, and it explains the increasing propensity to criticize the view of economic management as a technocratic pursuit.

Jospin's worldview insisted upon a *volontariste* state and the endurance of relatively generous welfare provision. Securing financial credibility through sound public finances and price stability *were* seen as imperatives of economic policy making in the contemporary international economic context. However, within these limits, they are much more convinced of the existence of "room to maneuver." The Socialists were more inclined to countenance demand-side activism, and indeed advocate and pursue activist state policies in a number of fields to try and boost employment.[16]

The PS under Jospin had a particular reading of the implications of globalization for social democratic economic strategy—*Réalisme de Gauche*. This rejected the orthodox assumption that "there is no alternative," as Cole and Drake put it: "The Jospin Government has insisted upon the need to protect the so-called European social model, under attack from neoliberalism and the invisible forces of globalization."[17] We will explore these changes within the cognitive framework, in particular how attempts have been made to bolt more social democratic aspirations onto the fundamentally neoliberal institutional framework of EMU.

Importing Ordo-liberal Credibility

We need not delve into the ins and outs of that regime-defining choice of 1983 here—it has been done admirably well elsewhere.[18] However, the strategic choice as construed by key actors such as Bérégovoy is instructive, revealing as it does the pervasive influence of an Ordo-liberal variant of neoliberal ideology (see the next chapter) on the cognitive frameworks of policy elites in the formulation of the choice of 1983.[19] The strategy of action—which pairs goals to available means within the key actor's cognitive framework[20]—offered a stark choice. On the one hand was the so-called Albanian solution, the *dirigiste* and protectionist *autre politique*, and on the other a European and Ordo-liberal solution, accepting EMS conditions for revaluation, and a distinctly German-influenced conception of what constituted sound macroeconomic policy, and indeed macropolicymaking institutions.[21]

This was a pivotal moment in the direction of French economic policy paradigm, the nature of engagement with the international economic context, and construction of, "external constraints." Once the decision to remain part of the EMS was taken, the "appropriate" path of development was conceived in very narrow Ordo-liberal terms, despite the absence in France of the wider framework of (corporatist) institutions upon which German Ordo-liberalism is predicated.

It is also important to note the at least partial congruence of external pressures for reform along neoliberal lines, and priorities of sectors of French policy elites, notably in the treasury section of the Finance Ministry and in the Banque de France. Recalling the "consolidation phase" of neoliberal restructuring (see chapter 1), Cohen sees the EMU project as the outcome of "a cartel of national administrative elites, sanctioned by politicians, who sought to 'naturalize' the demands of structural adjustment by invoking the European constraint."[22] Dyson insists upon the domestic as well as international origins of the prevalent economic orthodoxy enshrined in the Maastricht convergence criteria: "EMU can be seen as empowering Finance Ministry and Banque de France technocrats and rejuvenating and modernizing a domestic tradition of conservative liberalism that always been powerful in these two institutions."[23]

However, although the post-1983 policy choices were conceived in fairly narrow terms, it is important to distinguish in the French context between neoliberalism *pur et dur* and conservative liberalism within the French financial and administrative elite associated with the Tresor and Banque de France. According to Howarth, conservative liberals

> uphold the self-adjusting nature of the market mechanisms and reject state-led reflation. They seek exchange rate stability, low inflation, balanced budgets, and commercial and balance of payments surpluses . . . [and to] import German "sound" money policies and budget and wage discipline.[24]

The most significant dissonance for our discussion between French "conservative liberals" and full-blown neoliberalism is an attachment to a welfare state (with spending restrictions) and in general a more equivocal commitment to free markets and some residual *dirigiste* instincts.

At the root of this is the concern for some controls of free markets, given the potential social impact of the free play of market forces. French conservative liberals retain an attachment to a *dirigiste* state sustained by the French Republican tradition, which marks them out from German Ordo-liberals, who see the social market as being secured by the social partners more than by the state. As a technocratic doctrine, conservative liberalism is much more enthused by the importance, significance, and relevance of the expertise of state actors in managing economic and social policy than Ordo-liberalism would normally countenance.[25]

Dyson and Howarth are correct to insist that this, rather than full-blown neoliberalism, was the dominant ideology of financial and administrative elites in France, and provided the foundations of the cognitive framework through which the preparations for the EMU project were framed. However, what difference this distinction made on the impact of Ordo-liberalism and EMU on French politics and the French model is less clear-cut. The context in which the transition toward stage three of EMU occurred—of prolonged economic downturn and soaring public deficits—greatly reduced the ability to reconcile the apparently contradictory commitments *within* conservative liberalism. The less ambiguously neoliberal bottom line of the Maastricht criteria prioritized deficit reduction over welfare protection, the need for receipts from privatization favored advocacy of free markets over *dirigisme*. Furthermore, budget restrictions, allied to a wider neoliberal bias of the Single European Act (see later in this chapter), hemmed in the interventionist role of the state that conservative liberals favored.

This is why the ideational distinction between conservative liberalism and neoliberalism did not feed through into policy differences in the short to medium term. For example, Finance Minister (later Prime Minister) Bérégovoy was not conservative liberal, let alone a neoliberal, yet he mutated from a staunch left-wing proponent of *l'autre politique*[26] to the ultra-orthodox voice of neoliberal reason once installed as minister of finance. Bérégovoy, like other French Socialists involved in the 1983 decisions to adopt Ordo-liberalism, was committed to it as a necessary means to achieve European integration. The necessary accommodation to the German model was embraced on the understanding that increased influence once European integration advanced, and once eventually EMU was in place, might offer more scope for moving the goalposts. The French Socialists saw European economic integration and EMU as a long-run game.

Bérégovoy, like other French Socialists, saw Ordo-liberalism as a necessary means to achieve European integration, the endgame of which would, eventually, involve the recovery of Keynesian economic sovereignty at the supranational level. This perhaps explains the paradox reportedly noted by Mitterrand, "Why does he [Bérégovoy] let himself get swallowed by those people at Finance? When I see him, he's very much on the Left, when he writes to me, he's worse than Raymond Barre."[27] It was Bérégovoy who personally insisted on the criteria that public deficits should not exceed 3 percent of GDP,[28] a cause of such chagrin to the PS in the mid-1990s. The reason for this was not ideological conviction of the rectitude of neoliberal doctrine, but the overriding need to secure credibility with financial markets at all costs, having experienced firsthand the price to be paid for perceived financial profligacy in the 1981–1983 period.[29]

Competitive Disinflation

The causes of the paradigm shift in what French analysts call the *référential*—a doctrinal corpus or model of the world shared by political and administrative elites—from *dirigiste* macroeconomic framework and credit rationing to the market and rules-based Ordo-liberal regime span the domestic, European, and global dimensions, as outlined earlier in this chapter. The desire to facilitate European construction and shift the macroeconomic framework consistent with European priorities were reinforced by domestic priorities and budgetary constraints. Given the French state's severe lack of funds, it needed to find a new means of meeting its restructuring needs. As Cohen notes,

> Once the new government [in 1981] had emerged from its euphoria and faced up to the financial needs of an industrial apparatus weakened by 10 years of imposed restructuring, it realized that it had rapidly to allow nationalized companies to reenter the financial markets.[30]

This became all the more urgent when funds were diverted to defending the franc against repeated speculation.

The period 1981–1983 displayed an incompatibility with the changed international economic context. After 1983, the French response to this changed context, competitive disinflation, was to an extent a reflection of changed economic realities. It also reflected the singular reading of the implications of such changed realities of an elite in the capture of the *pensée unique*, the new economic orthodoxy. The overall aim was a fundamental departure from the traditional French model, bringing the pressures of market competitiveness explicitly to bear on an increasing number of social and economic actors.[31]

The logic of competitive disinflation is simple: "Under fixed exchange rates, a country with higher inflation loses competitiveness, and as a result demand for output falls. An increase in unemployment follows which makes inflation decrease sufficiently so that competitiveness is eventually reestablished."[32] The strategy was a crucial determinant of all aspects of economic policy from 1983 onwards. Competitive disinflation comprised three elements. The first was the nominal stability of the *franc fort*, pegged to the DM. The second was wage restraint and wage discipline, initially through a deindexation of wages, which aimed to tackle inflation and also to shift added value from labor to capital, improving profitability (and investment). The third priority was public deficit reduction, aiming both to bolster financial credibility and lower risk premia, and also to reduce "crowding out" effects, thus supposedly lowering interest rates.[33]

Competitive devaluation, and its attendant "moral hazard" problems, had been removed, and, as Lordon notes, "The publicly known restrictive orientations of monetary policy, which ceased to be accommodating, may have worked as a strong incentive on all social groups to radically change their price setting behaviour."[34] Restructuring and adjustment were achieved through market mechanisms, with firms obliged to pay extremely close attention to their costs and prices. Labor costs, the "social wage," and unemployment became the adjustment mechanisms. Indeed, Lordon goes so far as to claim that competitive disinflation "is not an economic policy, but reduces to the working of endogenous market adjustments."[35] Unemployment was transformed after 1983 from one of the main priorities of economic policy into the principle anti-inflationary tool and adjustment mechanism of the troubled French economy, about which the government tacitly accepted it could do little.

Competitive disinflation "worked" in the sense that credibility was eventually restored, and competitiveness of French firms improved in the 1990s. However, the myriad weaknesses, blind spots, and flaws at the theoretical level of this doctrine became all too apparent—not least the unrealistic expectations of interest rate reduction and its effects, and the soaring profitability, flagging investment, and low wages that generated a prolonged crisis of underconsumption. Weaknesses are perhaps more amply demonstrated at the practical level. The impact of competitive disinflation is more damningly demonstrated by its impact on French economy and society in the fifteen years following the U-turn, which saw structural unemployment rocket.[36]

Austerity dampened demand, and high interest rates discouraged productive investment. In the context of a downturn, the market medicine central to the competitive disinflation regime in many cases killed the patient. Persistent high unemployment produced "hysteresis" effects, with low activity and slow capital accumulation triggering bankruptcies and destroying productive capacity. The recovery process faltered, and the "natural" rate of structural unemployment was ratcheted up. This scenario obtained between 1983, when unemployment stood at 8.3 percent, until 1997, when it exceeded 12.6 percent. "The strategy followed has been, quite simply, to achieve disinflation and increased competitiveness through higher unemployment."[37]

ECONOMIC AND MONETARY UNION

Competitive disinflation established the frame of reference that set the parameters of economic policy making in France. EMU was entirely consistent with that frame of reference. However, within those parameters, EMU was a bid to rebalance the "asymmetric dependency" of Franco-German relations. EMU was seen by the French Socialist governments of the late 1980s and early 1990s as a means of regaining a degree of control over their monetary affairs that they had de facto "surrendered" to the Bundesbank within the ERM. In the context of free movement of capital, France lost its monetary policy autonomy vis-à-vis the deutschmark—the anchor currency of ERM. EMU became the cornerstone of a bid to shift the "terms of trade" of Franco-German relations and regain internal influence.[38] Furthermore, the aspiration for French Socialists was also to introduce jobs and growth-oriented elements into EMU's financial architecture. However, German cooperation was contingent upon the "German model" forming the basis for discussion.

The essentially neoliberal foundations of the EMU institutions, which, in Cohen's term, set in marble the strategy of competitive disinflation,[39] were not simply "imposed" upon France by Germany. Rather, it reflected a degree of elite-level domestic policy consensus, particularly amongst conservative liberals, that these were the right foundations. As Howarth notes, one reason why EMU bore the imprint in particular of the Tresor and the Banque de France was that this group was empowered within the French state by the EMS and then the ERM.[40] This subsequently hindered Socialist politicians' attempts to attenuate the influence of central bankers and introduce more growth and employment-oriented concerns into both the foundations of EMU and the policy mix, shifting away from exclusive focus on price stability and budget deficit reduction.

Attempts by French Socialists to shift the goalposts reflected a wide-ranging rejection of the *pensée unique* noted earlier in this chapter, but all were ultimately unsuccessful. The principal means to shift the parameters of economic policy making was the desire for an "economic government" designed to provide a "political counterweight" to the powers of the ECB. This aspiration had eventually to be sacrificed in the face of unstinting German hostility. Such political inference was counter to the German model, and the Maastricht Treaty explicitly outlaws such interference. However, in the mid-1990s political support increased for the kind of reorientations to EMU that the likes of Mitterrand and Bérégovoy had sought unsuccessfully at Maastricht.

The Politicization of the "Hidden Costs" of Maastricht: The *Mouvement Sociale*

The economic policy priorities that underpinned competitive disinflation, institutionalized into the Maastricht criteria, framed the nature of preparation for stage three of EMU. The reception that Maastricht received in France was frosty enough, as the 51 percent "petit oui" in the September 1992 referendum demonstrated. However, in the years that followed, hostility to the project, or at least the economic foundations on which it had been built, grew.

The enduring asymmetric dependency of Franco-German relations was graphically demonstrated in the post-reunification period. Germany decided to finance reunification through European borrowing and accordingly set very high interest rates. French interest rates were constrained to shadow sky-high German rates despite such a move, further crippling France's already sluggish growth. So dominant was the competitive disinflation *référential*, and its attendant sound money ethos, that when the Germans proposed a realignment of parities within the EMS, revaluing the mark, Bérégovoy refused.

The goal of competitive disinflation was clearly running counter to the declared justification of long-term job creation. This point is supported by OFCE studies of French competitiveness, which chart a 10 percent improvement in French unit costs and lesser improvements in price competitivity between 1987 and 1992. However, all these improvements were largely lost in the 1992–1993 period. The EMS crisis and its aftermath rumbled on until 1995.[41] The problems of sluggish growth, punitively high interest rates, an overvalued currency, and soaring unemployment levels began to take their toll on France's public finances. The 3 percent budget deficit requirement, insisted upon by Bérégovoy, now began to bite. The budget deficit was running at around 6 percent of GDP in 1993, hence, despite an economic downturn, further austerity measures appeared inevitable.

As if to further fan the flames of hostility to the EMU project, Chirac ran a Euro-ambivalent 1995 presidential campaign, in which he promised redistributive Keynesian and *dirigiste* solutions to France's "social fracture" that were manifestly incompatible with the EMU preparation. This was a calculated critique of his opponent Balladur—who, for Chirac, personified the *pensée unique*. On October 26, 1995, the inevitable U-turn came when President Chirac announced that the government would henceforth give priority to budget cutting in accordance with the Maastricht criteria. Having so recently unreasonably inflated expectations, Prime Minister Juppé's ill-timed announcements of austerity-oriented cuts in pensions and welfare provision caused outrage.[42]

Juppé's bull in a china shop tactics, moving on so many fronts at once, were *very* ill-thought out. They had the effect of uniting diverse groups behind cherished welfare provision, or *droits acquis*, and le *service publique*, both seen as integral parts of French citizenship. The demonstrations and strikes cohered around issues of "defense," "protection," and "maintenance" of Republican values, under threat not only from Juppé, but also, indirectly, from the neoliberal EU. Juppé's achievement was that he united the CGT and FO unions—an almost unique episode in French industrial relations, since they had been at loggerheads for forty years. Transportation workers and civil servants cooperated in calling a public sector general strike and in organizing mass demonstrations (the largest since May 1968), which partially paralyzed the country for six weeks.

As well as undermining Juppé, this episode made the issue of welfare reform almost untouchable. The episode was also counter-productive in the sense that economic growth was even slower than had been projected (1.3 percent), in part due to strikes, and as a result, the budget deficit remained stubbornly high at 5 percent in 1995. There was widespread public support for the strike (estimated 57 percent approval, including 45 percent of professional and managerial personnel)—even by those inconvenienced by it.[43] It was presented and seen as a protest against the neoliberal *pensée unique* and globalization. The defense of employment and public service resonated with the wider public—and deep-rooted French Republican political traditions. Chirac's mismanagement of the

European issue, and his unrealistic promises in 1995, thus brought home to the French electorate to a degree not hitherto seen the "hidden" costs of EMU.

THE AFTERMATH: *DIRIGISTE* ASPIRATIONS FOR A NEOLIBERAL EURO AREA

The 1995 *mouvement sociale* offered a graphic demonstration, both of the constraints on the welfare state imposed by Maastricht and of the constraints on welfare retrenchment placed by social and political forces in France. Although the Socialists were curiously reticent during the 1995 episode, Jospin was able to tap into the sentiments expressed at the time. In Gramscian terms, one government advisor identifies dissenters from the *pensée unique*:

> There were quite a number of people who did not integrate this dominant *"pensée unique."* There were efforts of resistance. For example, the unions, highly ideological in France, and who produce a lot of theory, a lot of general discourse. . . . There was always a pole of resistance—intellectual, not organic—on which Jospin could now build.[44]

This agenda found support beyond the ranks of the unions and the parties of the Left in France—a fact that hints at the limited acceptance of neoliberalism in France. Jospin's electoral strategy subsequently sought to exploit the Republican tradition and the instinctive hostility to neoliberalism it fosters. He cited as one of the three core principles of Socialist thinking that "social classes can be brought together through equality of opportunity." Jospin talked of the need to rally the middle classes, as well as those whom society has left behind, to the "cause of equality and social integration."[45] Jospin highlighted the need for redistribution of wealth between classes, toward those with a greater propensity to spend, to increase both social justice and demand in the economy.[46]

Jospin's project and policies aimed to forge a new alliance between "the excluded, the *classes populaires*, and the middle classes." These classes, Jospin accepted, had *specific, legitimate*, and at times *divergent* interests,

> but they also have common concerns. They have the same aspirations for the improvement of the employment situation, for the reduction of job insecurity, the improvement of the education system, and the consolidation of social protection. They can thus unite within our project of social transformation.[47]

This attachment to welfare provision, to state intervention and regulation of markets generally, and to the need to balance acceptance of the German model in the pursuit of "sound money" with more familiar, French *dirigiste* elements also extended to conservative liberals. Thus, as Howarth notes, one intellectual resistance to the *pensée unique* in its neoliberal form was the monetary policy committee of the newly independent Banque de France. Two of its members were actively calling for the addition of new Maastricht convergence criteria—for employment—to be added to the existing EMU preparation rules in 1996.[48] This was the main bone of contention between the German Ordo-liberal model and French Socialist conceptions of how macropolicy should be conceived.

This all increased hostility to a technical approach to economic questions, seen as excessively dominated by assumptions of the neoliberal worldview. Dyson notes that the French Socialists in particular "sought to draw a line between embracing rules of 'sound' public finance and money and taking on the whole apparatus of neoliberal and monetarist policy discourse."[49] Jospin tapped into anti–*pensée unique* sentiments of 1995, and he developed a subtle pro-European, but critical of current foundations of EMU, stance that was electorally successful in 1997. The four conditions imposed by Jospin on the advent of the euro articulated this new approach. Firstly, in a thinly veiled bid to limit German dominance, it was felt that the euro must include as many countries as possible, with Spain and Italy, states attached to the idea of political direction and accountability for economic policy, cited explicitly. Secondly, "Europe must be social and political"; therefore,

> We want the relations between participating Euro countries to be founded not on an austerity pact (this is an explicit reference to the German inspired "Stability Pact" of Dublin), but on a solidarity and growth pact, permitting policies in favour of job creation and social cohesion.[50]

Thirdly, there was a reiteration of the demand that, next to the European Central Bank, there must be established "a European economic government, representing the people and charged with coordinating the economic policies of the various nations." Finally, there was an insistence that the Euro must not be overvalued vis-à-vis the dollar and yen.

This hinted at a political role in the determination of exchange rates, and a balancing of stability with other economic priorities quite alien to German monetary arrangements. Here we see a reemergence of much of the French agenda from the Maastricht discussions. Former European Minister Moscovici highlighted that the price paid for monetary myopia, in terms of low growth, slowed down by prohibitive interest rates and mass unemployment, was too great. "That is why such dogmas are today seriously challenged, not only on the grounds of social justice, but also on the grounds of economic efficiency."[51] The Socialists aimed for a negotiated rebalancing of the policy mix, hoping to generate coordinated fiscal, monetary, and structural policies across the EU that would be geared toward jobs and growth. This is part of the French Socialists' long-run EMU game.[52] The necessary accommodation to the German model was accepted on the understanding that increased influence once EMU was in place might offer more scope for moving the goalposts. The strategy remained one of continued critical engagement from within—arguing at every turn for reorientations, such as a European Jobs and Growth Pact (Amsterdam) and a European Growth Fund (Portschach).

The issue of the economic government has always been the central plank of this ambition. As a 1996 Socialist Party conference text argues, a political structure, as a counterweight to the European Central Bank, was essential to avoid the single currency being "sacrificed to monetarism, the devolution pure and simple of monetary policymaking power to the governors of central banks."[53] This involved a shift away from the purely technical approach to policy underpinning Ordo-liberalism, toward a more "political" role for the ECB. The deflationary bias of the EMU foundations, institutionalized at Maastricht and reasserted with the stability pact agreed at Dublin, needed to be countered by neo-Keynesian inspired measures permitting governments under certain circumstances to reflate the economy to restore confidence. More generally, the aim was to bolster economic policy coordination, seeing the rules of convergence and stability as hedging, not binding, mechanisms.[54]

Given that a quite different model had already been set in marble at Maastricht, the Jospin government had no realistic prospect at the 1997 Amsterdam Summit of achieving fully such ambitions. However, the creation of an economic committee (Euro-11 Council, subsequently Euro-12 Council) to monitor the work of the ECB was a first step. Thereafter, French Socialist policymakers sought to give powers to the Euro-12 over economic and exchange rate policy. Where Amsterdam *was* more successful for the Jospin government was on the subject of the employment chapter, the growth and employment resolution, and the formulation of the European employment strategy. What followed as a result were the Luxembourg and Cardiff jobs summits and the 1999 Cologne Summit, which codified National Action Plans for employment. These were part of the Common Strategy for National Employment Policies (CSNEP), a surveillance and benchmarking process that emphasizes supply-side best practice measures to promote *employability*.[55]

The French Socialists' long game also involves more ambitious, Keynesian-inspired aspirations to cement the marriage of *l'Europe sociale* to monetarist EMU through coordinated fiscal activism at the European level advocated by Delors' white paper.[56] Out of a bipartite PS SPD declaration at Malmo on the appropriate European job creation policies grew the axis of Finance Ministers Strauss-Kahn and Lafontaine on social democratic coordination of economic policy to boost growth and jobs. Schröder, too, endorsed elements of this agenda.[57] This, according to Dyson, offered a "window of opportunity" at Portschach in 1998, coinciding as it did with fears of a global recession in the wake of the Asian and Russian financial crises, creating scope for challenging of the predominant neoliberal approach to economic policy in the EU.

Jospin articulated ambitious plans for European-level coordinated action on employment and growth, combining interest rate cuts to foster growth with large-scale public investment in infrastructural programs to boost demand and reduce unemployment. The centerpiece was a multibillion-pound development loan raised on Europe's financial markets.[58] This is the clearest and most consistent point of departure from the German model and the neoliberal foundations of EMU. The French Socialists have long argued that credibility can be retained while at the same time pursuing more activist, jobs- and growth-oriented macroeconomic policies at a European level.

Lafontaine and Strauss-Kahn were crucial to this reorientation process. Their departures partially undermined this agenda. The extent to which EMU between 1999 and 2002 conformed to certain social democratic aspirations (e.g., low interest rates and "soft" currency encouraging exports) owed more to economic conjuncture than reorientation of institutional design. The neoliberal bias of the institutions remains, as does that of the international financial markets whose structural power all governments and European financial institutions recognize. The monetary committee, and then the Cologne macroeconomic dialogue, were seen by the Jospin government as further evidence of the Euro-11 groups nascent "economic government" status. However, clearly the minimalist agenda won out. As a result, the Ordo-liberal exigencies of the process of European construction continued to constrain the government throughout Jospin's term, hemming in any Keynesian aspirations. Policy priorities, in Fitoussi's phrase, remain "inverted," with budget "regularization" misguidedly taking precedence over growth and employment.[59]

FINANCIAL SYSTEM REFORM IN FRANCE

If macroeconomic policy making underwent a fundamental overhaul in the 1980s, so too did microeconomic policy making. Changes to the French financial system were to have wider implications for the state–industry nexus, whereby long-term financing of private firms had been mediated, and at times subsidized, by the French state. As Cohen notes, "Until 1984, France's financial system was almost wholly nationalized, protected, and centrally controlled. The state was simultaneous regulator, owner, and interventionist."[60] The complements to competitive disinflation were deregulation to increase competition and the competitivity of firms, and the reconstruction of the French financial system. Although many commentators are skeptical about how influential neoliberalism (in its "pure," Anglo-Saxon articulation) has been in France, most agree that the influence has been most pervasive in the financial reforms enacted first by Bérégovoy and Delors, and then by Balladur. The changes in the incentive structure of the French financial system that these reforms heralded, bringing market discipline to bear on increasing numbers of economic actors and increasing the structural power of capital, dovetailed with the new ideological priorities— the *pensée unique*, or neoliberalism *à la Française*.

The process of European construction, and in particular the Single Market program, also played a significant role. Neoliberal nostrums about private capital markets being the most efficient allocators of resources, and of the public sector "crowding out" such investment, were in the ascendant. Financial integration was seen as an essential step in improving European firms' competitiveness, delivering a "competitive shock" to overpricing. Lower costs for capital would spill over into manufacturing and further help competitiveness. As Underhill notes, the Commission's white paper of 1985 "involved a conscious commitment to dismantling or at least severely restricting national prerogatives in favour of the construction of market decision-making processes and economic integration at the EU level."[61]

This was also seen partially as a need for European financial markets to respond to the competitive challenge that American deregulation presented. A desire to liberalize capital markets and free up capital movements across the EU was written into the Single European Act, which contained provisions to remove exchange controls on long-term credit and on buying and selling unlisted securities, unit trusts, and other financial instruments. Deregulation and liberalization went further in 1990, with removal of all capital and exchange controls (in accordance with an EU directive).[62]

The changes in France's financial system need to be understood in the context of troubles facing the French model and an international shift toward liberalization and deregulation (and a new neoliberal orthodoxy that accompanied it). As a result of deregulation and liberalization in the wake of Bretton Woods, there was a rapid expansion and "globalization of financial services markets," which saw the growth in relative importance of international banking and securities markets (including bonds, equities, foreign exchange, and derivatives). Rapid deregulation and internationalization of financial services brought external pressure to bear on the French financial system.[63]

This was compounded by the feeling that the French state had not always been the most efficient allocator of credit. The restructuring of the French financial system was in part the result of a realization that the French model was in need of reform—as flagging productivity, spiraling inflation, collapsed investment, and widening trade gaps demonstrated. France's financial system left areas of the economy undercapitalized and hindered the development of capital markets. The problem was exacerbated by developments in the international political economy. The oil price hikes and global downturn were catalysts of the 1974 industrial crisis, which exposed the chronic lack of investment and left French capitalism "without capital."[64]

The political expediency of "anxious conservative leaders who had no stomach for painful, if much-needed, rationalization of declining uncompetitive enterprises"[65] further hindered the efficient allocation of resources toward the supposed dynamic industrial core. The French state was "picking losers"! The French model had not reached limits wedded to its theoretical underpinnings, but suffered from the misallocation of funds that owed more to political expediency than economic strategy. Nevertheless, for some, the protectionist system was seen as a barrier to industrial development. Given the partial dysfunctionality of the existent French financial arrangements, and their mismatch with a changing international economic context, external pressure dovetailed with domestic impetus for change.

State elites saw financial liberalization as a means of removing the burden of business financing from the state.[66] The immediate context of the first phase of reform (1982–1983) was a time when the Socialist government keenly felt the commercial and financial demands for a balanced budget. This fiscal crisis of the state meant the state was much less inclined (and indeed less able) to foot the bill for industrial investment. Banking and financial sector reform was seen as a way of enabling firms to find alternative sources of investment income. With this in mind, Delors saw the bank nationalizations as an ideal opportunity to reduce compartmentalization and increase competition (both domestic and international) in the banking and financial services sector. Through financial deregulation, Loriaux insists, "The Socialists were not simply complying with or submitting to the dictates of the market, but were trying to regain control over the economy."[67]

Although the Banking Act of 1984 sought to enhance German-style close equity ties between banks and industrial corporations,[68] the context of liberalization and deregulation undermined the ability of policy elites to influence the overall direction of changes, which proved more Anglo-Saxon than Rhenish. French financial institutions, in part hampered by high-profile mismanagement scandals surrounding key players such as Crédit Lyonnais (which went bankrupt in 1993), were not able to play the same stabilizing orchestrator-of-restructuring role as their German counterparts were.

The French financial system's overhaul also saw the creation of a *Second Marché* of unlisted securities (designed to bring smaller firms into capital markets); a commercial paper market (allowing companies to raise capital directly from public through private bond issues); and the French futures market—the *Marché à terme des instruments financiers* (MATIF), opened in February 1986. Further deregulation involved freeing-up the securities and foreign exchange markets and facilitating the decompartmentalization of markets.[69] Banks were encouraged to raise capital beyond their deposit base; new instruments for interest rate, stock market, and currency hedging (copied from international markets) were introduced; and new institutions were created.[70] The Chirac government's deregulation also facilitated stock issues, leveraged management buyouts, and employee stock ownership plans.[71]

The impact on the French *dirigiste* model of this fundamental restructuring of the French financial system has been dramatic. State control, mediation, and subsidization of industrial financing all went into significant decline. Business financing from nonbanking sources rose from 30.7 percent of that of financial institutions in 1978 to 60.6 percent in 1985 and 153.6 percent in 1986. The opening of the markets under the Mauroy and Fabius governments enabled business to gain nongovernmental sources of financing through a wide variety of instruments, thus reducing their susceptibility to government pressure.[72] There was a sharp decline in the proportion of financial funds intermediated through the banking system.[73]

The policy implications of liberalized financial flows for macroeconomic policy have been explored earlier in this chapter. In addition to disciplinary neoliberalism operating on governments through financial markets, opening access to foreign capital to finance French debt has increased the reliance on foreign capital and thus the influence of the structural power of capital on the organization and operation of French capitalism. As Levy notes,

> The removal of price controls in 1986 allowed companies to reap the full benefits of successful competitive strategies. The elimination of capital controls in the late 1980s facilitated the expansion of production abroad and gave managers an "exit" option if domestic conditions were not to their liking. Taken together, these and other reforms helped boost corporate profitability from 9.8 percent of value added in 1982 to 17.3 percent in 1989.[74]

The internationally mobile capital that could now enter the French financial system was similarly structurally empowered by international liberalization. Policy elites keenly felt the disciplinary neoliberal pressures that accompanied increased reliance on foreign capital—the need to control inflation, secure credibility, and offer attractive interest rates and a strong currency.

In addition to a reduced direct state influence over private sector business finance, changes in the financial sector facilitated a more thoroughgoing restructuring of French capitalism as a result of the process of privatization that was contemporaneous to financial reform. The principal organizing feature of France's financial network economy[75] are *noyaux durs*—or hard cores of interlinked financial and industrial interests. Such networks span the public and private sectors, and cohere around a number of relatively stable "poles" or spheres of influence. The first phase of the restructuring process reinforced this financial network economy through such means as state selection of "golden share" recipients after privatization. Still amenable to state influence, and characterized by an antipredatory logic and well-established alliances, the makeup of the cores changed, but their influence endured.[76]

The state–firm relationship, however, is becoming more arms-length and indirect, involving the state inducing rather than directing change. As internationalization and liberalization of finance increases, Morin charts a decline in the size of the *noyaux durs*, and a growing presence of foreign investors. Whereas once the *noyaux durs* prevented foreign acquisition, in the 1990s they have increased the internationalization of French capital as the hard cores involve strategic European allies. Acquisitions, joint ventures, and participation in the capital of foreign firms have all increased. The recent expansion in foreign holdings on the French stock exchange is remarkable. Between 1985 and 1997, foreign owners increased their share of stock exchange capitalization from 10 percent to 35 percent (compared to 9 percent in Britain and 6 percent in the United States). This "highly significant trend," the increasing purchase by North American pension funds and fund managers of the stakes in French firms relinquished by the partial unraveling of the *noyaux durs*, may presage further restructuring of French capitalism.[77]

Thus far it has had a considerable impact on the corporate governance norms of French capitalism. While there has been no radical overhaul, with aspects such as the French social model still well entrenched, nevertheless Morin's analysis suggests that boardrooms are increasingly influenced by the shareholder value paradigm, the dominant strategic model of American institutional investors.[78] Financial deregulation has also led to significant shifts in the financing of French enterprises to patterns that are much more Anglo-Saxon. Internal sources of funds and equity have become proportionately more important and bank loans proportionately less important; of the funds available to enterprises, they now spend a smaller proportion on new investment in the firm and a higher proportion on purchasing financial assets, particularly equities.[79]

Industrial Policy, *Dirigisme*, and Anglo-Saxon Capitalism

Dirigisme involves a set of interventionist mechanisms and a directive approach to the policy process. In the field of industrial policy, French *dirigiste* mechanisms such as state aid, "assisted sectors," public procurement, and state-orchestrated mergers and acquisitions exist in tension with the norms of closer European integration as established in the Single European Act. In this sphere, EU integration can be more directly identified as the cause of policy change. The SEA logic draws on neoliberal economic theory and Anglo-Saxon norms of capitalist organization. This is perhaps most evident in antitrust (antimonopoly) directives, based directly on U.S. antitrust legislation.

The monopolistic, protectionist, and *dirigiste* norms of the French industrial policy, particularly in the public sector, appear at odds with EU rules on unfair competition, liberalization, and deregulation. Such constraints have compelled the French state to relinquish traditional instruments of *dirigisme*; for example, the EU stance on unfair competition calls into question public procurement policies, state aids and subsidies, and the notion of "assisted" sectors.[80] The SEA seeks to advance liberalization and deregulation by opening up markets, and in particular public sector monopoly utility providers, to competition, all of which threatens to alter the complexion of state–economy relations in France.[81]

The acquisition of subsidiaries, another arm of traditional *dirigisme*, has also been curtailed, as evidenced when Aérospatiale was prevented from buying De

Havilland.[82] Furthermore, high-profile cases such as Renault—forced to pay back 4 million francs of state aid in 1990 after a four-year dispute with the Commission—illustrates the threat to state subsidies. In terms of protected markets, Air Inter was forced to open up the domestic flights market to competition. Thus the traditional interventionist model of French industrial policy appears decreasingly viable, given the weakening of traditional policy instruments and advancing Europeanization. An equally powerful, though less overt, pressure on traditional French industrial policy has been the demands of budgetary retrenchment (see earlier in this chapter), which have provided the rationale for many of the privatizations undertaken by the French state in the last fifteen years.

However, one should not generalize too widely from the aforementioned cases. De Havilland, for example, was the only case of a merger being outlawed during three years of EU merger regulation between 1991 and 1994.[83] Scratch the surface and one sees that "certain nationalized industries continued to receive large infusions of capital while others were encouraged to merge, regardless of their anticompetitive effects and despite the possibility of censure by the European Community."[84] As for French public procurement norms, although an April 1989 decree applied a directive stating that the use of state contracts to support French firms was to cease and that bids from companies from any member state must be treated equally, by 1996 90 percent of state contracts *still* went to French firms. Furthermore, Air France and Crédit Lyonnais continued to receive sizeable state subsidies. As Guyomarch et al. note, "Theory has changed more than practice."[85] Kassim highlights how the picture varies across policy sectors, with the French state's "failure" in air transport contrasting with "success" in the audiovisual sector.[86]

In the public sector, there has been still more resistance to neoliberal influence and a desire to preserve the French state tradition's peculiar attributes, captured in the notion of *le service publique* (a more encompassing, egalitarian notion than "public sector"). The defense of French public services has been carried out under the auspices of subsidiarity. The French have sought to justify state funding of public service enterprises as defending "the hard core of French industrial patrimony."[87] Unease with the Anglo-Saxon approach to industrial policy led the Jospin government to invoke the EU's subsidiarity principle in relation to the *services publiques*. The move bore some fruit at Amsterdam.[88]

Exploiting such *service publique* constitutional prerogatives, the Jospin government also "defended" the EDF-GDF, SNCF, and *La Poste* against liberalization. The public service employment status of EDF-GDF workers was retained and only one-third of the market was opened up, with the state choosing which clients could shop around and imposing public service conditions on its competitors.[89] The Jospin government also staved off opening up the domestic energy market until 2003.

When the French state could not prevent liberalization and the opening up of markets, the Jospin government exploited the opportunity presented by EU pressures, the need for budgetary retrenchment, and the perceived need for "strategic" alliances with other major European firms. They engaged (with varying degrees of success) in restructuring the French defense, transport, and, with less success, telecommunications industries by quasi-*dirigiste* methods, thus pursuing industrial policy by another means. For example, France Télécom and Thomson-CSF were partially "opened up," with the state either retaining a majority interest or ensuring that majority shareholdings ended up in safe hands.[90]

In this hands-off, limited sense, French policy elites enjoyed some success in reinventing industrial policy on a European scale that at least in some respects reflects French traditions. French attempts to shift its traditional, interventionist *grands projets*–style industrial policy to a European level have been less fruitful. Despite isolated successes, such as the "carve-up" of EUREKA funding between Philips and Thomson,[91] "high-tech Colbertist" desires to establish "European champions" were hindered both by merger and acquisition directives and by a more general antipathy from the Commission.[92]

TOWARD NEOLIBERAL STABILIZATION?

This chapter has explored how the ascendant neoliberal orthodoxy that characterizes European integration has interacted with the *dirigiste* political traditions of the French model and the French state apparatus. These interactions have been situated in a wider international economic context to illustrate how the EU neoliberal hegemonic project must be understood in the context of a changing international political economy shaped by transnational neoliberalism. In macroeconomic policy, *dirigiste* instruments were dismantled and replaced by a German model in a (successful) Ordo-liberal bid to import credibility, which "normalized" the neoliberal macroeconomic paradigm. Given the neoliberal foundations of EMU's macroeconomic policy paradigm, *dirigiste* aspirations for a more politically directed policy mix have not been realized despite enduring high structural unemployment (although such aspirations continue to play a role in the French policy debate).

Similarly, in the field of structural reform of French capitalism, international trends toward liberalization that shaped the Single European Market program, compounded by a fiscal crisis of the French state, led policymakers to dismantle France's *dirigiste* model in favor of liberalized internationally open capital markets. This process has structurally empowered capital, and as a result it has significantly hemmed in the French state's *volontariste* potentialities. The upshot was a fundamental transformation not only of the state–industry nexus, but also of the structure of French capitalism, perhaps even threatening to alter the norms of corporate governance in France. The picture that emerges is of a French model considerably altered, more influenced by the neoliberal norms of the *pensée unique*. Markets play a more preponderant role and the structural power of capital is enhanced, shifting incentives structures in a manner consistent with the priorities of the neoliberal orthodoxy.

Can Neoliberalism Be Stabilized in France? Is There an End in Sight to the Organic Crisis?

French neoliberal restructuring has been a contested process, characterized by compromise and readjustment. The most spectacular manifestation of subordinated groups' shaping of the process came with the 1995 strikes that limited welfare retrenchment. Another area of struggle for a negotiated settlement was the Jospin government's attempts to reconcile this neoliberal bias to the French social model and social democratic aspirations for the euro area through measures such as economic government and a European Growth Fund, which were crucial to the Socialist's long game. Given the disappointing results of this attempt at negotiated settlement, it is difficult to see how unemployment (which stood at 9 percent in 2002) could be further reduced in a downward phase in the economic cycle given that macroeconomic policy remains hamstrung by the Growth and Stability Pact.

Nor does the period of restructuring appear over. Partially successful attempts to retain quasi-*dirigiste* influence over industrial policy by the Jospin government, particularly in the field of the *services publiques*, did not address some of the issues destabilizing the French model. Given the prioritizing of deficit reduction and budget balancing, further welfare state retrenchment appears likely to address problems caused by an unsustainable expansion of early retirement in the 1980s and 1990s, compounded by demographic trends reducing the size of the working population. These have created a pensions time bomb, which suggests that aspects of the organic crisis of the French model remain unresolved.

NOTES

1. Andrew Shonfield, *Modern Capitalism* (London: Oxford University Press, 1969), 86 and 128.

2. Elie Cohen, "France: National Champions in Search of a Mission," in Jack Hayward, ed., *Industrial Enterprise and European Integration: From National to International Champions in Europe* (Oxford: Oxford University Press, 1995), 27.

3. John Zysman, *Government, Markets, Growth: Financial Systems and the Politics of Industrial Change* (Ithaca, N.Y.: Cornell University Press, 1983).

4. See Alain Guyomarch, Howard Machin, and Ella Ritchie, *France in the European Union,* (Basingstoke, UK: Macmillan, 1998), 161–68; and Jonah Levy, "France: Directing Adjustment?" in Fritz Scharpf and Vivien Schmidt, eds., *Welfare and Work in the Open Economy,* vol. 2 (Oxford: Oxford University Press, 2000), 321. According to the latter, more than 75 percent of public aid went to fewer than half a dozen firms, most of which were uncompetitive and many of which were in declining sectors.

5. Christian Stoffaes, "Industrial Policy and the State: From Industry to Enterprise," in P. Godt, ed., *Policy-Making in France* (London: Pinter, 1989).

6. Cohen, "France: National Champions."

7. Elie Cohen, *La Tentation Hexagonale* (Paris: Fayard, 1996), 351.

8. Frédéric Lordon, "The Logic and Limits of Désinflation Competitive," *Oxford Review of Economic Policy* 14 no. 1. (1998): 96 and 102.

9. *Le Poing et la Rose*, no. 135 (January 1992): 18.

10. David Howarth, "The French State in the Euro Zone" in K. Dyson, ed., *The European State in the Euro-Zone* (Oxford: Oxford University Press, 2002), 12.

11. See David Held, Anthony McGrew, David Goldblatt, and Jonathon Perraton, *Global Transformations* (Cambridge: Polity, 1999), 2–14, for a discussion of the term.

12. (Parti Socialiste newspaper) *Vendredi*, December 17, 1993.

13. Lionel Jospin, *Modern Socialism* (London: Fabian Society, 1999).

14. Lionel Jospin, *L'Invention du Possible* (Paris: Flammarion 1991), 11.

15. Jospin, *Modern Socialism*, 4.

16. Parti Socialiste, final text of the National Convention *Mondialisation, Europe, France*, in *Vendredi*, April 5, 1996. See also Jospin, *Modern Socialism*.

17. Alistair Cole and Helen Drake, "The Europeanisation of the French Polity: Continuity, Change and Adaptation," *Journal of European Public Policy* 7, no. 1 (2000): 34.

18. Alain Fonteneau and Pierre-Alain Muet, *La gauche face à la Crise* (Paris: FNSP, 1985); Peter Hall, *Governing the Economy* (Cambridge: Polity, 1986); and David Cameron, "Exchange Rate Politics in France 1981–83: The Regime Defining Choices of the Mitterrand Presidency," in Anthony Daley, ed., *The Mitterrand Era* (London ; Macmillan 1996), 56–82.

19. Pierre Favier and Michel Martin-Roland, *La Decennie Mitterrand: 1 Les Ruptures (1981–1984)* (Paris: Seuil, 1990).

20. Fritz Scharpf, *Crisis and Choice in European Social Democracy* (Ithaca, N.Y.: Cornell University Press, 1991), 14.

21. Lordon, "Logic and Limits"; Olivier Blanchard and Pierre-Alain Muet, "Competitiveness through Disinflation: An Assessment of French Macro-economic Strategy," *Economic Policy*, no. 16 (1993): 12–50.

22. Cohen, *La Tentation Hexagonale*, 351.

23. Kenneth Dyson, "The Franco-German Relationship and Economic and Monetary Union: Using Europe to 'Bind Leviathan,'" *West European Politics* 22, no. 1 (1999): 37, 42.

24. Howarth, "The French State," 3.

25. See Howarth, "The French State," 3; and Dyson, "The Franco-German Relationship."

26. Bérégovoy had the left-wing stance while secretary-general of the Elysée staff and minister for social affairs.

27. Julius Friend, *The Long Presidency: France in the Mitterrand Years* (Boulder, Colo.: Westview Press, 1998), 191.

28. Friend, *The Long Presidency*, 190 and 220. It was a criterion that France easily met at the time of introduction: The level of public deficit as a proportion of GDP was about 1.5 percent in 1990–1991.

29. Friend, *The Long Presidency*, 30–46; and Dyson, "The Franco-German Relationship," 37 and 41–42. The importance of the ideologically charged concept of financial credibility, and the implications of this dominance of neoliberal economic orthodoxy, are

demonstrated by C. Aubin and J-D. Lafay's econometric analysis, which verifies that left-wing governments had to "over-compensate" in their pursuit of credibility. The "risk premia" paid by socialist governments under the EMS were consistently higher than those of Gaullists. See C. Aubin and J-D. Lafay, "Objectifs politiques et contraintes institutionnelles dans les decisions de politique monetaire. Analyse econometrique du cas français (1973.03–1993.12)," *Revue Economique* 46, no. 3 (1995): 869–78.

30. Elie Cohen, "A *Dirigiste* End to *Dirigisme?*" in Mairi Maclean, ed., *The Mitterrand Years: Legacy and Evaluation* (Basingstoke, UK: Macmillan 1998), 36–45, esp. 38.

31. Blanchard and Muet, "Competitiveness through Disinflation," 13.

32. Jean-Paul Fitoussi et al., *Competitive Disinflation* (Oxford: Oxford University Press, 1993), 25.

33. Lordon, "Logic and Limits," 103–5.

34. Lordon, "Logic and Limits," 106.

35. Lordon, "Logic and Limits," 109.

36. Jean-Paul Fitoussi, *Le Débat Interdit: Monnaie, Europe, Pauvreté* (Paris; Arléa, 1995); and Lordon, "Logic and Limits."

37. Fitoussi et al., *Competitive Disinflation*, 18; similar sentiments are expressed in Blanchard and Muet, "Competitiveness through Disinflation."

38. Cohen, *La Tentation Hexagonale*, 351–65.

39. Cohen, *La Tentation Hexagonale*, 343–47.

40. Howarth, "The French State."

41. OFCE, *L'Economie Française 1999* (Paris; La Découverte, 1999), 75.

42. Thus on November 15 Juppé announced the Plan Juppé, which reduced social security and health entitlements, and also threatened reduced public sector, and in particular civil service pension privileges, as well as the taxation of family allocations. On November 17, he announced changes to the railway workers' *contrat du plan*, changing working practices and reducing workers' benefits, and on November 19 the Finance Ministry announced an end to wage earners' 20 percent tax deduction.

43. George Ross, "Europe Becomes Domestic French Politics," in Michael Lewis-Beck, ed., *How France Votes* (London: Chatham House, 2000).

44. Jospin government advisor, interview with the author, December 17, 1997.

45. Jospin, *Modern Socialism*, 7, 14.

46. See Ben Clift, "The Jospin Way," *The Political Quarterly* 72, no. 2 (2001): 170–79. On redistributive record see Levy, "Directing Adjustment?" 337–44.

47. Jospin, closing speech to the PS *Universite d'Ete*, August 29, 1999. See Ben Clift, "Social Democracy in the 21st Century: *Still* a Class Act? The Place of Class in Jospinism and Blairism," *Journal of European Area Studies* 8, no. 2 (2001): 191–216.

48. Howarth, "The French State," 11.

49. Kenneth Dyson, "Benign or Malevolent Leviathan? Social Democratic Governments in a Neo-Liberal Area," *Political Quarterly* 70, no. 2 (1999): 202.

50. Parti Socialiste, *Changeons d'Avenir: Nos engagements pour la France*, election manifesto (1997), 12–13.

51. Pierre Moscovici, *L'Urgence: Plaidoyer pour une autre politique* (Paris: Plon, 1997), 58.

52. See Dyson, "The Franco-German Relationship," 36, 43–44.

53. *Vendredi*, March 8, 1996.

54. Dyson, "Benign or Malevolent Leviathan?" 206.

55. European Council, *Presidency Conclusion: Extraordinary European Council Meeting on Employment Luxembourg, 20 and 21 November 1997* (Brussels: European Council, 1997), 1.

56. Jacques Delors, *White Paper on Growth, Competitiveness and Employment* (Brussels: European Commission, 1993).

57. Dyson, "Benign or Malevolent Leviathan?" 205.

58. Dyson, "Benign or Malevolent Leviathan?" 203–4.

59. Fitoussi, *Le Débat Interdit*, 209–13.

60. Cohen, "A *Dirigiste* End to *Dirigisme?*" 42.

61. Geoffrey Underhill, "The Making of the European Financial Area: Global Market Integration and the EU Single Market for Financial Services," in Geoffrey Underhill, ed., *The New World Order in International Finance* (Basingstoke, UK: Macmillan, 1997), 105–6.

62. Philip Cerny, "The 'Little Big Bang' in Paris: Financial Deregulation in a *Dirigiste* System," *European Journal of Political Research* 17 (1989): 169–92, 186; and Guyomarch, Machin, and Ritchie, *France in the European Union*, 173.

63. William Coleman, "The French State, *Dirigisme*, and the Changing Global Financial Environment," in Geoffrey Underhill, ed., *The New World Order*, 274.

64. Stoffaes, "Industrial Policy and the State."

65. Levy, "Directing Adjustment?" 321.

66. For example, in 1983, under Finance Minister Delors, public firms and banks were authorized to raise private capital by issuing nonvoting shares (*titres participatifs*) and preferred stock (*certificats d'investissement*). Companies such as Saint-Gobain and Rhone Poulenc were quick to exploit the opportunity.

67. Michael Loriaux, *France after Hegemony* (Ithaca, N.Y.: Cornell University Press 1991), 238.

68. Coleman, "The French State," 284.

69. Coleman, "The French State," 280–84.

70. Loriaux, *France after Hegemony*, 224–25; and Cerny, "The 'Little Big Bang,'" 183.

71. Vivien Schmidt, *From State to Market? The Transformation of French Business and Government* (Cambridge: Cambridge University Press, 1996), 140.

72. Schmidt, *From State to Market?* 113.

73. OECD, *OECD Economic Surveys: France* (Paris, OECD, 1995), table 1.

74. Levy, "Directing Adjustment?" 325.

75. Francois Morin, "A Transformation in the French Model of Shareholding and Management," *Economy and Society* 29, no. 1 (2000): 36–53.

76. Schmidt, *From State to Market?* 370–86.

77. Morin, "A Transformation in the French Model," 38.

78. Morin, "A Transformation in the French Model," 45–49.

79. M. Schaberg, *Globalization and the Erosion of National Financial Systems* (Cheltenham, UK: Edward Elgar, 1999), chapter 2.

80. Guyomarch, Machin, and Ritchie, *France in the European Union*, 161–68, 172–76.

81. See Alistair Cole, "The *Service Publique* under Stress," *West European Politics* 22, no. 4 (1999): 166–84.

82. Schmidt, *From State to Market?* 182.

83. Schmidt, *From State to Market?* 230.

84. Schmidt, *From State to Market?* 176.

85. Guyomarch, Machin, and Ritchie, *France in the European Union*, 176.

86. Hussein Kassim, "French Autonomy and the European Union," *Modern and Contemporary France* 5 no. 2 (1997): 167–80, esp. 173.

87. Schmidt, *From State to Market?* 175.

88. Robert Ladrech, "Towards a Social Europe? Policy Issues and the French Socialist Government," paper presented at the PSA conference at Keele, 1998. See also Cole and Drake, "The Europeanisation of the French Polity."

89. Cole, "The *Service Publique* under Stress," 173.

90. Ben Clift, "The French Model of Capitalism: *Still* Exceptional?" in Ben Clift and Jonathon Perraton, eds., *Where Are National Capitalisms Now?* (Basingstoke, UK: Palgrave, 2003).

91. Guyomarch, Machin, and Ritchie, *France in the European Union*, 181.

92. Cohen, "France: National Champions."

8

⁓⁂⁓

Disciplinary Neoliberalism, Regionalization, and the Social Market in German Restructuring

MAGNUS RYNER

Previous chapters in this book have emphasized the importance of the diffusion of transnational norms of neoliberalism for the cementing of the contemporary European order. In this context transnational agency, especially capitalist class agency, "beyond" the nation state has been emphasized (see especially Gill, chapter 2, and Holman and van der Pijl, chapter 3). These works provide an important insight, but their arguments can only be sustained if the following qualifications are made clear:

- The transnationally hegemonic neoliberal norms establish above all a framework of *intersubjective meanings* and only to a lesser extent the collective images of a homogenous European social formation in toto.[1] Intersubjective meanings imply shared meanings and understanding between *different* actors, including the terms of contest and conflict between them. As Laclau points out, hegemony is not so much about the creation of a common perspective as it is about neutralizing the antagonisms between different perspectives.[2]
- This means that despite this "pan-European" and even "global" dimension, which ensures a measure of transnational coherence and prevents transnational relations to degenerate into anarchic conflict in the European Union and "the West," this perspective also allows for an important intergovernmental dimension where the nation-state and interstate relations still play an important role. Even in post-Maastricht Europe, despite qualified majority voting in the Council of Ministers, codecision powers of the European

Parliament, and the supremacy of the ECJ in the orbits of the treaties, the state remains the site of collectively binding authoritative (that is, sovereign) decision making. What is more, the institutions through which mass legitimacy is ensured and reproduced (corresponding to Gramsci's "ethico-political moment")—formal representative bodies such as national parliaments, political parties, interest organizations, and even mass media—are still primarily organized on a nation-state basis also in Europe.

On the basis of this theoretical statement on the multileveled nature of hegemony, one must acknowledge the crucial significance of Germany for neoliberal hegemony in Europe. On a very general level, the often-postulated importance of the Franco-German axis as a "motor" of integration has to be accepted. Furthermore, the German Ministry of Finance and Central Bank have been crucial *enforcers and guarantors* of what Stephen Gill calls disciplinary neoliberalism in Europe (see chapter 2) through its unique material capabilities and strategic location in the European Monetary System (EMS) and the forging of the EMU. In the terms we used in chapter 1, these agencies have been decisive for the consolidation and normalization of neoliberalism in Europe.

The importance of Germany for disciplinary neoliberalism in Europe contains an irony, which is the object of analysis of this chapter. The irony is that while Germany has this role, which its central bankers, finance ministers, and chancellors have played with great application, Germany has also one of the most highly developed and deeply entrenched apparatuses of labor protection and welfare states in Europe. This irony sometimes manifests itself as a social contradiction, which at times threatens to "spill over" (as it were) onto the European level and even global level as a challenge to the contemporary transnational neoliberal configuration. This became abundantly clear in late 1998 and 1999, when the German Finance Ministry, with Oskar Lafontaine at its helm, started to change policy in a direction that seemed more "French" than "German." Since it seems as if the French Socialist strategy of the long game has primarily been blocked by the German economic state apparatuses in the past (see Clift's chapter 7) and since it seems as if Lafontaine actually operated on the basis of a conscious alternative concept of governance, there was some substance to the claim of the British tabloid media that Lafontaine (from their point of view) was "the most dangerous man in Europe." After all, a Franco-German "Social Democratic Keynesian" axis would not be an inconsiderable force with which to reckon in the EU or even the G-7 (see Cafruny's chapter 11).

The aim of this chapter is to go beyond the superficialities of personalities and to explain the determinants of the contradictory equation of disciplinary neoliberalism and the social market in Germany. I will argue that at its social core it is based on a social mercantilist and corporatist class compromise between German export-oriented capital and organized labor, which is mediated in slightly different ways by the main German catchall parties, the Christian Democratic Union

(CDU) and the Social Democratic Party of Germany (SPD). Fundamentally, the intersubjective framework of this alliance is "economic-scientific" in form and is based on a broad elite-level acceptance of Ordo-liberalism. Ordo-liberalism found its most elaborate and conscious expression in the theories of the Freiburg School to which the legendary postwar minister of economics of West Germany, Ludwig Erhard, belonged. It is against the backdrop of the doctrine of Ordo-liberalism that the policy of Bundesbank monetarism is formulated. Its legitimacy in German civil society at large is in part based on the material goods that it is seen to have provided to various groups as well as on a deference to scientific experts in an "ideology of authorization."[3] Nevertheless, the hegemony of "Ordo-liberalism" "wears thin at the periphery"[4] of the social formation and it is more ambiguously reproduced in the mass parties, especially in the SPD and within the trade unions, than in its bastions of the German capitalist class and in the economic state apparatuses.

It is my thesis that Germany's social compromise has presupposed an exceedingly dynamic export sector, which has been able to serve as a catalyst of growth in the German national economy as a whole and whose rents have been available for a distributive bargain. For a variety of reasons, above all due to the path of post-Fordist restructuring pursued by German capital and German reunification, these conditions obtain to an ever lesser extent. This puts the equation of disciplinary neoliberalism and the social market under ever more stress, and it makes it ever harder for German political elites to render economic policy compatible with mass legitimacy. Overall, the main thrust of the strategies to cope with this problem has been based on retrenching the social market, but the social and ideological terrain is inadequately prepared for this and the CDU and the SPD have pursued retrenchment at high electoral cost. The "moment of Lafontaine" in 1998–1999 should be understood as an attempt to change the "disciplinary neoliberal" side of the equation rather than the social market in order to sustain a winning strategy of sociopolitical alliance formation in the wake of the collapse of Helmut Kohl's strategy. His has so far been the most comprehensive and provocative challenge to disciplinary neoliberalism emanating from the German state. It should be pointed out, however, that there have been more ad hoc, erratic, and subtler shifts in German policy that also point to the pressures German politicians face. This includes Theo Waigel's call to revalue Germany's gold reserves in 1997, Welteke's apparent "dovish" stance on euro interest rates, as well as Eichel's recent statement that it might be desirable to change the terms of the Stability and Growth Pact. Nevertheless, Schröder's resolve to stick to Ordo-liberal orthodoxy in the overall economic strategy despite the electoral risks and costs, and Lafontaine's abrupt departure, indicate how powerful transnational scientific-ideological discourse and the structural power of capital are. The question is whether it will be possible to reproduce this contradictory equation in the future. This remains a crucial question for the emerging neoliberal European order.

DISCIPLINARY NEOLIBERALISM AND THE SOCIAL MARKET: THE GERMAN MODEL

Germany has been able to project its economic policy priorities and strategy onto the European macroregional terrain in the past decades, and simultaneously it has served the more cosmopolitan and transnational ends of disciplinary neoliberalism in Europe. The German Bundesbank and Ministry of Finance have served as propagators and guarantors of neoliberal restructuring in Europe. But, at the same time, there is a significant social-mercantilist dimension to their actions that has ensured the integration of German welfare state constituencies. I suggest, then, that the EMU à la Maastricht is based on an implicit alliance of what Stephen Gill in chapter 2 has called "the rentier bloc"[5] and the distinct class compromise of the "German model."

The German state strategy of this power bloc can be traced back to the 1970s and the response of Helmut Schmidt's Social Democratic/Liberal (SPD/FDP) government to the effects of the collapse of Bretton Woods and the oil crisis. The aim of this strategy was to consolidate the competitive position of the German export sector while ensuring the consent of welfare constituencies, especially organized labor, and hence advance Germany's national interest. The critical link in this context was the importance of export competitiveness for the financing of the "social market."[6] The continued importance of organized labor should not be underestimated. It made, and continues to make, a Thatcherite strategy problematic in Germany. The role of organized labor has deep roots, going back to the patterns of Germany's "late" industrialization, which implied certain continuities with corporatist traditions in which trade unions have been able to secure an acknowledged role in socioeconomic integration (as *Ordnungsfaktor*). The trade unions were also important as institutions in the forging of a liberal democratic consciousness immediately after World War II, as they were one of the few categories of German institutions that had not been tainted by the Nazi period.[7] Organized labor has remained the single most important social faction underpinning the SPD, but also in the CDU it constitutes an important minority.[8]

The primary aim of the SPD/FDP strategy under Schmidt was price stability at home, a revaluation of the mark in relation to the dollar-denominated consumer- and industry-input imports (especially oil and other strategic raw materials). This benefited German export competitiveness because, on average, the costs of raw materials fell more than the rate of price increases for German exports. A second and intimately related aim was to prevent price competition to German products in Europe as a result of this revaluation; Europe was the largest market outlet for German producers but not proportionally significant for industrial input imports. Hence, after the collapse of Bretton Woods, Germany abandoned its pre–Werner Report skepticism toward a European monetary union and took the lead in instituting first the "currency snake" and then the EMS. Germany's position as the key surplus economy in Europe, which made it the key contributor to the foreign exchange reserve pool, gave it a decisive leverage in setting the terms for the EMS. Other EMS members agreed to German conditions because of their interest in stabilizing prices of their German-supplied investment goods.[9]

In the EMS, this policy was exerted through the Exchange Rate Mechanism (ERM). The ERM also served to generalize monetarist norms from the Bundesbank, regulating the "price-anchor" currency of the German mark on the basis of a strict norm of price stability (through money supply targets). Other states then managed their exchange rates through interest rate variations (determined by the "risk premium" of their exchange rate over the DM). They compensated perceived tendencies toward higher inflation through higher interest rates. Alternatively, they pursued deflationary fiscal policies. In the short to medium run, a common pool of reserves could prop up the currency, but the Bundesbank (as the main possessor of such reserves) had formidable leverage over the direction of adjustment, because in the last instance it could withhold its support. Germany had insisted on this unilateral right as a condition for providing the reserves in the first place. This "exit option" exerted formidable market discipline on states in the context of high-debt ratios. In the 1980s this regime was strengthened through an emerging consensus on new constitutionalism (see Gill's chapter 2).

This euro-centered hard-currency policy pursued since the Schmidt administration was central for ensuring an acceptance of low wage increases in Germany. Revaluations ensured access to cheaper import goods and contributed to retaining a high mass standard of living. At the same time, organized labor supported the fixed exchange rates to prevent wage competition–based devaluations. The CDU/FDP coalition under Kohl continued this strategy, although with a slightly greater emphasis on austerity, selectivity in social policy, and microlevel as opposed to macrolevel corporatism.[10]

The structural economic preconditions of this German strategy of economic policy and monetary diplomacy can be captured by a term that I, following Nordic regulation theory, previously have applied to the Nordic models of welfare capitalism: "disarticulated Fordism."[11] In contrast to the ideal typical Fordist model, in Germany the articulation of mass consumption and mass production was mediated by the world market.[12] A dynamic, high value-added producing, leading export industry generated earnings that could underwrite mass consumption at home. The investment-goods-producing engineering sector was predominant, but some consumer-durable industries also gained significance through the course of the postwar boom (especially automobiles and whiteware). Germany's export sector was tied together through an interlocking of manufacturing corporations to universal banks (so-called *Hausbank* relations), generating a handful of "spheres" of finance capital.[13] This centralized and highly organized economic structure allowed for informal coordination and corporate planning between individual capitals at the meso- and macro-levels, in terms of investments, research and development, wage bargaining, and economic policy advice. It also made businesses coherent and willing bargaining and discussion partners for governments and trade unions. In other words, it facilitated a corporatist form of regulation.

Organized, export-oriented capitalism, and also the imperative to integrate groups demanding social protection (trade unions and farmers), generated quite a particular mode of regulation in postwar Germany. It assigned from the beginning a great deal of importance to sound money, and restrictive fiscal policies, initially within the context of an undervalued currency.[14] Capitalism was instead regulated through the informal corporatist channels and through selective means (the state used selective tax exemptions and interest rate subsidies provided by the *Kreditanstalt für Wiederaufbau* [KfW], transmitted by banks as the chief steering mechanisms).[15]

By the early 1970s, the German export sector, specializing especially in high value-added industrial input production (especially engineering products), had achieved a dominant position in the emerging self-referential European division of labor, which explains why the switch to a high-value mark strategy was possible and rational after the collapse of Bretton Woods.[16] This composition of the export structure also helps explain why, in contrast to most other OECD cases, Germany's postwar settlement was remarkably stable during the phase of Fordist crisis in the 1970s and the 1980s.[17] It provided a framework in which unions could negotiate wage, work time, and labor process conditions associated with post-Fordist conditions, in a manner quite consistent with the social market economy.

Part of the story is also, however, that organized labor and social democracy marginalized the new Left and new social movements in Germany, and demands for welfare reform were moderated to meet the challenge of stagflation. One central aspect of this was that during the Schmidt administration, Social Democrats and unions definitely accommodated themselves to the "social conservative" aspect of the German welfare state emphasized by the CDU, in which, because of the continued central reproductive function of the patriarchal family, there has been less of a "need" to finance an expansion of public sector services and employment, and less intra-union rivalry between the "exposed" and (feminized and unionized) "sheltered" sectors qua Scandinavian social democracy (although one should not underestimate the significance of employment in the infrastructural public sector, and subsidies to declining industries like steel and coal for employment). While German unions favored a more expansionary and proactive employment policy, after the peak of their power during the brief spell of Keynesianism during the period of the Brandt administration, they accommodated themselves to monetarism and higher unemployment during the Schmidt administration and tried to influence wage policy, workplace organization, and terms of economic restructuring within this constraint. This general pattern continued during the Kohl years.[18] In particular, in the 1980s, unions tried to mitigate the pressure on unemployment increases as best they could through negotiations for work time reduction and early retirement.[19] This defensive policy of social protection that accepted a *narrowing* of active labor market participation for the sake of competitiveness has been labeled *Spaltungspolitik*.[20]

Unions, then, accepted a policy that prioritized price stability, even at the price of unemployment, and prioritized investment over consumption to ensure a high value-added restructuring of the German economy. High value-added capital accumulation nevertheless ensured that high rates of social insurance coverage and service consumption were retained.[21] Creative policies of job reduction and early retirement were also pursued, and unions and works councils exercised some influence over post-Fordist restructuring through the legally binding practice of codetermination. As a result, wage dispersion within the unionized core was contained and Germany avoided an increase of wage inequality.[22] From this perspective, the monetary diplomacy applied by Germany in relation to the EMS and the EMU can be seen as a "continuation of *Spaltungspolitik* through other means" (to slightly misquote Clausewitz).

THE EROSION OF THE GERMAN MODEL IN THE 1990s

In the 1980s, it seemed as if codetermination, and sector-specific "solidaristic" wage policy and work time reduction bargaining, might provide an institutional form in which the microeconomic and supply side aspects of a "progressive post-Fordism" might be realized in Germany. There were many cases that seemed to confirm that union constraints on corporate strategy had effects. Such constraints seemed to exert pressure on management to pursue high value-added strategies and to develop innovative production techniques that rendered collectively negotiated social and codetermined outcomes technologically feasible and economically competitive. The fact that collective bargaining legislation had made labor a more fixed factor of production and more expensive to dispose of seemed central to the explanation. At the same time, codetermination served enabling functions: It ensured labor consent to technological change and "functional flexibilization" of work time, and it provided one way in which "quality circles" could be organized. Moreover, publicly provided and subsidized "broad" skills that yet could be configured to firm-specific conditions provided positive externalities. Hence the economic foundations for ensuring the incorporation of organized labor into the German model seemed secure.[23]

But this happy combination of monetarism and the social market, based on an exceptionally dynamic export sector and favorable location in the global and European division of labor,[24] has been put under much stress since the mid-1990s. It seems to be an increasingly implausible equation. As of the late 1990s, Germany seemed to be standing at a crossroad: It could embark on a process of welfare state retrenchment and recommodification, which would threaten the acquiescence of unions and other welfare state constituencies (or union officials to lose rank and file legitimacy in their continued acquiescence). This was indeed the direction pursued by the Kohl administration in its last couple of years before its electoral defeat in 1998. After Lafontaine's resignation, it has also become the strategy of the Schröder administration, despite the electoral risks that it implies. Alternatively, Germany could begin to pursue a different type of economic policy and monetary diplomacy that challenges disciplinary neoliberalism, as favored by Lafontaine. Such a shift would have serious implications for the content and direction taken in the fledgling EMU and possibly for the politics of the transnational monetary regime in general.

The limitations of the macroeconomic aspects of the German model of social competitiveness became increasingly evident in the latter part of the 1990s. The micro- and meso-aspects of the German model began to erode, as corporations responded by implementing more flexible-liberal corporate solutions, and as unions were weakened by mounting unemployment. As of this time, it seems as if Germany was beginning to be seriously affected by the competitive austerity to which other European national economies had been subject for close to two decades because of the configuration of the German-led European monetary regime. Competitive austerity accentuates economic stagnation and unemployment, which biases post-Fordist restructuring in a neoliberal as opposed to a progressive negotiated involvement direction. Suffering from fiscal crisis, all European economies are trying to run current and budget surpluses to reduce their deficits and debts. But they are thereby undercutting each other's markets and denying themselves of important demand-determined dynamic economies that would be required for a progressive post-Fordism: adequate investment levels, returns of scale, and a stable environment for "learning by doing" in the production process.[25]

This highlights an often-neglected aspect of the German model: Although Germany has typically pursued a tight macroeconomic policy, it has also always had a Keynesian dimension insofar as it has been dependent on international reflation. American policies, from the Marshall Plan on to the Reagan boom boosted by military deficit spending, have been important.[26] But Germany has also relied on expansionary policies in consumer-product oriented countries in Europe, especially France, which developed a "symbiotic" balance of payments deficit and a subordinate structural relationship with Germany.[27] As the United States started to "put its house in order" in the 1990s, and especially as France as well as the other European countries increasingly copied German policy through the Convergence Criteria of the EMU, Germany found it increasingly difficult to find export outlets. The expansionary policies in the former GDR temporarily counteracted this tendency but as this market saturated, the recessions of 1992–1993 and then in 1995 generated the fiscal troubles with which Germany still struggles. Moreover, the import requirements of a deindustrialized former GDR, funded by an overextension of the transfer-payments systems (especially pensions and unemployment insurance[28]) in a strong mark environment, also limited the capacity to pursue an export-oriented strategy. Paradoxically, convergence to monetarist norms in Europe, as well as reunification, is undermining Germany's structural dominant relationship.[29] Consequently, by 1995 Germany would find itself in the embarrassing situation of having difficulties in meeting the Maastricht Convergence Criteria that it had insisted should be interpreted in the strictest sense and made legally binding in the Growth and Stability Pact. It was in this context that the Kohl administration introduced the austerity packages and made its moves to deregulate the labor market. It was these measures that would make the administration so vulnerable to critique by the SPD/Green opposition, and consequently it lost power in 1998.

More research on the implications of this changing macroeconomic environment in Germany on corporate and sectoral restructuring is needed. Bob Hancké's research on the automobile sector, however, indicates that the pressure on the export sector, caused by the change in macroeconomic conditions and policy stance in the 1990s, compelled German firms to begin to shift their corporate strategies toward an emphasis on outsourcing qua "lean production" in order to cut costs.[30] This is consistent with a more market-oriented approach to post-Fordism. Above all, this implies that final assemblers shift the cost of adaptation to its subcontractors by varying their demand for components (by avoiding stockpiling, while still preventing shortages). This tends to polarize market terms of employment among subcontractors and final assemblers, and makes it more difficult to synchronize and maintain equal terms of employment within and between sectors.[31]

In short, although German labor-process organization has continued to be a site of innovation, the new macroeconomic environment has compelled corporations into more defensive strategies, emphasizing price competition. Although foreign direct investment outflows are more a myth than reality in the German case,[32] corporations have successfully used the threat of exit to exert their new corporate strategy.[33] The exceptionally high rate of the German mark in the 1990s contributed significantly to this process, since it increased relative wage costs and made it cheaper to invest abroad.

These corporate developments have polarized the terms within and between sectors to grant wage increases. This has unleashed centrifugal forces in industrial relations that have put sectorally based bargaining solidarity under serious stress. This poses a threat for the trade union legitimacy. Cost-competition has increasingly compelled companies to define the terms for wages and work time at the level of the firm. At the same time, actual unemployment and the threat of future unemployment have put unions in an increasingly vulnerable position. Collective agreements on the sectoral level have become increasingly empty in content. This is not only in terms of creating an enabling framework for solidaristic work policy at the workplace, but there has also been a hollowing-out of minimum standards (especially in the former GDR). Moreover, there has since the 1990s been a notable increase of cases of Works Councils engaging in concession bargaining to maintain employment that contradicts German labor law.

Unions have been reluctant to legally challenge such practices, however, because of the costs involved and because this would not necessarily be considered legitimate among the rank and file facing the threat of unemployment. These developments constitute tendencies toward enterprise corporatism based on Works Councils, which might in the long run threaten unions as organizations.[34] This, in short, amounts to an erosion of the German model and the social market, and a tendency toward market-determined commodification also on the labor market.

Austerity and unemployment has also been eroding another central component of the social market, and this is a further indicator that the sole reliance on work time reduction is not a viable strategy. Given demographic developments, Germany's pension system will run into a serious deficit problem. There will be more pensioners, and the reduced number of employed will not be able to fund these in the pay-as-you-go system over the payroll. So far, the reaction has been to increase rates of wage surcharges. But this increases variable labor costs and serves as a further impediment on employment. To cope with this problem, it is argued that an increase of the rate of employment is needed and this requires labor market deregulation.[35] There is, however, another possible route: to expand public sector employment to "Scandinavian" levels and/or to fund pensions through other means than payroll taxes on labor.[36]

SOCIOPOLITICAL REALIGNMENT AND THE ELECTION OF 1998

Against the backdrop of the changing economic conditions, CDU's electoral defeat in 1998 signaled the exhaustion of their particular way of articulating the German power bloc. From 1982 up through the election of 1994, the CDU, together with its more conservative Bavarian "sister-party," the CSU, and the Liberal FDP, had managed to mobilize a heterogeneous majority social coalition in which disciplinary neoliberalism could be legitimated. This coalition certainly included the kind of "modern neoconservatives" who became hegemonic in Britain in the 1980s. It also included "value-conservative" rightist populist elements. But the secret of the electoral success of this coalition was the capacity of the CDU to recapture and hold on to the votes of workers in "sunrise" (especially small-scale) growth industries in the Catholic south, which the SPD had captured from the CDU under the leaderships of Brandt and Schmidt. It was also crucial that the coalition recaptured the vote of "the bourgeois center." (This was in many respects symbolized by the fact that the FDP abandoned Schmidt's government in favor of a coalition with the CDU and CSU.)[37]

The two latter groups are particularly pertinent for our understanding of the ambiguous relation between disciplinary neoliberalism and the social market. They constitute a category of voters for whom "economic-political competence" is decisive. But they also are reluctant to abandon notions of social security and social justice, and the imperative of catering to them prevented a radical and Thatcherite deregulation program in Germany in the mid-1980s. (To this, one should add that the right of the CDU/CSU, with roots in the protected agrarian sector, also has an ambiguous relation to self-regulating markets.)[38]

After German reunification, the coalition was rendered even more complex when the CDU routed the SPD in the former GDR: By 1989, the SPD thought it had found in Oskar Lafontaine a chancellor candidate and a political concept that would allow them to recapture the strategically decisive middle groups while being able to hold on to the traditional unionized vote as well as the emerging group of environmentalists. But the SPD was totally unprepared for the new situation they confronted after the collapse of the GDR. Instead, the CDU managed to become the party of choice in the east, obtaining the vote of over 50 percent of east German workers in the 1990 elections. CDU was successful in the east, which had been an SPD stronghold during the Weimar Republic, because it invoked German nationalism and promised a quick development to Western levels of prosperity through rapid reunification.[39]

From a Gramscian perspective, the CDU managed in 1989–1990 to adequately represent and articulate together a complex amalgam of civil societal interests and connect it with a concept of socioeconomic regulation based on monetarism and an innovation centered selective corporatism.[40] The 1990 election represented the height of CDU's achievement in bridging the contradictions between the groups it mobilized and sought to represent, and the low point in terms of SPD's incapacity to do the same. It was in this context that the Maastricht Treaty, the Convergence Criteria, and the EMU were formulated and implemented.

Subsequently, however, the economic basis for this coalition eroded, and the CDU did not manage to reformulate economic regulation within political constraints. In the election of 1998, they lost 6.2 percent of their vote compared to 1994. The predominant cause for the loss of votes was high levels of unemployment. The CDU lost 9.1 percent of their vote in the former GDR, where its working-class vote collapsed totally.[41] The analysis of the previous section of this chapter suggests that the extension of the CDU bloc into the former GDR was not consistent with the concept of socioeconomic regulation. Hence, Kohl's promise of "blossoming landscapes" could not be realized as promised through this concept and the CDU paid the political price. Indeed, the changing macroeconomic circumstances seriously undermined the prospects of maintaining the coalition also in western Germany.

The favored response of the Kohl administration to the changing economic circumstances in the latter part of the 1990s was to hold on to strict monetarism, to reduce income and corporate tax rates, and to finance these tax cuts through a reduction of social insurance replacement rates and benefits. Moreover, Kohl's government aimed to deregulate the labor market. For this, however, the government depended on the cooperation of trade unions in tripartite concertation.

Furthermore, for tax reform it depended on the cooperation of the Upper House (Bundesrat), which represents the constituent regions of the Federal Republic of Germany. But the Bundesrat had progressively fallen into the hands of the SPD in the latter part of the 1990s. The unions and the Bundesrat refused to cooperate with the government on its economic reform agenda. The result was a stalemate that remained until the 1998 election.

Much of the election debate of 1998 was about whether Germany's problems were due to the faulty policies of the CDU or due to the "blockage" of essential reforms by the SPD. The verdict of the elections was to endorse the SPD position, or at least to give it the benefit of the doubt. The SPD increased their share of the vote by 4.5 percent, and for the first time in German postwar history, the SPD and the Greens received more votes than the CDU, CSU, and FDP. To this, one should add that the East German ex-communist PDS managed to reach 5.1 percent of the total vote. With over 20 percent of the vote in the former GDR, the PDS hence established itself as a "third force" in that part of the country. The PDS had become a potent competitor to the SPD there, especially on issues of social policy. This upsurge of the PDS in 1998 was in a sense an expression of the exhaustion of the Kohl strategy toward reunification.[42]

According to surveys after the 1998 election, unemployment was considered the most important issue by the electorate (followed by "social problems" as a distant second). This underlines that although Germans have an aversion for inflation because of the 1920s, they also have an aversion for unemployment because of "1933." With 4 million unemployed, and particularly with difficulties in the former GDR, the situation was perceived as acute and potentially threatening for the democratic system there. Above all, it was considered necessary to tackle this problem because of the increased popularity of extreme-right groupings in the former GDR. The rise of the extreme right was indeed a more malignant expression of the representational vacuum in eastern Germany after the collapse of the Kohl strategy. It was indeed also primarily on the unemployment issue that SPD's successful electoral strategy focused and that it knew it would be judged. Immediately upon assuming office, the new government identified the reduction of unemployment as its primary goal. This was in part a goal sui generis; it was also formulated as the cornerstone of a budget consolidation strategy.[43]

A decisive contribution to the SPD victory was its capacity to reach 1.7 million former CDU/FDP voters, of which 1.3 million were from the west. Hence, the SPD managed to win back considerable support among the strategic middle stratum that has determined which party wins since the victory of Brandt (that is, white-collar wage earners, and workers in "high-tech" sectors). There is a certain affinity of these strata to disciplinary neoliberalism and the rentier bloc as discussed earlier in this chapter, but they also have a stake in German welfare state institutions and a welfarist ethos (not the least in the pension system). Here the strategy of promoting the personality of Schröder, photogenic in the mass media, as a pragmatic competent manager seems to have paid off. At the same time, the SPD managed to maintain the required majority among the western-German blue-collar working class, which already in 1994 had "returned" to the party. Together with the Green vote, they also managed to mobilize the environmentalists and pacifists with roots in the 1968 movement. SPD also did well among the unemployed. With regard to this, Oskar Lafontaine's consolidation of the party apparatus was important for the electoral victory. Finally, the SPD picked up considerable gains in the former GDR, and in 1998 the SPD was the largest party there. In the east, the main news was, however, the total collapse of the CDU vote. SPD continued to fare poorly in southern Germany—Bavaria and Baden-Würtemberg—also among the Catholic workers.[44]

The 1998 election, then, produced a new constellation behind the government. It included the western-German middle class, but the difference was now that the government was dependent on the support of workers, not in the innovation poles of the south but in the traditional industrial, heavily unionized centers with structural problems, such as North-Rhine Westphalia and northern Germany, as well as in eastern Germany, where it faced a challenge from the PDS and even by the far right. In addition, the government relied on the support of women and environmentalists. To this one needs to add, of course, the dependence that all governments in a capitalist state face with regard to business. In particular, the government made it quite clear from the outset that catering to the needs of small innovative business enterprises was the centerpiece in their economic strategy. [45] A partnership between Lafontaine, in charge of party organization and strategy, and Schröder, the chancellor candidate and media personality whose pragmatism appealed to the business community and the middle class, was seen as a centerpiece of the organization of this sociopolitical bloc.

THE RISE AND FALL OF LAFONTAINE: THE BRIEF SPRING OF GERMAN-LED EURO-KEYNESIANISM

It is against the backdrop of the need to synthesize this heterogeneous set of interests that one needs to analyze the search of the new government for a coherent economic policy stance. The internal reorganization and discipline imposed under the leadership of Lafontaine on the SPD was one precondition for this, which ensured the successful mobilization of the core constituencies. The fundamental challenge was to integrate this organizational cohesion with the interest and images that Schröder had invoked in his successful appeal to the strategic middle-class and eastern-German voters outside SPD's core orbit. Symbolically, this synthesis was captured by the notion of the *neue Mitte* (the New Center). In many respects, the ideological articulation of the *neue Mitte* expressed a continuation with old Ordo-liberal notions. The new element was the connotative link between the citizens' movement of the "new generation," which has come of age, and the innovation centers. In effect, this represented an attempt to forge a new "politics of productivity" between German capital and the generation of 1968 that had become "pragmatic" and "realistic."[46] This is an alliance that the SPD and, perhaps even more, the Greens are eager to forge. As such, it has strong parallels with the notion of the Third Way as formulated by Anthony Giddens.[47] It cannot be underlined enough that Lafontaine was also representing this political direction.[48]

The attendant economic policy stance, as formulated after the election, had a strong unambiguous supply-side dimension. But it also had an explicit demand-side dimension. The role of the demand side was, however, more ambiguously formulated, and subsequent events were to show that the new Minister of Finance, Lafontaine, did not have the support of Schröder to pursue the demand-side policies that he considered to be necessary. What I would like to demonstrate, however, is that the demand side was crucial for reproducing adequately the terms of the successful 1998 electoral coalition. Without the demand-side policies, the government was bound to fall back to a policy stance similar to that of the Kohl administration, despite the fact that the electoral base of the new government made it even more difficult to pursue such policies and sustain political success. It is against this backdrop that one can understand Lafontaine's determination to change the terms of European and even global economic governance.

Immediately after the election, an economic policy stance was formulated that contained the following:[49]

1. The reconvening of tripartite talks on an Alliance for Jobs (*Bündnis für Arbeit*), from which the unions had walked out when Kohl announced austerity measures in 1996. These were to be coordinated by the former vice president of the IG-Metall union, the new Minister of Labour, Walter Riester. Talks were to consider, inter alia, comprehensive reforms and interrelations of reforms in wage determination, working time, the social insurance system, vocational training, taxes, and economic policy in order to set a framework for employment promotion. Since this initiative was procedural, substantive outcomes were naturally contingent on the outcome of negotiations between parties with different interests and visions. As for Riester, he considered the Dutch Wassenaar Accord as a model, emphasizing supply-side solutions. While he did see a role for work time reduction and early retirement, he was on record as someone that believed that the potentials of this strategy had reached its limits in Germany. Rather, he pinned his hope on the extension of vocational training and on tax-financed subsidies of social benefits for a low-productivity private-service sector. This would allow the latter to develop in a "socially just" way. The paper in question identified the educational-service, family-service, and social-service sectors as possible growth areas.[50]

2. Two tax reforms, both of which were intended to boost the labor demand elasticity of growth. The first was a reform of income taxes: The emphasis

was on a reduction of taxes for low- and middle-income earners with the purpose of boosting demand. The government also pledged to reduce maximum corporate tax rates. Together with this, social benefit (e.g., pensions, sickness benefits, and maternity benefits) levels were restored to pre-1996 levels. The income and tax reform was to be financed by the elimination of (mainly) corporate write-offs to up to 73 percent.[51] This was to be followed by two further net tax reductions of the same magnitude in 2000 and 2002. The income effects were supposed to fully finance these reductions. In the second reform, employer and employee social benefits contributions, which are deducted on top of the wage bill (*Lohnnebenkosten*), were to be reduced to under 40 percent of the gross wage over the mandate period, and they were to be substituted for by increased energy taxes, touted as "ecological taxes."[52]

3. The intention of implementing a host of investment programs. The most concrete pronouncements envisaged the promotion of enterprises in new energy and conservation sector. This was to form part of a program to phase out nuclear power.[53]

4. Finally, with a distinct Lafontainesque signature, the government announced that it was to pursue a counter-cyclical but solid fiscal policy with a "future oriented" investment policy aimed at keeping investments "at the highest possible level" and aimed at better coordination and cooperation on fiscal, monetary, and exchange rate policy with EU partners.

The underlying rationale of this policy package seems to have been as follows: Employment was to be promoted without labor market deregulation through a set of demand-pull and substitution effects, driven by the tax reforms. This policy was to be flanked and supported by wage as well as monetary policy, the latter internationally coordinated within the EMU framework. The lowering of unemployment and the increase of employment would lead to a consolidation of the budget. The shift to ecological taxes (a relative shift to taxation of capital and land) was to reduce the burden of labor taxes, and hence help employment promotion as well as the finances of the strained pension system. This is a policy that was designed to appeal to productive capital (investments and selective tax brakes), organized labor (employment promotion and tripartite negotiations), as well as the middle classes and the unemployed, especially in eastern Germany.

But the policy package left many questions unanswered. Would the quantitative effects add up? Was there enough room for maneuver if highly contingent conditions did not obtain? Clearly there were tensions and potential policy conflicts in the package. One central question was if the aims of financial consolidation could be achieved through these means. The cornerstone of the strategy was that the substitution effects associated with the lowering of labor costs and the desired effects of boosting purchasing power indeed would materialize. The effects on employment would have to be sufficiently positive to not only neutralize but also substantially outweigh the negative effects on tax revenue of lower tax rates. What the government could ill afford was a slide into a world recession. One other striking feature about the strategy immediately after 1998 was the extent to which the government was prepared to make "big" transnationally mobile capital (such as the insurance industry and engineering industries) carry the costs of adjustment through the reduction of write-offs and increased energy taxes. This strategy was clearly risky in relation to the ambitions to boost investments. This made the government even more vulnerable to recessionary tendencies in Europe and the world as well as to investment exit options.

It is against this backdrop that one can make sense of Lafontaine's initiatives on the European stage. The economic policy was very much dependent on monetary policy that maintained low interest rates and did not dampen aggregate demand. Furthermore, tax harmonization in Europe would assist revenue-raising capacities in general, and it would reduce exit options for "big" transnationally mobile capital. If relief on these fronts were not forthcoming, the government would have to consider a return to Kohl's economic strategy of reducing social benefits to maintain economic stability.

Lafontaine took a number of initiatives on the European and world stage that attracted considerable attention and that provoked considerable hostility from the disciplinary neoliberal circles:

1. He challenged the ECB and the Bundesbank. Although he did not question Central Bank independence, he interpreted its meaning differently from his predecessors. He argued that monetary policy must not only support price stability, but also support employment-promoting growth. In the immediate juncture, he called for a reduction of interest rates. What was particularly alarming for his monetarist opponents was that these initiatives came at a time when a new president of the Bundesbank was to be appointed, and it was generally expected that his deputy minister and chief advisor, Dr. Heiner Flassbeck, would be appointed to the post.[54]

2. He joined his French and Italian colleagues in a call for a more "flexible" interpretation of the Growth and Stability Pact, arguing that the definition of the deficit norms should not include "structural" capital investment expenditure. It is reasonable to see this in context of his support for a more activist coordinated fiscal policy for employment promotion.[55]

3. He supported a call by the Japanese Minister of Finance, Obuchi, for target exchange rate zones between the dollar, yen, and euro. He then took this idea further by stating that he also would like to see a broader process of restabilization of the global financial system.[56] It should be noted that exchange rate policy is one method that could be used to force the ECB to (partly) accommodate itself to a more expansionist stance within the Maastricht Treaty, since exchange rate management is not an area of exclusive ECB responsibility—it is shared with the governments of the mem-

ber states of the European Union. This is because the Council of Ministers may, with qualified majority voting, seek to define "bands" of currency fluctuation for the euro.
4. Finally, Lafontaine began to push for European Union–level corporate tax harmonization, to prevent competitive tax depreciation and further pressure on the fiscal situation of European Union governments.[57]

But subsequent events that led to Lafontaine's resignation illustrate the power of disciplinary neoliberal hegemony. Lafontaine was subject to a concerted campaign by German business and the economic expert establishment for his tax plans and audacity to meddle in the matters of central bankers.[58] This was paralleled on the European level in pronouncements especially by the ECB, conflict in Ecofin, and scorn and ridicule not only in *The Sun* but also in the *Financial Times*. The decisive factor was, however, that Gerhard Schröder was not willing to back up his besieged finance minister. Rather, officials in the chancellor's office began to undermine Lafontaine through a whisper campaign. In such situations, the authority of the finance minister is undermined, and Lafontaine felt that his position had become unsustainable. He felt that Schröder had, from his position in the chancellor's office, reneged on a preelectoral agreement between the two men.[59] Subsequently, Schröder moved quickly to assert his authority by taking over Lafontaine's post as party leader and by appointing a more conservative minister of finance: Hans Eichel, former premier of the State of Hesse, which is the location of Frankfurt. This also paved the way for, from the point of view of the monetary policy establishment, a more congenial Bundesbank president than Flassbeck: The former head of the State Bank of Hesse, Ernst Welteke.[60] Lafontaine's former allies in the party and the unions were remarkably quiet, in part alienated by the manner in which he chose to go, and in part concerned with not further weakening the government.

It became clear very quickly in the subsequent period that the German government would retreat from its comprehensive and proactive demand side policy. Eichel quickly assured the ECB that he respected its authority and sought a more collaborative relationship.[61] In the meantime, Schröder's supply-side and "modernizing" credentials were explicitly defined in terms of Tony Blair's "Third Way" and the Dutch "Polder Model" with which the *neue Mitte* was now equated.[62] Not counting on a demand-side boost, Eichel steered the course more in the direction of a budget consolidation that was very reminiscent of that pursued during the last years of the Kohl administration.[63] Consequently, with a government pursuing a more business-friendly agenda, the Alliance for Jobs talks have also become mainly a forum of concession bargaining, emphasizing recommodification, as in the Dutch case.[64]

The central political question with regard to this development is whether the present course can be any more successful politically than when it was pursued

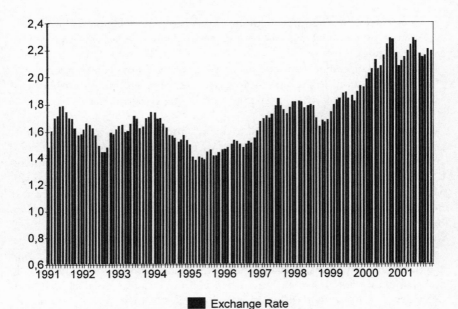

Exchange Rate

Figure 8.1.   Exchange Rate of German Marks to U.S. Dollar
Note: Since January 1999, euro converted to DM at the official rate of 1.95583DM/euro.
Source: Deutsche Bundesbank, www.bundesbank.de/de/statistik.

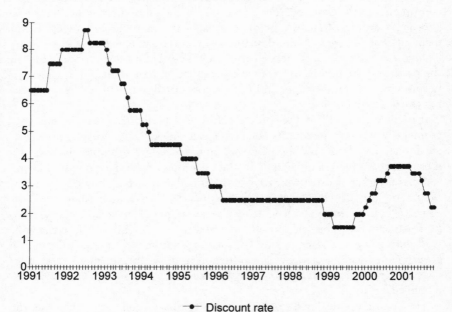

Discount rate

Figure 8.2.   German Discount Rate (Percentage)
Note: Since January 1999, this is the ECB discount rate.
Source: Deutsche Bundesbank, www.bundesbank.de/de/statistik.

by the Kohl government during its last years, especially considering the needs by the SPD to cater to the imperatives of social protection. Early indicators were that it cannot, as the SPD and the Greens lost a series of state elections, and lost control of the Bundesrat, because of a failure to mobilize its core constituencies. However, the corruption scandals of the CDU in 1999–2000 gave the government a new lease on life. In addition to this, in the absence of organized opposition from the Left, the government was ironically in a better position to pass business-friendly tax legislation. Hence, its bid to generate a more market-oriented growth strategy enjoyed better prospects of success.

But the greatest irony of all is that that the overall stance of monetary policy after the resignation of Lafontaine became more expansionary than Lafontaine himself could have hoped. In a development that echoes the French case in the 1980s (see Clift's chapter 7), when the leftist finance minister resigned, the euro was deemed to be a lower risk for financial markets, and this allowed the ECB to reduce interest rates after March 1999.[65] As figures 8.1 and 8.2 indicate, the interest rate subsequently increased in 2000, but this was against the backdrop of a rapidly depreciating euro. Moreover, in 2001 the rates of interest were progressively lowered at a continued low rate of the euro to the dollar; this policy stance has in effect ended the high-value mark policy of the EMS, and this ensured that Europe could be pulled away from recessionary tendencies through the "locomotive effect" of the American economy from 1999 through the first part of 2001.

This serendipitous effect, however, proved to be short-lived. After a brief recovery in 2000, following the American economy, the German economy has once again slowed down. In light of the need to reproduce its electoral coalition for the 2002 election, this is putting the German government under pressure. While there seems to be little sign of a return to an all-out Lafontainesque strategy, I suggest that it is in this context that we consider Eichel's pronouncements in August 2001 that he would like to make the fiscal terms of the growth and stability pact somewhat more flexible.[66] It is also in this context, I suggest, that one makes sense of Welteke's relatively dovish position on the question of the rate of interest of the euro and its rate of exchange to the dollar.[67]

NEOLIBERALISM AND THE "WAR OF POSITION" IN GERMAN POLITICS

This chapter has sought to complement neo-Gramscian works that emphasize the role of transnational agency in the construction of transnational hegemonic intersubjective norms. (I believe that these works are at their strongest when they reconstruct the relations between class formation and knowledge perspectives that indeed are essential to the intersubjective framework of transnational governance.) Drawing on the German case, I have done so by emphasizing the continuing

relevance of (inter-)state relations in socioeconomic regulation and in the organization of mass consent. One of the benefits of my perspective, I believe, is that it
allows me to point to the contradictions of neoliberal hegemony that in
1998–1999, in the form of the Franco-German axis, posed a real challenge to the
prevailing power bloc. I have argued that when Oskar Lafontaine challenged
the status quo of the EMU and sought to reform it in a Keynesian direction in alliance with the French Socialist government, he did so against the backdrop of
maintaining a broad electoral and social coalition in a context when economic restructuring in Germany had made a strong mark and monetarist strategy increasingly problematic, as indicated by the defeat of Kohl in 1998. The defeat of
Lafontaine does indeed point to the continuing power of neoliberal hegemony also
in German social democratic circles, which after all were responsible for getting rid
of Lafontaine. At the same time, I also pointed toward the importance of an expansionary monetary policy by stealth for keeping the present government on
course. Furthermore, when the slowdown is making this policy insufficient, we see
again indicators of inconsistency in the form of confusing "Keynesianesque" statements from Eichel and Welteke. In September 2001, Schröder even started a
Franco-German initiative to respond positively to antiglobalization protesters and
calls to investigate the merits of the Tobin Tax and other measures to reregulate
global financial markets.[68] Chances are that this will merely amount to a public
relations exercise. Nevertheless, the perceived need to respond is not without significance, and it points to the aforementioned difficulties in mediating economic
regulation with sociopolitical legitimacy.

Even in the absence of a challenge of the norms of transnational economic
governance of the type represented by Lafontaine, I think that German political
elites are going to continue to be tempted to use their position to soften the disciplinary nature of the European monetary regime. But these moves are likely to
be more narrowly of an economic-interest nature that will be presented as an
(acceptable) aberration from the prevailing norm as opposed to an all-out attempt to change these norms.[69] Such aberrations are connected to deficits in the
patterns of social representation in Germany, which are particularly acute in
eastern Germany where the principles of liberal democracy are far from firmly established. In the long run, however, one should not underestimate the prospects
of charismatic personalities such as Schröder to draw on ideology and mass media to change the economic expectations and incentives so as to weaken the
social market ethos in civil society. Possibly, a dualization strategy, which con-
solidates the rentier bloc while offering more low-wage, insecure, and precarious
work in especially the east, is a possible strategy. But it should be emphasized that
time scales are important. Trade unions, the social insurance systems, and the
sense of a social and redistributive solidarity are still not exhausted as "earth-
works and fortresses" against such a neoliberal movement. Given the prevailing
economic structural condition in Germany, these will continue to translate into
political pressure to reform the disciplinary neoliberal nature of the EMU as long

as the forces of neoliberal deepening have not decisively won the long-term "war of position" in German civil society itself.

POSTSCRIPT OCTOBER 2002

This chapter was completed just before the world recession deepened in the wake of the events of September 11, 2001, and the accounting scandals of Enron and Xerox. It was also written a year before the narrow reelection of the SPD/Green government in September 2002. The reelection of the government, despite maintaining the disciplinary neoliberal strategy through the slowdown, is in part to be explained by the fact that the CDU/CSU barely has recovered from a severe corruption scandal. It is also to be explained by the fact that the CDU/CSU decided to put forward the highly conservative and xenophobic CSU leader, Edmund Stoiber, as chancellor candidate. This limited the capacity of the CDU/CSU to forge a broad-based electoral appeal. The fear of a Stoiber victory also mobilized voters on the Left to vote for the SPD and Greens despite alienation from their economic and social policies. Despite this, the coalition almost lost the election, and victory was only secured through Schröder's populist response to short-term issues in the east (the Elbe floods of the summer of 2002) and through a pacifist stance on Iraq. This underlines the high electoral risks involved in maintaining the disciplinary neoliberal stance in Germany today, and recent pronouncements point to the difficulties of maintaining the macroeconomic stance. Although Eichel has backed down on reform on the Growth and Stability Pact, Germany will not be able to meet the 3 percent deficit target in 2003, and the new Coalition Agreement includes an explicit call on the ECB to lower its interest rate.

NOTES

1. On this distinction, see Robert W. Cox, "Social Forces, States and World Order: Beyond International Relations Theory," in Robert O. Keohane, ed., *Neorealism and Its Critics* (New York: Columbia University Press, 1986).

2. Ernesto Laclau, *Politics and Ideology in Marxist Theory* (London: Verso, 1977).

3. Pace Göran Therborn, *The Power of Ideology and the Ideology of Power* (London: New Left Books, 1976).

4. Pace Robert W. Cox, *Production, Power and World Order* (New York: Columbia University Press, 1987).

5. For a more elaborate account, see Stephen Gill, "European Governance and New Constitutionalism: Economic and Monetary Union and Alternatives to Neoliberalism in Europe," *New Political Economy* 3, no. 1 (1998).

6. Jeremiah Riemer, "Alterations in the Design of Model Germany: Critical Innovations in the Policy Machinery for Economic Steering," in Andrei Markovits, ed.,

The Political Economy of the German Model: Modell Deutschland (New York: Praeger, 1982).

7. Andrei Markovits and Christopher Allen, "The Legacy of Liberalism and Collectivism in the German Labour Movement: A Tense but Fruitful Compromise for Model Germany," in Peter Gourevitch et al., *Unions and Economic Crisis* (London: Allen and Unwin, 1984).

8. Josef Schmid, "Wandel der Konsensstrukturen: Die Volksparteien unter Anpassungsdrück," in Georg Simonis, ed., *Modell Deutschland nach der Wende* (Opladen, Germany: Leske & Budrich, 1998).

9. Carl Lankowski, "Modell Deutschland and the International Regionalization of the West German State," in Markovits, *The Political Economy of the German Model*, 95–97.

10. Bob Jessop, "Conservative Regimes and the Transition to Post-Fordism: The Cases of Great Britain and West Germany Compared," in Manfred Gottdiener and Nicos Komninos, eds., *Capitalist Development and Crisis Theory* (New York: St. Martin's Press, 1989).

11. Magnus Ryner, "Nordic Welfare Capitalism in the Emerging Global Political Economy," in Stephen Gill, ed., *Globalization, Democratization and Multilateralism* (Tokyo: UNU Press/Macmillan, 1997).

12. William Graf, ed., *The Internationalization of the German Political Economy: Evolution of a Hegemonic Project* (New York: St. Martin's Press, 1992), introduction.

13. Kurt Gossweiler, *Grossbanken, Industriemonopole, Staat* (Berlin: Das europäische Buch, 1971), cited in Josef Esser, "Bank Power in Germany Revisited," *West European Politics* 13, no. 4 (1990).

14. Willi Semmler, "Economic Aspects of Model Germany: A Comparison with the United States," in Markovits, *The Political Economy of the German Model*.

15. Richard Deeg, "Banks and Industrial Finance in the 1990s," *Industry and Innovation* 4, no. 1 (1997).

16. Christian Deubner, Udo Rehfeld, and Frieder Schlupp, "Franco-German Relations within the International Division of Labour: Interdependence, Divergence or Structural Dominance?" in Graf, *The Internationalization of the German Political Economy*.

17. Frieder Schlupp, "World Market Strategy and World Market Politics," in Graf, *The Internationalization of the German Political Economy*.

18. Inter alia Josef Esser, *Gewerkschaften in der Krise* (Frankfurt: Suhrkamp, 1982); Josef Esser, "Modell Deutschland in der 90er Jahren," in Simonis, *Modell Deutschland*; and Wolfgang Streeck, "Pay Restraint without Incomes Policy: Institutionalized Monetarism and Industrial Unionism in Germany," in Robert Boyer and Roland Doré, eds., *The Return to Incomes Policy* (London: Pinter, 1994).

19. Peter Swenson, *Fair Shares: Unions, Pay and Politics in Sweden and West Germany* (Ithaca, N.Y.: Cornell University Press, 1989).

20. Josef Esser, Wolfgang Fach, and Georg Simonis, "Grenzproblemen des 'Modell Deutschland,'" *Prokla* 40, no. 3 (1980).

21. Jens Alber, "Germany," in Peter Flora, ed., *Growth to Limits*, vol. 2 (Berlin: de Greuyter, 1986).

22. Wolfgang Streeck, "German Capitalism: Does it Exist? Can it Survive?" Discussion Paper. Max Planck Institut für Gesellschaftsforschung, Cologne (1995).

23. Wolfgang Streeck, *Social Institutions and Economic Performance* (London: Sage, 1992).

24. Schlupp, "World Market Strategy and World Power Politics."

25. Alain Lipietz, "The Debt Problem, European Integration and the New Phase of World Crisis," *New Left Review* 178 (1989); Robert Boyer and Pascal Petit, "Technical Change, Cumulative Causation and Growth," in *Technology and Productivity: The Challenge of Economic Policy* OECD (Paris: OECD, 1991); and Robert Boyer, "Capital–Labour Relations in OECD Countries: From the Fordist Golden Age to Contrasted National Trajectories," in Juliet Schor and J. Il You, eds., *Capital, the State and Labour: A Global Perspective* (Aldershot, UK: Edward Elgar, 1997).

26. Graf, *The Internationalization of the German Political Economy*, introduction.

27. Deubner, Rehfeld, and Schlupp, "Franco-German Relations."

28. Heiner Ganssmann, "Soziale Sicherheit als Standortsproblem," *Prokla* 106 (1997).

29. Christian Deubner, "Die Wiedervereinigungen der Deutschen und die Europäische Gemeinschaft," in Simonis, *Modell Deutschland*. OECD, *Economic Surveys: Germany* (Paris: OECD, 1993), 17 and passim, describes the concrete manifestations of this. The burden of unification was primarily carried by an unusually activist but procyclical and destabilizing fiscal policy in the early 1990s. But the attendant expansion of the economy took place in the context of high capacity utilization, which generated inflationary pressures. These were checked by the usual monetarist standard operational procedures of the Bundesbank, which resulted in an increase of short-term interest rates, which in turn resulted in an increase in the value of the German mark. This monetary tightening was then accompanied by progressive fiscal tightening as recessionary tendencies set in as of 1992. This amplified the downturn. The tendency toward short-term interest rate increases spread and was amplified throughout the EMS area (that is, to Germany's export outlets and especially France). There, they had even more of a deflationary effect than in Germany because of more elastic relationships between interest rates and investments. These deflationary factors were aggravated and made more persistent as a result of the Maastricht Convergence Criteria. Deflation in export markets, high interest rates, and an appreciation of the mark, OECD reported, put the German export sector under severe strain, especially the investment goods sector. Moreover, increased import penetration, which resulted from unification, high wage increases in eastern Germany, and a disproportional increase of activity in the building sector, contributed further to the undermining of export-oriented growth. The latter two contributed to increases in relative unit labor and factor costs. As a result of the first factor, export stimuli were now met with a withdrawal of activity through imports, leading to a "virtual disappearance of the contribution of the foreign sector to GDP growth."

30. Bob Hancké, "Reconfiguring the German Production System: Crisis and Adjustment in the Automobile Industry," paper presented at a symposium on "Modell Deutschland in the 1990s," Berlin, Wissenschaftszentrum, June 11, 1996.

31. An important question is whether a changing macroeconomic strategy as advocated by Lafontaine could have reversed this development. The opening of Eastern European labor markets in close proximity to Germany increases the scope for such labor market polarization, and hence it might be difficult to "turn the clock back." Moreover, Teague suggests that, since lean production allows competitors to compete on cost *and* quality, this post-Fordist production technique is now outcompeting the German model. This interpretation might, however, underestimate the degree to which the reduction of German competitiveness in the 1990s was due to currency appreciation and payroll tax increases to finance unification. Nevertheless, this might signal the limits to the German

post-Fordist restructuring, based on process innovation within "mature" sectors, as opposed to product innovation. It is within this context that one can view Germany's attempt to create new export growth industries through the privatization of public utilities such as telecommunications. Such privatization is Janus-faced from the point of view of the social market: It could provide the foundation for continued high value added competition in the export sector, but on the other hand, this privatization drive has negative effects on employment and on union clout in bargaining because it is intimately connected to labor shedding. See inter alia Paul Teague, "Lean Production and the German Model," *German Politics* 6, no. 2 (1997); Ganssman, "Soziale Sicherheit als Standortsproblem"; and Gilbert Ziebura, "Neue Herausforderungen für das Modell Deutschland," in Simonis, *Modell Deutschland*.

32. Michael Krätke, "Globalisierung und Standortskonkurrenz," *Leviathan* 25, no. 2 (1996).

33. Ziebura, "Neue Herausforderungen."

34. Jörg Flecker and Thorsten Schulten, "The End of Institutional Stability: What Future for the 'German Model'?" *Economic and Industrial Democracy* 20, no. 1 (1999).

35. Gösta Esping-Andersen, "Welfare States without Work: The Impasse of Labour Shedding and Familialism in Continental European Social Policy," in Gösta Esping-Andersen, ed., *Welfare States in Transition: National Adaptations in Global Economies* (London: Sage in association with UNRISD, 1996).

36. Gösta Esping-Andersen laid out these possible scenarios on the basis of his comparative research on the United States, Germany, and Sweden in 1990. In 1996, he retreated on his claim that the Swedish case represented a viable solution. However, I have shown elsewhere that that argument accepts on face value the spurious neoliberal argument that there is only one way to apply post-Fordist technology for sustained economic growth. See inter alia Gösta Esping-Andersen, *The Three Worlds of Welfare Capitalism* (Cambridge: Polity, 1990); Gösta Esping-Andersen, "After the Golden Age," in Esping-Andersen, ed., *Welfare States in Transition*; and Magnus Ryner, *Capitalist Restructuring, Globalisation and the Third Way* (London: Routledge, 2002), chap. 2.

37. Schmid, "Wandel der konsenstrukturen," 75; and Peter Lösche and Franz Walter, *Die SPD: Klassenpartei, Volkspartei, Quotenpartei* (Darmstadt, Germany: Wissenschaftlige Buchgesellschaft, 1992), 94–100.

38. Schmid, "Wandel der Konsensstrukturen," 77.

39. Schmid, "Wandel der Konsensstrukturen," 78–89; and Lösche and Walter, *Die SPD*, 100–107.

40. On the particular form of German catchall parties (*Volksparteien*) and their fundamental challenge to make compatible the representation of heterogeneous social groups with a coherent concept of socioeconomic regulation consistent with the prevailing regime of accumulation, see Häusler and Hirsch, "Political Regulation: The Crisis of Fordism and the Transformation of the Party System in West Germany," 306.

41. Wolfgang Hartenstein and Rita Müller-Hilmer, "Der Linksrück," *Die Zeit*, no. 41 (1998): 17–19.

42. Hartenstein and Müller-Hilmer, "Der Linksrück," 18–19.

43. Germany Bundeskanzleramt, *Regierungserklärung des Bundeskanzlers vor dem Deutschen Bundestag: "Weil wir Deutschlands Kraft Vertrauen"* (Bonn: Gerhard Schröder, 1998), 2–3; and SPD and Bündnis 90/Die Grünen, *Aufbruch und Erneuerung: Deutschlands*

Weg in 21. Jahrhundert: Koalitionsvereinbarung der Sozialdemokratische Partei Deutschland und Bündnis 90/Die Grünen, Bonn, October 20, 1998, 3–4.

44. Hartenstein and Müller-Hilmer "Der Linksrück."

45. Germany Bundeskanzleramt, *Regierungserklärung des Bundeskanzlers*.

46. The *neue Mitte* invokes "the innovative," "creative," and those "willing and able" to take up the challenge of "global competition." But it also invokes "social justice" and "solidarity," and it represents the new political generation, with roots in the "citizens' movements"—"east and west." See Germany Bundeskanzleramt, *Regierungserklärung des Bundeskanzlers*.

47. Anthony Giddens, *The Third Way: The Renewal of Social Democracy* (Cambridge: Polity Press, 1998).

48. Richard van der Wurff, "Neo-Liberalism in Germany? The 'Wende' in Perspective," in Henk Overbeek, ed., *Restructuring Hegemony* (London: Routledge, 1993).

49. For an overview, see Germany Bundeskanzleramt, *Regierungserklärung des Bundeskanzlers*; and SPD and Bündnis 90/Die Grünen, *Aufbruch und Erneuerung*, esp. 1–13.

50. Walter Riester and Wolgang Streeck, "Solidarität, Arbeit, Beschäftigung," Beitrag zur Schwerpunktskommission Gesellschaftspolitik beim Parteivostand der SPD ["Solidarity, Work, Employment," submission to the Commission for Social Policy of the Executive Committee of the SPD] (1997).

51. Germany Bundesfinanzministerium, *Entwurf eines Steuerentlastungsgesetzes 1999, 2000, 2002: Rede des Bundesministers der Finanzen Oskar Lafontaine anlässlich der Debatte im deutschen Bundestag*, www.Bundesfinanzministerium.de/s…doc_show.asp?dokumentid =549&kategorie=1 (accessed November 13, 1998).

52. SPD and Bündnis 90/Die Grünen, *Aufbruch und Erneuerung*, 12; and Germany Bundesfinanzministerium, *Rede des Bundesministers Oskar Lafontaine anlässlich einer Debatte über Ökologischen Steuerreform im deutschen Bundestag* www.Bundesfinanzministerium.de/s …doc_show.asp?dokumentid=557&kategorie=4 (accessed November 20, 1998), 4–5.

53. Germany Bundeskanzleramt, *Regierungserklärung des Bundeskanzlers*, 3–4.

54. Inter alia Oskar Lafontaine, *Koalitionsrede*, Ausserordentlicher Kongress der SPD www.spd.de/events/ptt_koalition/rede_ol.htm (accessed November 1998), 9–11; and Germany Bundesfinanzministerium, "Bekämpfung der Arbeitslosigkeit bleibt die vorrangige Aufgabe der wirtschaftspolitik," *Pressemitteilung*, www.bundesfinanzministerium.de/s …doc_show.asp?dokumentid=554&kategorie=1 (accessed November 1998); Germany Bundesfinanzministerium, *Entwurf eines Steuerentlastungsgesetzes*, 2–3; Ralph Atkins and Frederick Studemann, "Germany, Japan Eye Currency Coordination," *Financial Times*, January 13, 1999; and Ralph Atkins and Tony Barber, "Germany Urges ECB to Avert Slowdown," *Financial Times*, February 13, 1999.

55. Inter alia James Blitz and Michael Smith, "Germany: Lafontaine Beats the Drum for Euro-flexibility," *Financial Times*, November 20, 1998; and Oskar Lafontaine, "Globalisierung und internationale Zusammenarbeit," *Zeitschrift für sozialistische Politik und Wirtschaft 2* (1997): 5–6.

56. Inter alia Atkins and Studemann, "Germany, Japan Eye Currency Coordination"; Lafontaine, *Koalitionsrede*, 11–12; Germany Bundesfinanzministerium, "Bekämpfung der Arbeitslosigkeit"; and Germany Bundesfinanzministerium, *Entwurf eines Steuerentlastungsgesetzes*, 2.

57. Germany Bundesfinanzministerium, *Rede des Bundesministers Oskar Lafontaine anlässlich einer Debatte über Ökologischen Steuerreform*, 7–8; Peter Norman and Wolfgang

Münchau, "Germany to Push for EU Tax Harmonization," *Financial Times*, December 3, 1998.

58. Ralph Atkins and Uta Harnischfeger, "Lafontaine Fights a Rearguard Action to Defend Tax Ambitions," *Financial Times*, March 3, 1999; and John Plender, "Bosses on the Barricades: German Companies Are Leading an Unprecedented Revolt against High Taxes," *Financial Times*, March 6, 1999. Interestingly, Plender concedes that Lafontaine's strategy of broadening the tax base is not that "leftist": "The revolt is, in reality, as much about clipping Lafontaine's wings as tax. Business and the stock market are concerned that he is enfeebling corporate Germany and damaging the credibility of the European Central Bank."

59. Oskar Lafontaine, *Das Herz schlägt links* (Munich: Econ, 1999).

60. Ralph Atkins, "Bundesbank Job Set to Go to Minister's Ex-colleague," *Financial Times*, April 19, 1999.

61. Haig Simonian and Ralph Atkins, "Germany's Belt Tightener: Hans Eichel, the New Finance Minister Is Determined to Cut the Country's 'Debt Mountain,'" *Financial Times*, May 17, 1999; and Tony Barber, "Germany: Frictions with the ECB Have Eased," *Financial Times*, June 1, 1999.

62. Tony Blair and Gerhard Schröder, "Europe: The Third Way/Die neue Mitte," in Bodo Hombach, ed., *The Politics of the New Centre* (Cambridge: Polity, 2000).

63. On June 24, 1999, the government unveiled a package of budget cuts and tax cuts, which Schröder described as representing a "paradigm change." The measures were also designed to make up what it understood to be a 30 billion–mark gap in Lafontaine's plans (which Lafontaine had hoped to cover through the fiscal effects of an expansion of aggregate demand). The government announced a more specific and deeper corporate tax cut than previously announced: a fall of corporate taxes from 40 to 25 percent and an abolition of capital-gains tax for cross-holdings. This entailed reduced spending on social services and employment, including regional aid packages to the east and pensions. Later, a new plan to reduce the top level of income taxes was introduced, which was more rapid and substantial than those in Lafontaine's plans. More systematic reforms of the pension system have also been introduced, attenuating the pay-as-you-go system and compelling Germans to start their own pensions saving to make up the gap. This was, however, a direction that Lafontaine also indicated might be necessary to pursue. Inter alia Ralph Atkins and Haig Simonian, "German Economy: SPD-led Government in Rare Harmony with Industry on Wide-ranging Budget Cuts and Lower Taxes," *Financial Times*, June 24, 1999; Haig Simonian, "Berlin Plans Tax Cut to Lift Economy," *Financial Times*, December 21, 1999; Ralph Atkins, "German Banking, Finance and Investment: Ageing Population Forces a Rethink," *Financial Times*, October 23, 2000; and Lafontaine, *Koalitionsrede*.

64. Reinhard Bispnick and Thorsten Schulten, "Alliance for Jobs: Is Germany Following the Path of 'Competitive Corporatism'?" *WSI Discussion Paper No. 84, Institute of Economic and Social Research in the Hans Böckler Foundation* (Düsseldorf: WSI, 2000).

65. Alan Beattie and Melanie Carroll, "EURO Boosted after Lafontaine Exits," *Financial Times*, March 12, 1999; John Labate and Arkady Ostrovsky, "German Resignation Boosts Prices," *Financial Times*, March 12, 1999; Florian Gimbel, "Lafontaine Overshadows Oil and Bank Equities," *Financial Times*, March 12, 1999.

66. Lionel Barber, "Eichel's Second Thoughts," *Financial Times*, August 21, 2001.

67. Peter Hall, Michael Morgan, and Sathnam Sanghera, "World Stock Markets: Weak EURO Helps Halt Declines," *Financial Times*, July 28, 1999; Alan Beattie, "Wel-

teke remarks leave EURO standing," *Financial Times*, 28 July, 1999; Tony Barber, "A Banker Skilled in Diplomacy," *Financial Times*, September 10, 1999; Tony Barber, "Changing Places: Has France, Once Associated with State Intervention and High Inflation, Started to Displace Germany As Europe's Champion of a Strong Currency and As an Engine of Economic Expansion?" *Financial Times*, February 23, 2000; and Andrew Gowers, "Bundesbank President Sees no Need for Higher Interest Rates: Welteke Takes Dovish Line As Inflationary Pressures Build in the EURO-zone," *Financial Times*, March 27, 2000.

68. Haig Simonian, "Franco-German Summit to Look at World Market," *Financial Times*, September 2001.

69. In this context, it is worthwhile to note that business leaders state that their antagonism toward Lafontaine was just as much a question of tone and procedure questioning "credibility" as it was substantive; see Simonian, "Berlin Plans Tax Cut."

III

❧

THE EUROPEAN UNION BEYOND NEOLIBERALISM?

9

"Competitive Restructuring" and Industrial Relations within the European Union

Corporatist Involvement and Beyond

HANS-JÜRGEN BIELING AND THORSTEN SCHULTEN

The neoliberal hegemonic project is often understood with reference to an unhelpful dualism between the "market" and the "state." Here, neoliberalism is equated with the former category and understood as a "disorganized capitalist" phenomena.[1] The state, on the other hand, is understood as the opposite of neoliberalism, inherently associated with decommodification and social protection. This dualism ignores the fundamental role state functions play also in the social construction of market-capitalist society and in the mediation of social forces, power relations, and conflicts.

Discussions of the EU's social dialogue and corporatism in the emerging system of multilevel governance tend to assume this dualistic approach; hence these developments are often said to represent counter-tendencies toward an alternative "social Europe." In this chapter, we challenge the conventional approach to market and state and contend that such an approach is in fact part of what in chapter 1 was referred to as the "negotiated settlements" through which neoliberalism has been consolidated and normalized within the EU. The social dialogue and corporatism as institutional forms did not disappear in the 1990s. Rather, the content of corporatist regulation changed from the solidaristic welfarism of the Fordist period toward a depoliticized managerial mode of economic governance.[2] Unambiguously subordinated to the monetarist orientation of the ECB and the competitive exigencies of the single market, corporatism has in fact served to consolidate the new constitutionalism that was institutionalized in the Maastricht settlement (see chapter 2). Such a reconfiguration of corporatism has been made possible by the unprecedented weakness of the trade unions. Nowadays they constitute at best junior partners, which seem to have no other choice than to agree to a "new peace formula,"[3] essentially based on a joint commitment that the firm, the region, or the national economy has to improve its competitiveness under changed market conditions. This competitive corporatism is accompanied by an essentially symbolic Euro-corporatism, which offers next to nothing to trade unions in the here and now, but which maintains their loyalty to the system by holding out the promise of a social Europe in a vague, unspecified future.

In pursuit of this argument, we first outline the main moments of European integration and their impact on the reorganization of European power structures as well as for the transformation of industrial relations. We then discuss the character and the reproduction of the new multilevel structure of corporatist involvement, which seems to be an essential requirement for the (macro-)economic and political operation of the new European economy. We distinguish three main new forms of social concertation: first, "new social pacts" at the national level; second, new "competitive company alliances"; and, third, "symbolic Euro-corporatism" (the European Social Dialogue). The established fit between competitive restructuring and pyramid-shaped corporatist arrangements is, however, far from complete. Hence, we turn finally to the economic and political tensions and contradictions inherent in the complex arrangements of corporatist concertation.

THE NEW POLITICAL ECONOMY
OF COMPETITIVE RESTRUCTURING

A central dynamic force of competitive restructuring within Western Europe was of course the process of European integration itself. After many initiatives of sovereignty transfer, supranational state building, and the creation of an "organized European space,"[4] the area of common regulation and control has expanded to a wide range of political issues, among others social policy and industrial relations. Nevertheless, economic issues, above all monetary and market issues, have been and still are at the heart of the EU. The imbalance of economic and social integration gives the already present pressures of competitive restructuring—whether due to technological innovations, changes in the production chain, or more productive forms of work organization—an additional stimulus. Moreover, the renewal of European integration can be seen as an explicit attempt to revitalize capitalist accumulation in Western Europe by giving market forces a greater say within a rearranged, conditioning framework of neoliberal regulation. Common to all dimensions of this process is what Gill in chapter 2 called "new constitutionalism." The most decisive milestones in this context are the European projects of the European Monetary System (EMS), the Single European Market (SEM), the Economic and Monetary Union (EMU), and, more recently, the vision of a new finance-led information economy.

The EMS was established as a European response to the instability of liberalized international financial markets, which after the breakdown of the Bretton Woods system also increasingly affected the internal economic affairs of the European Community.[5] The high volatility of the dollar–deutschmark exchange rate made stable and economically calculable currency parities within Western Europe virtually impossible. Hence, after the defeat of the Werner Plan and the currency snake, Germany and France agreed to establish a new system of fixed but adjustable exchange rates, the EMS. It started to work from the beginning of 1979, and it operated fairly well for over a decade, despite increasingly liberalized capital and financial markets.[6] Although the fiscal imbalances induced by German unification plunged the system into serious trouble, its short history is seen by most observers as a success story. In fact, however, this success was not unconditional. Apart from all disputes,[7] due to the dominant and determining role of the deutschmark and the Bundesbank, it was based on the willingness of the participating governments to accept an asymmetrically distributed burden of adjustment and to pursue stability-oriented policies. In other words, the EMS provided a leverage to generalize the German stability culture and a monetarist approach of economic, financial, and monetary management.[8]

As neoliberal and monetarist ideas became generalized, the EMS proved to be a precondition for the Single Market project. Without the convergence of economic policy approaches, an encompassing constitutional rearrangement as agreed on in the Single European Act (SEA)—in other words, the abolishment of nontariff trade barriers, qualitative majority decisions with respect to the single market, and extended application of the principle of mutual recognition—would have been impossible. After the changes of governments in Great Britain and Germany, it was above all the French U-turn in early 1983 that enlarged the area of shared European interests and objectives.[9] The most important one was, of course, the widely acknowledged aim to overcome economic stagnation, the crises of public budgets and social security systems, and the so-called problems of Eurosclerosis, and to avoid falling further behind the more productive economies of Japan and the United States.[10] It is, however, not necessarily the case that a common perception of socioeconomic crisis and agreement about the main problems and objectives of European integration becomes translated into a coherent political program. Additional efforts were necessary before the vision of an integrated market, freed from technical, administrative, and political barriers, really entered and determined the European scene.

On the one hand, as described in chapter 3, there were incessant activities on the part of transnational capital, above all by the European Round Table of Industrialists (ERT), which insisted that a truly integrated European market was of utmost urgency.[11] On the other hand, there were, apart from the ERT but often in close cooperation with it, the entrepreneurial skills of the Delors Commission. The then-new Commission was very successful in synthesizing a broad range of neoliberal, mercantilist, and social democratic aspirations connected with the

Single Market project. In doing this, it succeeded in widening the public consensus and support for further initiatives of European integration. In this process, the trade unions were fairly important. First, in regard to the dangers of social dumping, they were rather skeptical or even hostile to the SEM. Such positions, however, changed after the engagement of Delors and some foreseeable progress in the social realm. Because of this, most trade unions were prompted to take a stance of "critical support."[12] This applied not only to the SEM, but also to the following EMU project.

The interests and motives for engaging in EMU have been far from uniform.[13] Whereas some emphasized the political control of unified Germany via EMU, others stressed the functional necessity to transcend the fragile EMS coordination, which seemed increasingly susceptible to speculative attacks. And a third group again put the accent on the chance of a more balanced economic governance vis-à-vis the economic and monetary authorities of Germany on the one hand and the United States on the other hand. Of course, there was also some disagreement—particularly in the course of intergovernmental bargaining—about how the different aspects should be stressed and realized in the final design and constitution of EMU. Apart from the British government, however, there was widespread consensus that EMU would further improve the advantages of the Single Market by providing lower transaction costs, greater market transparency, better conditions for business calculation, an improved European stance in global currency competition, and disciplinary incentives in terms of monetary and financial policies.[14]

The impact of EMU on the process of competitive restructuring and the transformation of industrial relations is principally twofold: It is due to both more transparent and better comparable market conditions, as well as some far-reaching changes in the macroeconomic framework. Concerning the latter, the old EMS was still stimulating tendencies of competitive austerity. This has changed, at least partly, with the transition to EMU. Externally, in other words in terms of Triad competition, such tendencies will prevail, but internally, within the euro area, competitive austerity will be a thing of the past. As the convergence criteria of the Maastricht treaty and, later on, the stability pact have shown, it has become, step by step, supplanted by a politically defined mode of "administrative austerity." How strict this will be handled depends eventually on the policy stance of the ECB, but also on some other constitutional and procedural elements of EMU, for example the definition of the new "policy mix," the broad economic guidelines, the macroeconomic coordination via Ecofin or the EURO 12 Group, the European macroeconomic dialogue, or even some national guidelines within the European employment strategy.

In principle, this provides the opportunity to widen the room for maneuver in governing EMU. So far, however, the disciplinary impact of EMU still works. This is partly due to the fact that in the nineties, trade unions had already internalized the threefold pressures of no inflation, budget consolidation, and improved capital profitability. As the statistics reveal, wage increases remained clearly below productivity gains,[15] which is a hint that trade unions consented to wage moderation and "competitive investment bargaining."[16] The latter indicates that disciplinary effects are not only exerted by the new macroeconomic framework, but also by new microeconomic strategies of competitive restructuring connected to it. During the second half of the eighties, the Single Market project had already stimulated a wave of mergers and acquisitions in the area of industrial production. This implies that pressures for industrial adjustment came not only from intensified intra-industrial trade, but also from the permanent threat to shift production sites. On the way to EMU, the volume and impact of cross-border capital mobility became even stronger. In the nineties, global foreign direct investment grew about 20 percent to 30 percent annually, and nearly two-thirds of worldwide capital outflows, in other words US$510 billion of US$800 billion, can be ascribed to TNCs based in the EU.[17] The increases here were partly stimulated by a second wave of mergers and acquisitions, which included more and more also financial actors, in other words large banks, insurance companies, and institutional investors.[18]

Until now, however, there has been at best a liberalized, not an integrated, capital market within Western Europe. Although the abolition of capital controls was one of the very first decisions of the Single Market program, serious regulatory hindrances did survive.[19] This applied less to the banking sector, where the Second Banking Coordination Directive had already been passed in 1989, but more to insurance services and even more to European security markets.[20] In the late nineties, the Financial Services Action Plan (FSAP) had been prominently placed on the European agenda to overcome still existing barriers in the financial realm.[21] It is obviously linked to the Lisbon strategy to create a competitive, shareholder value–oriented and knowledge-based "new economy." What this implies has been made very clear by Fritz Bolkestein, the commissioner responsible for the Single Market. From his point of view:

> Europe is adapting to the new world. We realize we have to create a more business-friendly environment to stimulate entrepreneurship, risk taking and innovation. Our fifteen Heads of Government met at a European Summit in Lisbon about a month ago. They set a clear strategic goal for the European Union for the next decade: to become "the most competitive and dynamic knowledge-based economy in the world." This is a bold objective. But achievable. In political terms the Lisbon Summit represents a sea change in European thinking. We have dates and timetables when market-opening measures have to be carried out. With benchmarking to accelerate inter-Member State competition.[22]

Besides all these proclamations, more recently their seriousness was even more underlined by recommendations of the so-called Lamfalussy Group to accelerate financial integration.[23] The suggestions, which were implemented in early 2002, refer to a new mode of regulatory governance based above all on two innovations:

first, an increased application of regulations instead of directives, which still must be implemented on the national level; and second, the establishment of two new committees—a European Securities Committee and a European Securities Regulators Committee—in order to accelerate the decision-making process in security market affairs at the cost of already weak democratic control.[24]

The more concrete measures taken so far do not only deal with financial market regulation, but also with investor relations and the mode of corporate governance. In this regard, they will seriously affect industrial relations regulation. It might be that the innovation and revitalization of the European economy are of topmost priority. At least as a side effect, however, the Anglo-Saxon business culture—in terms of shareholder and rentier interests—will get a stronger hold within European corporate governance systems. In principle, such tendencies have already unfolded on the way to EMU.[25] With the new common framework, which will include new rules for the operation of investment and pension funds, investor protection rules, accounting standards, takeover regulations, and, in a way also, a European regulation of employee participation, the reorganization process will certainly speed up. Of course, not all national regulations will become harmonized. Hence, in view of increased cross-border capital transactions and an emerging European market of corporate control, all the remaining national peculiarities—for example in the area of corporate governance—will increasingly be subjected to "best practice" comparison and, eventually, to the judgement of financial markets.[26]

CORPORATIST INVOLVEMENT WITHIN
THE EU SYSTEM OF MULTILEVEL REGULATION

The moments of the unfolding hegemonic project, which have been outlined above, indicate that the reorganization of European capitalism was not confined to the national level. It took place in an increasingly transnationalized arena and in an integrated European political economy.[27] As part of global or triadic capitalism, the European economy is based on a particular regime of capital accumulation, which is not only more transnational in terms of trade, transport, and foreign direct investment, but also increasingly finance led, in other words, determined by the development of financial markets, above all the stock market.[28] This path of transformation went hand in hand with the (trans-)formation of a hegemonic bloc of social and political forces—consisting of managers, bankers, insurance brokers, and real estate or financial services, as well as members of the European Commission, market-oriented politicians, neoliberal think tanks, and many journalists—largely integrated in a globalized business community, which meanwhile has created many links and (organized) channels of transnational communication.[29] Therefore, it is no accident that as far as economic governance issues are concerned, the contours of a European mode of regulation have become more and more clear-cut.

Despite the pressures of intensified transnational competition, most industrial relations systems in the EU have shown a remarkable stability regarding their national institutions, whereby changes and adjustments have followed a strong path dependency.[30] To a certain extent, there has even been a reinforcement of organized industrial relations and a restrengthening of trade union involvement in policy making at company, local, regional, national, and even European level. The latter can at least partly be interpreted as a reaction to the frictions and problems inherently associated with the new European economy. The conceptual motives for union involvement through various new forms of corporatist interest mediation are at least fourfold: Firstly, with respect to European growth and employment strategy, unions should provide only modest wage increases below productivity growth in order to stimulate investment and, as an effect of trickle-down, additional employment. Besides, they should participate in the political process to make a contribution to more employment-friendly, flexible labor market regulation and to a readjustment of social security systems. Secondly, with respect to monetary stability, wage moderation is again a decisive precondition. It should help to bring down or to maintain a low rate of inflation on the one hand and to support sound governmental budget strategies on the other hand. Thirdly, with respect to national economic problems—low productivity increases, an inflation-induced loss in competitiveness, or unforeseen shocks—trade unions should help to compensate for and balance uneven developments. Fourthly, and more generally, the incorporation of European trade unions or at least their leading representatives into a European hegemonic bloc of social alliances should strengthen and secure the political support and legitimation of market-led restructuring as the dominant form of European integration.

TRANSFORMATION OF CORPORATIST CONCERTATION

The concept of corporatism primarily provides a rather formal description of a particular mode of interaction between the state and a limited number of privileged organized interests, among them in particular trade unions and employers' and business organizations. Since its focus is on organizational and institutional arrangements and their influence on mediating different social interests, corporatism can principally be found under very different—including fascist and liberal-democratic—political regimes reflecting different political aims and outcomes. A basic common feature of all corporatist regimes, however, is the regulation of class conflicts regarding the distribution of national income and the structure of industrial relations through institutionalized forms of interest mediation, which are able to incorporate organized business and labor in political and economic governance.[31]

The concrete forms of corporatist arrangements, their major political projects and their substantial outcomes, depend on the concrete historical circumstances including the socioeconomic framework conditions, the power relations between different social classes, and the overall hegemonic political configuration. Although in its more authoritarian forms corporatism was a major tool to suppress an independent labor movement, in many countries the emergence of liberal corporatism went along with a significant strengthening of independent trade unions and an enforcement of political unionism.[32] Although corporatist arrangements were often ideologically accompanied by ideas of social harmony, which deny the existence of conflicting class interests, in practice these arrangements have always followed the logic of "antagonistic cooperation,"[33] according to which class conflicts are not surmounted but mediated on the basis of historically institutionalized class compromises.

The emergence of neocorporatism in the decades after World War II could therefore be interpreted as a specific political expression of the Fordist class compromise. The latter was generally based on a political exchange, whereby the trade unions gave up their more far-reaching goals of a socialist transformation through the socialization of capital and economic democracy in exchange for the establishment of a politically and socially highly regulated market economy composed of a macroeconomic regime of steady income growth, full employment, an extended welfare state, highly organized industrial relations, and a more or less extended involvement of trade unions in the overall process of policy making. The substantial core of corporatist arrangements in that period was the field of incomes policy, which aimed to keep price stability compatible with full employment within the overall framework of a Keynesian macroeconomic policy.[34]

The political exchange within Keynesian incomes policy had "largely the function of integrating organized labor into the economic status quo."[35] Trade unions were forced to give up their goal of a redistribution of national income through an expansive pay policy. Instead, they had to accept a policy of pay moderation according to which pay increases had to be in line with productivity growth and therewith should keep the given distribution between capital and labor income stable. In exchange, employers had to accept a more egalitarian pay structure, while the state agreed on tax reductions, the extension of welfare benefits or increased social participation, and codetermination rights.

The failure of Keynesian incomes policy in the seventies reflects in many respects the fragile character of corporatist arrangements. Under the conditions of full employment and economic prosperity, it was labor in particular that was often not able to fulfill its promises regarding moderate pay developments. The latter became most obvious in the late sixties and early seventies, when in many European countries a renewal of shop-floor trade union militancy rejected the demands of trade union leadership for pay moderation.

Under the conditions of rising mass unemployment from the mid-seventies on, however, the center of critique on Keynesian incomes policy passed over from labor to capital, which became less and less willing to accept the political price for corporatist cooperation and instead started to demand a more fundamental U-turn in social and economic policy including the deregulation and flexibilization of industrial relations. The change toward a more supply-side economic policy—mostly already introduced by social-democratic governments—ended up finally with a new neoliberal political hegemony in Europe, which fundamentally questioned the traditional Fordist class compromise.

Since Keynesian incomes policies were almost dead at the beginning of the eighties, many observers associated this with a principle crisis of the concept of corporatism. In contrast to that, however, from the mid-eighties many European countries saw the emergence of new forms of political concertation including a renaissance of national corporatism.[36] As will be outlined below, these new corporatist alliances have little in common with the corporatist arrangements of the Fordist period. Their principal aim is not to guarantee a smooth interaction of macroeconomic policy (as in the Keynesian concept) but to increase the overall national competitiveness. In order to underline the differences of Fordist and post-Fordist corporatism, many authors speak about a transformation from demand-side to supply-side corporatism[37] or from social corporatism to competitive corporatism.[38]

A EUROPEAN SYSTEM OF MULTILEVEL CONCERTATION

Industrial relations in Europe are faced with a new system of multilevel concertation, the overall aim of which is to promote the process of market-oriented restructuring through an active involvement of employees and trade unions in order to guarantee their political support and to safeguard a broad social acceptance. Therewith, the contours of a new hegemonic mode of regulating industrial relations in Europe have emerged as a specific combination of national competitive corporatism, competitive company alliances, and—to a large extent—symbolic Euro-corporatism (table 9.1).

National Level: Competitive Corporatism

At the end of the nineties, a social pact or another form of institutionalized tripartism at the national level was established in almost all EU member states—with the exception of France and the United Kingdom.[39] While in some countries (e.g., Austria and Denmark) national corporatism had continued to exist since the Fordist era, other countries (e.g., the Netherlands and Ireland) saw a reemergence of national corporatism as early as in the eighties. In the majority of the EU states, however, the new national social pacts were set up in the nineties, including the countries of southern Europe (Italy,

Table 9.1. European System of Multilevel Concertation

	National (regional/local) Level	Company Level	European Level
Characteristic Feature	Competitive Corporatism	Competitive Company Alliances	Symbolic Euro-corporatism
Institutions	Social pacts (at national level)	Company pacts for employment and competitiveness (PECs)	Social dialogue (at intersectoral and sectoral levels)
	Territorial pacts (at regional/local level)		Macroeconomic dialogue
			Various tripartite consultation bodies in the areas of employment policy, regional and structural policy, industrial policy, and the like
Major Aims	Improving national/regional competitiveness by: • Pay restraint • Reduction of social cost and company taxes	Improving company competitiveness by employee concessions in pay and working conditions	Strengthening political acceptance and legitimation for the major EU projects
	Fulfillment of EMU	Introduction of new forms of work organization	Integration of trade unions in restructuring of European capitalism
	Convergence Criteria and Stability Pact	Labor's involvement in and support of transnational restructuring	

Influence of European Politics

European benchmarking of "national models"

Involvement of "Social Partners" in
- Implementation of European agreements
- National Action Plans (NAP)
- Regional development projects funded by the EU (at regional/local level)

"European model": Partnership for a new organization of work

Social dialogue in the management of industrial change and corporate social responsibility

Information and consultation rights

European Works Councils

Financial and institutional support to European trade unions and employers' organizations

Source: Author.

Spain, Portugal, and Greece), which had no strong tradition of Fordist corporatism.

The reemergence of national corporatism was mainly due to three developments: First, in the transition to Economic and Monetary Union (EMU)—in view of the convergence criteria—almost all member states had to intensify their efforts to adapt their whole macroeconomic arrangement of monetary, fiscal, social, and wage policies, which seemed to be facilitated by the involvement of trade unions.[40] Second, the electoral success of new Social Democratic Parties and the formation of center-left coalitions stimulated corporatist alliances not only for practical, but also for ideological reasons.[41] And third, it became increasingly clear that those countries whose economic management had shown enduring corporatist features of interest mediation—for example the Netherlands, Ireland, and Denmark—had been most successful with respect to competitiveness and employment creation.[42] Against the background of the new political benchmarking procedure in the European Union, they became models in the discussion on so-called best practices.

Despite all the existing national particularities of the new social pacts, there are at least three closely connected policy areas that can be found in one form or another in almost every country and that could be interpreted as the core of competitive corporatism:

1. The commitment of the unions to a policy of pay restraint based on pay levels remaining below productivity increases, a (partial) opening of pay bargaining from sector to company level, and the acceptance of higher pay differentials;
2. The reconstruction of Fordist labor market and welfare state institutions in order to make the labor markets more flexible and to achieve a significant reduction in social security contributions and welfare expenditure; and
3. The reform of the tax system geared toward achieving a gradual shift of focus from direct to indirect taxation and in particular a comprehensive reduction in company taxes.

The most visible policy area within competitive corporatism is pay policy. Whereas it has always been a central aim of corporatist arrangements to guarantee moderate or restrained pay developments, the terms "moderate pay policy" and "restrained pay policy" have undergone a fundamental change in meaning and today are no longer associated with a productivity-oriented pay policy (as in the Keynesian regime), but instead with a competition-oriented pay policy aiming at a strengthening of investment and employment through the improvement of national competitiveness.[43] As a result, almost all new social pacts have contained more or less binding wage policy guidelines that either aim to undercut the average wage trend in the most important rival countries or generally seek to lower national labor costs by concluding pay settlements below the growth of productivity (table 9.2).

Table 9.2.   **Pay Guidelines or Recommendations in National Competitive Corporatism**

Country	Agreement(s)	Pay Guidelines or Recommendations
Belgium	Cross-sectoral bipartite agreements (1998, 2001)	Defining a maximum pay increase, which should correspond with the average wage increases in France, Germany, and the Netherlands.
Denmark	National tripartite declaration (1987)	Developments of Danish labor costs should not exceed the development of labor costs in competing countries.
Finland	Agreement of the national tripartite incomes policy commission (1995)	Pay increases should be in line with the total sum of the target inflation of the Bank of Finland (today the European Central Bank) and the national productivity growth.
Germany	Statement of the national tripartite "Alliance for Jobs" (2000)	Results of collective bargaining should be based on productivity growth and should be primarily used for job-creation measures.
Greece	National tripartite "Confidence Pact" agreement (1997)	Pay should rise along with inflation and should also reflect part of national productivity growth.
Ireland	National tripartite agreements (1987, 1990, 1994, 1997, 2000)	Determining of maximum pay increases in line with the European Stability Pact.
Italy	National tripartite agreements (1993, 1998)	Nationally agreed pay increases should reflect national and average European inflation, and additional pay agreements at company-level should reflect productivity.
Netherlands	National bipartite agreements within the labor foundation (1982, 1993, 1999)	Recommendation of moderate pay increases in order to improve overall competitiveness.
Norway	National tripartite incomes policy agreements (1992, 1999)	Pay increases should be in line with average pay developments of Norway's main trading partners.
Portugal	National tripartite agreement, a.k.a. "employment pact" (1996)	Pay increases should reflect inflation and productivity growth.
Sweden	Bipartite agreement for the industry sector (1997)	Recommendation for a "European norm," according to which Swedish pay should not rise faster than the EU average.

Source: Thorsten Schulten and Angelika Stückler, "Wage Policy and EMU," *EIRObserver*, no. 4 (2000).

The shift in pay policy primarily reflects a changed configuration of interests and bargaining power between trade unions and employers due to the transition from a full employment economy to a situation of mass unemployment.[44] In addition to that, it has also been promoted by the establishment of an institutionalized monetarism in Europe through EMS and EMU, which automatically counteract "immoderate" pay developments by a tough monetary policy.

Besides pay developments, the reconstruction of the Fordist labor market and welfare state institutions have been the most important issue on the agenda of competitive corporatism.[45] In comparison to the corporatist arrangements of the sixties and seventies, however, the new social pacts of the eighties and nineties are not about extensions of welfare state benefits (in exchange for the union's pay moderation) but about their limitation. A particular focus, thereby, was on the reorganization of the social security systems aiming at cuts in social benefits, a reduction of nonwage labor costs, and a privatization of parts of social security in order to reduce the financial burdens of both the employers and the state.

Against that background, the political exchange within competitive corporatism has become distinctly asymmetrical. Usually the unions are expected to make advance concessions, particularly in the form of pay restraint, which only rarely contain clearly defined quid pro quos (e.g., working time or tax reductions) and which are frequently balanced against nothing more than a vague hope of job growth induced by wage restraint.[46] The unions are, in principle, expected to adopt the neoliberal creed that considers economic problems to be caused by an overregulation of the economy and by generally excessive labor and welfare costs. From the trade union perspective, however, the most important core of the new competitive corporatism is that it may contribute toward stabilizing the national institutions of industrial relations, thereby politically maintaining the importance of the unions as an accepted social actor at national level despite a significant loss of power.[47]

The establishment of new social pacts at the national level has often been accompanied by the emergence of new forms of tripartite concertation at the subnational level, for example at the level of federal states, regions, provinces, or local areas. Some of them took the form of so-called territorial employment pacts, which became politically promoted and financially supported by the European Commission as part of the EU structural and regional policy.[48] Although these regional pacts vary a lot regarding their mode of operation and concrete policy projects, their core aim is to improve regional attractiveness for new business and investments. In that sense, the regional pacts complement the social pacts at the national level as a kind of "competitive meso-corporatism."

Company Level: Competitive Company Alliances

The market-led restructuring of European capitalism at the national level was accompanied by the emergence of a new "post-Fordist production model" at company level.[49] The latter was developed as a result of a fundamental corporate restructuring process, which includes various aspects such as the introduction of new information technologies, new forms of work organization, the acceleration of (transnational) mergers and acquisitions, the emergence of internationally integrated value chains, the reorganization of companies as widely independent business units and profit centers, permanent changes in the company organization as the result of in- and outsourcing of economic activities, as well as the introduction of shareholder-value orientation as the dominant form of corporate governance. Altogether, these developments had an enormous impact on the development of industrial relations and led to a fundamental questioning of the traditional Fordist class compromise.

Although the traditional Fordist production model was embedded in a strong national labor regulation provided either by national labor law or by multi-employer collective agreements at the sectoral or national level, post-Fordist production became widely associated with deregulated and decentralized industrial relations. Since the whole restructuring process took place under the conditions of globally deregulated financial markets, increased fierce competition, and mass unemployment, at least in three respects the new post-Fordist production model is based on a fundamental shift in power relations within the company.

First of all, there has been a fundamental shift in the power relations between capital and labor. Capital has more and more (actual or potential) "exit options" to undermine or change existing labor regulation. By using threats of layoffs, relocation, or modification of investment plans, it can force labor to accept concessions in respect to collectively agreed-upon or statutory employment conditions. Secondly, there has been a shift in power relations between local and central management. Since the governance methods within companies have become more and more market oriented, the local management is under increasing competitive pressure to fulfill its short-term profit targets. Especially within transnational corporations, local business units are centrally monitored under a permanent benchmarking process that aims at the global dissemination of "best practices" and the enforcement of competition between the different units within the corporation. In recent years, labor-related issues such as overall labor costs, labor productivity, absenteeism, pay settlements, duration and flexibility of working time, and new forms of work organization have become increasingly part of such benchmarking processes and provide an important tool for central management to put pressure on their local managers who then pass the pressure on to the local workforce.[50] Thirdly, there has been a shift in power relations between management and shareholders (in the form of institutionalized investors such as banks, investment funds, and the like) as far as the increase of stock market quotations have become the company's prime goal. Since the latter always depends on current company performance, the shareholder-value orientation produces a structural short-termism in companies' behavior, which enforces a permanent organizational restructuring and an elimination of those parts of the companies that cannot fulfill the profit targets.

Against that background, a new type of concertation has been developed at the company level that has often taken the form of so-called pacts for employment and competitiveness.[51] These new company pacts, which have been found in many European countries, are based on company alliances between the local management and the core workforce mostly supported by local labor representatives and sometimes also by local trade unions.[52] The general pattern behind all these new company pacts is the integration of labor into a company strategy that aims at the permanent improvement of the competitive performance of the local business unit. There are, of course, many different ways how this improvement can be reached, and so the outcome of the company pacts has shown many differences in detail. However, they also widely reflect the changed power relations within the company, which give them a highly asymmetrical character and put labor in many respects on the defensive.

One major area that the company pacts dealt with has been the introduction of new forms of work organization. At the beginning of the nineties, the transformation toward a new post-Fordist production model was widely regarded as an opportunity to overcome the old Taylorist form of work organization, with its strongly hierarchical work relations, by the introduction of a new more employee-oriented system of work organization including more "democratic" forms of direct employee participation. The introduction of a new organization of work was expected to improve both working conditions and productivity and therewith to create a new "win-win" basis for the integration of labor at company level. During the last decade, however, these expectations have often been disappointed.[53] Although there have been some innovative examples of new work organization, the prevailing trend so far seems to be that external economic pressures coming from fierce competition and shareholder-value orientation create a significant barrier to more substantial changes in work organization and sometimes have even promoted a re-Taylorization of work.

The basis for the integration of labor into the new competitive company pacts was, therefore, not so much the introduction of more employee-oriented work organization but instead the establishment of a new form of concession bargaining.[54] In order to avoid possible job losses, the employees' representatives—often with great support from the workforce—made concessions regarding pay levels, work time arrangements, and other working conditions, and in exchange they received from the employer a guarantee not to make compulsory redundancies for a certain period of time, which in some cases went along with promises for new investments. Although many of these company pacts originally emerged in a situation where the company was in a significant economic crisis, in the meantime they have also been applied in better performing companies and therewith have become established, more and more, as a "normal" type of labor regulation at company level.[55]

All in all, the new competitive company alliances have contributed to a significant decentralization of industrial relations in Europe. In various cases they even openly contravene valid labor laws or collective agreements and therewith represent a new form of "wildcat cooperation" at the company level. Moreover, the spread of the new company pacts has increased the pressure to change existing labor regulation in order to give more regulatory competence to the company level. Indeed, almost all European countries have seen a process of organized decentralization, according to which many provisions of existing labor law or collective agreements have been opened for a more flexible implementation or even a "regulated departure" at company level.[56] Therefore, the development of new competitive company alliances is also not in contradiction to the renaissance of national competitive corporatism. On the contrary, national social pacts have often promoted the process of organized decentralization, while both forms of concertation have helped to integrate labor in the overall process of competitive restructuring.[57]

European Level: Symbolic Euro-corporatism

Since the core political projects of recent European integration were identified as a central dynamic force for the new political economy of competitive restructuring, they have been to a certain extent accompanied by a new European social and labor policy that promoted the emergence of quasi-corporatist structures at the European level as a new mode of tripartite concertation.[58] The growing importance of European social and labor policy can be interpreted as a political compromise with those social forces, who criticized the existing imbalance between economic and social integration and who might refuse—at least potentially—their political support for the core economic integration projects.

It has been, in particular, the European trade unions who emphasized the possible negative effects of SEM and EMU, which might increase the danger of social dumping and downward competition within national social and labor standards. These complaints had already been taken up in the mid-1980s by the Delors Commission, which developed its vision of a strong social dimension of the European integration process.[59] Jacques Delors presented this vision in 1988, first at the Congress of the European Trade Union Confederation (ETUC) in Stockholm and then at the Congress of the British Trade Union Congress (TUC) in Bournemouth, and received strong support from the European trade unions who since then have taken a much more positive attitude toward European integration.[60] Initially, the concept of a social dimension was little more than a programmatic declaration to mobilize sympathy among trade unions and other social actors. However, in 1989 it materialized first in the so-called European Social Charter and the successive Social Action Program and later on in the Social Protocol of the Maastricht Treaty of 1991. All these initiatives followed the idea of setting up certain European minimum standards in the field of social conditions and labor rights in order to avoid social dumping.

Apart from that, the European Commission developed new initiatives to strengthen tripartite cooperation at European level. The first was the 1985 Val Duchesse initiative, with which the European Commission aimed to establish the so-called social dialogue as a permanent European forum for those European peak associations of employers and trade unions that had been designated by the Commission as "European social partners." This initiative did institutionalize regular meetings between representatives of the ETUC on the one hand and UNICE (Union of Industrial and Employers'— Confederations of Europe) as well as CEEP (European Center of Enterprises with Public Participation) on the other hand. These meetings resulted in a number of joint-position papers that have been of little consequence, however, since they only took the form of general, advisory, and voluntary documents without any binding effect.

The Social Chapter of the 1991 Maastricht Treaty (which was incorporated without any significant changes into the Treaty of Amsterdam in 1997) gave the social dialogue a much broader legal basis. For the first time, the European social partners were not only granted extensive consultation rights in all European social policy initiatives, but the treaty also made it possible for them to substitute the Commission's draft directives with their own agreements or else to enter into agreements on their own initiative. Subsequently, the social dialogue became considerably intensified, both at the cross-sectoral level (between the ETUC and UNICE and CEEP) and at the sectoral level (between the sectoral trade union and employers' organizations).[61] In the meantime, "four European social partner agreements" have been successfully concluded between the ETUC, UNICE, and CEEP, covering the areas of parental leave (1996), part-time work (1997), nonstandard employment contracts (1999), and more recently on telework (2002). In addition, three other sectoral accords concerned with sector-specific adaptation to the EU Working Time Directive have also materialized. The substantive results of these agreements are, however, rather modest and entail an improvement to existing national standards in only a very few EU member states.

The experiences of the social dialogue so far emphasize the "structural superiority of capital at transnational level,"[62] which holds that labor can seek its class interest only through supranational protection against competitive deregulation while capital can seek its class interest by simply rejecting and blocking a European-wide social regulation. The latter has been proved by the fact that the European employers' associations were only prepared to negotiate a European agreement under the social dialogue when they might have been able to avoid what, in their eyes, was a "less favorable" EU directive. Yet even this new form of European bargaining between the social partners "in the shadow of the law" has so far not proved very resilient, and has generally been limited to less controversial subjects. As soon as more controversial issues were involved, such as the introduction of European Works Councils (EWCs) or the issue of general employees' information and consultation rights at company level, negotiations failed because of the employers' resistance, although the European Commission had presented a draft legal arrangement beforehand.

Apart from the European social dialogue in the core of labor and social policy, during the nineties European tripartite cooperation structures were also developed in other policy areas. In particular, the European Employment Policy as a newly established policy field at European level led to a further increase of social partners' participation in European policy making.[63] European trade unions and employers' associations became structurally involved in the development of the annual European Employment Guidelines and are part of the new macroeconomic dialogue between the national governments, the European Commission, and the European Central Bank (ECB). The institutionalized involvement of the European social partners has also further increased in the areas of regional and structural policy as far as they have become more closely linked with employment policy.

Although in the past decade Europe has seen the emergence of a widely branched "corporatist policy community,"[64] the core political projects of European integration have remained largely unaffected by these developments and continue to follow the logic of competitive restructuring. The actual political significance of the European social dialogue and other forms of European tripartite concertation has therefore less to do with its few substantial results than with its political function to integrate European trade unions, at least symbolically, into the EU system of policy making. Such symbolic Euro-corporatism serves to a large extent the institutional self-interests of the European trade union organizations in Brussels and has been further stabilized by the development of a rather comprehensive informal network between representatives of the European employers' associations and trade unions and officials of EU institutions. A particularly close-knit network has been developed between the ETUC, its sectoral affiliates, and the Directorate-General for Employment and Social Affairs (former DG V) of the European Commission. Thereby, the European trade union organizations have strongly profited from the Commission's political and financial support, which has allowed them to expand their political and organizational infrastructure in Brussels to a remarkable extent over the last few years.[65] Today, they are reliant on EU funding for a substantial number of their activities, ranging from the organizational and translation costs for European meetings to considerable funding provided for European trade union institutions such as the European Trade Union Institute or the European Trade Union College.

The far-reaching political and sometimes even financial support of EU institutions for the European trade unions has, of course, ambivalent effects. On the one hand, it increases the scope for union activity at the European level, but on the other hand it also creates political dependencies that are of considerable consequence for the formulation of positions and strategies within the European trade unions. Regarding the core political projects of European integration such as SEM and EMU, European trade unions have always taken a "Yes, but" position.[66] They have usually supported the projects in principle, but have claimed to give them a less neoliberal direction by compensating the negative effects through the extension of European social regulation. Although the substance of what the unions have got so far is not at all able to fulfill this compensatory function, the emergence of symbolic Euro-corporatism has proved a relatively successful way to integrate them into a hegemonic bloc at European level while keeping alive their functionalist hopes of a slow but steady and continual expansion of European social regulation.

Finally, the EU institutions—among them in particular the European Commission—have also started to influence the development of industrial relations also at the national and company levels by actively supporting the idea of a European system of multilevel concertation. In particular, the European employment policy has become an important policy area through which the idea of "a strong partnership at all appropriate levels (European, national, sectoral, local and enterprise levels)"[67] has been promoted. Although the EU Council has always recommended extensive participation of social partners in the implementation of the European Employment Guidelines, the European Commission has evaluated, in detail, to what extent the social partners have actually been involved.[68] Based on this evaluation, the Commission came to the result that, for example, the social partners' involvement in the development of the National Action Plans (NAPs) has been inadequate, especially in those countries that have more decentralized collective bargaining systems.[69] The Commission called on the governments of France, Greece, the UK, and Portugal to improve cooperation with the social partners at national level.[70] In addition to that, the European Commission also took various initiatives that aim at the promotion of the "partnership approach" at the company level, such as the 1997 green paper, "Partnership for a New Organization of Work,"[71] or more recently the *green* paper, "Corporate Social Responsibility."[72] All these initiatives try to establish a new model of company-level concertation in order to involve the employees in the process of corporate restructuring.

Finally, in 2000 the European Commission established a so-called High-level Group on Industrial Relations composed of representatives of trade unions and employers' associations and of industrial relation experts who would make an evaluation on the future role of industrial relations in Europe. In its final report to the European Commission, the High-level Group emphasized the importance of industrial relations that

> can make an important contribution to good governance and push forward the European strategy, fostering modernization based on a social contract, exploring new ways to strengthen competitiveness with social cohesion, creating better prospects for employment and improving living and working conditions.[73]

Considering this, the High-level Group recommended the strengthening of social concertation at various levels.[74]

CORPORATIST INVOLVEMENT AND BEYOND?

Even under conditions of intensified, market-driven economic restructuring, the traditional forms of corporatist interest mediation and social concertation in Europe did not simply dissolve. They did rather undergo a fundamental transformation, above all in terms of their content. Institutionally, corporatist involvement at the national level is still most important, but evidently is simultaneously influenced by new modes of social concertation at the firm or regional level on the one hand and at the European and transnational level on the other hand. Of course, all these dispersed but interacting dimensions cannot be reduced to one single content; depending on the nation-state and the level of concertation, the bargaining issues and concrete power configurations are too different.[75] All in all, however, they have a general, and in a way ambiguous, effect: Although they might contribute to or perhaps even strengthen the acceptance of employees' representatives and trade unions as reliable political actors, they help to mediate a way of socioeconomic restructuring, which tends to favor a world market-oriented, cost-cutting competition strategy.

This holds true for most of the EU countries, at least. Apart from those societies without any significant mode of concertation, the character of corporatist arrangements, including the role of trade unions, has changed along the general lines of a market-led process of socioeconomic restructuring and political regulation. For the so-called social partners, this potentially implies some new or additional arenas of information exchange and political bargaining—and, by this, a strengthening of the logic of political influence vis-à-vis the logic of membership—but further also a weakening of autonomously defined interests on the part of trade unions.[76] There is, of course, no immediate trade-off between corporatist involvement and autonomous trade union politics. But if trade unions rely almost exclusively on their formal or procedural participation in political decision making and not on their original power resources—for example interest representation at the workplace, membership mobilization, and the capacity to strike or to organize public campaigns—they run the risk of becoming highly dependent on the willingness of other political actors—political parties, associations, and governments—to take the aspirations of trade unions into consideration.

From a trade union point of view, such a strategy of involvement is a not necessarily desperate but eventually unsuccessful attempt to overcome its own political and organizational problems. On the contrary, some national unions manage even to (re-)gain some organizational strength by the corporatist adaptation to the disciplinary pressures of competitive restructuring. Mostly, however, such strategic orientations are accompanied by political self-restraint, in other words the renunciation of vivid internal debates and any autonomous definition of trade union interests. It is far from certain what this will eventually mean in a medium- to long-term perspective. At present, however, there are at least some indications that a politically subordinate and dependent strategy of union involvement is becoming more and more unsustainable. Within the unions' membership base, there are signs of political discontent emerging in various European countries, since the GDP and enterprise profits have tended to increase substantially while—as far as social policy and wage relations are concerned—the claims, expectations, and interests of employees have failed to keep up. Forms of employee and union membership disappointment seem to be stimulated by the following developments:

First, at the onset of the new millennium, wage bargaining within the EU took place in a different socioeconomic and political configuration. On the one hand, the new configuration is still determined by the labor markets as well as by social and fiscal policy requirements to stabilize EMU.[77] Hence, it has to keep going along with the new policy mix and the EU Broad Economic Guidelines, which are mainly defined by business interests, in other words wage restraint, low inflation, low interest rates, and high enterprise profits. On the other hand, now that the transition toward EMU has been almost completed, there are some indications of a change of criteria and concerns of political action. There is already some talk of a post-EMU agenda, since wage bargaining has become more and more relieved of the burden of supporting the fulfillment of monetary and fiscal convergence. Moreover, there seems to be an emerging consensus among European trade unions that the coming focus should be on "the sharing of productivity gains" and the management of pressing social issues such as employment conditions, social exclusion, and pensions.[78]

Secondly, besides the changed (post-)EMU configuration, the consensus of wage moderation seems to be dissolving due to improved labor market conditions. The economic upswing in the second half of the nineties brought many European countries—although not the larger ones such as Germany, Italy, France, and Spain—close to a situation of full employment. Without doubt, this amended the bargaining position of employees and trade unions. Even if the unions are cautious and hesitate to take advantage of this modified power configuration, they are confronted with rising membership claims. After about two decades of wage restraint and redistribution of income in favor of capital, the recent collective bargaining rounds in Europe have shown that particularly in the economically successful countries, as for example the Netherlands, Ireland, Denmark, or Norway, the demand for more distributive justice is back on the bargaining agenda again.[79]

Thirdly, from the point of view of union membership, many of the recent forms of social concertation and corporatist involvement seem to be exhausted. Since management and investors make use of their capacities to play off the employees of different plants, on the firm level concertation is often associated with deteriorating work and employment conditions, while on the national and European level there are only few signs of social progress. Without a macroeconomic dimension, national corporatism—in other words wage bargaining, labor market policies, and social reform—is strongly determined by competitive issues, and the European social agenda contains hardly any issues of substantial regulation, but mostly issues of procedural coordination.[80] How such weak, often only symbolic forms of concertation will create sufficient consent on the part of union membership remains therefore rather unclear and uncertain.

Finally, the political constellations that have gone along with the reemergence of national corporatism are far from stable. After almost all EU governments were led by social democratic parties at the end of the nineties, in the meantime it seems to be that New Labour has already exceeded its zenith. In recent years, social-democratic led governments have lost the general elections in most European countries (Austria, Denmark, France, Italy, Portugal, Norway, and the Netherlands) and became replaced by more right-wing governments that often include not only traditional conservative but also right-wing populist parties. As in particular the example of Italy has indicated, the failure of New Labour in Europe might lead to new political alliances that take a much more anticorporatist attitude in favor of a more radical approach toward neoliberal policies.

So far, there are only some weak signs that the emerging discontent will lead to both: to a comprehensive and progressive critique of the European socioeconomic order and to autonomously defined trade union strategies. The main problem is that the (often rather diffuse) discontent is neither analytically nor politically linked to the most serious contradictions and potential conflicts inherent to the prevailing mode of market-driven disciplinary restructuring of capitalist societies. Analyzing the Seattle Movement, Stephen Gill refers to four main contradictions,[81] all of them driven by a market-oriented transnational constitutionalism: The first one is between *global capital* and *democracy*, since most powerful governments and TNCs try to evade public and parliamentary control by "locking in" neoliberal policies in supra- or transnational arrangements. The second contradiction—an economic and social one—is due to the *intensified discipline on labor*, in other words worsened social work and employment conditions as an accompanying result of transnational economic, social, and political restructuring. This discipline is, thirdly, stretching beyond the work and production site to the *sphere of social reproduction* so that family or community relations and social welfare regulation are also subjected increasingly to the flexibilizing pressures of market competition and profit criteria. And, finally, corporate domination tends to establish a kind of monoculture or *cultural imperialism*, which affects more or less directly the given diversity of sociocultural and biological relations.

It is this broader context that must be taken into account if unions are to rethink their recent political initiatives and strategies, and look for ways to mobilize more autonomously social and political capabilities. This means, above all, to strengthen transnational class alliances by cross-border union cooperation while simultaneously taking a more critical and self-reliant approach in terms of national corporatist arrangements.[82] The same is true for the idea of European social dialogue that Richard Hyman has described as

> one of the more fatuous of recent rhetorical devices within the European Union . . . (which) effect in the real world is imperceptible. But *within* and *between* trade unions themselves, the pursuit of dialogue and search for common opinion are vital requirements. Hence the task of European trade unions today may be encapsulated in the slogan: *develop the internal social dialogue!*[83]

In recent years, some initiatives toward more autonomous European trade union cooperation have already emerged that could be referred to as such a strategy. The most important can probably be found in the field of collective bargaining, where almost all European trade union organizations have followed the approach of the European Metalworkers' Federation (EMF) to coordinate their bargaining policy.[84] In order to avoid a European downward competition on wages and working conditions, the EMF has started to define political criteria for a solidaristic bargaining policy at national and local levels.[85] Besides this, there are also some broader discussions on an alternative macroeconomic approach of governing the European economy, for example by a growth and employment friendly monetary policy, a strengthened fiscal base for upgrading the public infrastructure, flexible work time reduction, and more binding and substantial European commitments in the area of social regulation.[86]

Whether such issues will seriously be placed on the European agenda depends eventually also on the capability of the unions to form together with other initiatives a bloc of progressive social and political forces. In order to do so, one of the pivotal tasks is to link the objective of solidaristic collective bargaining and macroeconomic policy to the concerns of progressive social movements, for example to the critique of deteriorated social and ecological living conditions or the development of unfettered global capitalism. For progressive unions, such issues cannot be an anathema. Some of them have shown this by their engagement in transnational campaigns and demonstrations in Seattle, Prague, Nice, Gothenburg, and Genoa. Such engagement is, however, only a first important step. In a mid- to long-term perspective, it is essential to develop alternative political projects to give momentum—against the prevailing mode of market-oriented constitutionalism and disciplinary competitive restructuring—to a solidaristic and ecologically defined "progressive constitutionalism."[87]

NOTES

1. Scott Lash and John Urry, *The End of Organized Capitalism* (Oxford: Polity Press, 1987), 232–84.

2. Peter Burnham, "The Politics of Economic Management," *New Political Economy* 4, no. 1 (1999): 37–54; see also Martin Rhodes, "Globalization, Labour Markets and Welfare States: A Future of Competitive Corporatism?" in Martin Rhodes and Yves Meny, eds., *The Future of Welfare: A New Social Contract?* (London: Macmillan, 1998), 178–203.

3. Wolfgang Streeck, *The Internationalization of Industrial Relations in Europe: Prospects and Problems*, MPIFG Discussion Paper, no. 2 (Cologne: MPIFG, 1998).

4. George Ross, *Jacques Delors and European Integration* (Cambridge: Polity Press, 1995), 107–35.

5. Loukas Tsoukalis, *The New European Economy Revisited*, 3rd ed. (Oxford: Oxford University Press, 1997), 138–42.

6. Eric Helleiner, *States and the Reemergence of Global Finance: From Bretton Woods to the 1990s* (Ithaca, N.Y.: Cornell University Press, 1994), 146–68.

7. Tsoukalis, *The New European Economy*, 152–62.

8. Kathleen R. McNamara, *The Currency of Ideas: Monetary Politics in the European Union* (Ithaca, N.Y.: Cornell University Press, 1998), 125–58.

9. Helleiner, *States and the Reemergence of Global Finance*, 140–43.

10. Wayne Sandholtz and John Zysman, "1992: Recasting the European Bargain," *World Politics* 17, no. 1 (1989): 95–128.

11. Maria Green Cowles, "Setting the Agenda for a New Europe: The ERT and the EC 1992," *Journal of Common Market Studies* 33, no. 4 (1995): 501–26; and Bastiaan van Apeldoorn, *Transnational Capitalism and the Struggle over European Order* (London: Routledge, 2002).

12. David Foden, "EMU, Employment and Social Cohesion," *Transfer: European Review of Labour and Research* 2, no. 2 (1996): 273–86.

13. Wayne Sandholtz, "Choosing Union: Monetary Politics and Maastricht," *International Organization* 47, no. 1 (Winter 1993): 18–25.

14. McNamara, *Currency*, 159–78.

15. Thorsten Schulten and Angelika Stückler, *Wage Policy and EMU* (Dublin: Foundation for the Improvement of Working and Living Conditions, 2000).

16. Frank Mueller, "National Stakeholders in the Global Contest for Corporate Investment," *European Journal of Industrial Relations* 2, no. 3 (1996): 345–68.

17. UNCTAD, *World Investment Report: Cross-border Mergers and Acquisitions and Development* (New York: United Nations, 2000), xxi.

18. Jörg Huffschmid, *Politische Ökonomie der Finanzmärkte* (Hamburg: VSA, 1999), 72–79.

19. Jonathan Story and Ingo Walter, *Political Economy of Financial Integration in Europe: The Battle of the Systems* (Cambridge, Mass.: MIT Press, 1997), 250–74.

20. William D. Coleman and Geoffrey R. D. Underhill, "Globalization, Regionalism and the Regulation of Securities Markets," in William D. Coleman and Geoffrey R. D. Underhill, eds., *Regionalism and Global Economic Integration: Europe, Asia and the Americas* (London: Routledge, 1998), 223–48.

21. European Commission, *Financial Services: Implementing the Framework for Financial Markets: Action Plan* (Brussels: Author, 1999), 232 final.

22. Frits Bolkenstein, "Financial Integration after the Euro," speech at Harvard Business School, April 27, 2000, www.europa.eu.int/comm/internal_market/en/speeches/spch149.html (accessed June 14, 2000).

23. Committee of Wise Men, *Final Report of the Committee of Wise Men on the Regulation of European Securities Markets* (Brussels: European Commission, 2001).

24. For a more detailed account of financial market integration see Hans-Jürgen Bieling, "Social Forces in the Making of the New European Economy: The Case of Financial Market Integration," *New Political Economy* 8, no. 2 (2003): forthcoming.

25. Story and Walter, *Financial Integration*; Martin Rhodes and Bastiaan van Apeldoorn, "Capital Unbound? The Transformation of European Corporate Governance," *Journal of European Public Policy* 5, no. 3 (1998): 406–27.

26. Hans-Jürgen Bieling and Jochen Steinhilber, "Finanzmarktintegration und Corporate Governance in der Europäischen Union," *Zeitschrift für Internationale Beziehungen* 9, no. 1 (June 2002): 39–74; and Karel Lannoo, "A European Perspective on Corporate Governance," *Journal of Common Market Studies* 37, no. 2 (June 1999): 269–94.

27. Hans-Jürgen Bieling and Jochen Steinhilber, eds., *Die Europäische Konfiguration: Dimensionen einer kritischen Integrationstheorie* (Münster: Westfälisches Dampfboot, 2000).

28. Robert Boyer, "Is a Finance-led Growth Regime a Viable Alternative to Fordism? A Preliminary Analysis," *Economy and Society* 29, no. 1 (Feb. 2000): 111–45.

29. Belén Balanyá et al., *Europe Inc.: Regional and Global Restructuring and the Rise of Corporate Power* (London: Pluto Press, 2000).

30. Franz Traxler, Sabine Blaschke, and Bernhard Kittel, *National Labour Relations in Internationalized Markets* (Oxford: Oxford University Press, 2001).

31. Philippe C. Schmitter and Gerhard Lehmbruch, eds., *Trends towards Corporatist Intermediation* (London: Sage, 1979), esp. 7–52, 147–83, 151–52.

32. Winton Higgins, "Political Unionism and the Corporatist Thesis," *Economic and Industrial Democracy* 6 (1985): 349–81.

33. Peter Glotz, *Die Beweglichkeit des Tankers: Die Sozialdemokratie zwischen Staat und neuen sozialen Bewegungen* (Munich: Bertelsmann, 1982).

34. Lehmbruch, "Liberal Corporatism and Party Government," in Lehmbruch and Schmitter, eds., *Trends towards Corporatist Intermediation*; and Michael Mesch, "Einkommenspolitik in Westeuropa 1945–80," *Wirtschaft und Gesellschaft* 10, no. 2 (1984): 237–69.

35. Lehmbruch, "Liberal Corporatism," 171.

36. Grote and Schmitter, "The Renaissance of National Corporatism"; and Giuseppe Fajertag and Philippe Pochet, eds., *Social Pacts in Europe—New Dynamics* (Brussels: ETUC, 2000).

37. Franz Traxler, "National Pacts and Wage Regulation in Europe: A Comparative Analysis," in Fajertag and Pochet, eds., *Social Pacts*, 401–18.

38. Rhodes, "Globalisation."

39. Fajertag and Pochet, *Social Pacts*; and European Commission, *Industrial Relations in Europe 2000* (Luxembourg: Office for Official Publications of the European Communities, 2000), 80–85.

40. Anke Hassel, "Bündnisse für Arbeit: Nationale Handlungsfähigkeit im europäischem Regimewettbewerb," *Politische Vierteljahresschrift* 41, no. 3 (2000): 498–524.

41. Hans-Jürgen Bieling, *Sozialdemokratische Wirtschafts- und Beschäftigungspolitik in der neoliberalen Konstellation* (Marburg: FEG-Arbeitspapier 20, 2000).

42. Paul Teague, *Economic Citizenship in the European Union: Employment Relations in the New Europe* (London: Routledge, 1999).

43. Thorsten Schulten, "A European Solidaristic Wage Policy?" *European Journal of Industrial Relations* 8, no. 2 (2002): 173–96.

44. Traxler, "National Pacts," 411.

45. Anke Hassel and Bernhard Ebbinghaus, "From Means to Ends: Linking Wage Moderation and Social Policy Reform," in Fajertag and Pochet, ed., Social Pacts, 61–84.

46. Hassel, "Bündnisse für Arbeit," 30.

47. Colin Crouch, "The Snakes and Ladders of Twenty-First-Century Trade Unionism," Oxford Review of Economic Policy 16, no. 1 (2000): 770–83; and Frank Deppe, "Sozialpartnerschaft ohne Alternative?" in Udo Klitzke, Heinrich Betz, and Mathias Möreke, eds., Vom Klassenkampf zum Co-Management? (Hamburg: VSA, 2000), 179–213.

48. European Commission, Second Interim Report on the Territorial Employment Pacts (Brussels: Author, November 1999), www.inforegio.cec.eu.int/pacts/DOWN/rap_en/rapp_en.doc.

49. Klaus Dörre, "Gibt es ein nachfordistisches Produktionsmodell?" in Mario Candeias and Frank Deppe, eds., Ein neuer Kapitalismus? (Hamburg: VSA, 2001), 83–107.

50. Paul Marginson and Thorsten Schulten, "The 'Europeanisation' of Collective Bargaining," EIRObserver no. 4 (1999): i–viii.

51. Keith Sisson et al., Pacts for Employment and Competitiveness: Concepts and Issues (Luxembourg: Office for Official Publications of the European Communities, European Foundation for the Improvement of Working and Living Conditions, 1999).

52. Keith Sisson and Antonio Martín Artiles, Handling Restructuring: Collective Agreements on Employment and Competitiveness (Luxembourg: Office for Official Publications of the European Communities, European Foundation for the Improvement of Working and Living Conditions, 2000).

53. Dörre, "Gibt es ein nachfordistisches Produktionsmodell?" 85–94.

54. Sisson and Artiles, Handling Restructuring, 117–18. Although the authors take a more positive view on the progressive potentials of the new company pacts, in the end they leave it open if the existing company pacts are little more than "concession bargaining by another name."

55. Andreas Maurer and Hartmut Seifert, "Betriebliche Beschäftigungs—und Wettbewerbsbündnisse—Vom Kriseninstrument zur regelungspolitischen Normalität?" WSI-Mitteilungen 54, no. 8 (2001): 490–500.

56. Traxler et al., National Labour Relations, 119–35.

57. Hassel, "Bündnissse für Arbeit."

58. Gerda Falkner, EU Social Policy in the 1990s: Towards a Corporatist Policy Community (London: Routledge, 1998).

59. George Ross, Jacques Delors; Patrick Ziltener, "Social Policy—The Defeat of the Delorist Project," in State-building in Europe: The Revitalization of Western European Integration, ed. Volker Bornschier (Cambridge: Cambridge University Press, 2000), 152–83.

60. Jon Eric Dølvik, An Emerging Island? ETUC, Social Dialogue and the Europeanisation of Trade Unions in the 1990s (Brussels: ETUI, 1999).

61. For an overview on the various social dialogue initiatives see Berndt Keller and Michael Bansbach, "Social Dialogues: An Interim Report on Recent Results and Prospects," Industrial Relations Journal 31, no. 4 (2000): 291–307; and European Commission, Industrial Relations in Europe 2000.

62. Wolfgang Streeck, "Entscheidung durch Nichtentscheidung: Zur Logik transnationaler Interessenpolitik," in Wolfgang Streeck, ed., Korporatismus in Deutschland (Frankfurt: Campus, 1999), 112–23.

63. Frank Deppe and Stefan Tidow, eds., Europäische Beschäftigungspolitik, FEG-Studie, no. 15 (Marburg: FEG, 2000).

64. Falkner, *EU Social Policy in the 1990s*, 186–207.

65. Andrew Martin and George Ross, "In the Line of the Fire: The Europeanization of Labour Representation," in Andrew Martin and George Ross, eds., *The Brave New World of European Labour: European Trade Unions at the Millennium* (New York: Berghan Books, 1999), 312–67.

66. Dølvik, *An Emerging Island?*

67. European Commission, *Guidelines for Member States' Employment Policies for the Year 2000 and Council Recommendation on the Implementation of Member States' Employment Policies* (Brussels: Author, 2000), europa.eu.int/comm/employment_social/empl&esf/line2000/line2000_en.pdf, 12.

68. European Commission, *Joint Employment Report 2000* (Brussels: Author, 2000), europa.eu.int/comm/employment_social/empl&esf/Emplpack/En/jointreport_en.pdf.

69. European Commission, *Joint Employment Report 2000*, 55.

70. European Commission, *Guidelines for Member States' Employment Policies*.

71. European Commission, *Partnership for a New Organisation of Work*, green paper (Brussels: Author, 1997), 128 final.

72. European Commission, *Promoting a European Framework for Corporate Social Responsibility*, green paper (Brussels: Author, 2001), 366 final.

73. European Commission, *Report of the High Level Group on Industrial Relations and Change in the European Union* (Luxembourg: Author, 2002), 5.

74. At the supranational level, the European Union should create new instruments and institutions in order to enlarge tripartite social dialogue. For example, the High-level Group took over a proposal originally made by the European trade unions and the employers' association to have an annual common meeting between the European Council and the European social partners. In the meantime, the European Commission has made an official proposal to establish an annual "Tripartite Social Summit for Growth and Employment"; see European Commission, *The European Social Dialog: A Force for Innovation and Change* (Brussels: Author, 2002), 341 final. Apart from that, the High-level Group demanded the European institutions to extend their instruments for European coordination of the development in industrial relations at national and company level, and to enlarge the use of monitoring and benchmarking methods in order to enhance a cross border spreading of best practices.

75. John Grahl, "'Social Europe' and the Governance of Labor Relations," in Grahame Thompson, ed., *Governing the European Economy* (London: Sage, 2001), 133–64.

76. Claus Offe and Helmuth Wiesenthal, "Two Logics of Collective Action," *Political Power and Social Theory* 1, no. 2 (1980): 67–115.

77. Kenneth Dyson, "EMU As Europeanization: Convergence, Diversity and Contingency," *Journal of Common Market Studies* 38, no. 4 (2000): 645–66.

78. Giuseppe Fajertag and Philippe Pochet, "A New Era for Social Pacts in Europe," in Fajertag and Pochet, eds., *Social Pacts* (Brussels: ETUC, 2000), 22–23.

79. Thorsten Schulten, "Tarifpolitik in Europa 2000/2001—1. Europäischer Tarifbericht des WSI," *WSI-Mitteilungen* 54, no. 7 (2001): 407–19.

80. Gerda Falkner, "EG-Sozialpolitik nach Verflechtungsfalle und Entscheidungslücke: Bewertungsmaßstäbe und Entwicklungstrends," *Politische Vierteljahresschrift* 41, no. 2 (2000): 279–91.

81. Stephen Gill, "Toward a Postmodern Prince? The Battle in Seattle as a Moment in the New Politics of Globalisation," *Millennium: Journal of International Studies* 29, no. 1

(2000): 134–35; see also Kees van der Pijl, *Transnational Classes and International Relations* (London: Routledge, 1998): 31–63.

82. Thorsten Schulten, "Barrieren und Perspektiven eines 'neuen Internationalismus' der Gewerkschaften," in Hans-Jürgen Bieling, Klaus Dörre, Jochen Steinhilber, and Hans-Jürgen Urban, eds., *Flexibler Kapitalismus* (Hamburg: VSA, 2001), 193–206.

83. Richard Hyman, *Understanding European Trade Unionism: Between Market, Class and Society* (London: Sage, 2001), 174.

84. Thorsten Schulten, "Europeanisation of Collective Bargaining: An Overview on Trade Union Initiatives for a Transnational Coordination of Collective Bargaining Policy," *WSI Discussion Paper*, no. 101 (Düsseldorf: WSI, 2002).

85. Thorsten Schulten, "A European Solidaristic Wage Policy?"

86. Memorandum of European Economists, *Full Employment with a Strong Social Constitution: Alternatives for a New Economy in Europe* (n.l.: n.p., 2001).

87. Hans-Jürgen Bieling and Frank Deppe, "Europäische Integration und industrielle Beziehungen: Gewerkschaftspolitik in der 'Regime-Konkurrenz,'" *Supplement der Zeitschrift Sozialismus* no. 4 (2001): 22–40.

10

❧

Cultural Policy and Citizenship in the European Union

An Answer to the Legitimation Problem?

GILES SCOTT-SMITH

> Legitimation becomes visible as a problem and an object of study only at the point in which it is called into question.
>
> —Frederic Jameson[1]

As previous chapters have indicated, from Gill's argument about a weakening of the "hegemonic aura" of the embedded liberal period and Cafruny's conception of a "minimal hegemony" and onwards, the issue of legitimacy, or, more specifically, its absence, is a major issue of contemporary EU governance. This issue has also become a major discussion point in much analysis of both the operations of the European Union institutions and the processes of European integration since the 1990s. In line with the general approach of the other contributions to this collection, this chapter analyzes how and why new forms of governance have arisen at the European level, and how new identities have been promoted in the context of a developing neoliberal socioeconomic order and its search for legitimacy. Claiming that the European Union is now some (unique) form of polity points to the fact that there are important additional dimensions to do with social, cultural, and political identities that have emerged and that also need serious consideration. As discussed in chapter 1 of this volume, whereas the introduction of constructivist approaches to the integration process has brought fresh insight into the analysis of changing actor identities in Europe, they avoid any consideration of material interests or power relations in this process.[2] The forces driving market integration, in order to achieve hegemony, have necessarily promoted the introduction of new, compatible identities to

261

achieve coherence within the emerging European social body. As indicated by the importance for hegemony of the ethico-political moment of Gramsci's concept of relations of force (see chapter 2), any investigation of European integration from a critical political economy perspective needs to take this wider sociocultural context into consideration.

The chapter is structured according to the following pattern. First, the issue of legitimacy itself is discussed, especially its relation to democratic systems of government. The starting point is taken to be that the problems of superimposing the national model of parliamentary democracy onto the supranational European landscape are essentially insuperable. This points toward a necessary examination of the possibilities for securing legitimacy and trust via other means. The chapter proceeds by charting and criticizing two important developments in this terrain of nonparliamentary legitimacy: European cultural policy and European citizenship. In the 1990s, these topics have received a great deal of attention, since it was their formal clarification in the Treaty of Maastricht that brought their significance (and potential) into the spotlight. However, the fundamental contradiction that this contribution seeks to highlight is that, although the forces of market integration require new identities (e.g., European citizenship) with which to legitimate and secure allegiance to the (neoliberal) European project, these alternative forms of legitimation are blocked by either national chauvinism or narrow neoliberal interests themselves.

The field that this contribution discusses is vast and the following analysis therefore does not claim to be a comprehensive review of the issues or problems (or relevant literature) involved. Instead, it aims to point out some of the paradoxes to do with "nonparliamentary legitimacy" within the context of the constructive phase of neoliberal hegemony in Europe. As emphasized in the opening chapter, the processes of integration as confined by neoliberal interests necessarily involve constant negotiation, compromise, and adjustment between opposing forces, and this is as true in relation to the construction of new identities as it is for every other field.

MAASTRICHT AND LEGITIMACY

Although questions of legitimacy have certainly arisen before in relation to European integration (concerning the right of the national veto in the 1960s, for example), there has never before been such sustained attention given to the social and democratic consequences of integration and the place of the public within its processes. Hence in February 2000 the Commission identified one of its strategic objectives as the need to promote "new forms of European governance," a central part of which will be improving accountability and "the effective involvement of citizens in devising and implementing decisions that affect them."[3] The immediate cause, or in Weiler's phrase the "constitutional moment," of these changed circumstances has generally been regarded as the signing of the Treaty on European Union (TEU) at Maastricht at the end of 1991.[4] Above all, Maastricht symbolized the "completion" of the Single Market and the introduction of the next stage of integration: EMU and the creation of the second and third "pillars" to do with the CFSP and Justice and Home Affairs. However, this broadening of competences at the European level can also be seen within the overall context of the Single Market imperative, since the necessary management of this project at the supranational level has pushed the EU's regulatory powers into ever-increasing fields of activity (such as immigration, policing, and security). In other words, the three separate pillars are part of, and are generated by, the same economically driven dynamic of integration. Thus Kees van der Pijl's description of socialization (*Vergesellschaftung*) as "the planned or otherwise normatively unified interdependence of functionally divided social activity" within the logic of market forces.[5] Socialization is not an automatic process, and as it incorporates new fields of social life it also opens up more sites of contention.

By extending the processes of supranational management within the EU, Maastricht caused considerable debate as to the existing apparatus for democratic accountability and popular representation in the European Union, and how this might be improved. Above all, the European Parliament notwithstanding, the traditional mechanisms for channeling the democratic consent of the governed remained framed in a national context. For the first time in the history of European integration, therefore, there was a sense, widespread across all member-state societies, that the pace and scale of integration were occurring without sufficient attention being given to the possibilities for the democratic participation of the European public. What is more, the room for sociopolitical maneuver to resolve this problem is small under the conditions of fiscal discipline as encased by EMU. As Stephen Gill framed it in chapter 2, EMU is a form of supranational neoliberal "new constitutionalism" that aims to secure monetary stability in the euro zone while simultaneously delimiting the space for the operation of democracy.[6]

However, Maastricht also included two other significant extensions of governance on the European level that relate to the processes of socialization and the question of legitimacy in important ways. Firstly, there was the outline of some form of cultural policy to coordinate the cultural interests of the member states. Secondly, there was the introduction of a form of European citizenship, with the intention of enhancing rather than replacing the currently existing national citizenship characteristics. Taken together, despite their relatively minimal and fragmentary nature at present, these developments point toward the potential formation of a European consciousness in line with the gradual evolution of the EU into a single economic, financial, and political space. Although the EU is more than an arena for intergovernmental problem solving, as a functionalist or liberal perspective might have it, and more than the simple sum of state interests, as realists would argue, it is also not a constitutional European state. Within this scenario, European cultural policy and citizenship could potentially provide important elements of some form of postnational legitimacy[7] parallel to Castell's notion of the development of the Europe-wide "network state"[8] and the transformation of the European Union, especially since Maastricht, into a realm of post-parliamentary or multilevel governance.[9] Yet the contours and consequences of any claim to postnational legitimacy on behalf of the EU, particularly under the prevailing political and economic conditions, remain vague and uncertain. Is it right, for instance, to transpose the qualities of nation-state legitimacy onto the EU and expect a direct match? Should the EU not be considered as a unique arrangement requiring a different response? The aim here is to examine the problems related to this situation and to present some of the major dilemmas of the EU legitimacy question in the context of ongoing integration.

LEGITIMACY, DEMOCRACY, AND IDEALS

In contemporary debate, there is a close linkage between the functioning of a democratic apparatus within a political system and the level of legitimacy accorded to that system. If one takes democracy to represent a political apparatus that guarantees the participation of the governed (whether directly or via representatives) in the decision-making process, then it is rightly considered to be an important, if not essential, element within the modern conception of self-determination and freedom. Such a claim has only been reinforced since the collapse of the communist world and the decline of practical alternatives. Yet these apparently triumphant circumstances have to be matched with two evident drawbacks. Firstly, there are question marks over the efficacy and effectiveness of national democratic models when an increasing amount of decisions are taken within regional, international, or global fora outside of the control of the singular nation-state. Secondly, there is the ancient problem related to who should actually be included as a participant within any democratic system. As Robert Dahl has pointed out,

> although the root meaning of [demokratia] is simple enough, even self-evident—
> *demos*, people, and *kratia*, rule or authority, thus "rule by the people"—the very roots
> themselves raise urgent questions: who ought to comprise "the people" and what
> does it mean for them "to rule"?[10]

The problems of efficacy and the existence of a demos both apply closely to the issue of democracy in the EU, and they raise some important questions: How can democratic legitimacy be secured in the context of widening and deepening integration? To what extent can, or should, the European public be granted a seat at the decision-making table? And who is included in the "European public"?

From the point of view of a political system's democratic accountability, "parliaments are considered to be strongholds and symbols of legitimacy."[11] Yet analyses of the relative legitimacy of the organs of the European Union and the oft-cited "democratic deficit" that exists between governance and governed rarely emphasize the possibilities for an enhanced European Parliament to fulfill this role. Although in the national context the executive branch is subject to parliamentary oversight, at the European level this symbiotic relationship between executive and legislature breaks down. Why is this? Partly it has to do with the constitutional status of the European Union itself. As "the key principles and practices of liberal democracy are associated almost exclusively with the principles and institutions of the sovereign nation state,"[12] these principles and practices could only be transferred to an enhanced European Parliament within the context of some form of a European state. Before this stage is reached, the structural operation of the Parliament in European governance prevents it from assuming the responsibilities associated with assemblies in liberal democratic nation-states. Since the advent of direct elections to the European Parliament in 1979, the powers of this body in the decision-making process of the EU have been progressively expanded in its transition from "consultation" under the Treaty of Rome to "cooperation" (Single European Act) and "co-decision" (Treaty on European Union). Yet the declining election turnouts show that these increased powers have not resulted in any changed perception of the assembly by European voters. Consequently, "while legitimacy understood as an attribute of the political system of the EU has been strengthened, legitimacy as an orientation among the citizens has decreased."[13] The lack of meaningful Europe-wide political coalitions, and the continuing focus of the media and political debate at the national level, also contribute to the stagnation of the Parliament in public consciousness.[14] Likewise, the increased powers also have major qualifications, such as the exclusion of any real parliamentary competence in relation to EMU and the second and third pillars of the Maastricht Treaty. The European Parliament will always be more of an administrative than a legislative assembly, its most important work being carried out by a committee in Brussels and not at the Strasbourg parliamentary chamber. Commenting on the supposed powers of scrutiny of the European assembly, Chris Shore has stated that "while interinstitutional rivalry no doubt exists, members of the Parliament and the Commission have a shared interest in protecting and defending each other from those outside the EU institutions."[15] It is therefore unlikely that, whatever the visions of federalists, the Parliament can be recreated as a fully operational check on the European "executive" (i.e., Commission/Council of Ministers) in the manner of national assemblies.

Clearly, if the democracy–legitimacy issue is going to be successfully addressed, there have to be other options available alongside the European Parliament. As Desmond Dinan stated in 1994,

Will the democratic deficit ever be rectified? Certainly not simply by giving more power to the European Parliament. . . . The Community is a unique system with unique institutions; the solution to the democratic deficit will be equally novel and unconventional. . . . Undoubtedly the European Parliament will remain an essential ingredient of political accountability in the European Community. But in an evolving European Community of traditional or transformed nation-states, the democratic deficit will have to be resolved by an imaginative blend of public representation and involvement at the regional, national and Community levels.[16]

Traditional approaches to democratic theory, democratic decision making, and the importance of popular consent, all of which have been developed in the context of the nation-state, are therefore lacking with regard to the evolution of the EU as some form of supranational polity. We are now entering, as some have claimed, an era of post-parliamentary governance in Europe, whereby the declining abilities of national assemblies to provide a level of democratic scrutiny of European affairs are further supplemented by the inadequacies of the European Parliament, as discussed earlier in this chapter.[17] Yet this does not mean that legitimacy is therefore an impossible goal, since if legitimacy "means a generalized degree of trust of the addressees of decisions towards the political system" then it follows that "the legitimacy of a political system is not exclusively linked to democracy and certainly not to parliamentary democracy."[18] In contrast to an understandable debate in the public realm over the need to democratize the EU, significantly enough, much academic discussion has in recent years begun to take the relative impossibility of representative democracy in the EU as its starting point, since, on a fundamental level, "Democracy requires the existence of a collective identity which does not exist on the European level."[19] In other words, alongside the structural deficiencies of the European Parliament lies another, arguably more far-reaching weakness—the lack of a European demos. Thus Chris Shore has gone so far as to say recently that

> by far the greatest obstacle to European integration today hinges around the problem of *legitimacy*. The credibility and authority of the European Union's supranational institutions . . . rests upon their claim to represent the "European interest" over and above that of the individual member states. This, however, presupposes a transnational European public whose "general will" arises from common interests that can be represented and championed by these supranational bodies.[20]

The classic theory of European integration, functionalism, has been based on the presumption that integration was a matter of enlightened self-interest for the states of (Western) Europe in order to overcome the destructive tendencies of nationalism.[21] Thus it was assumed that sociopolitical integration would follow from economic and legal integration, that popular loyalties would turn away from the nation-state and follow the developing supranational networks of power. The neofunctionalism of Ernst Haas and Leon Lindberg started from the same premises, but both these authors recognized that efforts had to be made to encourage the shift in public opinion away from a purely national outlook.[22] Yet neither functionalism nor neofunctionalism allowed space for any doubts as to the *reasons* for these processes to occur.[23] The promotion of integration in all areas was so patently in the general European interest after two world wars that concerns over the lack of a European demos did not arise. It was the business of the pro-European technocratic elites, first and foremost, to create a stable political-economic-social environment, a task that was meant to (and, for many, did) preempt questions of democratic legitimacy.

What then were the ideals of the Treaty of Rome and the early years of integration? Weiler has convincingly identified three primary motives: the securing of peace, the achievement of prosperity, and the undermining of nationalism within the formation of a supranational political economy.[24] Clearly, all three fit together closely, and all three were dominant motives when set against the European experience of the first half of the twentieth century and the need to recreate the European landscape after World War II. If integration could satisfy these three criteria, then it would naturally be deemed a success. But these postwar circumstances are now several decades in the past, and the legitimacy problem that emerged around the Maastricht TEU had to do with the fact that the underlying basis for continuing integration had shifted considerably. In other words, behind the crisis of legitimacy lies a crisis of "European ideals" as a popular mobilizing factor in the integration narrative. Above all, the functionalist belief in European integration as a relatively smooth, logical transition toward an expanding framework of European governance cannot sufficiently incorporate the tensions introduced by neoliberal supranationalism.

Basing its analysis on problem-solving capacities at the European level, functionalism requires that the European system be judged through its performance and its ability to meet specific goals and satisfy member-state interests. Building on this position, Fritz Scharpf has referred to "two distinct but complementary perspectives" on the issue of democracy and legitimacy:

> Input-oriented democratic thought emphasizes "government *by the people*." Political choices are legitimate if and because they reflect the "will of the people"—that is, if they can be derived from the authentic preferences of the members of a community. By contrast, the output perspective emphasizes "government *for the people*." Here, political choices are legitimate if and because they effectively promote the common welfare of the constituency in question.[25]

Although these two factors necessarily operate alongside each other in any democratic system, in terms of the EU there is clearly a tension between input-oriented and output-oriented legitimation. For a start, although government by the people involves the democratic norms of participation and consensus, for the "tyranny of the majority" to be avoided there has to be a widely accepted notion of the general welfare and the values of collectivity. In other words, a relatively strong sense of collective identity has to already exist. Therefore, even if the input-oriented democratic apparatus of the EU could be improved, the lack of a continent-wide collective identity would prevent it from fulfilling the requirements of legitimacy (for instance, Scharpf mentions that this dilemma negates the possibilities of increased Europe-wide referenda). This shifts the focus to the operation of government for the people, since this is *interest-based rather than identity-based* and requires the identification of long-term common interests ahead of any concerns over the collective identity of the community in question. However, assuming that the EU could rely solely on output-oriented legitimacy raises several problems. Firstly, it brings to light once more the question of what common Europe-wide interests consist of. Secondly, without the balance of input-oriented legitimacy, such common interests can still be discerned by the policy-making technocracy alone. Thirdly, without the back-up of a durable, "thick" collective identity, government for the people on the European level can only compensate for this lack and achieve its goal of securing legitimacy if "all interests [are] considered in the definition of the public interest, and . . . the costs and benefits of measures serving the public interest [are] allocated according to plausible norms of distributive justice."[26] In other words, the original ideals of prosperity and supranationalism in particular have to live up to their possibilities as ideals in the interests of all. Before turning to this issue in more detail, the contours of EU cultural policy need to be examined.

CULTURAL POLICY, CULTURAL IDENTITY, AND THE EU

> In its widest sense, culture may now be said to be the whole complex of distinctive spiritual, material, intellectual and emotional features that characterise a society or social group. It includes not only the arts and letters, but also modes of life, the fundamental rights of the human being, value systems, traditions and beliefs.
>
> —Declaration of Mondiacult[27]

> Culture, it is being argued more and more frequently these days, is the one thing that will help sustain and develop democracy in Europe today. . . . It has the power to unite rather than divide, to democratize rather than dictate.
>
> —"Culture and Democracy"[28]

The purpose of the Common Market was to remove barriers to the movement of goods, services, capital, and persons (labor), as exemplified by the Single European Act (SEA) of 1987. With these conditions being deepened and widened since Maastricht, the processes of integration continue despite the relative lack of a corresponding Europe-wide allegiance to what is being created. The EU as a supranational body therefore has had to promote and emphasize the collective values that should be (but are not) self-evident to the European peoples themselves.

Therefore, the goal has to be "a collective identity that can transcend exclusively parochial and nationalistic loyalties and lay the foundation for a higher level of consciousness based on allegiance to European, rather than national, institutions and ideals."[29] But clearly this is much easier said than done, and there are considerable problems related to projecting a common cultural identity "from above." Committed as it is to forging "ever-closer union among the peoples of Europe," the intricate balance between unity and diversity remains at the heart of any notion of a Europe-wide cultural identity. Resting on this slippery foundation is the question of what collective values that cultural identity can be based upon, and how far it can go toward being socially inclusive without being constructed at the expense of others. Added to this is the determination that the EU is not so much *creating* a cultural identity or collective values as it is realizing their already latent characteristics. This is a crucial point. Although the operation of a semidemocratic technocracy will be accepted in the realm of economics (if it delivers results and satisfies key interest groups), the same techniques applied to the social-cultural realm expose the EU to severe criticism from civil society groups and national political interests concerned about unjust and unaccountable manipulation. The necessity to "involve people in their own destiny" is therefore fraught with dangers.[30]

Prior to the 1970s, responsibility for Europe-wide cooperation in the fields of culture, education, human rights, and related matters was seen as the task of the Council of Europe in Strasbourg. Since the early 1970s, however, the EC/EU has taken on increasing responsibilities, transforming the Council's role into more of a think tank or pressure group on these issues. The catalyst for this expanded responsibility was the commitment, shaky at first but nevertheless present, to European economic and monetary union as outlined by the Werner Report of October 1970. Intended as the answer to intra-European price differentials (especially within the Common Agricultural Policy) and the growing instability of the dollar, Werner recognized that any moves in this direction must simultaneously involve an expansion of powers for the European Parliament to ensure an improved level of democratic control.[31] But subsequent declarations and studies of the future configurations of the proposed European Union began to stress other aspects of the legitimacy issue. In 1973, coinciding with the first enlargement, came the Declaration on the European Identity, which stated the determination of the member states to promote the rule of law, social justice, and respect for human rights. At the 1974 EC summit, attention was given for the first time at this level to what Europe-wide rights could be given to member-state citizens. The 1975 Report on European Union by Leo Tindemans introduced the need to encourage solidarity within a "People's Europe" by means of citizen's rights and democratic legitimacy, the latter to be satisfied "with greater powers being vested in a directly elected European Parliament, for instance." As the "for instance" demonstrates, the Parliament was not intended to be the only answer to the legitimacy issue.[32] It is noticeable how this interest in legitimacy coincided with the efforts in the early 1970s to put the Werner Plan for monetary union into effect by 1980. During this period, however, "the combination of an unfavourable international environment, divergent national policies, a half-baked economic strategy, and a very weak political commitment ensured the quick death of EMU."[33] But the effort would be renewed in the 1980s.

Even prior to the scripting of the SEA in 1985–1986, it was the low turnout and interest in the European Parliament elections of 1979 and 1984 that caused the Commission to focus more on how to promote the transition from national to supranational identity. The Solemn Declaration on European Union in 1983 put the need to encourage action in cultural areas on a Europe-wide basis on the agendas of the member states. This new opening was developed by the Committee for a People's Europe, chaired by Pietro Adonnino, which delivered a report in 1985 recommending the adoption of an EC flag, a European anthem, the designation of May 9 (commemorating the announcement of the Schuman Plan in 1950) as Europe Day, and the harmonizing of all member-state passports. Other proposals demonstrated the Commission's wish to bring to the fore the common European heritage and civilizational attributes, such as through a European Academy of Science, by emphasizing the history of European development in education programs and by creating a Euro-wide information and audiovisual network. These moves were an attempt to implement Karl Deutsch's influential argument that a social community could be created via an extensive and intensive development of all forms of social communication.[34] The importance of promoting shared allegiance to European cultural values to foster a supranational identity and greater social cohesion is demonstrated by a Commission paper from 1988 that states, "The European Union which is being constructed cannot have economic and social objectives as its only aim[,] it also involves *new kinds of solidarity* based on belonging to European culture."[35] Thus the scripting of a European narrative of linear historical development, with its just and rational culmination in the EC/EU, reached a high point with the Commission's support for Jean-Baptiste Duroselle's *Europe: A History of its Peoples*, published in 1990. Such an attempt to almost codify European history from the point of view of Brussels has to be seen in the context of Jacques Delors's Commission not only looking to secure the progress of the SEA toward 1992, but also keeping an eye on the next stage of integration that was to be thrashed out in Maastricht. But this approach has major drawbacks. As one observer has noted, it leads to "the idea of a predestination for Europe rooted in an ancient legitimacy, unity, and fixed identity . . . which can only function to exclude others and close off the possibility of change and adaptation to 'outsiders.'"[36]

Significantly enough, such interventionism on the part of the Commission was at this stage not backed up by any legal mandate in the treaties for a European cultural policy, leading to "a grey zone [being] created by invoking economic reasons for achieving cultural ends, and the Ministers of Culture adopted a series of nonbinding resolutions, for which the Commission could find small amounts of money under its own authority."[37] The Maastricht TEU of 1992 finally formalized the Commission's role by introducing actual prerogatives for culture at the EU level. Aimed at fostering a "common cultural heritage" while simultaneously "respecting . . . national and regional diversity" and contributing "to the flowering of the cultures of the Member States," the EU's areas of cultural competency as outlined in Article 128 included improving knowledge of European history, practicing heritage conservation, encouraging cultural exchanges, and supporting artistic and literary creation.[38] Yet the application of the principle of subsidiarity on this issue prevents the Commission from acting prior to consideration of whether the objectives can be achieved by the member states themselves. The Community's sanctioned role is therefore limited to offering "incentive measures" and making recommendations without having any powers to enforce harmonization via Regulations or Directives. Even then, the Council will act on recommendations of the Commission only after a unanimous vote. Therefore, despite the interest of the Commission to assume responsibilities in this area, "Article 128 is widely regarded as much as a device to control Commission activity in this sector as encourage it, some countries believing that cultural action at a European level could threaten the independence of national cultural policies."[39] The balance that was struck between supranational and national interests in the cultural realm therefore produced the result that "there is no Community cultural 'policy,' but Community encouragement of action among member states, supporting and supplementing their action 'if necessary.'"[40] This perspective has been reinforced by the fact that the Community's powers in the cultural realm were further curtailed in the Amsterdam Treaty in 1997, when Clause 4, stating that "the Community shall take cultural aspects into account in its action under other provisions of this Treaty," was amended to include "in particular in order to respect and to promote the diversity of its cultures."

Therefore, due to subsidiarity and the dangers of such an enterprise, the explicit aim of formalizing a European cultural identity has been downplayed since Jacques Delors left the Commission. Cultural policy has since then emphasized the need to fulfill the goal of fostering joint cultural initiatives between the member states, thereby staying within the bounds of subsidiarity (but maintaining an influential presence).[41]

Other aspects to this field, demonstrating an enhanced awareness of the importance of cultural policy in coordination with other EU goals, have also been emphasized since Maastricht. In 2000, Dutch sociologist Abram de Swaan presented a research plan to the Commission to investigate the reasons for the absence of a European cultural elite (read: "European intellectuals developing the European idea") and what could be done about it. To his dismay, he received the reply that the EU avoids cultural questions such as this, particularly those having to do with "elites."[42] For de Swaan (and many others), there can be no narrowing of the democratic deficit without the deliberate formation of a

European intellectual network, especially via Europe-wide journals, that can transcend national borders, create a continent-wide public space, and solidify the perception of cultural-intellectual unity alongside the continuing processes of economic and political integration. For the Commission, however, such a move is problematic. It wants to avoid any suggestion that an elite-controlled European cultural framework is to be put into place, instead attempting to utilize an interpretation of culture that stretches beyond elites to incorporate European society in general. This was demonstrated by the First European Community Framework Programme in Support of Culture (2000–2004). Remarking that "culture is no longer considered a subsidiary activity but a driving force in society, making for creativity, vitality, dialogue and cohesion," it outlined how it was a vital component in the following challenging issues: the acceleration of European integration, globalization, the information society, employment, and social cohesion. The focus on social cohesion is particularly interesting, since the report states that

> as a result of unemployment and insecurity, social ties are being loosened and exclusion is becoming a serious issue, particularly in and around our cities. Social exclusion means cultural exclusion too. In many cases, cultural activities help the marginalised, particularly young people, to reintegrate into society.[43]

Clearly, cultural initiatives are now being explicitly positioned in terms of their importance for facilitating social cohesion within the European Single Market. At this point, it becomes apparent that fostering a sense of cultural identity and belonging within a European space is not just a necessary addendum (or, perhaps, prerequisite) for the political economy of integration, but that *it adds to the possibilities for coping with potentially adverse socioeconomic conditions within the EU*. Specifically, the pressures to deregulate national economies, scale back on welfare costs, and prioritize monetarist goals above all else, processes that the SEA encouraged and EMU virtually codified, have created conditions whereby the reduced ability of member states to protect their citizens from adverse economic circumstances has *not* been replaced by additional powers at the level of the EU. In this context, it is hard to avoid the shrewdness of Pierre Bourdieu when he states that "the breaking of the bonds of social integration which culture is asked to reconstruct is the direct consequence of a policy, an economic policy."[44]

EUROPEAN CITIZENSHIP: A FALSE START?

The restricted room for maneuver in the cultural realm has led to the EU presenting "an ambivalent idea of culture: as an economic asset at the local and regional level, where nationalism is embedded, and as a form of civic identity or

"Europeanness" to supplement transnational citizenship."[45] Cultural identity and citizenship are closely entwined, since

> the very idea of *European* integration suggests that integration is only imaginable by reference to the closure provided by an identity, a boundary that is normative rather than merely geographical. . . . Bluntly, there is no integration without inclusion and, also, no integration without exclusion.[46]

Consequently, one would imagine that a broad interpretation of European citizenship rights and duties could potentially offer a path toward developing supranational allegiance and identity within the EU.[47] The introduction of European citizenship has opened up a Pandora's box of possibilities and caused considerable debate—and many demands—amongst academics and interest groups within civil society.[48] For Robert Dahl, democracy can be viewed from two sides: by concentrating on the sovereignty of the people (ultimately via the electoral process) and by focusing on the body of rights that define democratic society, from freedom of speech through to "rights to privacy, property, a minimum wage, nondiscrimination in employment, and the like."[49] Therefore, in the context of Scharpf's output-oriented legitimacy, European citizenship would seem a potentially vital element.

However, at present the rights of European citizens, introduced at Maastricht, seem fairly rudimentary: for example freedom of movement, the right to stand and vote in local and European elections, and the right to petition the European Parliament or apply to an ombudsman over grievances. As one would expect, national prerogatives still dictate the outlines of this embryonic European legal identity. Clause 1 states that "every person holding the nationality of a Member State shall be a citizen of the Union," thus making it clear at which level the "granting" of identity takes place.[50] Similar to the reaction against European cultural initiatives, this position was strengthened in the Amsterdam Treaty with the added sentence that "citizenship of the Union shall complement and not replace national citizenship." Likewise, "the right to move and reside freely within the territory of the Member States" remains at the mercy of national directives, with the result that "European citizens still encounter real obstacles, both practical and legal, when they wish to exercise their rights to free movement and residence in the Union."[51] The only extension of rights offered by the Amsterdam Treaty was the availability for any citizen to write to any EU institution and receive an answer in any one of the twelve official European languages.

The introduction of European citizenship, with its desultory list of rights set against its weight as a crucial element of democratic politics, has been described as "an embarrassment." The rights of European citizens were basically present before Maastricht, so it is not as if the new status offers any added value at the supranational level. Simply put, the expanding framework of EC law was leading to the point where clarification of an individual's status vis-à-vis the Community treaties was becoming necessary.[52] The linkage between the simultaneous arrival of citizenship status and the completion of the Single Market has led to understandable cynicism about how European citizens have more consumer rights than anything else. Nevertheless, the fact that a legal status has been given to a form of citizenship that operates beyond the borders of a single nation-state is a significant development, since it points toward a scenario where the linkages between citizenship, nationality, and identity could be broken, or at least loosened—with significant consequences for the EU legitimacy issue.

Nationality obviously has a deep substance within European polities, tied up as it is with a profound sense of belonging and identity, loyalty, and uniqueness. From the perspective of the formation of nation-states, "The state is to be seen principally as an instrument, the organizational framework within which the nation is to realize its potential."[53] Within this scenario, citizenship became not only the codification of rights and duties but also the demarcation of individuals within a political community. In modern times, this led to the blending of nationality and citizenship, of cultural identity and formal rights, so that the concept of citizenship provides a political subjectivity that is deeply implicated with the sovereignty and legitimacy of the nation-state framework. Citizenship, as with every element of democratic theory, has been formulated and understood in the context of nation-state politics. Introducing the concept at the European level is clearly beset with problems.

Although the member states hold the keys to European citizenship, the EU's development within the framework of increasing supranational governance does suggest that the concept will evolve beyond its current status into something more meaningful. One would expect that multilevel governance, the strength of regional or minority allegiances, and the effects of migration and the resulting cultural diversity of national societies might weaken the nation–state linkage in Europe. There seem to be three possible developments in these conditions. Firstly, multilayered governance and the overlapping of structures of governance in Europe could encourage the development of multilayered identities and forms of citizenship.[54] Yet, although this might be a flexible arrangement, it is unclear how it might affect allegiance and legitimacy in relation to the EU institutions themselves. A second development could be the gradual evolution of a European (federal) state, involving enough official transfer of sovereignty from the national level to allow an enhanced European citizenship and, potentially, the recreation of the cultural identity–formal rights dichotomy at the European level. However, the image of a European "superstate," federal or not, remains anathema to many, as recent debate has demonstrated.[55]

Before turning to the third possible development, it is apposite to consider at this point how an enhanced version of European citizenship could go some way toward overcoming the democratic deficit and the legitimacy gap in the EU. Although it may well indicate "a step towards a new concept of politics inside and simultaneously beyond the framework of the traditional notion of politics defined by the nation-state," European citizenship remains a long way short of providing the kind of security that would secure allegiance to the European idea.[56] The answer could lie in the provision of social rights. One of the key texts in the analysis of citizenship is that by T. H. Marshall from 1950, the time of the European welfare state's entrenchment after World War II.[57] For Marshall, the development of citizenship was something of an evolutionary process, from civil rights (freedom from the state) in the eighteenth century to political rights (universal suffrage) prior to World War II, culminating in social rights (access to health, education, and welfare facilities) in the late twentieth century. Marshall emphasized an important aspect to citizenship—its normative role in formalizing equal status or solidarity between citizens in all areas of social life.

This provides the background to the third potential development for European citizenship. Rather than imagining a European superstate, the possibility is there for the enhancement of one of European integration's founding ideals: supranationalism. For Weiler, this involves an apparatus for the "policing" of the worst behavior of nation-states.

> In the supranational vision, the community as a transnational regime will not simply be a neutral arena in which states will seek to pursue the national interest and maximise their benefits. . . . Crucially, the community idea is not meant to eliminate the nation state but to create a regime which seeks to tame the national interest with a new discipline.[58]

The supranationalist ideal therefore aims to overcome the negative boundaries that nationalism can create, be that expressed via the exclusion of "aliens" at the external border, the abuse of domestic powers by the state, or the perversion of cultural identity into notions of superiority and xenophobia. Within this construct of supranationalism, the nation-state remains intact but the concept of European citizenship could potentially offer the means to promote and defend a code of civic values that are preeminent over the potential prejudices of nationalism. As Weiler admits, it is the potential fulfillment of the Kantian Enlightenment "project." The outline of this remains fragmentary at present, but it does exist. The freedom of movement provisions, however unfulfilled, is one example. Also, any form of citizenship should include duties as well as rights on the part of the citizen, and the treaties have been criticized for stating this but not being explicit regarding what these duties are. Indeed, with the EU it is obviously awkward to say to whom or what citizens it should have duties toward. Yet Article 6 of the Treaty of Amsterdam states that "the Union is founded on the principles of liberty, democracy, respect for human rights and fundamental freedoms, and the rule of law," and that these rights are "guaranteed by the European Convention for the Protection of Human Rights and Fundamental Freedoms signed in Rome on 4 November 1950." The uncoordinated response of EU member states to the inclusion of Jorge Haider's Freedom Party in the Austrian government in 1999 was a messy but nevertheless significant example of what this interpretation of supranationalism might represent. By building on this, an extension of the supranational ideal in combination with Marshall's conception of social rights could potentially create a form of European citizenship that would deliver not only greater security but also allegiance and recognition within a single European social space.

The problem with this vision is not necessarily the blockage of nationalism. It is more the fact that the political economy of integration is basically being driven by a neoliberal outlook that has at best an uneasy and at worst an antagonistic relationship with the principles of social welfare. As some have pointed out, the EU's commitment to solidarity is questionable, particularly as it is not a very popular word within the neoliberal lexicon.[59] This has been apparent since the enactment of the Single European Act (SEA) and its commitment to a "European internal market" devoid of internal barriers. Apparently not fully realized at the time, the SEA effectively

> rules out all national measures and existing regulations that might be capable of restricting the freedom of the border-crossing movement of goods, persons, services and capital, or of distorting free and equal competition between domestic and foreign suppliers or demanders. At national level, thus, European integration amounts to a twofold, *de jure* and *de facto*, compulsion to deregulate.[60]

The SEA revived the relatively moribund integration process and has contributed to the establishment of European "champions of industry" in the global marketplace. The SEA and EMU have together introduced a new level of supranational governance in Europe, but these are Europe-wide agreements enforced by member states without any significant corresponding extension of the Europe-wide apparatus for democratic scrutiny. As Stephen Gill has put it, EMU works by "'locking in' political commitments to orthodox market-monetarist fiscal and monetary policies that are perceived to increase government credibility in the eyes of financial market players." The result is to "make governments more responsive to the discipline of market forces, and correspondingly less responsive to popular-democratic forces and processes."[61] The transformation of socioeconomic conditions in this way, by a neoliberal drive for deregulation, privatization, and cost-cutting efficiency, has further exposed the democracy–legitimacy problem, something that the introduction of European citizenship has only highlighted more. As Habermas has pointed out,

> An increasing number of measures decided at a supranational level affect more and more citizens over an ever increasing area of life. Given that the role of citizen has hitherto only been institutionalized at the level of nation-states, citizens have no effective means of debating European decisions and influencing the decision-making processes.[62]

It is important to recall Dahl's two sides to democracy: the influence of the demos in the decision-making process, and the provision of rights. Could an enhanced European citizenship overcome the lack of popular participation in the EU decision-making process and the absence of a fully functional European assembly? Not for nothing did former Spanish Socialist Premier Felipe Gonzalez suggest in a letter to the European Council that European citizenship should be made one of the pillars of the EU, alongside EMU and the CFSP (the third pillar that came into existence is, of course, Home Affairs), and the Commission declared that the citizenship concept introduced in Maastricht would improve the democratic legitimacy of the EU and its goals.[63] These statements of concern can be matched with the Delors Report of 1989, which stressed the need for mechanisms to ensure a greater distribution of resources within the EU in order to counter the destabilizing effects of regional disparities under EMU.[64] It is important to consider the view that "the democracy gap does not only stem from outdated constitutionalist assumptions about popular sovereignty in a nation-state, but it is also in part a consequence of crumbling welfare state regimes."[65] However, both Gonzalez and Delors were defeated by both member-state national interests that did not perceive such a transfer of power to either citizens or Brussels as desirable, and a neoliberal ideology that rejects *dirigiste* redistribution or extensive social rights.

NEOLIBERALISM VERSUS DEMOCRACY IN THE EU

This chapter has sought to understand the development of new forms of socialization in the context of the "deepening" of EU competences according to neoliberal doctrine. While highlighting some of the positive elements of these developments, the aim has been to show how a unity can never be achieved between the material and sociocultural elements involved. Hegemony can never be complete, and lacunae and sites of contestation will always remain. Thus, although Marshall's conception of social rights might offer a promising option to achieve greater coherence within the EU, it conflicts directly with an economic landscape defined by the "retreat" of the state at the national level, and obstacles of subsidiarity, the national veto, and neoliberal doctrine preventing reregulation at the European level. As several observers have pointed out, the market imperative has been central to the development of citizenship rights in the EU, such that "the most highly developed rights—the freedom of movement and residence—are closely linked to the creation of a single market; indeed, they guarantee its efficiency."[66] The extension of these rights in the interests of solidarity and cohesion, for instance in the direction of redistribution (with corresponding duties such as "European taxes"), is not going to happen under current conditions. Although Marshall's interpretation of citizenship is still regarded by many as the norm, it is difficult to see how this can be realized. Yet as Pierre Bourdieu has rightly claimed:

> Monetary integration cannot be expected to secure social integration. On the contrary: for we know that countries that want to maintain their competitiveness

within the euro zone relative to their partners will have no option but to reduce wage costs by reducing welfare contributions. "Social dumping" and wage-cutting, the "flexibilisation" of the labour market, will be the only devices left to states which can no longer play on exchange rates. Only a European social state would be capable of countering the *disintegratory* effects of monetary economics.[67]

Where does this leave the issue of democracy and legitimacy in the EU? Clearly, if fewer and fewer decisions are left open for national electorates to decide upon, the will to express political participation via the ballot box can only decline. After all, "While democratic self-determination is not to be equated with the fulfilment of each and every wish, it does imply freedom and therefore the possibility of choice," and an enforced orthodoxy of "deregulation, flexibilisation and cost reduction" can only lead to democracy losing "its function of securing acceptance for political choices that could go one way or the other."[68] In this scenario, the processes of integration can be regarded as a *fait accompli,* and democracy in any significantly participatory form no more than a *risk* to be avoided. The ideal of prosperity might be secured, but it will arise in conditions of inequality guaranteed by a neoliberalism that puts a low priority on collective welfare and security. European citizenship, with its limited effectiveness, is therefore at present not a concept to prevent further social alienation under the current political-economic consensus.

Such a situation has not been greatly altered by the EU's Charter of Fundamental Rights, which was included in the final declaration of the 2000 Nice Summit, but not in the treaty. The Charter originated at the Cologne Summit in June 1999, where it was decided "to establish a Charter of fundamental rights in order to make their overriding importance and relevance more *visible* to the citizens."[69] The fifty-four articles are divided into sections on dignity, freedoms, equality, solidarity, citizens' rights, and justice, and the Charter is intended to "counterbalance the Euro[,] become part of the iconography of European integration and contribute both to the identity of and identification with Europe."[70] As European Parliamentarian Inigo Mendes de Vigo claimed, the Charter should demonstrate that the EU is "not just a market but a community of values."[71] The determination of Europe as a privileged space, exemplified by the ideal of the euro as a currency immune from the potential shocks of the global financial system, would then be further solidified. However, the Charter's provisions were heavily diluted by business groups keen to undermine the emphasis on social welfare commitments, and the more awkward decision over its legal status was then shelved for a later date. In particular, the Charter became caught between those member states who wanted it to represent a major shift toward political union, and those that rejected its constitutional pretensions in favor of a statement of intent. The result is that the final document remains in an ambiguous legal position. The vague wording of its provisions offers the potential for more extensive citizens' rights in the future, but only if the European Court of Justice is prepared to take an interventionist stance in its interpretation.[72]

Clearly, then, the EU has entered something of a double bind. The scale and scope of integration, and the corresponding necessity for increasing governance at the European level, demand that efforts be made to secure a greater level of social cohesion, allegiance, and belonging from the European peoples. The transfer or extension of identity from the national to the European level has not, however, occurred as a natural process. Yet the equally powerful demands of neo-liberal economic and financial orthodoxy, which have been the dominant logic behind the integration process since the SEA in the mid-1980s, effectively block the formation of the democratic rights that could legitimize the whole project. Attempts by the Commission to utilize cultural policy to overcome the legitimacy question have instead highlighted the limits to how far the EU can actually go to form a European identity. It is to be expected that, instead of unblocking some of these issues, the current European Convention on the Future of Europe will probably only illuminate how intractable they actually are.

NOTES

1. Frederic Jameson, "Foreword," in Jean-François Lyotard, ed., *The Postmodern Condition: A Report on Knowledge* (Minneapolis: University of Minnesota Press, 1999), viii.

2. See for instance Jeffrey Checkel, "Social Construction and Integration," *Journal of European Public Policy* 6 (December 1999): 545–60.

3. "Enhancing Democracy in the European Union," white paper on European governance (Brussels: SEC, 2000), 1547/7 final, europa.eu.int/comm/governance/work/en.pdf (accessed May 3, 2001).

4. J. H. H. Weiler, *The Constitution of Europe: "Do the New Clothes Have an Emperor?" and Other Essays on European Integration* (Cambridge: Cambridge University Press, 1999), 3–4.

5. Kees van der Pijl, *Transnational Classes and International Relations* (London: Routledge, 1998), 15.

6. See also Stephen Gill, "European Governance and New Constitutionalism: EMU and Alternatives to Disciplinary Neo-Liberalism in Europe," *New Political Economy* (March 1998): 1.

7. Erik Oddvar Eriksen and John Erik Fossum, "Legitimation through Deliberation: The EU and Post-National Legitimacy," paper presented at the biannual conference of the International Society for the Study of European Ideas, Bergen University, Norway, August 2000.

8. Manuel Castells, *The Information Age: Economy, Society and Culture*, vol. 3: *End of Millennium* (Oxford: Blackwell, 1999), 350–52.

9. William Wallace, "Europe after the Cold War: Interstate Order or Post-Sovereign Regional System?" in "The Interregnum: Controversies in World Politics 1989–1999," *Review of International Studies* 25, Special Issue (December 1999): 203:

It is arguable that the region within which the modern state system emerged is now moving towards a post-modern and post-sovereign political system, in which authority will be shared among different levels of government—and in which the Westphalian concept of sovereignty will have disappeared, with a more diverse and open international civil society emerging in its place, with multiple levels of authority and governance.

10. Robert A. Dahl, *Democracy and Its Critics* (New Haven, Conn.: Yale University Press, 1989), 3.

11. Wolfgang Wessels and Udo Diedrichs, "A New Kind of Legitimacy for a New Kind of Parliament—The Evolution of the European Parliament," *European Integration Online Papers* 1, no. 6 (1997): eiop.or.at/eiop/texte/1997-006a.htm (accessed May 10, 2001), 1.

12. David Held, "The Transformation of Political Community: Rethinking Democracy in the Context of Globalization," in Ian Shapiro and Casiano Hacker-Cordon, eds., *Democracy's Edges* (Cambridge: Cambridge University Press, 1999), 91.

13. Wessels and Diedrichs, "Legitimacy," 1.

14. Weiler, *Constitution*, 266.

15. Cris Shore, *Building Europe: The Cultural Politics of European Integration* (London: Routledge, 2000), 218.

16. Desmond Dinan, *Ever Closer Union? An Introduction to European Integration* (Basingstoke, UK: Macmillan, 1994), 292.

17. Andreas Follesdal, "Theories of Democracy for Europe: Multi-level Challenges for Multi-level Governance," paper presented at the biannual conference of the International Society for the Study of European Ideas, Bergen University, Norway, August 2000; and S. Andersen and T. Burns, "The EU and the Erosion of Parliamentary Democracy: A Study of Post-Parliamentary Governance," in S. Andersen and K. Eliassen, *The European Union: How Democratic Is It?* (London: Sage, 1996).

18. Markus Jachtenfuchs, "Democracy and Governance in the European Union," *European Integration Online Papers* 1, no. 2 (1997): eiop.or.at/eiop/texte/1997-002a.htm (accessed May 9, 2001), 6.

19. Jachtenfuchs, "Democracy," 6.

20. Shore, *Building Europe*, 18–19.

21. See David Mitrany, *A Working Peace System* (Chicago: Quadrangle, 1966).

22. See Ernst B. Haas, "The Challenge of Regionalism," *International Organization* 12 (1958); and Leon N. Lindberg, *The Political Dynamics of European Economic Integration* (Stanford, Calif.: Stanford University Press, 1963).

23. See the arguments on functionalism presented in chapter 1.

24. Weiler, *Constitution of Europe*, 240–41, 244–46.

25. Fritz Scharpf, *Governing in Europe: Effective and Democratic?* (Oxford: Oxford University Press, 1999), 6.

26. Scharpf, *Governing in Europe*, 11, 12, 13.

27. Declaration of Mondiacult, UNESCO World Conference on Cultural Policies 1982, quoted in *In from the Margins: A Contribution to the Debate on Culture and Development in Europe* (Strasbourg: Council of Europe, 1997), 28.

28. Editorial, "Culture and Democracy," *European Cultural Foundation Newsletter* 21, no. 2 (May 1998): 3.

29. Shore, *Building Europe*, 21.

30. Shore, *Building Europe*, 44.

31. Richard McAllister, *From EC to EU: An Historical and Political Survey* (London: Routledge, 1997), 66–67.

32. McAllister, *From EC to EU*, 110–11; and Shore, *Building Europe*, 44–45.

33. Loukas Tsoukalis, *The New European Economy Revisited* (Oxford: Oxford University Press, 1997), 142.

34. See Karl Deutsch, *Nationalism and Social Communication* (Cambridge, Mass.: MIT Press, 1966); and Cris Shore, "Governing Europe: European Union Audio-Visual Policy and the Politics of Identity," in Cris Shore and Susan Wright, eds., *Anthropology of Policy: Critical Perspectives on Governance and Power* (London: Routledge, 1997).

35. Commission of the European Communities, *A People's Europe: Communication from the Commission to the European Parliament* (Brussels: Author, 1988), 331/final, quoted in Shore, *Building Europe*, 26 (emphasis added).

36. J. Bloomfield, "The New Europe: A New Agenda for Research," in Mary Fulbrook, ed., *National Histories and European History* (London: UCL Press, 1993), 256.

37. Alan Forrest, "A New Start for Cultural Action in the European Community: Genesis and Implications of Article 128 of the Treaty on European Union," *European Journal of Cultural Policy* 1, no. 1 (1994): 12. See "Culture, Cultural Industries and Employment," Commission Staff Working Paper (Brussels: SEC, 1998), 837.

38. Treaty on European Union, "Culture," Title IX, Article 128.

39. *In from the Margins*, 37.

40. Forrest, "A New Start," 17–18.

41. See for instance Council of Ministers Press Release, "The Role of Culture in the Development of the European Union," November 5, 2001, Press: 377, Nr: 13126/01, ue.eu.int/Newsroom/LoadDoc.asp?MAX=1&BID=95&DID=68667&LANG=1 (accessed August 28, 2002); and Council of Ministers, "Future of European Cultural Cooperation—Resolution," May 23, 2002, 8846/1/02 REV 1, Presse 140, ue.eu.int/pressData/en/cult/70787.pdf (accessed August 28, 2002). The European Parliament has been influential in pushing this field forward. A recent resolution, "Cultural Cooperation in the European Union," European Parliament Resolution A5-0281/2001, September 5, 2001, stated that "it is one of this Parliament's duties to make progress in the search for a common cultural basis, a European civil area, that will increase citizen's sense of belonging to that European area," since

> in an increasingly multi-ethnic Europe, cultural policy needs to be an integral part of economic and social development, to perform a role of social cohesion and mutual enrichment, and to be a factor that is essential for belonging to a European citizenship.

Contrary to this important role, the report also notes that only 0.1 percent of the Community budget was allocated to culture and the audiovisual sector in 2000.

42. Abraam de Swaan, "We hebben Europese Intellectuelen Nodig!" *Vrij Nederland* 61, no. 49 (9 December 2000): 34–37.

43. Commission of the European Communities, *First European Community Framework Programme in Support of Culture 2000–2004* (Brussels: European Commission, 1998), 266 final, 2.

44. Pierre Bourdieu, *Acts of Resistance: Against the New Myths of Our Time* (Cambridge: Polity Press, 1998), 45.

45. J. Moreira, "Cohesion and Citizenship in EU Cultural Policy," *Journal of Common Market Studies* 38, no. 3 (September 2000): 457.

46. H. Lindahl, "European Integration: Popular Sovereignty and a Politics of Boundaries," *European Law Journal* 6, no. 3 (September 2000): 253.

47. There is a considerable literature on European citizenship. See in particular Jennifer Welsh, "A People's Europe? European Citizenship and European Identity," *EUI*

Working Paper, 93/2 (1993); Elizabeth Meehan, *Citizenship and the European Community* (London: Sage, 1993); Josephine Shaw, "Citizenship of the Union: Towards Post-National Membership?" *Jean Monnet Paper* (1997): www.jeanmonnetprogram.org/papers/97 /97-06-.rtf (accessed August 29, 2002); Richard Bellamy and Alex Warleigh, eds., *Citizenship and Governance in the European Union* (London: Continuum, 2001); and Klaus Eder and Bernhard Giesen, eds., *European Citizenship: Between National Legacies and Postnational Projects* (Oxford: Oxford University Press, 2001).

48. For instance see Tony Venables, "Time has come to turn the Rhetoric on 'European Citizenship' into a Reality," *European Voice* 6, no. 1 (6–12 January 2000).

49. Robert Dahl, "Can International Organizations be Democratic? A Skeptic's View," in Shapiro and Hacker-Cordon, ed., *Democracy's Edges*, 20.

50. Treaty on European Union, "Citizenship of the Union," Title II, Article 8.

51. *The Amsterdam Treaty: A Comprehensive Guide* (Brussels: Directorate-General for Education and Culture, 1999), 30.

52. Shore, *Building Europe*, 74.

53. Weiler, *Constitution of Europe*, 338–39.

54. See Joe Painter, "Multi-level Citizenship, Identity and Regions in Contemporary Europe," in J. Anderson, ed., *Transnational Democracy* (London: Routledge, 2001).

55. See for instance the speech by Joschka Fischer at the Humboldt University in Berlin, May 12, 2000, and the many reactions it caused. "From Confederacy to Federation—Thoughts on the Finality of European Integration," www.germanembassy.org.au/eu-fisch.htm (accessed May 16, 2000).

56. Ulrich Preuss, "Problems of a Concept of European Citizenship," *European Law Journal* 1, no. 3 (November 1995): 280.

57. T. H. Marshall, *Citizenship and Social Class* (Cambridge: Cambridge University Press, 1950).

58. Weiler, *Constitution of Europe*, 342.

59. See on this point Carlos Closa, "A New Social Contract? EU Citizenship as the Institutional Basis of a New Social Contract—Some Sceptical Remarks," *EUI Working Paper*, 96/48 (1996); and Shaw, "Citizenship of the Union."

60. Fritz Scharpf, "Democratic Policy in Europe." *European Law Journal* 2, no. 2 (July 1996): 142.

61. Gill, "European Governance," 1.

62. Jurgen Habermas, "Citizenship and National Identity: Some Reflections on the Future of Europe," *Praxis International* 12, no. 1 (April 1992): 9.

63. Shore, *Building Europe*, 74.

64. Tsoukalis, *New European Economy*, 221.

65. A. Wiener and V. Sala, "Constitution-making and Citizenship Practice—Bridging the Democracy Gap in the EU," *Journal of Common Market Studies* 35, no. 4 (December 1997): 606.

66. Closa, "A New Social Contract?" 8.

67. Bourdieu, *Acts of Resistance*, 62.

68. Scharpf, "Democratic Policy," 50.

69. Xenophon A. Yataganas, "The Treaty of Nice: The Sharing of Power and the Institutional Balance in the European Union," *Jean Monnet Papers* (2001): www.jeanmonnetprogram.org/papers/01/010101.html (accessed May 17, 2001).

70. J. Weiler, "Editorial: Does the European Union Need a Charter of Rights?" *European Law Journal* 6, no. 2 (June 2000): 95.

71. Quoted in Peter Norman, "Europe's Charter of Rights Given a Smooth Passage," *Financial Times*, October 3, 2000, 1.

72. Yataganas, "The Treaty of Nice." At present, the only "fundamental right" that the EU Treaty contains concerns equal pay for men and women. As a European Parliament document states, "There are limits to the protection of fundamental rights. . . . They must always be considered with regard to the social function of the protected activity." See "Respect for Fundamental Rights in the EU," www.europarl.eu.int/factsheets/2_1_1_en.htm (accessed August 29, 2002).

11

֍֎

Europe, the United States, and Neoliberal (Dis)Order

Is There a Coming Crisis of the Euro?

Alan W. Cafruny

The history of the European Union is littered with failed visions and discarded or moribund institutions. As previous chapters in this volume show, integrative institutions and policies have developed when they have helped to consolidate a given capitalist regulatory framework or "comprehensive concept of control."[1] During the Bretton Woods era, the key institutions of the European Community buttressed the "embedded liberal" framework in which market forces were constrained by the postwar settlement.[2] The Treaty of Rome promoted regional economic integration but was also compatible with substantial legal and informal barriers to trade as well as relatively high levels of state intervention and corporatist involvement. The Common Agricultural Policy (CAP) utilized regional cooperation to cement the postwar social compromise and enhance social welfare and state power. As van Apeldoorn, Overbeek, and Ryner (chapter 1) and Gill (chapter 2) show, the crisis arising from the collapse of the Bretton Woods system led ultimately to the abandonment of Keynesianism and the "relaunch" of integration in the 1980s within a new regulatory framework of neoliberalism.[3] The Single European Act (SEA), which liberalized trade and capital markets, was the central feature of this process and led directly to EMU.[4]

The defining feature of the present phase of European integration is the monetary union, a point that deserves emphasis in view of the prevalence of teleological assumptions concerning the scope and significance of "Europeanization."[5] As a result of pressures deriving from the Doha Round of WTO negotiations and the budgetary implications of future enlargement, the CAP in its present form is endangered, and it is possible that agricultural policy will be re-nationalized.[6]

Holman and van der Pijl (chapter 3) show that European capital has during the last decade achieved a significant level of regional cohesion and begun to acquire some of the features of a transnational class through the construction of the single market and a "juridical Europe." However, the single market is also losing its distinctiveness as it is inserted into the process of global trade liberalization and regulation under the auspices of the WTO. As Scott-Smith demonstrates (chapter 10), the democratic potentialities of the Union are undermined by the absence of a European demos or a conception of Marshallian social rights. Bieling and Schulten (chapter 9) find that the concept of "social Europe" is essentially devoid of content. In chapter 4 of this volume, I show that even modest steps toward European political and military cooperation have been taken under the umbrella of American geopolitical power.

Throughout the post–World War II period, European countries have had to contend with overwhelming U.S. monetary power. Since the early 1970s, a series of attempts to establish a European zone of monetary stability have been frustrated by American policy and European weakness and fragmentation. However, although the significance of EMU as presently constituted derives primarily from its "constitutional" and disciplinary functions (see Gill, chapter 2), a single economic and monetary bloc encompassing one-fifth of global GDP and a plurality of votes in the IMF also has the potential to transform the Euro-American relationship. In this chapter I argue that the aspiration of European capital—both collectively and as constituent national fractions—to build a monetary union designed to promote competitiveness and regional autonomy is inconsistent with the neoliberal underpinnings of the system as it has developed since the Maastricht Treaty.

The first part of this chapter reviews the history of attempts to build a European zone of monetary stability in response to the collapse of the Bretton Woods system. In Gramscian terms, the Atlantic political economy of the Bretton Woods period can be conceived as a form of integral hegemony, a highly consolidated form of domination characterized by a well-developed sense of common purpose and lack of overt antagonism. The breakdown of the Bretton Woods system has resulted in a form of minimal hegemony, in which conflicts of interest are more visible, underlying power relations are more transparent as consent gives way to compulsion, and the system rests on a narrower social base and becomes increasingly unstable.[7] Thus during the 1970s U.S. international policies became more immediately self-interested; expansionary fiscal and monetary policies transmitted inflation to Western Europe and undermined attempts to maintain stable exchange rates. The deregulation of American and global financial markets beginning in the 1980s greatly increased America's structural power and placed limits on Europe's ability to counteract the emergent Anglo-American neoliberal offensive.

The second part of this chapter explores the double-sided and contradictory nature of EMU. On one hand, it expresses the strategic orientation of an embryonic transnational class. On the other hand, the decision to participate in the monetary union derived from national class strategies. It reflected domestic social settlements and political calculations and as such remains contingent. In its present form, EMU does not serve to reduce Europe's dependence on the United States. The conflicts over the Stability and Growth Pact are the inevitable result of a monetary union bereft of strong federal institutions and social solidarity. The final part of this chapter considers the possibility that alternative European projects, including either re-nationalization or the restructuring of the EU along social democratic and Keynesian lines, might emerge in the context of an organic crisis of the system as a whole.

IMPLICATIONS OF U.S. MONETARY POWER FOR EUROPE

The post–World War II form of integral transatlantic hegemony rested on two pillars: The first was the pattern of Fordist regulation that had emerged in the United States during the 1930s and became generalized throughout the OECD area after the war.[8] Fordism depended on the linkage of mass production and consumption, sustained by Keynesian policies of demand management. Technological innovation and collective agreements made it possible to build the welfare state and distribute the gains from productivity. The second pillar was U.S. hegemony expressed in the form of interdependent monetary and trade policies. Through the establishment of the dollar–gold standard at Bretton Woods, the United States provided stability and liquidity, laying the basis for the expansion of trade and investment that, however, throughout the "golden age" lagged behind the growth of output. The system remained stable as long as the dollar was strong enough to generate a constant supply of liquidity and international capital flows remained relatively low in proportion to GDP.

By the late 1960s it had become apparent that both of these pillars were crumbling. As the supply of dollars began to outrace existing gold stocks, confidence in the dollar was undermined and Europe and Japan became increasingly unwilling to finance U.S. deficits. In establishing a blueprint for a European zone of regional stability, the Werner Plan of 1970 reflected the changing nature of Atlantic power relations. It bore the imprint of German interest, viewing EMU as a means of reducing intra-European conflicts caused by French devaluation in the wake of 1968, but it also reflected Europe's resistance to growing U.S. unilateralism, especially after the failure to impose an alternative international currency in the form of special drawing rights on the United States.[9] At the same time, Fordism began to experience strains as two decades of full employment eroded wage restraint, especially in the context of inflationary U.S. policies, and the rate of profit fell.

The initial response to these problems on both sides of the Atlantic was to seek to preserve the framework of embedded liberalism in the context of a revision of the terms of agreement between the United States and Europe. However, America's unilateral decision to decouple the dollar from gold in 1971 did not lead to a multilateral balance of power, as assumed by numerous American scholars, but rather the more predatory use of power by the United States as policies began to reflect more narrowly defined national objectives and interests and a narrower social base.[10] The Carter administration's attempts to stimulate growth led initially to low interest rates and a depreciating dollar. By 1980, however, U.S. inflation was in double digits, and speculation against the dollar began to mount. U.S. expansionary policies greatly exacerbated Europe's problems. The "currency snake" deriving from the Werner Plan represented the first attempt to coordinate exchange rates, but the appreciation of the DM in relation to the dollar placed massive deflationary pressures on other currencies and ultimately made the system untenable. The decline of the dollar and the resulting global inflation also impeded Europe's attempts to recover from the recession by increasing exports and eventually provoked a new European response in the form of a Franco-German bid for a zone of European monetary stability in 1978. But this initiative also collapsed as once again European currencies appreciated at different rates and attempts to coordinate policy failed.

During the postwar boom, Western European countries "internalized" U.S. monetary hegemony as they relied on both fixed exchange rates to provide an anchor for the price system and on external adjustment to underwrite Keynesian strategies that supported class compromises. In France, for example, the ability to devalue without serious short-term cost helped to create what Michael Loriaux calls the "overdraft economy" based on "institutional structures that were designed not to control monetary growth but to facilitate mercantilist policies of industrial development,"[11] unlimited credit, and the possibility of external adjustment. The inability to control credit generated a social compromise that automatically generated inflation and required periodic devaluations.

The primary rationale offered for floating exchange rates was that they would relieve countries from having to pursue domestic austerity in order to fulfill international obligations. In principle, a country seeking to maintain full employment could inflate its domestic economy without having to defend the existing exchange rate by buying its own currency. Instead, the falling currency would boost exports, further stimulating growth. However, as the case of France demonstrated, floating exchange rates in the context of international capital mobility made it increasingly difficult to reflate by any means without setting of speculative runs on the currency. In this context, the inability to maintain a viable EMS and the collapse in 1983 of France's nationalist and Keynesian strategy would serve to redirect the embryonic European transnational class toward a neoliberal strategy under the leadership of Jacques Delors, who, as Mitterrand's finance minister, had experienced the full force of international speculative attacks on the franc.

The Bases of U.S. Monetary and Financial Power and the Neoliberal Offensive

Mainstream theorists of American hegemonic decline based their analysis on a conception of a "basic force model," which conceives of power in terms of resources. Thus, for example, when the Bretton Woods system collapsed scholars of hegemonic decline argued that U.S. monetary power was in decline because gold stocks were diminishing,[12] the United States was beginning to experience chronic balance of payments deficits,[13] or the United States was moving from a position of net creditor to net debtor.[14] Yet, such a conception of power misses the most salient features of U.S.–European relations, especially since the end of the Bretton Woods system. To be sure, in some respects U.S. power had declined: Postwar recovery in Japan and Germany and the decline of U.S. steel and auto rendered the prevailing dollar–gold standard obsolete, especially in the context of America's inflationary financing of Viet Nam. However, if trade deficits constituted an adequate measure of power, then Japan would presumably have increased its power over the course of the 1990s. Since World War II, moreover, the United States and Britain have been net debtors while Japan and Germany have been net creditors.

The concept of structural power provides a more comprehensive and satisfactory approach to international economic relations in general, and to the particular constraints operating on European economic and monetary policies. As Susan Strange has written, the progressive deregulation of finance and the consolidation of the "structural power of capital" were generally facilitated by technological developments but resulted in "certain specific political decisions or non-decisions taken by the leading financial authorities, especially in the United States."[15] These decisions flowed from a logic that was as much political as economic or technological: The size and power of the United States economy made it possible—in the context of floating exchange rates—to pursue economic policies according to the logic of domestic politics, a privilege that no single European country enjoys. Since 1971, U.S. monetary power conceived in structural terms has increased dramatically. As the traditional industries such as steel and auto declined, in part as a result of a geopolitical decision to remain open to Japanese imports, the U.S. government sought to establish liberal regimes in sectors that it could dominate, including not only finance but also telecommunications (and services more generally) and even agriculture.[16] This tendency was reinforced by the progressive dominance of financial capital over industrial capital and deregulatory policies that produced the collapse of the S & Ls in the late 1980s; the stock market bubble of the late 1990s; and the bursting of the bubble amid boardroom scandals at Enron, WorldCom, and a host of other corporations.[17]

U.S. monetary and financial power is ultimately grounded in the ability to create capital through credit, and not simply or primarily through the accumulation of resources. Such a power has depended on national policies designed to make Wall Street the center of global credit, to impose an open door on the rest of the world to allow U.S. access to domestic financial systems, and to eliminate barriers on the free flow of capital into the United States. Indeed, as Leonard Seabrooke shows, America's structural power enabled it to transform indebtedness into a strength by creating the necessity to develop financial innovation, thereby enabling the United States essentially to tax the resources of the major holders of U.S. debt: Japan, Germany, and Britain. Expansion of the euro–dollar market "provided a way of increasing the attractiveness of dollar holdings to foreigners" while facilitating the spread of offshore financial markets. The United States "sought to avoid undertaking adjustment measures by encouraging foreign governments and private investors to finance these deficits."[18] Beginning in the 1980s, the United States began to attract massive capital inflows from the rest of the world. In 2000, for example, the United States' current account deficit grew to US$450 billion, 4.5 percent of its national income. The United States accounted for 31 percent of global GDP and absorbed 64 percent of the world's net capital flows or almost 8 percent of the world's gross national savings.[19] These inflows not only enabled the United States to exert power over global capital markets but also to finance a defense budget that serves as a powerful Keynesian stimulant as well as a source of technological innovation.

Since 1971, U.S. international monetary power has not been expressed through formal monetary regimes, but rather through a combination of "international passivity and national activism" resulting from the "interactive embeddedness of Washington and Wall Street."[20] At the national level, the United States has deregulated its domestic financial markets in order to make them more competitive internationally. The process of deregulation began in the 1960s with the reopening of the City of London and the growth of the euro–dollar market, but a new wave began in the 1980s with the International Banking Act of 1980, which allowed U.S. banks parity with U.S. subsidiaries of foreign banks; the lifting of controls on interstate banking; the Deregulation and Monetary Control Act of 1980; the Garn–St. Germain Act, which allowed banks to extend beyond their traditional spheres into property development, insurance, and mortgages; and culminating in the Financial Services Modernization Act of 1998, which repealed the last vestiges of New Deal legislation deriving from the Glass Steagall Act. At the international level, the United States has resisted attempts to diminish the role of the dollar—such as special drawing rights in the late 1960s, enabling it to continue to enjoy "exorbitant privileges" while resisting capital controls and thereby promoting the expansion of private capital in international finance. Through its effective leadership of the IMF and World Bank, the United States has blocked attempts to establish or maintain capital controls on a national or regional basis, paving the way for a wholesale penetration of U.S. banks and financial corporations into Asian markets. The U.S. Treasury used the Asian financial crisis of 1997–1998 to restructure and liberalize the South Korean economy while blocking Japanese attempts to establish an Asian Monetary Fund that would have reduced the role of the IMF and undermined the "Washington Consensus."[21]

THE DOLLAR VERSUS THE EURO

The scope of U.S. power within global financial circuits is illustrated by a dramatic increase in international bank and bond lending over the last two decades, more than three-quarters of which is now denominated in dollars. By the mid-1990s, the dollar accounted for 61.5 percent of all central bank foreign exchange reserves, 76.8 percent of all international bank loans, 39.5 percent of all international bond issues, and 44.3 percent of all euro currency deposits.[22] Since the early 1990s, moreover, the trend toward dollarization has strengthened. Dollarization increases the advantages from seignorage because it extends the role of the dollar as the key international source of credit, confers advantages on U.S. exporters and importers, and enhances the ability of Washington and Wall Street to influence the price of the dollar. By the end of 2001, official or semi-official dollarization had extended throughout much of Latin America, including Argentina where it produced disastrous results. Dollarization, furthermore, reinforces pressures for structural adjustment: No longer able to devalue their currencies, underdeveloped countries become competitive by cutting wages.[23] And the trend toward dollarization serves to maintain the primacy of the dollar against the euro.[24]

Given the exorbitant privileges that the dollar bestows on the United States, the central role of the dollar in enabling the United States to restructure global finance, and the importance of dollar hegemony to U.S. geopolitical power, it is not surprising that since 1944 the United States has energetically defended the preeminent status of the dollar. At Bretton Woods, the United States resisted Keynes's proposal for an international currency, "bancor," and although the ensuing dollar–gold system was formally multilateral in practice it depended for its stability on American policy: Marshall Plan aid, foreign direct investment, and overseas military spending. During the 1960s as the dollar came under attack, the United States rejected calls, especially from France, to return to the gold standard, and prevented the use of SDRs as a significant alternative source of liquidity.[25]

Beginning in the early 1970s, the EU mounted a number of unsuccessful attempts to establish a "zone of stability" against the dollar. As noted above, the currency snake of 1972, the European Monetary System (EMS), and the subsequent Exchange Rate Mechanism (ERM) all sought to maintain a system of internal fixed exchange rates. Yet these initiatives were undermined by Europe's collective vulnerability to U.S. monetary unilateralism, chronic uneven development among the member states, and high levels of labor militancy, which made it impossible to maintain sufficient discipline or "internal adjustment" and thereby pass the cost of adjustment on to labor. As a result, currencies were eventually pushed out of fixed parities.

Prior to EMU, the imbalance between Germany and the rest of the EU meant that the DM was a powerful magnet for international capital seeking a safe and noninflationary haven. The 1992 collapse of the ERM, considered by the Bank of International Settlements to be the most significant international monetary crisis since the fall of the BW system in 1971, exemplified this tendency.[26] As long as European economies were expanding, ERM members were able to raise their interest rates in order to maintain parity with the rising DM. Reunification, however, precipitated a crisis both for Germany and the EU as a whole. The cost of reunification (5.5 percent of German annual GNP) resulted in a serious budgetary shortfall. At the same time, Chancellor Kohl promised *Ossis* that he would establish a 1–1 parity for DM–OstMark, despite having pledged to the German people that there would be no permanent tax increase. The Bundesbank raised interest rates to historically unprecedented levels, thus playing the role in relation to the rest of the EU analogous to that which the United States played in relation to Europe during the 1980s when high interest rates attracted massive infusions of capital from abroad. At the same time, the U.S. Federal Reserve cut interest rates, a decision that France called an "Anglo-Saxon plot to undermine the movement towards European unity."[27] Despite spending half of its reserves to buy pounds and a five-point increase in interest rates on September 16, 1992 (Black Wednesday), Britain was forced to exit the ERM. After similar massive and costly intervention, Italy followed suit. Speculation against the franc during the summer of 1993 necessitated the widening of ERM margins of fluctuation to 30 percent as the EMU appeared headed for disaster. Between September 1992 and March 1995, the lira fell by 35 percent against the mark, the peseta dropped 29 percent, and the pound lost 19 percent of its value. These currency fluctuations not only rendered EMU doubtful, but also threatened the Single Market itself. Despite French accusations of Anglo-Saxon responsibility, the fear of German monetary nationalism remains throughout the EU, especially in Britain.

EMU in Permanent Crisis?

The EMU, of course, goes far beyond the ERM because it demands greater macroeconomic cohesion and thereby seeks to institutionalize a new balance of power between capital and labor. In some respects, EMU, in contrast to previous attempts at monetary cooperation, is potentially a policy of reregulation, including a federal structure based on the German model and a strong commitment to price stability. The Maastricht Treaty compelled member states to harmonize their fiscal policies as a condition of entry, and limited budget deficits to 3 percent of GDP and accumulated debt to no more than 60 percent of GDP. The Stability Pact additionally called for the phasing out of all budget deficits by 2004 and the imposition of punitive measures against recalcitrant governments. The disciplinary and procyclical features of the Stability Pact reflected, at least at the outset, the interest of the stronger economies, especially Germany.[28] Subsequent developments, however, have shown that the Stability Pact contains the seeds of instability and future conflict.

Between 1995 and 2000, Italy experienced the second-lowest growth rate among the fifteen member states as it pursued radical financial and monetary policies in order to qualify for inclusion in EMU. But the weak economy generated increasing budget deficits, so much so that Finance Minister Giulio Tremonti announced a 2.4 percent budget deficit for 2001, well above the voluntary ceiling that EU finance ministers had agreed on (but still below the 10 percent average for Italy between 1975 and 1995). Tremonti was ultimately compelled to reduce the targets, but did so only by assuming unreasonably high expected growth rates for 2001–2004. Italy's record was not exceptional; by mid-2001, every state in the euro zone had broken the 2 percent barrier. Italy and Belgium continue to maintain debt to GDP ratios in excess of 100 percent.

It is widely recognized that the Stability and Growth Pact not only places pressure on weaker economies, but also no longer accords with the interest of the stronger economies, including Germany. During the decade since Germany signed the Maastricht Treaty in 1992 its unemployment rate increased from 4.5 percent to 9.9 percent. Germany's growth rates for 2001 and 2002 were the lowest of all fifteen member states, and unemployment reached 4 million by mid-2002. Despite relatively high worker productivity (2.6 percent per year through the 1990s), the dampening of demand has prevented a decrease in unemployment. Given the size of the German economy (31 percent of Union GDP), low growth greatly impacted the French economy and rippled throughout the euro zone as a whole, which registered a growth rate of only 1 percent for 2002. German Finance Minister Hans Eichel suggested in August 2001 that the constraints of the Stability Pact should be abandoned in favor of targets on public spending (see Ryner, chapter 8). Although Chancellor Schröder overruled him after strong protests from the ECB, it is notable that opposition is arising in the core and not just in the periphery. By the end of 2002, President of the Commission Romano Prodi and Trade Commissioner Pascal Lamy variously proclaimed the Stability Pact to be "stupid" and "medieval"; France and Germany both stated their intention to violate the deficit rules. If the Stability Pact were to be abandoned, then international financial markets would be even more dependent on a monetarist ECB to maintain the value of the euro. Yet, even under the terms of the Stability Pact, despite unprecedented unemployment, the ECB has less flexibility than the Federal Reserve Board, which in 2001 cut interest rates eleven times even as the United States' current account deficit exceeded $400 billion.[29]

More generally, the neoliberal agenda is self-limiting because it does not provide necessary institutional and political foundations for stability. In contrast to the United States, the EU still has no centralized fiscal policy. Whereas the power to set interest rates lies with the ECB, national finance ministers still nominally control exchange rate policy, but they are heavily influenced by the ECB as well as potentially by the G-8. The Stability Pact demands steep cuts in social spending throughout the Union, but low growth places pressure on government budgets. The virtual absence of a Union budget does not allow for the extensive redistributive policies necessary to minimize uneven development by compensating weaker economies that have lost the option of devaluation. Current EU revenues are 1.3 percent of member-state GNP, much less even than the 5–7 percent viewed as the minimum necessary budget called for in the McDougall Report of 1977.

It is of course widely assumed that the imperatives of monetary union mean there is "no alternative" to the adoption of Anglo-Saxon models of deregulated labor markets, which, together with deregulated product markets and removal of other barriers to competition, will reduce instability and uneven development in the euro zone.[30] To be sure, flexibility has made significant inroads, especially in Britain and in the Mediterranean.[31] However, even on its own terms, deregulation of labor markets is not an effective means of counteracting uneven development within a single currency area. Variations in growth and productivity will increase as a result of enlargement, and there are strong cultural barriers to labor mobility. Moreover, the correlation between deregulated labor markets, on the one hand, and either employment[32] or productivity[33] on the other hand is very weak. The problem of insufficient demand is central to Europe's economic problems over the last decade. Unless the Union budget increases substantially and a European fiscal policy is developed, the realities of uneven national development will always sooner or later threaten the stability of an integrated market and place limits on the cohesion of a transnational European capitalist class.

The United States and the Euro

The foregoing suggests why, in view of the claims and predictions that a European monetary union constitutes a fundamental challenge to U.S. monetary hegemony, and given the overall context of aggressive assertion of American financial interests in the 1990s, the U.S. response toward EMU has been rather muted. American official and semi-official commentary with respect to the euro during the 1990s in fact replicated the response toward the single market a decade earlier. At the outset of the single market program, there was substantial opposition in Washington toward an anticipated French model of "fortress Europe" that had the potential to exclude American capital and trade. When it became clear by the early 1990s that the single market would in fact promote Atlantic economic integration, opposition evaporated. A similar process appears to have taken place with respect to the euro.[34] To be sure, Washington's attitude of benign neglect toward the EMU has numerous proximate causes, including widespread skepticism until recently that EMU could survive, Britain's decision to remain outside euroland, and the preference of the United States to influence international monetary policy through domestic policy and unilateral actions rather than through multilateral negotiations. More fundamentally, however, the monetary union as presently constituted is subordinated to the U.S. policy of financial liberalization, and is inextricably linked to broader U.S. geopolitical hegemony. As Charles Pasqua has written,

> the good will that [the United States] shows for the process of European monetary integration is the counterpart to the strategic advantage that it expects from the now generalized acceptance in Europe of the preeminence of NATO in the matter of European defense. . . . [T]he *European model* which is appearing before our eyes is a whole—monetarist, federal, Atlanticist—and it is impossible to accept one part of it without being forced to accept the other, nor to reject one part without renouncing the other.[35]

Although the prospect of monetary union does not appear to have produced widespread alarm in Wall Street or an antagonistic policy response in Washington, there are nevertheless two significant long-term sources of American concern with respect to EMU. First, much of the commentary in congressional and academic circles has focused in the issue of seignorage and the possibility that the euro will reduce this benefit to the United States. However, although the euro will certainly displace the dollar in some areas, especially in Central and Eastern Europe, it is doubtful that in the absence of a more generalized global economic crisis the overall impact will be large enough to constitute a major challenge to the dollar. Moreover, the increased regional cohesion of the European economy has not been accompanied by a reduction of dependence on the United States either in terms of trade and investment or the ripple effects of American macroeconomic policies. The process of transatlantic integration has accelerated dramatically over the last twenty-five years. Between 1990 and 2001, two-way (merchandise and services) trade between the EU and the United States increased from $273 billion to $573 billion. The share of U.S. imports from the EU remained steady (22 percent in 1990 and 21 percent in 2000), as did EU imports from the United States (16 percent in 1990 and 17 percent in 2000). The trend in foreign direct investment shows more evidence of Atlantic integration: In 1990, 58 percent of foreign investment controlled by EU firms went to the United States, increasing to 65 percent by 2000. During the same period, approximately 25 percent of U.S. FDI went to the EU. In 2000, two-way foreign direct investment stock was US$1.376 trillion.[36] The speed and intensity with which developments in the U.S. economy and financial markets impact on Europe underscores the lack of autonomous European growth trajectory.

A second source of potential transatlantic tension is the protectionist potential of EMU. Between its launch in 1999 and the spring of 2002, the euro declined by 25 percent against the dollar. A number of factors can be cited to account for this decline, including the position of financial markets toward a new and uncertain currency. However, there is also substantial evidence that the ECB has sought to accommodate EU export interests and to moderate the conflicts arising from tight fiscal policies.[37] What amounts to a policy of covert "neoliberal mercantilism" highlights the contradictions and limitations in the monetary union. It suggests that the ECB is torn between the particular national interests of strong states—in this case, Franco-German interests—and the more general project of European capital as a whole, including the viability of the euro as a rival to the dollar. It also highlights the dependency on and vulnerability to U.S. policies. A devaluation of 25 percent against the dollar was not inconsistent with U.S. policy, which has sought to expand domestic capital markets and privileged finance at the expense of industry.[38] However, the strong dollar policy depends on the ability of the United States to continue to finance massive deficits. During the summer and fall of 2002, the dollar declined significantly against the euro as the stock market bubble burst amid boardroom scandals.

ALTERNATIVES TO NEOLIBERAL EUROPE: RE-NATIONALIZATION OR A SOCIAL-DEMOCRATIC EU?

There is considerable tension between the goal of greater regional autonomy and the monetary union as presently conceived. The neoliberal underpinnings of EMU serve to reinforce Europe's subordinate relationship within the Atlantic area. At the same time, the EU has neither the internal cohesion and political will, the characteristics of a polity, nor the geopolitical power to promote greater regional autonomy and a return to Europe's distinctive social market traditions. This section examines the longer-term possibilities for an alternative political project designed to transcend the limitations of minimal hegemony. Such a project would necessarily have both national and European dimensions, although these would not be mutually exclusive.

Re-nationalization

The assertion that national autonomy is constrained by globalization is by now commonplace, and it is a central assumption of the politics of the "third way." Yet, the experiences of Britain, Germany, and France over the last three decades suggest that such an assertion needs to be advanced with caution. As Hay and Watson (see chapter 6) write,

> The impact of globalization on the British political economy may be more rhetorical than substantive. . . . It is the political discourse of globalization rather than globalization *per se*, we argue, that summons the inexorable "logic of no alternative. . . .
> It is the political deployment of the discourse of globalization, rather than the transformation of the international political economy which such a discourse purports to

represent, that is the most significant factor in restricting the parameters of that considered politically and economically possible.

Social democratic governments in Britain and France sought unsuccessfully to pursue national Keynesian strategies in the 1970s and 1980s. More recently, Oscar Lafontaine challenged the Stability and Growth Pact through the mechanism of an alternative Franco-German alliance (see Ryner, chapter 8). Have these strategies failed as a result of "necessity" in the form of the hypermobility of financial markets, offering decisive proof that national Keynesian strategies are no longer viable?

In the case of Britain, the origins of New Labour arose from the failure of the Alternative Economic Strategy of the mid-1970s. The centerpiece of this strategy was a National Enterprise Board, which would have extended public ownership and provided leverage for tripartite negotiations or "sector planning agreements." In exchange for wage restraint, the Labour Party promised expansionary public financing, basing its hopes on increased oil revenues to balance the external trade account. By mid-1975, however, a balance of payments crisis resulted as reflation caused a surge in imports and a run on the pound. Pressed by central bankers and especially the IMF, Prime Minister Harold Wilson imposed an austerity program, rejecting the alternative of capital and import controls.

The fate of the French Socialists in 1981–1983 was very similar, although the "lessons" have been less fully internalized in the PS. In the French version of the AES, Mitterrand implemented a *programme commun* based on extensive nationalization, Keynesian fiscal stimulus, and modest expansion of the money supply. As with the British experience, however, the program was pursued in the teeth of a worldwide recession and was greatly influenced by France's desire to remain within the EMS. Once again, a socialist government retreated in the face of speculative attacks. In the French case, the European dimension was more important (see Clift, chapter 7). Whereas Britain looked unsuccessfully to the United States for support, France expected Germany to reflate in response to its growing current account deficit. Germany's refusal reinforced the crisis of confidence of French business and led the government to devalue the franc and accommodate to global finance.

The case of Germany is more complex: As the strongest and most competitive economy in Europe, Germany has a clear interest in fixed exchange rates and "sound money." The Bundesbank and the Ministry of Finance have been enforcers of monetary orthodoxy through successive European monetary regimes; yet, the tradition of ordo-liberalism has permitted a deeply entrenched system of social protection on the basis of highly developed corporatism and a dynamic export sector. As Ryner shows (chapter 8), the "moment of Lafontaine" highlighted these contradictions as mounting unemployment in the summer of 1999 led the now-deposed minister of finance to seek to "change the terms of European and even global economic governance" through

a more "flexible" interpretation of the Stability Pact and an international exchange rate regime. Lafontaine sought to develop a program emphasizing employment through supply-side measures, but not the deregulation of labor,
demand stimulus through tax reduction, and fiscal policy. He recognized that
such a policy would require regional support. Yet the program met with stiff resistance not only in Germany but also throughout the EU, ultimately leading
to Lafontaine's dismissal.

The capitulation to neoliberalism was repeated on a smaller scale virtually
everywhere else in Europe throughout the 1980s. At the beginning of the
decade, it appeared that the smaller European countries might prove more successful in adapting corporatist structures to the liberalization of production and
finance. Yet by 1986 Norway had embarked on a "turning operation" in which
the commitment to full employment was abandoned and foreign exchange controls were lifted. Sweden followed suit as the Social Democrats pushed through
a massive program of financial deregulation in the late 1980s. The krona was
pegged to the EMS, where it became vulnerable to speculation and finally collapsed in November 1992.

The analysis of the failure of "Keynesianism in one country" helps to clarify
the political and theoretical implications of the thesis of declining sovereignty.
At what point is it possible to argue that national economic autonomy no longer
exists and that national strategies that seek to respond to and influence international market forces are no longer feasible? In the case of Britain in 1975, for example, standard accounts cite the central role of the IMF in the collapse of the
AES; as Hay and Watson show (chapter 6), the alleged imperatives of global financial liberalization have become the defensive armor of New Labour. Yet, the
key political debates and vital political maneuvers within the cabinet took place
not in the heat of the IMF crisis but at least a year before. As Steven Ludlam
notes, "The IMF deal merely codified a change of political course already well
underway and proceeding under the stewardship of British social democracy."[39]
In France, similarly, the new policy of *rigueur* was justified with reference to the
imperatives of globalization. Yet, there is no evidence that the French government ever seriously contemplated operating outside EMS guidelines, much less
risking a sharp political confrontation with capital, or that it sought to mobilize
its supporters for this purpose.[40] The case of the rise and fall of Oskar Lafontaine
is particularly instructive in this regard, clearly illustrating the limitations of an
argument from the point of view of international imperatives as well as the limits of neoliberal legitimation in Germany. Although his initiative was defeated,
nevertheless "Lafontainism without Lafontaine" persisted in the form of what
Ryner (chapter 8) terms "expansionary monetary policy by stealth" in the form
of a weakening euro.

In principle, European governments could have resisted monetarist pressures
arising from central bankers and international markets: Apart from the legal and
institutional commitments entailed by EMU, there is no prima facie reason why

Keynesian strategies could not be employed either unilaterally or in combination.[41] As Fred Block writes, the thesis of globalization

> tends to naturalize the world economy—that is, to see it as having a life of its own independent of politics. . . . The alternative view is that the particular structure of the world economy—the rules of the game that determine international economic transactions—emerge out of political negotiations and conflicts among nation-states. The balance of political forces within and among nations shapes, and can re-shape, the structure of the international economy.[42]

The internationalization of production and capital has been established and policed by nation-states, especially the United States, and is therefore subject to political control and modification. As Hay and Watson (chapter 6) argue, that the reintroduction of capital controls and other forms of regulation are seldom considered as serious options in medium-sized economies such as Britain, France, and Germany at least partly reflects the self-imposed limitations of social democracy, and not simply the internationalization of production and capital.

EMU beyond Neoliberalism?

If the thesis of declining sovereignty is overstated, it is nonetheless the case that European national capitalist strategies have inevitably encountered serious limitations if they sought to swim against the neoliberal tide. With the exception of Britain, Denmark, and Sweden, of course, this type of strategy would now require a very different conception of EMU. As the second part of this chapter indicated, U.S. fiscal and monetary policies have imposed serious costs and constraints on medium-sized economies. That capital controls and the reintroduction of financial regulation have lost favor at least partly reflects the historical role of social democratic parties as managers of capital; although globalization does not in principle preclude interventionist strategies, it raises the stakes of political conflict for opponents of neoliberalism, especially where capital is emboldened by its own mobility as well as chronic low growth. In comparison to medium-sized economies, the United States clearly retains a great deal of room for maneuver. However, by virtue of its size and level of economic integration as well as its residual social traditions, the EU has the capacity in principle to mount a challenge to neoliberalism. Such a challenge, which would require a fundamental revision of the Stability Pact and the underlying regulatory framework, would inevitably provoke conflict with the United States. Is "social democracy in one continent" a viable strategy?

The economic and monetary provisions of the Maastricht Treaty were quite specific and carefully drafted, standing in marked contrast both to the common foreign and security policy and to social policy. Article 5 of the Treaty states categorically that "the primary objective of the ECB shall be to maintain price stability."

Yet Article 5 also mandates that "without prejudice to the objective of price stability, the ECB shall support the general economic policies of the community," and article 2 explicitly provides for a social framework:

> The Community shall have as its task . . . to promote throughout the Community a harmonious and balanced development of economic activities, sustainable and non-inflationary growth respecting the environment, a high degree of convergence of economic performance, a high level of employment and of social protection, the raising of the standard of living and the quality of life, and economic and social cohesion and solidarity among member states.[43]

Thus, the Maastricht Treaty incorporated some of the ideological forms of the postwar settlement, even though, of course, the Stability and Growth Pact clearly removed any ambiguities concerning the underlying social purpose of EMU. At the same time, however, slow growth and mass unemployment have begun to isolate the Bundesbank and ECB even from finance ministries, and the Stability Pact itself is routinely evaded.

At the international level, Europe would need to establish regulatory policies across a wide array of international regimes. Such policies would need to include restrictions on speculative capital flows, as with the Tobin Tax, which has recently received support from Germany and France; sponsorship of debt repudiation and alternatives to structural adjustment; and the abandonment of neomercantilist trade policies toward the third world, especially with respect to agricultural. More generally, the EU would need to shift the focus of policy from monetarism to development, especially as it expands into Eastern Europe. A strategy for reform would make monetary and fiscal policy subsidiary to employment: It would go beyond "competitive restructuring" and implement tax reforms to expand demand, and state-led investment programs, counter-cyclical fiscal policy, and labor market reforms that stop short of deregulation. Such a program would almost certainly include capital controls.

Of course, a fundamental change in orientation would demand a return to Keynesian and corporatist traditions represented in the Werner Plan and not in Maastricht.[44] A regional project of this magnitude would require a centralized authority to compensate for the loss of national autonomy, even if the impetus for reform would need to include mass movements still organized at the level of the nation-state. A political union capable of carrying out structural reforms would require a substantial increase in the budget, a single fiscal policy including taxation and substantially higher levels of interregional redistribution, and a common foreign and defense policy. Such a program would certainly trigger a strong U.S. reaction.

The political conditions for such a program do not exist at the present time. Indeed, framing the issue in this way underlines the extent to which the Left has during the last two decades surrendered the ideological terrain to capital. In electoral terms, the 1990s were largely a social democratic era, and ruling parties were at the forefront of the construction of neoliberal Europe, either justifying these programs with slogans such as the third way and *neue Mitte*, as in Britain and Germany, or acquiescing to them, as in France. Despite their virtual monopoly of power throughout the second half of the 1990s European social democratic parties were unwilling or unable to develop transnational cohesion or challenge the neoliberal consensus, as indicated most vividly by the collapse of Lafontaine's Franco-German project. The explanation for the abandonment of distinctive social democratic aims and principles (as opposed to electoral success) would need to address a range of material factors, including the shrinking of the industrial working class, the changing nature of work, and the fact that in many countries the labor movement retains considerable defensive strength. But the collapse of the Left also needs to be understood on the terrain of theory. As Robin Varghese has recently proposed, "It may be this pessimism about the reascendance of working-class interests to a hegemonic position that places the social democratic project's future in question far more than capital flows or the structure of wage bargains."[45] Recent antiglobalization demonstrations in Gothenburg and Genoa have, however, placed alternatives on the agenda and shown that neoliberalism is still far from having achieved unchallenged ideological hegemony.

The impact on Europe of America's financial meltdown in 2002 showed that the fate of neoliberal Europe continues to be tied to an inherently unstable "American model." Through its global power, the financial sector of U.S. capital has thus far been able to resolve problems and contradictions arising from this model, which include a massive trade deficit, chronically low savings, continuing dependence on inflows of foreign capital, and dramatic increases in levels of poverty and inequality. However, despite the size and centrality of U.S. capital markets, it may not be possible to finance trade deficits of this magnitude indefinitely, and a prolonged U.S. recession would send shock waves throughout the world economy. At the same time, there is little evidence that America's sclerotic and corrupted political establishment has the capacity to articulate a coherent imperial vision or recreate the underlying conditions for a return to a more integral global hegemony. A full-blown crisis of the American model would inevitably present Europe with novel political dangers as well as opportunities.

If, on the other hand, the present trajectory of slow growth and mass unemployment continues, conflict over the terms of the monetary union is likely to increase. The institutional architecture of the EU inevitably pits strong cultural and political units against an unaccountable Central Bank. The result is a legacy of growing nationalism: opposition to the Maastricht Treaty, resistance to the Stability and Growth Pact, and a divisive and inconclusive constitutional process aggravated by the pressures of enlargement. Indeed, given its aspiration to construct a political union, European capital has not been entirely well served by labor's conditional surrender: The absence of countervailing social pressures provides no incentive to transcend its own short-term interests and establish integrative regional institutions that might underwrite social stability and global monetary autonomy. Absent such institutions, neoliberal Europe is condemned to confront a mutually reinforcing combination of market rationality and resurgent nationalism.

NOTES

1. On this concept see Kees van der Pijl, *Transnational Classes and International Relations* (London: Routledge, 1998), esp. 4, 5. See also chapters 1 and 2 of this volume.

2. On the concept of embedded liberalism see John Ruggie, "International Regimes, Transactions, and Change: Embedded Liberalism in the Postwar Economic Order," in Stephen Krasner, ed., *International Regimes* (Ithaca, N.Y.: Cornell University Press, 1983). See also Alan Milward, *The European Rescue of the Nation-State*, 2nd ed. (London: Routledge, 2000).

3. See also Bastiaan van Apeldoorn, *Transnational Capitalism and the Struggle over European Order* (London: Routledge, 2002).

4. Although Franco-German relations may have influenced the timing and specific form of EMU, the economic imperative was crucial, a point made by Tomasso Padoa-Schioppa, "Engineering the Single Currency," in Peter Gowan and Perry Anderson, eds., *The Question of Europe* (London: Verso, 1997). See also Commission of the European Communities, *Report on Economic and Monetary Union, Delors Committee Report* (Brussels: Author, 1989). To stress the interrelationship of the single market and single currency, especially for the continental countries, does not imply a more general neofunctionalist argument. On this point see Talani, chapter 5 of this volume. Of course, the original blueprint for EMU expressed the still-ascendant Keynesian orientation of the late 1960s. See Lars Magnusson and Bo Strath, "From the Werner Plan to the EMU: In Search of European Political Economy: Historical Perspectives and Future Prospects," in Lars Magnusson and Bo Strath, eds., *From the Werner Plan to EMU: In Search of a Political Economy for Europe* (Brussels: P.I.E. Peter Lang, 2001).

5. Lloy Wylie, "EMU: A Neoliberal Construction," in Amy Verdun, ed., *The Euro: European Integration Theory and Economic and Monetary Union* (Lanham, Md.: Rowman & Littlefield, 2002).

6. Marjoleine Hennis, "Europeanization and Globalization: The Missing Link," *Journal of Common Market Studies* 39 (2001).

7. On the distinction between integral and minimal hegemony see Alan W. Cafruny, "A Gramscian Concept of Declining Hegemony: Stages of U.S. Power and the Evolution of International Relations," in David P. Rapkin, ed., *World Leadership and Hegemony* (Boulder, Colo.: Lynne Rienner, 1990).

8. Kees van der Pijl, *The Making of an Atlantic Ruling Class* (London: Verso, 1984).

9. Riccardo Parboni, *The Dollar and Its Rivals: Recession, Inflation, and International Finance* (London: Verso, 1982).

10. David Calleo, *The Imperious Economy* (Cambridge, Mass.: Harvard University Press, 1982).

11. Michael Loriaux, *France after Hegemony: International Change and Financial Reform* (Ithaca, N.Y.: Cornell University Press, 1991), 10.

12. Robert O. Keohane, "The Theory of Hegemonic Stability and Changes in International Economic Regimes, 1967–77," in O. R. Holsti, R. M. Siverson, and A. L. George, eds., *Change in the International System* (Boulder, Colo.: Westview Press, 1980).

13. Robert Gilpin, U.S. *Power and the Multinational Corporations: The Political Economy of U.S. Foreign Direct Investment* (New York: Basic Books, 1975).

14. Michael Webb and Stephen Krasner, "Hegemonic Stability Theory: An Empirical Assessment," *Review of International Studies* 15, no. 2 (1989).

15. Susan Strange, *Casino Capitalism* (London: Basil Blackwell, 1986), 60. See also Eric Helleiner, *States and the Reemergence of Global Finance: From Bretton Woods to the 1990s* (Ithaca, N.Y.: Cornell University Press, 1994).

16. Alan Cafruny, "Economic Conflicts and the Transformation of the Atlantic Order: The USA, Europe, and the Liberalisation of Agriculture and Services," in Stephen Gill, ed., *Atlantic Relations: Beyond the Reagan Era* (London: Harvester Wheatsheaf, 1989).

17. On the rise of finance capital and the emergence of a *rentier bloc* see van Apeldoorn, Overbeek, and Ryner, chapter 1 of this volume; and van der Pijl, *The Making of an Atlantic Ruling Class*. See also Kevin Philips, *Wealth and Democracy: A Political History of the American Rich* (New York: Broadway Books, 2002).

18. Leonard Seabrooke, U.S. *Power in International Finance: The Victory of Dividends* (Basingstoke, UK: Palgrave, 2001), 10. Gowan's "dollar–Wall Street regime" advances a similar argument: the financial regime evolves not as a result of multilateral negotiation, but as an expression of U.S. policy. See Peter Gowan, *The Global Gamble: Washington's Faustian Bid for World Dominance* (London: Verso, 1999).

19. Eric Altbach, "The Asian Monetary Fund Proposal: A Case Study of Japanese Regional Leadership," *Japan Economic Institute Report* 47 (December 19, 1997). Stephen Gill, "The Geopolitics of the Asian Crisis," *Monthly Review* 50, 10 (March, 1999).

20. Seabrooke, U.S. *Power*, 19.

21. Joseph Stiglitz, *Globalization and Its Discontents* (New York: W. W. Norton, 2002), 112–13. See also Gowan, *The Global Gamble*, especially chapter 6.

22. Gowan, *The Global Gamble*, 35–36.

23. Guglielmo Carchedi, *For Another Europe: A Class Analysis of European Economic Integration* (London: Verso, 2001), especially 145–56.

24. Kenneth Schuler, *Basics of Dollarization*, Joint Economic Committee Staff Report (Washington, D.C.: U.S. GPO, 1999). See also Robert Mundell, "What the Euro Means for the Dollar and the International Monetary System," *Atlantic Economic Journal* (September 1998). *The Economist* estimates that seignorage represents as much as 0.1 percent of American GDP; see *The Economist*, "The International Euro" (November 14, 1998). See also Parboni, *The Dollar and Its Rivals*, 40–58.

25. Barry Eichengreen, *Globalizing Capital: A History of the International Monetary System* (Princeton, N.J.: Princeton University Press, 1996), 115–17; and Parboni, *The Dollar and Its Rivals*, 62–63.

26. Seabrooke, U.S. *Power in International Finance*, 162.

27. Seabrooke, U.S. *Power in International Finance*, 163.

28. Jeffrey Frieden, David Gros, and Eric Jones, eds., *The New Political Economy of EMU* (Lanham, Md.: Rowman & Littlefield, 1998).

29. In this respect the situation confronting the Federal Reserve Bank and the ECB at the end of 2002 reveals the potential for instability. The Fed cut interest rates by a half-point, a move that was deemed necessary to revive economic growth and thereby

continue to sustain capital flows into the United States to finance the current account deficit. However, the minutes of the Fed's open market committee indicate fears that "further sizeable disinflation that resulted in a nominal inflation rate near zero could create problems for the implementation of monetary policy through conventional means in the event of an adverse shock to the economy that called for negative real policy interest rates" (*New York Times*, November 8, 2002, sec. C3).

After twelve rate cuts over the last two years, the federal funds rate declined to 1.25 percent, virtually eliminating rate cuts as a policy tool. Responding to concerns about German deflation, Wim Duisenberg insisted that "the bank's primary mission is not to spur growth, but to curb inflation."

30. European Commission, *White Paper on Growth, Competitiveness, and Employment: The Challenges and Ways Forward into the 21st Century* (Brussels, 1993).

31. Leila Simona Talani, "Mediterranean Labour and the Impact of EMU: Mass Unemployment or Labour Market Flexibility," in Henk Overbeek, ed., *The Political Economy of European Employment* (London: Routledge, 2003).

32. When levels of incarceration are taken into account, U.S. and European unemployment rates are similar. See, for example, OECD *Employment Outlook* (Paris: OECD, 2000); and Robert Buchele and Jens Christiansen, "Do Employment and Income Security Cause Unemployment? A Comparative Study of the United States and the E-4," *Cambridge Journal of Economics* 22 (1998).

33. European Commission, Eurostat, *Structural Indicators: Labor Productivity* (Brussels: Author, 2001). See also S. Nickell, "Unemployment and Labor Market Rigidities: Europe vs. North America," *Journal of Economic Perspectives* 11 (1997).

34. Official and quasi-official Washington has of course issued very strong warnings about the euro since the early 1990s. As late as 1997 Martin Feldstein warned, "If EMU does come into existence . . . it will change the political character of Europe in ways that could lead to conflicts in Europe and confrontations with the United States." "EMU and International Conflict," *Foreign Affairs* 76 (November-December 1997): 60.

35. Charles Pasqua, "Which France for Which Europe?" in Ronald Tiersky, ed., *Euro-Skepticism: A Reader* (Lanham, Md.: Rowman & Littlefield, 2001), 210.

36. Statistics derived from Gary Hufbauer and Frederick Neumann, "U.S.–EU Trade and Investment: An American Perspective" (Washington, D.C.: Institute for International Economics, 2002); and U.S. Bureau of Economic Analysis, "U.S. International Transactions Accounts Data" (Washington, D.C.: U.S. Department of Commerce, 2002).

37. See especially Miriam Campanella, "Euro Weakness and the ECB Economic Governance: A Strategic Institutionalist Perspective," in Miriam Campanella and Sylvester Eijffinger, eds., *EU Economic Governance and Globalization* (London: Edward Elgar, 2002); and Leila Simona Talani, "The ECB between Growth and Stability," unpublished manuscript.

38. Between 1997 and 2001, the dollar appreciated by 30 percent in value against all other currencies. The United States experienced a $140 billion drop in manufactured exports between August 2000 and December 2001, leading to an estimated loss of 500,000 jobs. See National Association of Manufacturers, "Overvalued Dollar Puts Hundreds of Thousands out of Work," www.nam.org/docs/itia/24415Dollar_Paper.

39. Steven Ludlam, "The Gnomes of Washington: Four Myths of the 1976 IMF Crisis," *Political Studies* 40 (1992): 727.

40. Marc Lombard, "A Re-examination of the Reasons for the Failure of Keynesian Expansionary Policies in France, 1981–3," *Cambridge Journal of Economics* 19 (1995): 371.

41. Geoffrey Garret provides data that refute the strong globalization thesis. "Shrinking States? Globalization and National Autonomy," in N. Woods, ed., *The Political Economy of Globalization* (Houndsmills, UK: MacMillan, 2000). See also Robert Kudrle, "Market Globalization and the Future Policies of the Industrial States," in A. Prakash and J. Hart, eds., *Globalization and Governance* (London: Routledge, 1999).

42. Fred Block, *Postindustrial Possibilities: A Critique of Economic Discourse* (Berkeley: University of California Press, 1991), 16, 17.

43. Commission of the European Communities, *Treaty on European Union* (Luxembourg: Publications of the EC, 1992).

44. Tom Notermans, "The Werner Plan as a Blueprint for EMU?" in Magnusson and Strath, eds., *From the Werner Plan to the EMU*.

45. Robin Varghese, "The Operation Was a Success . . . But the Patient Is Dead: Theorizing Social Democracy in an Era of Globalization," *Review of International Political Economy* 8 (Winter 2001): 737.

Index

About the Contributors

Bastiaan van Apeldoorn is lecturer in International Relations at the Free University of Amsterdam, Netherlands. He earned his Ph.D. (1999) from the European University Institute in Florence, and was formerly a postdoctoral fellow at the Max Planck Institute in Cologne. His main research interests are within the fields of international political economy and European integration. He is the author of *Transnational Capitalism and the Struggle over European Integration* (2002).

Hans-Jürgen Bieling is junior professor for European Integration in the Political Science Department at the Phillips University of Marburg, Germany. His main fields of interest are international political economy, European integration, and industrial relations. His publications include *Dynamiken Sozialer Spaltung und Ausgrenzung: Gesellschaftstheorien und Zeitdiagnosen* (2000) and *Arbeitslosigkeit und Wohlfahrtsstaat in Westeuropa* (coedited with Frank Deppe, 1997).

Alan W. Cafruny is Henry Platt Bristol Professor and Chair of the Department of Government at Hamilton College, United States. He is a former visiting professor and external professor at the European University Institute in Florence. He is the author or editor of a number of books and articles in the areas of international political economy and European integration.

Ben Clift was lecturer in French and comparative politics at Brunel University, UK, until August 2003, when he commenced a lectureship in international political economy in the Department of Politics and International Studies at the

University of Warwick. He has written numerous articles on the French Socialist Party and the comparative political economy of social democracy. He is the
author of *French Socialism in the Global Era: The Political Economy of the New Social Democracy in France* (2003).

Stephen Gill is professor of political science at York University, Canada. His
publications include *Global Political Economy: Perspectives, Problems, and Policies*
(1988), *American Hegemony and the Trilateral Commission* (1990), *Gramsci, Historical Materialism, and International Relations* (1993), and, most recently, *Power
and Resistance in the New World Order* (2002).

Colin Hay is professor of political analysis and head of the Department of Political Science and International Relations at the University of Birmingham, UK.
He is the author or editor of a number of volumes, including most recently *Political Analysis* (2002), *British Politics Today* (2002), *De-Mystifying Globalization*
(2000), and *The Political Economy of New Labour* (1999). He is coeditor of the
Journal of Comparative European Politics.

Otto Holman is reader in international relations in the Department of Political Science at the University of Amsterdam. His publications include *Integrating Southern
Europe* (1996) and *Political and Economic Transformations in Central and Eastern Europe: The International Dimension* (in Dutch, 1995). He was also coeditor (with
Henk Overbeek and Magnus Ryner) of *Neo-liberal Hegemony and the Political Economy of European Restructuring* in the *International Journal of Political Economy* (1998).

Henk Overbeek is associate professor of international relations in the Department of Political Science at the Free University of Amsterdam. He is the author
of a number of books and articles on International Relations and European politics, including *Global Capitalism and National Decline: The Thatcher Decade in
Perspective* (1990), and he edited *The Political Economy of European Employment*
(2003). He is a member of the editorial board of the *Review of International Political Economy*.

Kees van der Pijl took up the chair in international relations at the University
of Sussex, UK, in 2000, coming from the University of Amsterdam. His work
deals with transnational class formation and the history of international theory.

Magnus Ryner is lecturer in the Department of Political Science and International Studies at the University of Birmingham, UK. He is the author of *Capitalist Restructuring, Globalization, and the Third Way: Lessons from the Swedish
Model* (2002) and coeditor of *Neo-liberal Hegemony and the Political Economy of
European Restructuring* in the *International Journal of Political Economy* (1998).

Thorsten Schulten is a researcher at the Wirtschafts un Sozialwissenschaftliches Institut (WSI) within the Hans Bockler Foundation in Düsseldorf, Germany. His main fields of interest are IPE, comparative industrial relations, and European trade union policy. He recently published "Solidaristic Wage Policy" in the *European Industrial Relations Journal* (2002) and coedited *Collective Bargaining under the Euro* (with Reinhard Bispinck, 2001).

Giles Scott-Smith received his Ph.D. in international relations from the University of Lancaster in 1998. He is a postdoctoral researcher with the Roosevelt Study Center in Middleburg, The Netherlands. For several years his research has focused on the links between culture, politics, and political economy.

Leila Simona Talani is a lecturer in European politics and political economy in the Department of European Studies at the University of Bath, UK. She received her Ph.D. from the European University Institute in Florence. She was previously a research fellow and then lecturer in the Government Department and at the European Institute of the LSE. She is the author of *Betting for and against EMU: Who Wins and Who Loses in Italy and the UK from the Process of European Monetary Integration* (2000).

Matthew Watson directs the Political Economy Research Group at the University of Birmingham, UK, where he is a lecturer. He has published widely in peer-reviewed academic journals in the areas of European and international political economy. His research interests include the history of economic thought, the idea of economic exchange within general equilibrium analysis, and changing patterns of economic change at a range of spatial scales.